THE UNFINISHED REVOLUTION

School of History

University of
St Andrews

Awarded to

Hannah Norfolk

for performance in

HI2001 - 2014/2015

THE UNFINISHED REVOLUTION

MAKING SENSE OF THE COMMUNIST
PAST IN CENTRAL-EASTERN EUROPE

JAMES MARK

YALE UNIVERSITY PRESS
NEW HAVEN AND LONDON

For information about this and other Yale University Press publications, please contact:
U.S. Office: sales.press@yale.edu   www.yalebooks.com
Europe Office: sales @yaleup.co.uk   www.yaleup.co.uk

Set in Minion by IDSUK (DataConnection) Ltd
Printed in Great Britain by TJ International Ltd, Padstow, Cornwall

Library of Congress Cataloging-in-Publication Data

Mark, James.
    The unfinished revolution: making sense of the communist past in Central-Eastern Europe/James Mark.
       p. cm.
    Includes bibliographical references.
    ISBN 978-0-300-16716-0 (cloth:alk. paper)
    1. Europe, Central—Social conditions—1989-2. Europe, Eastern—Social conditions—1989-3. Communism—Social aspects—Europe, Central.
4. Communism—Social aspects—Europe, Eastern. 5. Post-communism—Europe, Central. 6. Post-communism—Europe, Eastern. 7. Memory—Social aspects—Europe, Central. 8. Memory—Social aspects—Europe, Eastern. 9. Collective memory—Europe, Central. 10. Collective memory—Europe, Eastern. I. Title.
    HN380.7.A8M365 2010
    943.705—dc22

                                                                           2010020687

A catalogue record for this book is available from the British Library.

10 9 8 7 6 5 4 3 2 1

CONTENTS

FIGURES

ACKNOWLEDGEMENTS

I am pleased to record here my thanks not only for the help and support I have enjoyed through the long gestation of this book, but also for the part colleagues and others have played in stimulating my professional and intellectual journey during this time. At this project's inception I was a social historian who wanted to uncover voices from everyday life during the Communist period in central-eastern Europe. Its pursuit has led me to become a scholar of memory too, concerned with how the values of a new era determine what can and cannot be said about previous political systems, and how ordinary people, with complex, rich and multifaceted pasts, attempt to fit themselves to a radically changed world in which they are pressed to make sense of their lives anew.

I am grateful to my D.Phil. supervisors at Oxford, Robert Evans and Richard Crampton who encouraged me to question governing paradigms. In the years since, I have benefitted from the advice and intellectual support of many researchers. In particular, I am indebted to a new generation of scholars in former Communist countries, many of whose intellectual journeys have been shaped by the culture of the Central European University, and who have developed novel critical approaches to the dominant historical forms of post-Communism. In doing so they have invigorated the study of memory, post-Communist politics and culture, and historical studies more widely – and have strongly shaped my own scholarship.

This book represents the culmination of several projects, made possible by an AHRB D.Phil. Studentship, a British Academy Small Research Grant, research funding from the Universities of Exeter and Plymouth, and an AHRC Research Leave Award. I thank *Past and Present* for allowing me to use parts of 'Remembering Rape', and the Central European University Press for permission to reproduce a significant part of the chapter, 'Containing Fascism'.

This work is broad in scope, and has taken me beyond my immediate specialism and familiar academic territory – as a consequence I am most grateful to all those who have generously provided me with practical assistance and specialist advice. I offer my thanks to Piotr Filipkowski, Dragoş Petrescu, János M. Rainer, Krzysztof Persak, David Weber and Miroslav Vanek for their help developing the research project and especially for locating oral history respondents. For reading and commenting perceptively on my work I am indebted to Péter Apor, Timothy Ashplant, Marie Černá, Kate Fisher, Nick Fisher, Csilla Kiss, Daniela Koleva, Martha Lampland, Maria Mälksoo, Małgorzata Mazurek, András Mink, Bill Niven, Ewa Ochman, Krzysztof Persak, Steve Smith, Lavinia Stan, Alexandra Walsham, Meike Wulf and Magdalena Zolkos. I also thank Victoria Patch, Victoria Bates and Nic Bilham for their assistance in producing the final text, Robert Shore for his exquisite copy-editing, Jane Horton for indexing, and the anonymous Yale University Press reader – as well as the Yale London team, including Robert Baldock, Rachael Lonsdale, Tami Halliday and Candida Brazil, who have been very helpful and supportive.

My colleagues on the 'Around 1968' project have been generous in allowing me the time and space to complete this project, and have furnished me with a stimulating and supportive environment. Colleagues in the History Department at the University of Exeter also contributed to this fertile environment, as did my MA and undergraduate students, many of whom have themselves taken up the study of memory with an enthusiasm which has delighted me.

I am hugely grateful to my family for all their support throughout the project. Edmund, Isaac and Kit, who were all born during its lifetime, may not yet have any idea what it is about, but have developed an impressive knowledge of the playgrounds of the capitals of central-eastern Europe. I thank Kate especially, who not only has been an unwavering source of invaluable intellectual and emotional support, but also had the opportunity to experience those playgrounds too.

Finally, I wish to record my heartfelt thanks to all those who gave their time to talk to me about their own lives under Communism, and to those who were willing to discuss the professional endeavours through which they seek to make sense of the past for a post-Communist public. Without their time, patience and generosity, not only would I have little of the material that forms the basis of my work, I would have been deprived of much of the rich dialogue which has inspired and challenged me in developing its intellectual content.

INTRODUCTION

On 12 June 2007, the Monument to the Victims of Communism was unveiled in Washington, D.C. It was dedicated to the memory of the many millions of Communist citizens who died in the Soviet Gulag, the Ukrainian Famine, Mao's Great Leap Forward, Ho Chi Minh's terror in Vietnam and other catastrophes caused by, and atrocities committed under, Communist dictatorships worldwide. Lee Edwards, one of the leading historians of the American conservative movement, and prime mover behind the memorial, viewed the commemoration of Communism's victims as a necessity in the western world, where, he believed, an unhealthy amnesia had settled over the crimes of Communism to a degree unthinkable for the victims of the Holocaust.[1] Yet the memorial evoked far more than simply the remembrance of Communism's brutality; it was also an embodiment of western triumphalism after the end of the Cold War, and a strident assertion of the inevitability of liberal democracy's eventual victory over totalitarian ideology everywhere. While the monument itself was dedicated to the 'one hundred million victims' (a debated figure the contestation of which was not noted),[2] the form they chose to adorn its pedestal did not illustrate mass suffering at all. It was a 'Goddess of Democracy', a copy of the model built by the student demonstrators who protested against the Chinese Communist government in Tiananmen Square in 1989, and whose democratic movement was eventually suppressed. The monument's American sponsors chose it as they believed the goddess's form to have been inspired by the Statue of Liberty, a claim its Chinese creators refuted, saying they had modelled it on socialist realist sculpture and had deliberately avoided employing a form that could be associated with western culture or politics and hence might be used to demonize them in their homeland.[3] However, in its setting in Washington, D.C., the goddess's similarity to the Statue of Liberty was obvious and entirely in harmony with the monument's sponsors' ideological intentions: to present a world divided between those who enjoyed American-style freedoms, and those who yearned for them. As Lee Edwards put it, 'we selected it because it is a graphic reminder of how Communism suppresses anyone who challenges its authority, and because the statue has become a global symbol of man's innate desire for freedom.'[4] Though illustrating a defeated democratic movement, the monument nevertheless expressed the inevitability of victory over left-wing dictatorships. Even the dedication to those who had died as a result of the worldwide Communist experiment – 'To the more than one hundred million victims of Communism and to those who love liberty' – hinted that their mass sacrifice was made on behalf of freedom's global mission.[5]

At the unveiling ceremony in 2007, President George W. Bush framed the collapse of Communism in Europe as an important staging post on the journey towards the worldwide spread of freedom; the example of the collapse of the Soviet bloc would inspire others towards the inevitable final victory. All totalitarian and violent non-democratic political ideologies would eventually be trounced: 'We can have confidence in the power of freedom because we've seen freedom overcome tyranny and terror before. . . . President Reagan went to Berlin. He was clear in his statement. He said, "tear down the wall," and two years later the wall fell.'[6] As the seemingly last major ideological competitor to western systems, the story of Communism's defeat in Europe bolstered the idea that liberal democracy, free markets and human rights were the only possible models for human development. All their ideological rivals had supposedly failed.[7] In dominant western public discourses after 1989, Communism was thus most commonly invoked as a defeated ideology in order to assert the inherent superiority of liberal democratic development.[8] Yet while most western observers were sure that they had seen Communism crushed and liberty and democracy triumph, many within the former Soviet bloc were not convinced of the finality of Communism's demise, or were unsure about the precise ideological nature of the 'post-Communist' system that had emerged.[9]

Communism was also frequently remembered and memorialized in the former Communist countries of central-eastern Europe. The development of sites, institutions and processes devoted to remembering, commemorating and working through the Communist past, such as Institutes of National Memory, History Commissions, lustration bureaux, museums and commemorative memorials, were regarded by some elites as fundamental to the democratic re-education of post-Communist societies. Debates over the meaning of the Communist past were to play important roles in defining both domestic political cleavages and new geopolitical orientations. A large number of autobiographies and oral histories were published, reflecting the desire of many to remember the former dictatorship. The range of memory practices adopted after 1989, especially by elites, was a continental novelty. In neither the aftermath of the defeat of the Fascist regimes in Italy and Germany at the end of World War II, nor in the wake of the collapse of the southern European dictatorships in Greece, Portugal or Spain in the 1970s, was there a widespread attempt to remember dictatorship or its origins, or to establish public institutions that could aid the public 'working through' of difficult pasts. This book is an attempt to explore the extent to which the region between the former Soviet Union and Germany, commonly called 'central-eastern Europe',[10] differed from this pattern and examine how certain elites sought to confront post-Communist societies with their recent past at a wide range of sites of memory. It will first explore the ways in which changing political and social conditions created the very idea that Communism needed to be remembered in the public sphere. Then it will examine the relationship between these new public cultures of memory and the frameworks that individuals drew upon in rethinking their own histories and life stories. In doing so, it will not attempt to examine all nations in central-eastern Europe, but rather will employ relevant case studies to illustrate debates over memory that often had wider resonances across the region. It will draw on research into cultural, judicial, political and personal forms of remembering conducted in a selection of countries – Poland, the Czech Republic, Hungary, Romania, Estonia, Latvia and Lithuania – between 1998 and 2009.

Increasingly, scholars recognize that the act of remembering the past should not be essentialized as a universal phenomenon but rather viewed as having its own specific history: they assert that particular cultures invoke historical memory only at certain times, and often for very different purposes. Indeed, practitioners of memory studies have become as interested in the reasons for the absence of cultures of remembrance, and the existence of enforced silences in public memory, as they are about its active articulation.[11] The impulses that propelled the memory of Communism to the forefront of national debate in central-eastern Europe were not the same as those in North America. Unlike their western counterparts, eastern European elites did not commemorate the victory over Communism: few freedom monuments, or days of liberation marking the end of Communism, were established in the region.[12] Indeed, during that brief interlude after its collapse, when 'victory' was assumed to have been achieved, Communism was often forgotten or not thought worthy of invocation. The impulse to remember only developed with the growing perception in the mid-1990s that the former system had not in fact been fully overcome. Some post-Communist elites only sought to remember Communism in significant ways when doubt started to emerge about the degree to which it had genuinely been defeated and the revolutions of 1989 began to be viewed as unfinished. Thus, the practitioners of a new 'memory politics' in post-Communist central-eastern Europe invoked, commemorated and reflected upon their Communist pasts, not to confirm their mastery over a now demonized and banished political system, but in order to confront and weaken its continuing hold on the present.[13]

The idea that Communism was a problematic historical object that had to be dealt with by democratizing societies was not immediately apparent everywhere in the region after 1989. Despite the fact that Communists had survived the negotiated transition in some countries – in part because they agreed to give up power in return for a promise that they would not be excluded from political life – 1989 was still regarded as representing a defeat for former dictators.[14] Liberal oppositionists who had been involved in these transitions as partners at the so-called 'Round Table' settlements argued that the absence of violence and the peaceful incorporation of former enemies into the new 'democratic game' was a sign of the mature and civilized nature of central-eastern Europe:[15] the very survival of Communists represented the overcoming of totalitarian practices and thus an effective closure of the Communist period. Conservative anti-Communists, who made up the first post-Communist administrations in Hungary and Poland, also took the victory over Communism as assured, and invoked its memory infrequently. They preached the politics of restoration rather than revenge: 1989 was envisaged as the starting point where history began again after a painful forty-year detour from the proper trajectory of national development. In these countries, memorial practices adopted in this period often looked to connect post-Communism to the prewar era in order to re-establish the 'continuity of the nation'. Governments and memorial institutions looked to re-assert traditions that they believed had been erased under the Communist regime, rather than deal directly with the legacies of the previous four Communist decades.[16] The bones and bodies of interwar leaders, anti-Communists and nationalists who had been exiled from their homeland were returned and reburied at great expense.[17] The absence of discussion about the Communist past was often part of a process whereby nationalists attempted to erase the memory of the previous era.

Yet, as the 1990s wore on, the idea that the revolution had not been completed grew stronger and provoked many to consider the Communist era as a problematic period that needed to be revisited in order to be fully overcome. This impulse came from two main sources, one domestic and one international. At home, anti-Communist nationalist and liberal parties, confronted by the return of ex-Communists to power and the growing realization of the continued strength of former apparatchiks within the economic sphere and state bureaucracy, increasingly invoked the idea of the 'unfinished revolution'.[18] They developed strident critiques of the negotiated transitions which had allowed the former Communist elite and bureaucracy to remain within the political system. The presence of former Communists and the continuation of earlier attitudes and outlooks derived from the Communist period were deemed to be having a negative impact on the course of democratization and the establishment of a new post-Communist national identity.[19] The completion of the revolution was increasingly called for, either through the physical purge of former Communists, or through the creation of institutions that could help forge new democratic national identities for their citizens.[20]

The notion of central-eastern Europe's incapacity to overcome the legacies of its totalitarian past was also propagated outside the region itself. Western Europeans – and in particular German elites – promoted the idea that eastern Europeans had a problematic relationship with their recent history that needed to be addressed.[21] The seeds of this had in fact been germinating for two decades in liberal-leftist circles, particularly in West Germany. Here, a new postwar generation were increasingly critical of the failure of their parents to deal adequately with the legacies of the Nazi past; in their view, the absence of a politics that diligently 'worked through' the country's experience of Fascism was responsible not only for the inadequacies and shallowness of the postwar democratic system but also for important continuities in social attitudes and political practices, as well as a residual regard for the 'authoritarian personality'. Their critique was historically inaccurate in some ways: 'coming to terms' with the Nazi past had begun in important ways in the 1950s.[22] Nevertheless, radicals in the late 1960s extensively employed memories of Nazism to frame and enable social and political change.[23] In the long term it contributed to the creation of a powerful new discourse which asserted that difficult pasts were collective experiences that needed to be addressed and overcome in order for a society to be truly democratic, and that a post-dictatorial democracy needed to develop a 'critical memory culture' by establishing processes and institutions that would force the past into the public domain, and in doing so embed the idea of an ongoing (and, some would say, never-ending) engagement with the dictatorial past as an absolute public good.[24] It was the legacies of these approaches, still present two decades later, that 'easterners' were confronted with in their early encounters with the western elites after 1989. As part of the unification process with West Germany, the citizens of the former Communist German Democratic Republic were the first to experience this. Although the right and left in the political elites of the unified Germany had very different ideas about what the GDR had been – a totalitarian dictatorship or a failed experiment in modernization and equality – there was nevertheless consensus that a post-Communist society needed a set of institutions to help it overcome its history.[25] Although it was initially oppositionists from the former East Germany who set about coming to terms with the experience of dictatorship, it was primarily debates derived from the former West Germany concerning its own failure to deal with its Nazi past with sufficient haste that played the greatest role in shaping how the easterners' experience of Communism was to be understood. Moreover, the former West Germany had not only a ready-made western court system but also funding and personnel equipped to address the legacies of dictatorship.[26] This led some to regard this historical reckoning as a form of western ideological colonization, in particular because its processes often involved western judges and bureaucrats sitting in judge-ment over citizens of the east.[27] Of all the countries in central-eastern Europe, Germany engaged in the earliest and deepest confrontation with its past, purging up to fifty thousand members of the public service for their connec-tions to the Stasi, pursuing public trials for former Communists who had committed prosecutable crimes, establishing parliamentary commissions to investigate the nature of the GDR, and setting up an institution charged with holding the records of the former secret police (the so-called 'Gauck Office', latterly the 'Birthler Office').

The memory of Communist dictatorship was not the only part of central-eastern Europeans' pasts that was problematized from outside the region. Western elites, particularly those in the European Union, considered it essen-tial that central-eastern Europeans 'face up' to their experience of Fascism and, in particular, the Holocaust, as part of their return to the European fold. By the 1990s, western European political elites considered remembering the Holocaust a vital part of 'being European'. The Jewish genocide was conceived of as an absolute moral evil against which to define those values – tolerance and diversity – that were seen as essential characteristics of modern civilization. This was particularly the case in the European Union: as the integrative effects of the fear of Communism fell away after the end of the Cold War, so its leaders increasingly presented the EU as emerging out of the horrors of genocide and as an insurance against it occurring again.[28] Western elites often perceived central-eastern European countries' early reluctance to place the Holocaust at the forefront of their post-Communist public memories as a moral failing or as a sign of their backwardness, and insisted that they rectify this as part of a 'return to Europe'.[29] Moreover, they increasingly pressurized eastern European elites to control what they considered to be inappropriate memories of Fascism, such as nationalists' willingness to celebrate figures of the right and far right for their anti-Communism: Marshall Antonescu in Romania, Baltic 'freedom fighters' and Hungarian conscripts who had fought alongside Nazi Germany were all commemorated by patriotic groupings and veteran bodies after 1989 for their part in the struggle to 'save Europe from Bolshevism'.

These new pressures to remember and invoke the past in appropriate ways were variously received in former Communist countries. In some cases, these western templates were selectively appropriated by anti-Communists who viewed them as politically useful; in other cases, they were experienced as the imposition of a colonial ideology on eastern European countries. The model of the unified Germany provided inspiration for those anti-Communists who accepted the region's democratic shortfalls, the need to overcome its past and 'become European' through a condemnation of Communism. No country looked outside Europe to the South African model of reconciliation or to Latin American and Asian History Commissions.[30] Instead, new Institutes of National Memory in the region took Germany's Gauck Office as a model, while History Commissions in Romania and the Baltic States took some of their inspiration from Germany's Enquete Commissions.[31] Western Europe's universalizing discourse on the Holocaust, which was often transferred to central-eastern European nations as part of their integration into the European Union and NATO, was regarded as more problematic. The willingness of former Communist countries to adopt Holocaust discourses was often taken as an important sign by 'old' European elites of their readiness to westernize themselves. The outward signs of Holocaust remembrance – such as Holocaust days and memorials – were established in many countries in the region. However, the western insistence that the Holocaust was unique in its violence, and the failure of western Europeans to reciprocate with an understanding of the brutality of Communism in the construction of a 'common European memory', often meant that recalling the Jewish genocide was regarded as an assertion of the innate superiority of western European politics and culture (see Chapter 4).

The Reach of the Unfinished Revolution

The idea of the unfinished revolution, and the necessity of overcoming a problematic past, did not appear everywhere in the former eastern bloc. This work focuses on those smaller nations formerly on the western borderlands of the Soviet Empire where a growing anti-Communist culture, and a willingness by some elites to accept that 'difficult histories' were something that European cultures looked to overcome, meant the Communist past was increasingly invoked as something to reject. Further to the east, however, this was not the case. This study will not consider the very different approaches that dominated post-Communist Russia.[32] Although some liberal groups there tried to revive the memory of the victims of Stalinism and present Communism as a traumatic and criminal moment that post-Communist Russia now had to signal its distance from, this view was not widely shared.[33] Many powerful voices rejected the idea that the Soviet past was aberrant. Some post-Communist Russian elites, particularly from nationalist and Communist traditions, refuted the idea that the western liberal model should be essentialized as *the* natural form of historical development. Hence the Communist past, although it had ended in failure, was simply regarded as a form of modernization and certainly not as a deviation from the correct model: as such, future Russian development was not reliant on learning to reject Communism as an anomalous detour from the norms of global development.[34] Rather, the Communist past was no more than a failure in economic management that had now been dealt with by the adoption of a capitalist model. Under the presidency of Vladimir Putin from 2000 onwards, the need for a proud national identity was increasingly asserted after the decade of economic and social decline that had followed the collapse of the Soviet Union. In this context, some Russian historians argued that it was unhelpful to suggest to the generations who had lived through Communism that they had in fact supported a criminal project. In fact, they suggested, it was better to present the Soviet period as a legitimate part of national history.[35] Putin himself often went even further, reviving heroic memories from the Soviet period as a source for a new Russian national pride. In particular, Stalin and the Red Army re-emerged in political discourse as heroic figures who had led the fight to save Europe from Fascism. This did not mean that Russians had forgotten the terror and the Gulag; unlike many in the west, however, they did not regard them as *the* symbols of a criminal and abhorrent system. Rather, many Russians historicized these phenomena, weighing up whether they were historical necessities and assessing whether they had strengthened the country and thus helped it to 'save Europe from Fascism' in World War II.[36] Many opinion polls found that post-Communist Russians retained a very positive attitude towards the Communist past, especially the Stalinist period.[37]

Sites of Memory and Completing the Revolution

Attempts at completing the revolution in central-eastern Europe took many forms. Key to this study is an exploration of the elite contestations over how the Communist past should be overcome and how the various factions in these 'memory wars' sought to make their accounts of the past, and their suggested means to master it, plausible in the public arena. To this end, this book is divided into chapters dealing with different sites of memory: political, judicial and cultural spaces where debates over the manner in which the past should be dealt with were played out. It examines why some groups thought particular spaces conducive to their models of remembering, and how they used specialists connected with them to make their stories and solutions convincing. This part of the book uses interviews with thirty-four professionals who were involved in the production of the past in History Commissions and Institutes of National Memory, and at the excavations of mass graves, terror sites, statue parks and museums across the region.[38] In each of these arenas, different groups attempted to establish convincing accounts of the 'true nature' of the Communist experience, and show how present-day society had to learn to relate to that past in order to overcome its legacies. They were to use the varied techniques of the lawyer, museologist, archivist, archaeologist and historian to make their accounts of the past, and their remedies for overcoming it, appear convincing in the spaces in which they chose to produce, uncover, interrogate or display Communism. Most research on remembering focuses on one particular manifestation of memory; one of the advantages of examining this phenomenon at multiple political and cultural levels, as in the current work, is that it allows the scholar to explore why and how traditions select (or reject) particular spaces in which to establish their versions of collective memory, and to assess how and why collaborations are formed between various political forces and the professions that are needed to produce credible accounts of the recent past.

For some radical anti-Communists, completing the revolution meant purging the former *nomenklatura* from the political elite and bureaucracy. They initially looked to the judicial sphere, hoping to establish bodies that could carry out lustration and exclude certain portions of the former Communist elite from public service or, in some cases, the professions. Outside unified Germany, these procedures were seldom established and, even where they were, had limited impact (see Chapter 2). In the wake of their failure to establish a 'Communist Nuremberg Trial', some radical anti-Communists instead transferred their judicial impulses to the fields of cultural display and forensic excavation. They established memorial museums at sites of former Communist terror, turning them into 'cultural courtrooms' where Communism could be put on trial (see Chapter 3). They also looked to the science of forensic archaeology to uncover those Communist-era mass graves that would provide powerful evidence of the criminality of the previous era for a new generation. The hopes they invested in forensic science were often repaid with ambiguous results: excavations often unexpectedly revealed the legacies of the region's other histories – including those of the Holocaust – that threatened to undermine their exclusively anti-Communist accounts (see Chapters 3 and 4).

For less radical (often liberal) anti-Communists, completing the revolution was not a question of purging the regime's remnants, which from their perspective constituted a return to the violence of Communist-era practices, but rather required the 'democratization of national memory'. For them, the revolution was incomplete because totalitarian attitudes remained and 'the people' did not fully identify with the post-Communist political system. A new liberal account of the past had to be created with which post-Communist citizens could identify, and into which they would be prepared to rewrite their own lives, reconceptualizing themselves as victims of Communist criminality who had been liberated by democracy in 1989. In their view, the absence of popular involvement during the collapse of Communism had led to a lack of identification with the new system, because people had not actually experienced 1989 themselves as an important historical break. They therefore looked to 'narrative reshaping' bodies, such as History Commissions and Institutes of National Memory, to provide powerful new official accounts that chronicled the recent past as a period of revolutionary change from the criminality of Communism to the legal protections of the liberal democratic system.

Others argued that the revolution *had* been completed in 1989. Some former dissidents, who framed themselves as 'anti-Communists with a human face',[39] viewed the pursuit of radical policies to 'complete the revolution' as deleterious to democratic development. Ex-Communists for the most part tried to distance themselves from various debates over memory that they encountered after 1989: they often held ambivalent or negative views about 'truth-telling procedures', such as History Commissions and Institutes of National Memory, which criminalized the Communist past. In some ways they could turn this unwillingness to engage with the struggles over memory to their advantage, presenting themselves as the embodiment of the nation's future, and their anti-Communist opponents as refighting the tired battles of the past. Yet they did engage in 'memory practices' in minor ways. A number of ex-Communists suggested reconciliation commissions based on the South African model, proposals that were often regarded by their political opponents as manipulative attempts to avoid a proper reckoning with the past. More importantly, and surprisingly perhaps, ex-Communists were at the forefront of the organization of public commemorations for those who resisted the Communist state before 1989. Their legitimacy in the post-Communist era was dependent on making their assertions that they had democratized themselves convincing. Stories of the victory of anti-Communist resistance over the former system provided them with persuasive evidence of their own defeat that could frame their rebirth as democratic socialists, and thus confirmed that they were no longer a threat to democratic development (see Chapter 1).

Oral History and the Unfinished Revolution

This book begins with the assumption that telling stories about a dictatorship should not be seen as an obvious or natural act: indeed, many historians have charted the social silences that followed the demise of other authoritarian regimes.[40] Post-Communist central-eastern Europe, by contrast, saw the production of a significant amount of personal testimony concerning the Communist period. This was in part a result of the timing of Communism's demise: it collapsed at a moment when the individual witnessing of traumatic pasts (in particular the Holocaust) was considered vital to the preservation of democratic values and history writing, especially in the western world.[41] Moreover, following years of manipulation of public memory by the Communist state, the personal account was ascribed an authority to embody the realities of past experiences that even a reformed public history lacked.[42] Nor was the act of remembering considered dangerous. This was not a culture marked by a fear of return to civil violence if historical memories and grievances were put on display, as was the case in Spain after the collapse of the Franco dictatorship.[43] There was little sense that dictatorship could return; hence there was little fear that testimonies might later be used against the witnesses who produced them.[44]

Moreover, those who had problematic pasts were not encouraged to forget them, or socialized to expect punishment on account of them, but rather pressurized to retell them with a new ideological gloss. Aside from the German case, anti-Communists failed to enact purges of those with politically demonized histories who had served the former regime.[45] Rather, some post-Communist elites created institutions that encouraged all citizens to reframe their own pasts in democratic terms. Many could refashion themselves as 'victims' or 'resistors'; those who had worked for the Communist-era security apparatus were put under pressure to regard themselves as 'collaborators' (Chapter 2). These processes were framed as a necessary form of democratic re-education, rather than as a deliberate evasion of the complex realities of the Communist past. Individual memory thus became an object of interest for many of those who sought to 'complete the revolution'. Personal memories framed in inappropriate forms were regarded as evidence of the unfinished nature of the democratic transformation, while the level of assimilation of nationalist or democratic tropes into individuals' life stories became important indicators of the extent of the revolution's success. Indeed, this fascination with the erasure of Communist values from individual autobiographies was illustrated by the frequency of post-1989 opinion polls commissioned to assess the legacies of Communist-era public memory in individuals' post-Communist representations of their own, and their families', experiences under Communism.[46]

In cultures that prize the reframing of autobiography and identity, oral history has an interesting role to play. It allows the historian to examine the impact of new public memories on individuals' conceptions of their own lives, and the way in which these interacted with, and in some cases replaced, the ways that they had learnt to think about their lives under the previous regime. Did post-Communist citizens modify their life stories to adjust to new nationalist and democratic public memories? Could the autobiography be used as a defence against them? Were there new taboos that replaced Communist-era enforced silences, which in turn affected how individuals could present themselves to their post-Communist audiences? Which parts of the Communist-era autobiography remained socially acceptable after 1989, and which had to be purged? Despite this, oral history scholars who conducted interviews as part of their research did not pay a great deal of attention to the way in which individuals adjusted their autobiographies after 1989.[47] Work on the remaking of memory after 1989 was mainly the preserve of political and cultural historians, and cultural and literary scholars, who explored how new public narratives embedded themselves in museums, cinema, political ritual, literature and history writing, but who did not engage with individual memory or oral history.[48] Anthropologists and sociologists extensively researched the 'unmaking' of Communist-era identities and new social practices, but they too were less concerned with questions of personal autobiography and memory.[49]

This absence was also attributable to the absence of dialogue between the practitioners of oral history and memory studies. Since the period of the discipline's initial growth in the 1970s, many oral historians have justified their work in terms of uncovering hidden and marginalized stories, often within the context of political activism and radical social movements. Issues of how societies alter their memories have commonly been of secondary importance. Even where oral practitioners have incorporated sophisticated analyses of the impact of memory on the testimony they have gathered, these reflections on collective remembering are usually included to provide a more convincing account of the manner in which the oral testimony can lead the historian to the realities of past social experience.[50] Likewise, scholars of public memory avoid oral history in the main. They come from fields such as cultural studies, literary theory and political history, and are for the most part interested in the forms of remembrance that occur at a national or public level and show little enthusiasm for the recovery of individual memories.[51]

In central-eastern Europe, oral history emerged as part of the political activism of dissident groups in the early 1980s, when the first informal oral history groups were established in Warsaw (the Karta Centre) and in Budapest (the 1956 Institute).[52] They were founded by liberal and leftist members of the opposition, and regarded the recovery of individual memory as a means to challenge the dominant public narrative of the Communist state. Both aimed to uncover sets of experiences – particularly from members of certain political traditions: reform socialism in the case of Budapest and, in the case of Warsaw, the experience of Solidarity activists and those Poles in the eastern provinces that had been absorbed into the Soviet Union – that had been denied a place in official historiography.[53] After 1989, oral historians in the former Communist bloc used interview techniques to recover the voices of those groups whose histories had previously not been able to find public expression. Some saw this as important for the rebuilding of the nation: these practitioners frequently collected the memories of alternative national traditions whose representatives had been brutalized under Communism.[54] Here, the voice of the victim or resister was often ascribed a greater authenticity as a witness to the realities of Communism than those of the socially mobile or party members.[55] Others presented their work as a significant contribution to the creation of a democratic culture. The collection of multiple voices from non-elite groups was an important democratizing activity because it not only broke the myth of societal homogeneity propagated by the Communists but also encouraged society to regard diversity and tolerance for a plurality of memories and identities as positive values.[56] The idea that oral history could assist in the creation of a tolerant multiculturalism as part of a 'return to European values' was popular too.[57] This appreciation of diversity only extended so far, however: unlike some of oral history's western founding fathers, central-eastern Europeans shied away from the examination of groups that had been valorized by the Communist state such as the working classes. Rather, they focused on the politically persecuted, those involved in dissident movements, women and intellectuals, and on using individual testimony to create regional histories.[58] Moreover, the idea of reconciliation through 'oral history dialogues' never became popular. While 'joint witnessing' by formerly opposed groups was seen as fundamental to attempts to heal historical wounds in South Africa, neither post-Communist oral historians nor producers of new national memories considered this method to be meaningful.[59] Indeed, neither of the two most popular forms of 'memory reshaping' institutions that emerged in the region after 1989 – the History Commission and the Institute of National

Memory – embraced oral witnessing as a means to gather evidence about the past. Instead, they employed politically reliable scholars to research and write new national histories 'from above', based primarily on the documentary remnants of the former security services (see Chapter 2). There were only a few individual initiatives that presented clashing or multiple perspectives on the Communist past, using interviews between former opponents or oral histories of multiple sides in the struggle.[60]

In other parts of the world, scholars were becoming interested in using oral testimony to examine the ways in which historical memory changed over time. From the 1980s onwards, historians such as Alessandro Portelli, Luisa Passerini and Al Thomson employed oral testimony to explore why people remembered in certain ways, and how group memories shifted over time when faced with different public ways of remembering the past.[61] They became as interested in what was forgotten, or misremembered, as in what was accurately recalled. In some post-Communist oral history, silences or episodes of inaccurate recollection were not regarded as interesting in themselves, but rather as problematic by-products of mentalities inherited from the era of dictatorship, which needed to be overcome through the heroic intervention of the oral historian.[62] Practitioners therefore presented themselves as actively creating memories within peoples who had been socialized into amnesia by the manipulations of Communist public memory, or as professionals who could access traumatic memories that individuals had hidden, even from their own family members.[63] They were not detached analysts of silence but active memory-makers who enabled societies to overcome their taboos. There were a substantial number of post-Communist oral historians who became interested in the relationship between public and individual memory, but their work usually focused only on the ways in which Communist – rather than post-Communist – ideology and public histories affected individuals' own value systems and sense of self.[64] These practitioners were often critical of those who sought out only alternative non-Communist memories; rather, they wanted to show how many groups had been captured by Communist ideology, and that there was no liberal democratic subject or nascent nationalist simply waiting to break free in 1989.[65] Yet they shared the assumption that the main function of oral history was to uncover the realities of the experience and mentalities of the Communist era. While the majority of oral historians address post-1989 memory as part of their research, their analyses of the pressures of post-Communist memory are usually subsumed within broader works concerned with the recovery of the Communist experience itself. Only a few scholars have focused specifically on how new public memories altered what could, and could not, be said after 1989.[66]

One of the main aims of this book is to combine the agendas of memory studies and oral history in order to explore the relationship between new public memories and the way in which individuals could relate their lives after 1989. While oral historians have long recognized that oral history interviews are necessarily dialogues between past and present that do not provide direct access to historical experiences, this book will bring the interrogation of that process to the fore. It employs personal testimony not primarily to uncover the realities of interviewees' Communist pasts, but rather to investigate how the values of post-Communism and liberal democracy have shaped what it is permissible to say about their experiences of dictatorship after 1989. The oral history analysis presented here draws upon the narratives revealed in interviews with 118 people from Hungary, Czechoslovakia and Poland, originally collected as part of three separate pieces of research.[67] Unlike those projects, this book does not primarily dissect particular groups' attitudes and experiences in the past. Instead, it investigates the ways in which interviewees chose to present their life stories after 1989 as they attempted to come to terms with their experiences of dictatorship in a new political context. Its focus is on the range of acceptable stories available to individuals in the post-Communist period, highlighting the clashes between past experiences and new ideas of what is politically or morally appropriate. Thus, the focus is not on the individuals themselves but rather on the stories they silenced, revived or reformulated after 1989.

Oral historians interested in the memory of Communism also need to pay attention to the ways in which former Communist subjects were socialized to think about the very function of *telling their life stories*. Before 1989, individuals had been required to write their own family pasts into official Communist histories in public autobiographical writings necessary for job applications or to gain entry to tertiary education. A person's willingness to write a politically appropriate life story was taken as a mark of loyalty to the system, and could determine whether an individual achieved social mobility or avoided discrimination. Moreover, for those who were born in the interwar period – the focus of the oral history conducted for this work – their young lives were marked by a particularly intense encounter with these procedures immediately after the establishment of Communist rule in the region: they faced immense pressure to reshape their life stories to fit the historical templates of the class and anti-Fascist struggles from Communist states which saw these autobiographical procedures as essential to the absorption of individuals' own identities into their own ideological orbits, and to the creation of the ideal socialist citizen. Research has begun to suggest that, by the late Communist period, these procedures were increasingly routinized and emptied of real meaning; even for those who still believed in the system, the production of autobiographical texts privileged form over content, and did not signal the interweaving of personal and public to the same degree as for older generations.[68] By contrast, writing the correct autobiography in the age of Communist mass mobilization in the 1940s and 1950s was experienced as an intensely political and meaningful act, through which supporters of the regime interwove their personal experiences with official narratives to produce life stories that signalled their identification with the new socialist project, and through which opponents feared contamination of their pre-Communist life stories as they too were offered opportunities to integrate themselves into rapidly modernizing and expanding economies, if they were prepared to reshape their identities, at least in public.[69] Thus – even if many regarded such procedures as inauthentic assaults on their identities – this cohort was drawn into understanding autobiographical production as innately ideological, and into viewing even family story-telling as a political act. This study shows in Chapter 6 that even anti-Communist nationalists who were deeply opposed to the Communist state and sought to withdraw from its ideological realm were shaped by these experiences: before 1989, they produced politicized life stories in private which integrated their family histories into the anti-Communist struggle, thus echoing – but simultaneously reversing – the formulas that they had been taught to produce in public Communist-era curricula vitae.

It was this intensely political conception of the life story that those socialized in the 1940s and 1950s transferred to the post-1989 era.[70] Indeed, the post-Communist period was ideologically recognizable as such to this group because they were suddenly faced with a new set of politically determined autobiographical procedures, albeit ones not linked with extreme punishments, and ones which could now be publicly contested. In some countries of the former eastern bloc – as mentioned above – institutions pressurized post-Communist citizens to categorize their pasts in terms of their relationship to the Communist regime, and to use the totalitarian terminology of 'victim', 'collaborator' and 'resister' when doing so.[71] Thus, after 1989, former Communist subjects were again asked to produce autobiographies, the forms of which were supposed to determine their relationship with the dominant power. Indeed, many ex-party members who wished to display their new political credentials now used their life stories to show how they had democratized themselves and come to support the post-Communist system. Interestingly, they still often drew on autobiographical templates from the 1940s and 1950s – specifically, the teleological narrative in which the individual's whole life was presented as an anticipation of an identification with the Communist project – which they simply reversed. Their identification with liberal democracy was, in a striking inversion, related as a story of inevitability in which the individual's choices had frequently anticipated their eventual belief in the newly established dominant ideology; life stories were often accounts of resistance against the excesses of both right and left which foretold the eventual arrival of democracy in 1989 (see Chapter 5). Anti-Communist nationalists gave their life stories other types of political meaning. They presented their personal autobiographies as sites where stories of the nation were kept safe. The act of articulating their autobiographies after 1989 was, for them, about the transmission to a new generation of a set of national political values that they claimed to have preserved within their families from the threat of pollution by Communist public historical narratives. Their family stories wrote the history of their ancestors into the history of the nation, and revealed how they had protected these accounts from contamination by Communist ideology (see Chapter 6).[72] The great politicization of life story that this group had experienced in the postwar period re-emerged powerfully after 1989; personal autobiographies were deployed in post-Communism in a deeply political fashion, to assist the construction of new identities based on claims about the truths of experiences that lay deep in the Communist past.

Thus, 1989 did not see a sudden emergence of previously unacceptable 'truthful' narratives, but rather a new set of political and cultural values determining what could and could not be said.[73] The oral method can be used to explore what had to remain hidden, or was newly suppressed, assessing which experiences from their Communist pasts individuals thought it worth making public, which they should keep private and which should be reshaped into newly acceptable narratives. Ex-party members, for example, narrated a painful process of deciding which aspects of their Communist life stories had to be discarded, and which could be remade, for the post-Communist era. Most no longer presented their lives in terms of the class struggle, but still battled to discover a way of relating their anti-Nazi stories in a democratic form in order not to appear to be parroting a set of clichéd anti-Fascist formulas that would mark them out as unreconstructed Communists (see Chapter 5).

Others found their experiences shaming to relate after 1989: Catholic and conservative interviewees sought to forget, or downplay, their stories of social mobility and professional success for fear of being branded collaborators who had given in to the Communist regime and who had not properly fulfilled their historic task of preserving national values for the next generation. More surprisingly, they could not use their resistance activities to evidence their anti-Communism after 1989. They viewed the public expression of opposition as a form of collaboration – in that it involved a dialogue with the Communist state – through which they might become ideologically 'contaminated'. Thus many pushed their involvement in the 1956 revolution in Hungary, or the Solidarity movement in Poland, into the background of their autobiographies (see Chapter 6). It was only the left (and some liberals) who placed their resistance activities at the forefront of their autobiographies: such stories could be used to demonstrate their commitment to the reform or destruction of dictatorship in advance of its collapse, and provided them with a 'biographical compensation' for their now demonized participation in dictatorship.

Other groups kept quiet about experiences of suffering even when offered the opportunity to testify to them after 1989. New dominant nationalist discourses on the 'martyrdom of the nation' under Communism meant that bearing witness to one's victimization had the potential to align individuals' experiences with a right-wing analysis of the past that they might not support. Chapter 6 deals with those who were marginalized professionally on the basis of class or political background, but who now refuse to construct themselves as victims of the system. Chapter 7 explores those victims of Red Army atrocities committed in 1945 who declined to relate stories of trauma and suffering that more dominant voices within their culture expected them to narrate.[74] Thus, even those who had suffered or been marginalized under Communist regimes often refused to present themselves as victims, fearing that such narratives would serve to confirm a new political agenda and a form of witnessing that they had no wish to support. As such, new democratic and nationalist public memories both opened up and closed down the possibilities of what could be said after 1989. The post-Communist totalitarian language of 'victim', 'collaborator' and 'resister' was understood by all, but only accepted and appropriated by some in their post-Communist autobiographies; others sought to reconstitute themselves autobiographically by refusing this new dominant democratic or nationalist language to describe their lives, and by rooting around in their earlier stores of memories for that which could be saved from their Communist-era autobiographical selves.

CHAPTER ONE

THE UNFINISHED REVOLUTION

In 1989, scenes of West and East Germans vandalizing and crossing the Berlin Wall became *the* images denoting the collapse of Communism in central-eastern Europe. This was in part because they seemed to conform to what a popular anti-Communist revolution was expected to be: crowds borne along by the desire to be free and to overthrow a spent dictatorship. Moreover, the Berlin Wall had been *the* emblem of Cold War division; its destruction by 'the people' became a powerful symbol of the end of a bipolar world. These pictures were to become a global visual shorthand for the popular defeat of Communism and the establishment of liberal democratic hegemony. Yet the world media's choice of the Wall as an object of revolutionary anger was also determined by the lack of other options: by and large, the events of 1989 were characterized by a visible absence of real Communists to overthrow. Only footage from Romania – where Nicolae Ceauşescu was forced to flee by helicopter from the roof of the party headquarters after a rally turned against him in central Bucharest – provided the world with scenes of actual conflict and defeated, powerless Communists. This absence was not incidental: in many central-eastern European countries, ruling Communists did not violently oppose a change of system. At the point of Communism's collapse, many were sitting down with the opposition for the so-called 'Round Table' talks and negotiating themselves a place in the new democratic political order.[1] Even in Romania, a majority of the former Communist *nomenklatura* backed the ousting of Ceauşescu, and saw in their support for the toppling of the dictator the possibility of remaining a significant force within the newly emerging political system.[2]

In the years after 1989, the defeat of Communism and the fall of the Wall were officially remembered much more readily outside central-eastern Europe than within the countries that experienced the collapse themselves. On the tenth and twentieth anniversaries of the fall of Communism there were few major commemorations within the former Soviet bloc. Where they did occur, in Berlin and Prague, they were as much *transnational* affairs celebrating the end of a bipolar world and the nuclear threat as they were *domestic* events commemorating the struggles of Germans and Czechoslovaks to overcome Communism in their own country.[3] Indeed, they were led by international actors from outside central-eastern Europe, with comparatively little representation from the region itself.[4] In fact, most post-Communist countries have not marked the end of Communism by instituting 'independence days' or 'freedom monuments'.[5] Movements such as Solidarity in Poland, which played a large role in undermining the legitimacy of Communism, failed to gain a significant place in post-Communist public memory, and the prospect of their memorialization was often a source of deep political and social division.

Only a few former dissidents – such as Adam Michnik in Poland – argued that the Round Table talks of 1989 should be used to provide a powerful foundation myth for the post-Communist system. They viewed the absence of revolution, the negotiated nature of the transition and the survival of Communists in the new system as something to be celebrated.[6] For them, the negotiated process was a symbol of the maturity and civilized nature of central-eastern European countries in which authoritarianism had been discarded without bloodshed and former Communists had been incorporated into the new order without instability. Despite these marginal voices, however, the memory of the overthrow of Communism failed to become a source of national cohesion. The unrevolutionary, negotiated, elite, non-participatory nature of the system change proved incapable of symbolizing a new beginning around which post-Communist societies could coalesce. Instead, different political movements sought to ascribe their own very particular meanings to the events of 1989, frequently blocking any wider, nationally consensual understandings of the past from emerging.[7]

Differences in the understanding of the nature of the collapse of Communism came to define deep divisions within the political elites after 1989, and played a significant role in shaping new alliances in the post-Communist period, often trumping variations in economic or social ideologies as the main determinant of fresh political cleavages.[8] By the mid-1990s, anti-Communist parties and electoral alliances were coalescing around the idea of the 'unfinished revolution'.[9] For these groups, the 'founding sin' of the new system was the negotiated transition, which had failed to remove the Communists from the political arena. This was blamed for the maintenance of corrupt clientelist networks in sectors of the economy and for crises of moral faith in the new system, which had not managed to remove former 'criminals' and 'perpetrators'. Anti-Communist governments, such as Fidesz (1998–2002, 2010-) in Hungary, Solidarity Electoral Action (1997–2001) and Law and Justice (2005–07) in Poland, and the Justice and Truth Alliance (2004–08) in Romania, all came to power claiming to be able to complete the unfinished revolutions of 1989. To make their case, they often revived the memory of resistance to Communism. On the one hand, the meaning of opposition was shaped to justify the necessity of continuing the anti-Communist struggle: thus, episodes of resistance were narrated in a story of successive failures to defeat Communists which culminated in the opposition's inability to remove them from the political arena in 1989. On the other, they needed to be rousing illustrations of heroic action that would inspire their constituencies to continue this unfinished struggle. Thus the story of valiant failure was at the centre of their new account of history.[10]

By contrast, it was the post-Communist left – including many ex-Communists – for whom the story of the victory of the anti-Communist struggle was most important. For them, their legitimacy after 1989 rested on the idea that Communism had been overcome and provided no threat to the present demo-cratic development of their country. Thus, in some places, they invoked the memory of the glorious, heroic anti-Communist struggle as evidence of their own defeat. In other cases, ex-Communist elites went further, identifying them-selves with resistance movements. They pointed to their role in allowing opposi-tion to flourish in the late years of Communism and ultimately considered themselves as the true liberators of their countries from dictatorship owing to their participation in the creation of the Round Tables.[11] As such, they became the revolutionary handmaidens of democracy and legitimate players in the post-Communist system. This chapter will explore the way in which these different political actors on the right and left, working within a post-Communist system whose nature and legitimacy were often contested, sought to narrate both the resistance to, and the collapse of, Communism in very different ways in order to mobilize support in favour of their political visions.

Politics, Anti-Communism and the Memory of Resistance

The dismantling of Communism in both Hungary and Poland was accom-plished almost entirely without popular participation, having been the negoti-ated result of so-called 'Round Table' agreements between Communist parties and elites drawn from the opposition. In Poland, where this process began in February 1989, the ruling Communists initiated negotiations not in order to dismantle the system, but rather to find a way of incorporating the opposition movement Solidarity into the political decision-making process. After ten years of existence, Solidarity was deemed to have proved its 'staying power' and was viewed as a political and social force that could not be ignored.[12] Against a background of an economically disruptive wave of strikes in spring and summer 1988, the Communists invited Lech Wałęsa and Solidarity to negotiations on condition that they brought the industrial unrest under control. In the winter of 1988–89, Round Table discussions between the regime and Solidarity began: it was for the most part the liberal wing of the movement that got involved; representatives of its nationalist wing, who would later be at the forefront in making complaints about the unfinished nature of the transition, were excluded. Reform Communists viewed the co-optation of Solidarity as necessary if plans for the renewal of an increasingly inefficient economic system were to be successful. Moreover, Solidarity had been weakened (it now enjoyed only a tenth of the membership it had had in the early 1980s) and was thus no longer perceived as a political threat. The regime agreed to allow Solidarity to contest a minority of seats in the lower house and all the seats in the Senate in the elections of June 1989. Against the regime's expectations, Solidarity was victorious in nearly all cases. Reform Communist elites soon recognized that a fatal blow had been delivered to their own legitimacy and, as the Soviets were no longer prepared to intervene, allowed Poland's first non-Communist government to be formed in September 1989.

Hungary's Round Table sat in the summer of 1989 in the wake of Solidarity's partial victory in Poland, by which point Soviet intervention there also seemed unlikely: thus from the start the discussions went beyond 'socialist pluralism' and accepted that the eventual outcome would be multiparty elections.[13] Different parties focused their efforts on establishing the form of democratic system that would best represent their particular agendas.[14]

In the immediate wake of the collapse, the first post-Communist governments in Hungary and Poland, despite their anti-Communist credentials, did not invoke the idea of the unfinished revolution. Instead, they championed the idea of compromise. In Poland, Tadeusz Mazowiecki's liberal Catholic administration supported the idea of continued reconciliation, the foundations of which had been laid in the negotiated settlement. Mazowiecki, informed by both his religious convictions and sense of social responsibility, believed that the Round Table agreement should be honoured; hence he argued that a 'thick line' should be drawn between past and present, and that revenge should not be pursued.[15] He was supported by prominent liberal oppositionists such as Adam Michnik, who argued that compromise and the absence of bloodshed should be celebrated as evidence of the region's political maturity and the rejection of Communist practices of confrontation and violence. The first post-Communist Hungarian government – the national-conservative

Hungarian Democratic Forum – defined its anti-Communism not through references to a continuing struggle, but through a return to a politics guided by the example of the pre-Communist anti-Communists such as Admiral Horthy, whose construction of a socially stable and bourgeois Hungary could provide inspiration for a new conservative politics. For them, anti-Communism was not the politics of contemporary revenge, but the restoration of an 'eternal Hungary', as if Communism had never existed.[16] The first governments in both Hungary and Poland thus tied their political identities to the Round Table agreements and continued to defend them as a mode of transition to democracy.

In this context, the founders of the new post-Communist order were careful to shape stories of the Communist past that framed the elite negotiated transitions as legitimate culminations of earlier (often violent and confrontational) anti-Communist struggles. This was particularly the case in Hungary, where the revival of the memory of the 1956 Uprising played a significant role in the collapse of Communism. In October 1956, a range of political forces – reformist socialists led by the Communist Imre Nagy who wanted an end to Stalinism while maintaining the socialist system; conservatives and working-class radicals wanting political independence; and factory organizations who wanted 'workers' democracy' – had provided the first serious challenge to the power of a Communist state in eastern Europe, until their protest was crushed by the Soviet intervention of 4 November 1956. The re-established Communist state had very effectively silenced public discussion of the so-called 'October events' between 1956 and 1989, officially characterizing the Uprising as a 'Fascist counter-revolution' intent on restoring the right-wing authoritarianism of the interwar and World War II period, and its leader – Imre Nagy – as a national traitor. Meanwhile, it presented itself as the only political force that could prevent the return of Fascism. In June 1989, both the Round Table opposition and the Communists agreed to the reburial of Nagy, the head of the government in 1956, with the aim of recasting him as a hero of what was now considered a legitimate 'popular uprising'. This revision of the meaning of the 1956 events exposed the Communists' claim to legitimacy – as the protectors of their country from a Fascist counter-revolution – as a lie, a shift that soon came to be viewed as the beginning of the end for the regime in Hungary. Yet while this revision of the way in which 1956 was remembered was important for the toppling of the system, the revival of the memory of violent confrontation was nevertheless perceived as a threat by both Hungarian reform Communists and the opposition, who wanted a peaceful, elite-guided transition. They feared a return to the tradition of armed struggle, and were concerned that Imre Nagy's reburial might provide the context for a revolutionary situation to emerge; their fears, however, proved false.[17] Both sides tried to keep radical anti-Communists – including representatives of the armed struggle in 1956 – away from the nego-tiations, or forced them to renounce earlier commitments to violence.[18] Moreover, new conservative elites were careful to present the peaceful transition as the 'respectable culmination' of the Uprising.[19] At the first sitting of the freely-elected post-Communist Hungarian parliament, this idea of '1956 fulfilled' was expressed vividly. Its first act was to declare the following: 'The Uprising of 1956 lays the foundation for the hope that it is possible to achieve a democratic social order, and that no sacrifice for our country's independence is made in vain. Although the ensuing suppression reinstated the old power structure, it could not eradicate the spirit of 1956 from people's minds.'[20] Indeed, aware of the threat of revolution, the framers of the new republic instigated commemorative days that alluded to the restoration of historical continuity (choosing St Stephen's Day, 20 August, the founding date of the Hungarian state, as the main national holiday) rather than revolutionary anniversaries such as 15 March (the anniversary of the 1848 revolution against the Habsburgs) or 23 October (the date of the outbreak of the 1956 Uprising).[21]

However, by the mid-1990s, the idea of 1989 as an 'unfinished revolution' had begun to dominate anti-Communist political discourse. This was a response both to the resurgence of the ex-Communist left, who had returned to govern-ment as dominant partners in liberal-left alliances in both Poland (1993) and Hungary (1994), and to the splintering of the right, for whom the concept was to provide a valuable ideological glue. New political formations – such as Fidesz in Hungary and Solidarity Electoral Action in Poland – developed unifying programmes based on powerful critiques of the transition process. For them, the failure of the negotiated collapse to exclude Communists, and their subse-quent return to positions of power, indicated the powerful hold that the left still had on both the political and economic spheres. For them, this continued grip was the cause of a moral malaise and of the inability of post-Communist popu-lations to identify completely with the new political system. Corrupt patronage networks drawn from the Communist era had been insufficiently challenged and had firmly embedded themselves within the new political system, while earlier Communist-era mindsets had also been left unconfronted. Moreover, the ideology of the 'unfinished revolution' allowed these new right-wing form-ations to combine forces while ignoring the social and economic cleavages within their movements.[22]

Historical memory was at the centre of this new rightist politics; their assault on the ex-Communist left would be fought rhetorically through the re-creation of the conditions of the anti-Communist struggle before 1989. They pointed to the failure to defeat Communism in 1989 and the need to continue the traditions of resistance that had existed before the negotiated transition, reshaping the great moments of opposition to dictatorship – such as the 1956 Uprising and the Solidarity movement – in their own image, and imagining themselves to be their direct successors. Simultaneously, they recast the liberal-left coalitions as the enemy, the post-Communist left as the successor to movements that had suppressed national resistance, and liberals as their willing collaborators. This of course necessitated a redrawing of the barricades of history; memories of liberals' roles as anti-Communist dissidents and of the reformist socialist opposition to Stalinism were either erased or delegitimized.

In Hungary, by the mid-1990s, the negotiated settlements of summer 1989 were increasingly under attack from the anti-Communist right,[23] headed by a newly emerging populist conservative party, Fidesz, led by Viktor Orbán.[24] Fidesz itself had never been reconciled to the negotiated transition. At the reburial of Imre Nagy in June 1989, Orbán had called for political forces not to compromise in their dealings with the Communists, and for the withdrawal of Soviet troops; moreover, his party, alongside the liberals, refused to sign the transitional pact that had guaranteed former Communists' survival into a new era.[25] Orbán was critical of the first post-Communist conservative administration. He viewed its anti-Communism – which sought a return to the conservatism of the interwar period rather than a fight with the leftist threat of the present – as an anachronism. In a speech in 1992, Orbán criticized its invocations of anti-Communist semi-feudal interwar Hungary as 'by and large represent[ing] a rotten, decaying world that would never again return to Hungary'.[26] Nevertheless, during the first years after the collapse of Communism, Fidesz eschewed the engineering of history for political gain. The party initially adopted a non-nationalist liberal agenda, arguing in 1991 that attempts to enact retroactive justice for Communist-era crimes were contrary to the rule of law, and famously quitting the parliamentary chamber en masse during a debate over the commemoration of Hungarian troops who had served alongside the German army on the Don Bend in World War II. By 1995, in response to both the return of former Communists to power, and the emergence of an opening on the right side of Hungarian politics, Fidesz turned itself into a conservative-nationalist party and from then on viewed history as a legitimate source from which to define its political identity.[27] It now promised to overturn the terms of the transition that had been established in 1989 and instigate a new revolution. It would build a new 'civic-bourgeois (polgári) Hungary' based on the support of the middle classes. From its viewpoint, both the anti-bourgeois state socialist policies of the Communist period and the neo-liberal shock therapy of the first ex-Communist coalition government (1994–98) had undermined the security and status of the Hungarian bourgeoisie.[28] Fidesz leaders argued that the middle classes, despite being the embodiment of the values of patriotism and self-reliance, had continued to be victimized long after the collapse of Communism.[29] To rectify this, they needed to purge the country of the leftist elites who had monopolized political and economic power since the 1940s, and whose influence had not declined since 1989. Thus Fidesz rejected the terms of the transition and promised a new revolution to compensate for its inadequacies.[30]

The memory of the 1956 Uprising played a substantial part in the construction of a newly aggressive form of anti-Communist conservatism.[31] Unlike the Spanish transition to democracy in the 1970s, in which both sides of the political spectrum were afraid of reviving memories of fratricidal conflict in the Spanish Civil War, Fidesz rejected the consensual memory of the 1956 Uprising that had dominated the immediate transition period, and replaced it with a story that presented the earlier revolution as part of an ongoing, still unresolved, struggle between Hungarians. Its rhetoric reversed the claim, dominant in the immediate wake of the transition, that the national aspirations of the Hungarian people expressed in the Uprising had been realized by the system change in 1989. Its more divisive interpretation identified the post-Communist left with those who suppressed the revolution in 1956; the negotiated transition in 1989 thus became the betrayal of 1956 as it had allowed the guilty to continue within the political system. For Fidesz, Hungarian politics was a struggle between the anti-Communist right, who were the true inheritors of the values of the 1956 Uprising, and the Communist successor party on the left, which was directly linked to those who had brutally suppressed the revolution. In particular, anti-Communists targeted the first post-Communist socialist prime minister, Gyula Horn, as emblematic of this historical link. In 1956, Horn had been a young member of the revolutionary militia called the Pufajkások, some of whose members had played a role in the suppression of the Uprising. He had admitted his membership in his autobiography, although he never elaborated on the exact nature of his role. Conservatives sought to attack Horn by including post-1956 militias in the 'screening law' introduced just before the 1994 election;[32] his 'vetting' in 1996 revealed that he had been part of the Budapest militia and had guarded bridges and prisons, although no direct evidence of violence against revolutionaries could be found. Horn himself argued that he had revealed his involvement before standing for election, and hence had no moral or legal obligation to resign.[33]

While the memory of the 1956 Uprising was used by conservatives to support the idea of the incomplete revolution, it was also re-imagined as a struggle that could provide inspiration for a new anti-Communist crusade. This rhetoric was powerfully deployed in Fidesz's successful electoral campaign in 1998, in which it presented the system change of 1989 as a betrayal of 1956, and itself as the contemporary successor to the revolutionaries of 1956, whose values would finally be realized with Fidesz's assumption of power nine years after the formal end of one-party rule. Its fight for a bourgeois Hungary was a continuation of the struggle for the values that were embodied in the Uprising of 1956. It therefore identified the conservative, bourgeois and religious forces, which emerged towards the end of the Uprising, as the true revolutionaries, while dismissing those left-wing forces – such as reformers who wanted a more representative and locally responsive socialism, and proletarian groups who fought for workers' democracy within factories – who had played a significant role in resisting Stalinism in 1956.[34] If the revolution was henceforth to be considered a failed attempt to create a Christian bourgeois Hungary, then it followed that there was no meaningful difference between those left-wing revolutionaries who took part in the Uprising in the name of 'democratic socialism', and those hardline Communists who suppressed it. Rather, they were lumped together as merely two different kinds of jailers who had prevented Hungarians from building a religious middle-class country.[35]

Some conservatives also viewed themselves as part of a long-term battle between the forces of the 'east' and those who desired a westernized Hungary. Indeed, Fidesz leader Viktor Orbán painted the anti-Communist fight, of both the Communist and the post-Communist period, onto an even broader historical canvas where the Hungarian nation had played a centuries-long historic role as a bastion of Europe against threats from the Orient.[36] In his view, Hungarian forces, which had once protected the rest of the continent from the Mongols and Turks, had again, in 1956, resisted an eastern power. Despite failing to eject the 'influence of the Communist East' from the country, Orbán argued that the Uprising had dissuaded the Soviets from further advances into the West. From this perspective, the socialists were not fully Hungarian; they were demonized as national traitors who had allied themselves with an 'eastern ideology' – Bolshevism – which was alien to 'true patriots'. Their political project had prevented Hungarians from rejoining their proper alliance with the Christian, capitalist and bourgeois societies of the West. On the anniversary of the outbreak of the revolution on 23 October 2007, Orbán characterized 1956 as

a revolution against the East . . . [that] restored Hungarians' self-esteem, ushering in a new era all across Europe and causing severe damage to the Eastern Colossus that had once planned to conquer the West. . . . [R]ight from the moment of its foundation, Hungary has always been a Western country which has never wished to belong to the East. The very reason our ancestors came here was because we did not want to stay there[37]

... although the Soviet Empire has disappeared, it has not vanished entirely. A renewed, vigorous Eastern power arises in its place. It is getting stronger every day by supporting its former partners [i.e. the ex-Communist socialist parties] from the Ukraine through Central Europe [and] all the way to the Balkans.[38]

As it still considered socialists to be the agents of the east, so Fidesz imagined itself as part of an ongoing struggle to free Hungary from the grasp of the Orient. This mindset identified an important continuity between the role of some Communists in 1956 and that of ex-Communists after 1989. Those who had opposed a bourgeois Hungary in 1956 continued to do so in a new political context after 1989: for Fidesz, socialists were responsible not only for the suppression of bourgeois interests and liberal democracy in 1956, but also for the weakness of civil society and democracy in post-Communist Hungary. It was thus necessary for anti-Communist forces to complete a struggle against the east that had begun in the sixteenth century, continued in the 1956 Uprising and was still being fought in the post-Communist period.

This idea of 'finishing 1956' was graphically played out during the riots sparked by the leaked confessions of the socialist prime minister, Ferenc Gyurcsány, and then shaped by the revelation's proximity to the commemorations of the fiftieth anniversary of the Uprising in October 2006.[39] The protests themselves were a direct reaction to the disclosure on 17 September 2006 that Gyurcsány had lied about the state of the public finances to ensure his party's re-election earlier that year. His anti-Communist opponents, who began to organize protests in late September 2006, attempted to identify the socialist government as the direct successor of those who had suppressed the revolutionaries in 1956. They often invoked Gyurcsány's own past as a KISz (Communist youth) leader, and seized on the fact that he had appeared to echo a radio broadcast from the Uprising itself in which a broad-caster from Hungarian national radio had admitted that the station had, under the Stalinists, 'lied in the morning, lied in the evening, and . . . lied the whole day'. Gyurcsány had employed an approximation of this phrase, in a secretly taped private political speech, to describe the socialists' cover-up of the parlous state of the government's finances earlier that year. His incendiary comments, which appeared to link Stalinist-era cover-ups with the machina-tions of the post-Communist socialists, were publicly leaked only weeks before the fiftieth anniversary of the Uprising. For many anti-Communists, the socialist government, which had played a major role in the organization of the 1956 commemorations and the commissioning of new memorials to the revolutionaries, thereby forfeited its right to lead the festivities.

Radical Hungarian anti-Communists attempted (symbolically at least) to re-create the 1956 revolution on the streets in Budapest, imagining themselves to be the true revolutionaries and members of the socialist government the successors to those Communists who had lied to the Hungarian people in the 1950s.[40]

These protestors sought to take control of the public space in Budapest in the weeks prior to the socialist-led fiftieth-anniversary celebrations. Fidesz, the opposition party, called for mass protests 'in the spirit of 1956'.[41] Daily street demonstrations took place in Kossuth Square, outside the Hungarian parliament, from 17 September. Protestestors consisted of both Fidesz supporters and followers of the far right, who collectively cast themselves as revolutionaries from 1956 come back to break the ongoing leftist stranglehold on Hungarian politics. Demonstrators frequently imagined themselves to be 're-creating 1956', and developed their own strategies of protest drawn from collectively remembered scripts from the Uprising itself. Earlier in the year, Hungarian state television had run a series of promotional advertisements that had invoked the memory of the storming of the radio station, one of the first major political acts of the 1956 revolution. The advertisements had asked: 'Which television station would you storm now?' The right-wing protesters' answer to that question was Hungarian state television, and they penetrated the broadcaster's building on the night of 18 September, demanding the opportunity to publicize their demands in a live transmission.[42] Others sought to remind the government of the suppression of the 1956 revolution by Soviet tanks, stealing one from an exhibition about the Uprising and, delighted to discover that it still worked, riding it through the streets of Budapest as part of the public protests (see Figure 1). They thus fashioned themselves as heroic revolutionaries, inspired by the struggles of 1956 and devoted to the 'real regime change' that had been blocked since 1989.[43]

Right-wing protestors also understood the socialists' attempts to commemorate 1956 as the expression of a tradition that had suppressed the true aims of the Uprising. Thus, socialist efforts to celebrate the revolutionaries could be interpreted as a disguised attempt to legitimize the destruction of the revolution. A major new memorial to the 1956 revolutionaries (see Figure 2) was commissioned by the socialist government at the site where the Stalin statue had been pulled down during the Uprising (this was one of the best-remembered moments of iconoclasm from the 1956 events in Hungary). The new monument eschewed the traditional heroic romantic fighting figure that was normally used to commemorate the 1956 struggle, and instead drew upon an abstract form of a rising wave, inspired, according to some observers, by the Holocaust memorial in Berlin. Yet some anti-Communists wished to interpret it as a monument commemorating the successful suppression of the revolution, an affront to the Hungarian nation that even the Communist regime, re-established after 1956, had not attempted.[44] Some likened the steel columns that make up the monument to the gallows on which revolutionaries were hanged, arguing that it should be regarded as a monument to the Workers' Militia which had enforced the clampdown which had followed the defeat of the revolution.[45]

Unlike Hungary, where Communist-era resistance, especially the 1956 Uprising, was extensively commemorated, Poland paid remarkably scant public attention to its own history of political resistance. Solidarity, despite once having been the largest Communist-era opposition movement in central-eastern Europe, was afforded no major national monument, museum or commemoration for the first fifteen years after the collapse of Communism.[46] In 2005, it finally received attention on the occasion of the twenty-fifth anniversary of the shipyard strikes that had led to its formation. Yet even then it was an international affair involving thirty world leaders, who celebrated Solidarity's contribution to European freedom and unity rather than its part in the collapse of Communism in Poland. The date of the movement's formation in 1980, 31 August, was declared the European Day of Solidarity and Freedom, and a 'European Solidarity Centre', to celebrate Poland's contribution to the continent's march towards liberty, was established in Gdańsk, the industrial city port on the Baltic Sea where Solidarity first emerged.[47] Domestic attempts to commemorate the independent trade union frequently failed, however, and plans to celebrate its leader – Lech Wałęsa – were regularly dismissed.

The fact that Solidarity had been the largest opposition movement to emerge in Communist eastern Europe, had been very adept at symbolic politics and public memorialization before 1989, and in many accounts was ascribed a leading role in the destruction of dictatorship, made the absence of public commemorations of it in Poland particularly striking.[48] Solidarity developed into a broad non-Communist movement, gaining at its peak reputedly ten million members who united a number of powerful bases of opposition to the Communist regime: Catholic nationalists, liberal intellectuals and working-class trade unionists. In the brief period during 1980–81 when it was legalized, it established a significant series of public memorials honouring the tradition of workers' protests across Poland, and developed a sophisticated symbolic language to articulate an alternative value system to that of the Communist state.[49] It was a broad social movement that gave shape to a range of social and cultural identities that were distinct from the official ideology; however, it also explicitly chose not to challenge the power of the state. Without its philosophy of the so-called 'self-limiting revolution', it believed its actions might have invited Soviet intervention.[50] The movement was outlawed in December 1981, when martial law was declared in Poland, but re-emerged in the late 1980s. Liberals within the movement were eventually invited by the Communists to the Round Table discussions that would lead to the dissolution of the dictatorship.

Yet the absence of any domestic state commemoration for Solidarity was mainly due to the deeply divided (and often ambiguous) ways its legacy was understood by the successors to the liberal and right wings of the Solidarity movement. Liberals understood Solidarity's achievement as a heroic victory over Communism in 1989. The negotiated end to the system was seen as the inevitable culmination of the ideology of the 'self-limiting revolution', which prized dialogue and negotiations and rejected armed struggle as a way of achieving gains for the Polish population.[51] The survival of Communists after 1989 was not seen as a defeat; rather, it was considered a testament to the power of Solidarity that former Communists had been converted into democrats. Moreover, it was a sign of the mature and civilized nature of Polish society that such a significant political change occurred without bloodshed, and that old enemies could be incorporated into the democratic game without destabilizing the new political system. Thus some Polish liberals rejected this new anti-Communism that sought to reconstitute older struggles in the post-Communist period. They began to define themselves as 'anti-anti-Communists' or 'anti-Communists with a human face', signalling that they rejected not only Communism but also the radical anti-Communist mobilization of historical memory which appeared to them divisive and inauthentic.[52]

The anti-Communist nationalist right understood Solidarity differently; for them, it was Solidarity, rather than its Communist opponents, that had been defeated in 1989, as it had not managed to end the participation of Communists in Polish politics.[53] According to this view, Solidarity's participation in the Round Table negotiations of 1989 was not an expression of the movement's self-limiting nature, but rather was a betrayal on the part of its liberal wing who had been prepared to reach a deal with the Communists. Indeed, the very preparedness of some Solidarity activists to compromise with the regime in 1989 served to remind the right that the movement had been initially concerned with reforming the Communist system rather than over-throwing it. Thus, some later considered Solidarity to have been insufficiently democratic during the Communist period to provide a model for politically appropriate behaviour after 1989.[54] Even those nationalists who accepted that the Round Table was an initial necessity on the road to dismantling Communism argued that, once Solidarity had proved its popularity in the first

elections, there was no need to keep to the terms of the Round Table agreements, and that ex-Communists should have been thoroughly cleansed from
public life.[55] Liberal activists were seen to have failed, not only because they
had not fought to remove former Communists, but also because the negotiations themselves had given the Communists a political legitimacy that they
had never enjoyed in over four decades of one-party rule.

The nationalist critique went further still, accusing the liberals not of being
naïve or politically inept, but rather of being closer in ideological outlook to
former Communists than to the rest of the Solidarity movement. Thus, for
some right-wingers, their former colleagues in Solidarity were now recast as
Communist collaborators. They pointed to the Communist family backgrounds from which liberal dissidents such as Adam Michnik and Jacek Kuroń
had emerged, and made accusations that prominent Solidarity activists had
been secret-police informants. They claimed that the Round Table was
effectively a compact between liberals from Solidarity (the so-called 'pinks')
and Communists (the 'reds') to engineer a political system that favoured
the liberal left and diminished the role of nationalism, the Catholic Church
and traditional Polish culture.[56] Their agreement had paved the way for secu-
larism, individualism, neo-liberal economics and a morally neutral state that
'protected pluralism' but not national values. From this viewpoint, liberalism
was seen not as the rejection of Communism but rather as its obvious successor
and ally, an anti-religious, modernizing, anti-traditional, anti-national political
ideology that united liberals and ex-Communists against the right.[57]

On the one hand, anti-Communists seldom supported the commemoration
of Solidarity because of its failure to banish Communists which was interpreted as a betrayal of the struggle under dictatorship. On the other hand,
from the mid-1990s, its memory was invoked as a form of unifying political
rhetoric. Faced with a resurgent ex-Communist left, which became a dominant partner in government in 1994 and took the presidency in 1995, some
now looked to the memory of Solidarity to provide ideological glue for a right
wing that was weak and splintered between proponents of free-market liberalism, more traditional nationalist conservatism and German-style Christian
democracy.[58] For the Polish right, reviving the memory of the struggle – in
which the Catholic nationalists were imagined as the sole inheritors of the
Solidarity revolution, and the liberal-left as its destroyers[59] – was effective in
creating a common enemy, providing an otherwise ideologically diverse coalition with a powerful historical identity around which to coalesce. Solidarity
Electoral Action, founded in 1996 as a coalition of mainstream trade unions
and minor rightist parties, and the winner of the 1997 elections, was an excellent illustration of this: it represented a number of diverse and antagonistic

political platforms which were united by a pact, centred on their shared Catholicism, anti-Communism and desire to create a 'broad electoral bloc, capable of winning the next parliamentary elections', that could complete the 'Solidarity revolution'.[60] A 'genuine' revolution was required, based on Catholic anti-Communist values, to realise the political change that had failed to be fully implemented in 1989. After its election, Solidarity Electoral Action embarked on a programme that sought to tear Poland from its Communist past. It introduced the country's first post-Communist constitution, initiated the first (failed) attempts at widespread screening of former security-service collaborators who stood for post-Communist public office, and created the first new state institution since 1989 – the Institute of National Remembrance – in order to reshape Polish collective memory (see Chapter 2). A liberal-left government re-took power in 2001, after which the idea of the unfinished revolution was revived again by the Law and Justice party, which became the dominant partner in a new governing coalition from 2005 to 2007. It promised to replace the immoral, corrupt and anti-national nature of the post-Communist 'Third Republic' with a new 'Fourth Republic' that valued moral community and would place Catholicism at the core of public life. It would complete the revolution of 1989 by instigating widespread purges of ex-Communists, not merely from the state bureaucracy but also from within the professions. According to one of its proponents, Bronisław Wildstein:

> The Fourth Republic of Poland was supposed be a cure for its predecessor's faults. Its starting point was supposed to be moral regeneration . . . [the] rebuilding of the civic commonwealth, [and] . . . modern patriotism was supposed to be awakened. This is why memories of the remarkable Solidarity revolution had to be restored. A debate was started around 'historical policy', in which the past was viewed as fundamental for integration [into the post-Communist system]. Unlike the inferiority complex caused by the Third Republic pedagogues, the proclaimers of the Fourth Republic of Poland appealed to national pride.[61]

In order to support this idea of a new revolution, anti-Communist ideologues referred to Catholic, conservative ideals as those of the 'true Solidarity' of the early 1980s (simultaneously characterizing the liberal wing of the movement as inauthentic). In this reading, Solidarity became the starting point and inspiration for a traditional Catholic revival in Poland. It had once provided an alternative to the anti-traditionalism of Communism in 1980, but also articulated an ideology of resistance to the 'moral, individualistic emptiness' of the liberal-left, secular and anti-national modernizing consensus of the post-Communist Polish Republic. According to Zdzisław Krasnodębski, one of the new right wing's most prominent intellectuals, Solidarity represented an alternative to the anti-Catholicism, feminism and uncritical assumptions about progress that were part of both Communism and liberal modernity:

> Solidarność [Solidarity] ended the 'red decades', or even the 'red centuries'. Poles need to be taught that the political language used by the left is irrelevant, dishonest and dangerous. At the same time they need to know that national consciousness is not the same as nationalism; that religion is not the opium of the masses; that the Catholic church is not a totalitarian institution; that the idea of progress can be oppressive and lead to crimes; that feminism can be funny and vulgar and that the Holocaust was not the only twentieth-century massacre worth remembering.[62]

In refashioning Solidarity, these anti-Communists did not seek to celebrate its history fully since they believed that it had not been victorious – yet. Indeed, rather than promoting Solidarity's achievements in ending Communism in central-eastern Europe, Polish anti-Communists turned back much further to the story of the Warsaw Uprising of 1944. It is striking that anti-Communists should have looked to the story of a defeat of the Warsaw population by the Germans in 1944 to promote the myth of the heroic struggle against Communism, rather than to Solidarity, which had (at least to many outside Poland) appeared to have played a direct role in ending left-wing dictatorship. For anti-Communist groups – and in particular the Law and Justice party – it was the heroic efforts of the population of Warsaw in the summer of 1944, rather than the 'betrayed and defeated' Solidarity, that could be written into a longer-term national narrative of resistance against occupation and the fight for independent statehood. The Uprising provided the subject for Poland's first major post-Communist museum, initiated by Jarosław Kaczyński, a member of the right-wing Law and Justice party, then mayor of Warsaw and later prime minister (2005–07). The museum was supposed to provide a message about the sacrifice and heroism of previous generations.[63] It told the story of Warsaw's patriotic Home Army insurgency against the Germans in August and September 1944, alongside that of the Red Army's betrayal of the city as it halted at its eastern outskirts for over two months, waiting for both the German and Polish forces to weaken themselves. Warsaw's insurgents eventually capitulated on 2 October 1944. The clear military defeat of an unsupported yet heroic uprising was, for anti-Communists, a story free from the messy compromises with the 'occupier' that characterized the end of the Solidarity movement. Moreover, the emphasis on both the heroism of the insurgents and the betrayal of the Soviet forces (who both refused to provide assistance during the Uprising and then persecuted its leaders as bourgeois nationalists afterwards) led some Polish commentators to conclude that an uninformed visitor might leave the museum with the impression that the true enemies of the insurgents had been the Communists,[64] and that the Uprising had actually been victorious. Thus, anti-Communists had turned the story from a defeat by the Nazis into a heroic struggle against the Communists, in which the combatants, unlike Solidarity, had refused to compromise themselves.[65] For them, only the story of the Warsaw Uprising could be accommodated to the radical anti-Communist traditions of romantic nationalist resistance. By contrast, that of Solidarity was too ambiguous; its Catholic wing had been let down by liberals who had negotiated with the regime to dismantle Communism but in doing so had failed to exclude actual Communists, whose continued presence morally tainted the new political system. Solidarity embodied the failure to forge a new moral, Catholic, anti-Communist Poland: its memory could not therefore become the basis for post-Communist national commemoration.

Ex-Communists and the Memory of Resistance

In most countries in central-eastern Europe, the post-Communist left was dominated by ex-Communists who survived the revolutions of 1989. In many cases, they jettisoned much of their former ideological outlook: the ex-Communists who came to power in Hungary (1994, 2002, 2006) and Poland (1993, 2001), for instance, formed economically liberal parties that embraced globalization and were often far less statist than their anti-Communist opponents. To a certain extent, they avoided discussions of recent history. First, they renounced their own pasts: ex-Communists were only successful electorally when they managed to expunge the remnants of Marxist-Leninist ideology and symbolism from their party. Where leaders were unable to purge their parties in this way, as in the Czech Republic, their electoral appeal withered and political space opened up for other left-wing alternatives.[66] Second, they often developed strategies to deal with the negative influences of their association with the 'crimes of Communism': some parties preferred amnesia, while others engaged in partial apologies which were seen by their critics as momentary and insincere, rather than as indicative of a genuine atonement for the past. Third, they turned their rejection of 'memory politics' to their advantage: the ex-Communist president of Poland between 1995 and 2005, Aleksander Kwaśniewski, often presented himself as the embodiment of Poland's future, while his opponents were characterized as refighting the now irrelevant anti-Communist struggles of the past.

Some former Communists did engage with debates over the meaning of the pre-1989 anti-Communist struggle, however. This was particularly the case for those who had to remake themselves for the new political game. Whereas older Communists who had withdrawn from political life could defend former positions, those who entered the post-Communist political arena often carefully crafted new stories about their pasts directed at a democratic audience. For figures such as Kwaśniewski, or for ex-Communist elite members of the Hungarian Socialist Party such as Ferenc Gyurcsány, former Communist youth leader and then post-Communist prime minister (2002–08), constructing a politically appealing, story that explained the party's transition from its dictatorial past was key. A central issue was how to gain democratic legitimacy after four decades of association with dictatorship. Unlike those anti-Communists who saw 1989 as an incomplete revolution, some ex-Communists argued that Communism had been defeated and that they had genuinely changed their political orientation, and hence were no longer a threat to liberal democratic development. Thus, while anti-Communists constructed a narrative of a decades-long struggle against Communism that was still to be completed, some ex-Communists told the story of a triumphant battle for democracy that had seen Communism truly vanquished in 1989. In Poland, some ex-Communist Social Democrats embraced the story of Solidarity, in so far as it allowed them to tell the story of their own defeat and their ideological conversion from dictators to democrats. In Hungary, some former Communists went even further, presenting themselves as the true architects of their country's liberation from dictatorship.[67]

Hungary: Communists as Liberators

The post-Communist Hungarian Socialist Party was the successor to the pre-1989 Hungarian Socialist Workers' Party: the latter was never officially dissolved, and its Communist-era membership and financial resources remained intact.[68] The Socialist Party became the dominant force in the first two decades of post-Communist politics, winning elections in 1994, 2002 and 2006. In the process of recasting itself for democratic politics, it had to deal with the legacy of four decades of association with dictatorship. Hungarian ex-Communists publicly regretted and renounced their authoritarian traditions with more vigour than most other central-eastern European successor movements during the transition process. In October 1989, they apologized for aspects of their party's past: the forced incorporation of the Social Democratic Party into the Communist Party after World War II; the violence of the Stalinist period; the suppression of the 1956 revolution; and Kádár's refusal to liberalize the system in 1985. These public expressions of regret, in part, led to the breakaway of the Workers' Party, a repository for orthodox Communists who did not want to give up their political heritage and who remained a tiny electoral presence. The formation of a breakaway Communist group was useful to the new Hungarian Socialist Party in that it set its own abandonment of one-party rule and centralized planning into starker relief.[69] Yet, while condemning dictatorship and apologizing for its former role in it, it also began to construct a democratic heritage for itself. Communists' involvement in the Round Table at the re-birth of Hungarian democracy was central to their depiction of themselves as convincing democrats after 1989. The negotiated transition, in which they had played a major role, became an important end-point to a new set of stories about their pasts, which anticipated their commitment to democracy after 1989. Central to these were their claims on the legacies of the 1956 Uprising. At different moments, ex-Communists placed themselves on either side of the barricades in 1956 in order to paint themselves as the handmaidens of democracy in Hungary. Sometimes they were resisters against Stalinist dictatorship, at others they were the necessary suppressors of revolution, who nonetheless recognized the legitimacy of its democratic claims and sought to facilitate them in the longer term.

In some accounts, ex-Communists aligned themselves with the heroic struggle against Stalinist dictatorship in 1956. This shift to an identification with the democratic socialist aspect of the Uprising had in fact occurred within the Hungarian Socialist Workers' Party immediately *before* the fall of the system. In February 1989, eight months before the end of one-party rule, the Communists altered their official line on the 1956 Uprising. Their Central Committee wanted to switch sides with regard to 1956; no longer were they the party of János Kádár who, they had formerly claimed in official histories, had saved Hungary from the restoration of Fascism in 1956 by suppressing the so-called 'counter-revolutionaries'. The Central Committee members tried to work out how to enable their party, which had been responsible for crushing the revolution and for the execution of its reformist leader, Imre Nagy, to lay claim to the democratic socialist traditions of the party.[70] In June 1989, they agreed to re-bury Nagy as a national hero in an attempt to re-legitimize the party by claiming him as the antecedent for the party's new reformed socialist path.[71] Thenceforth, the Uprising would be characterized as a popular revolt against the illegitimate use of power by the Stalinists, and the Hungarian Socialist Workers' Party would now attempt to identify itself with the reform socialists led by Nagy, who fought in the revolution for national independence and democratic socialism.[72] Although the Communists had initially embraced the democratic tradition of the 1956 Uprising in order to stabilize the one-party system, after the Round Table and the beginning of multiparty democracy, it became a way for ex-Communist elites to discover a democratic heritage and a commitment to the Hungarian nation, and divorce their successor party from a movement associated with dictatorship and Soviet domination.[73] In 1996, two years after its first post-Communist electoral victory, the Hungarian Socialist Party successfully proposed a law enshrining Nagy's status as a martyr of the revolution. This was an attempt to repudiate the idea that it was the ideological descendant of those who had suppressed the revolution, and instead to assert that it was the inheritor of a legitimate left-wing movement that had struggled against the excesses of dictatorship in Hungary and, at least by the end of the revolution, had embraced multiparty democracy.[74] It was also a way in which Communists could claim to be victims of Communism too: Nagy's execution in 1958 reinforced a historical account in which their movement had fought for a reformed version of socialism, but which had in turn been brutally suppressed.

Yet, at other moments, ex-Communists placed themselves on the other side of the revolutionary barricades, identifying themselves with the Kádár regime which had crushed the revolution in 1956. This was possible partly because there was still a residual public affection for the Kádár period; indeed, it is esti-mated that up to 100,000 people attended the leader's funeral in 1989.[75] In the 1990s, nostalgia for the social and economic stability of those years was common.[76] It was also possible because of what András Mink called the 'Faustian legend of Kádár': the idea that, post-1956, leaders had realized that the goals of the revolution – independence, democracy and so on – were impos-sible in the context of the Cold War. Nevertheless, Kádár had then been prepared to 'dirty' his hands and sacrifice his moral integrity in order to secure material progress and relative freedom for his people. Thus, Kádár and the Kádárist elite were seen as having carried out a secret, underground mission to accomplish the goals of 1956: no less than the gradual self-liquidation of the regime behind the Soviet leaders' backs.[77] Ex-Communists pointed to their role as the greatest liberalizers within the Soviet bloc, introducing market conditions and reaching out to western institutions from the late 1960s onwards. They presented the late Communist period as a steady inevitable evolution towards social democracy in the context of the constrained geopolitical environment of the period.[78] In this version of history, Hungarian Communists – as soon as the rise of Gorbachev allowed it – transformed their reformist agenda into a democratic one, organizing multiparty local elections from 1984, enabling the growth of opposition movements and transforming themselves into 'Europeanized' social democrats in the late 1980s.[79] This was a convincing historical narrative for some: the Hungarian Communists had been at the forefront of reforms within the eastern bloc in the late Communist period, had a less antagonistic relationship with society than in neighbouring socialist states, and had played a prominent role in the regime's dismantling. However, this historical narrative was also essentially a myth. Before the Round Tables of 1989, any movements towards economic liberalization and social reforms were aimed at stabilizing the one-party system, not forging a path to liberal democracy. As Ferenc Laczó argued, Hungarian Communists' reformism was not thought to have led to the collapse of the system, so 'their failure (to reform the system) should not be accepted as their success (in overcoming it)'.[80]

These complex historical constructions, which celebrated both Imre Nagy *and* János Kádár, were part of a wider argument that it was the left, rather than the conservatives, who were the true harbingers of democracy in Hungary. Socialists often accused the right of idolizing those fighters in 1956 whose agendas were linked to a return to the 'reactionary', 'neo-feudal' Hungary of the interwar years, rather than the liberal democratic system that emerged after 1989.[81] In this version of events, it was only the left that could claim a legitimate progressive heritage in post-Communist Hungary: the socialists claimed that they had been advocates for democratic developments in Hungary since 1945. They constructed a story that began with their support for the Red Army's liberation of Hungary from Fascism and the conservative, 'reactionary' political system that had preceded it,[82] and continued with their embrace of a progressive political system after 1945, which had sought to advance social equality. When that experiment degenerated into Stalinist oppression after 1948, the reformed left played a leading role in forging resistance to that dictatorship, which eventually led to the Uprising of 1956.[83] Although their attempts to democratize Hungary – embodied in the figure of Imre Nagy – had failed, they had – in the figure of János Kádár – nevertheless sought reform within a constrained international environment, and worked to prepare the country for the eventual arrival of liberal democracy. This strategy offered a subtle reminder that although ex-Communists were now fully committed to democracy and had rejected the practice of dictatorship, they nevertheless understood that the reasons for the maintenance of autocratic rule were comprehensible in a different historical context. Even if one party rule were to be condemned, the Communist movement had steered Hungary away from Fascism in 1945 to the realization of liberal democracy in 1989, and in doing so had sought both to protect the Hungarian nation from the excesses of dictatorship and to enable the maximum amount of personal freedom given the geopolitical constraints of the Cold War. Just as Franco's Spanish supporters after the transition presented his dictatorship as an unfortunate necessity on the road from civil war to democracy, so ex-Communists in Hungary presented dictatorship as an unwanted, but nevertheless understandable, stage on the national journey to liberal democracy.[84]

Poland: Ex-Communists as Converted Democrats

Polish Communists had also played a part in the dismantling of Communism at Round Table negotiations. Thus, after 1989, they had a basis upon which they could construct a claim to a prior commitment to democracy and, as in Hungary, they searched for evidence of their earlier attraction to liberal democratic development. However, ex-Communists in Poland – who dominated the post-Communist coalition governments (as social democrats) in 1993–97 and 2001–05 – found it far more difficult to demonstrate a long-term history of resistance to dictatorship. They had no equivalent of the socialist involvement in the Hungarian Uprising of 1956 by which they could present themselves as having fought against dictatorship in advance of Communism's collapse.[85] In fact, Polish Communists' suppression of Solidarity – the largest opposition movement in the eastern bloc – in December 1981 had the potential to undermine any claim they might later make to having been committed to ending the Communist system before 1989. Yet, despite this, ex-Communists commemorated anti-Communist resistance, and in particular Solidarity, to a far greater extent, and with far less ambiguity, than those who had constituted Solidarity's membership.[86] This was because ex-Communists could use the story of Solidarity to forge an account of their conversion from dictators to democrats. Solidarity was the heroic and powerful movement that defeated Communism ideologically, and in doing so made democrats out of a Communist elite, who previously had been uncommitted to change.

In this account, ex-Communists did not depict themselves as democrats before the arrival of Solidarity, but rather as non-ideological patriots who had protected ordinary Poles from the impositions of the Soviet Union wherever possible. Thus they had fought for Polish sovereignty, resisting the incorporation of Poland as a seventeenth republic of the Soviet Union in the 1940s and threats to Polish borders from the Germans and Russians in the 1950s and 1960s.[87] Some ex-Communists claimed that after 1956 there had been no ideological Communists in Poland, only patriots pretending to be Communists for the sake of the Polish nation.[88] They had served as a necessary and constructive buffer between the Soviet imperialists, on the one hand, and the needs of Polish society, on the other. In the late Communist period, they argued, the gap between society and the regime was much narrower than in other Communist countries. In this version of events, the real dividing line was between the Communist elite and Polish society on one side, and Moscow on the other.[89] Before the late 1970s, though essentially non-ideological, the party had lacked a commitment to change; it was Solidarity that converted its members. Solidarity was presented as important for the Communists in that it showed them that peaceful change was possible, that dictatorship could be ended and that gradualism could be embraced. At the twenty-fifth-anniversary celebrations of Solidarity in 2005, Aleksander Kwaśniewski, the former Communist minister of youth and the post-Communist president between 1995 and 2005, declared:

> Twenty-five years ago people in the Gdańsk shipyard formed Solidarity. Out of their courage was born a movement of ten million people, which changed the course of history. Today I want to thank all those brave people. I believe that all Poles owe you their gratitude. Also those who were not in Solidarity then. [We] who did not understand that you were right. Who did not want to or could not support your cause. And even those who fought against you then. Since we all, I stress all, live in a free Poland. . . . As the president of the Republic of Poland I wish to dedicate words of admiration and respect to the great leader of the Polish August, Mr. Lech Wałęsa. Twenty-five years ago I did not stand on the same side as you, but today I have no doubts that your vision of Poland led us in a good direction. And thanks to your courage, today we can build together the wellbeing of our homeland.[90]

For many anti-Communists, this historical narrative was inauthentic: the Communist regime's initial crushing of Solidarity in December 1981 with the imposition of Martial Law illustrated that the real dividing line lay between Moscow and Polish Communists on one side, and Polish society on the other. Polish Communists were quislings who had neither the best interests of the nation at heart, nor any intention of dismantling the Communist system. Yet for Kwaśniewski, the suppression of Solidarity and the imposition of Martial Law in December 1981 were not evidence of their anti-democratic nature. Indeed, he credited ex-Communists with the creation of Solidarity itself: their liberalizing dictatorship of the 1970s had allowed dissent to flourish. Polish Communists had then been converted to democratic change by Solidarity in 1980, had been prepared to come to terms with Solidarity in 1981, but had been unable to do so because of the threat of invasion from the Soviet Union.[91] Kwaśniewski argued that Solidarity was thus quashed only temporarily in order to maintain Polish independence; as soon as the international situation made reconciliation feasible, the Communists worked alongside Solidarity to dismantle the system. Thus, 1989 was the realization of the spirit of 1980–81, which had been briefly suppressed owing to international pressures that could not be blamed on home Communists. According to Kwaśniewski in 2005:

> In a certain sense, 1989 was a test of the intentions of 1981. For the external conditions had changed drastically, the Brezhnev doctrine had disappeared, Poland started to regain its sovereignty. And then we came out of this test exceptionally well. We found the strength, the indispensable trust and imagination, capable of breaking down walls .... Lech Wałęsa and Wojciech Jaruzelski, yesterday's enemies, became co-architects of the Polish accord. There is one lesson for us in this: we must always speak with each other, be capable of finding agreement as to how to protect our freedom, sovereignty and democratic rights.[92]

In this account, ex-Communists did not need to be attacked, or a new anti-Communist revolution attempted, because Communist ideology had in fact been defeated in 1981, and its demise confirmed in 1989. Although individual ex-Communists had remained in power, they had long rejected their commitment to Communism and dictatorship. Solidarity had destroyed their belief in the system and had created the potential for reconciliation between former enemies who dismantled the system together. Thus, ex-Communists such as Kwaśniewski often regarded the past as 'mastered', rejecting the right's questioning of 1989 as an incomplete revolution.[93] Indeed, Kwaśniewski owed his own electoral success in part to his ability to frame his opponents as incapable of moving on from their anti-Communism, to the detriment of Poland's current economic and political development. As the sociologist Andrzej Rychard put it, Kwaśniewski was 'the personification of the dream about an elegant and painless departure from the Communist past'.[94]

Conclusion

Across the twentieth century, it was often the case that opponents of a former political system – such as anti-Fascists after the collapse of Fascism, or anti-colonialists after the collapse of the European empires – remembered their resistance to the previous political system. They did this as a way of celebrating the overcoming of a rejected ideology, and of providing a heroic narrative that could form the basis for political consensus in the present, no matter how small that opposition might have been.[95] Hungary and Poland experienced moments of opposition to Communist regimes on a scale unmatched elsewhere in the eastern bloc, yet stories of resistance and revolution could not easily be invoked to provide a founding myth for the new political system after 1989. Rather, historical memory divided right and left in post-Communist politics, and became a vital tool through which new political movements sought to legitimize themselves, define their political enemies and frame new political struggles.

Some anti-Communists invoked a version of the past that justified their struggle to finish an incomplete revolution. They saw the negotiated settlements of 1989, which had left the Communists unscathed, as a betrayal of earlier struggles against the regime. Thus they invoked the memory of the unfinished struggles of 1956 and of the Solidarity revolution in order to re-create the anti-Communist struggle in the post-Communist present. Some prominent ex-Communists, by contrast, either invoked their participation in anti-Communist resistance (the 1956 Uprising) to bolster their pre-1989 democratic credentials, or told stories of their ideological defeat at the hands of heroic anti-Communist forces which had converted them from dictators to convinced democrats (Solidarity). The victory of anti-Communist resistance was related in order to frame the 1989 settlements as essentially complete, and hence to bolster ex-Communists' claims to be genuinely converted democrats who did not need to be purged from the post-Communist political arena. Historical memory was invoked for partisan advantage. By contrast, 'anti-anti-Communist' arguments that the 1989 settlements and the resistance that preceded them could be sculpted into cohesive national mythologies bore little fruit.[96]

To find such heroic unified narratives, one would need to look outside central-eastern Europe to dominant western discourses, which placed stories of courageous resistance – the 1956 Hungarian Uprising, the Prague Spring, Solidarity and late Communist dissidence – into a linear narrative that charted the frequent and powerful expressions of an anti-Communist popular will that eventually found expression with the final defeat of Communism in 1989.[97] Indeed, for western European politicians, the stories of those who *resisted* dictatorship were frequently much easier to deal with than the experience of those who were *victimized* by it; the memory of the participants in Solidarity and the 1956 Uprising could easily be re-imagined for a new globalized, post-Cold War history of Communism overcome and the triumph of democracy, the free market and European integration. Victims of Communism were, by contrast, often perceived to be in competition with those who had suffered under Nazism and in the Holocaust.[98] Stories of resistance to dictatorship fitted smoothly into a narrative of European unity founded on the story of struggle against dictatorships of both left and right. The European Union president José Manuel Barroso, who attended commemorations for the fiftieth anniversary of the 1956 Uprising and the twenty-fifth anniversary of the Solidarity movement, wrote both events into a narrative that started with anti-Communist resistance and finished with the political unity of the European continent. Speaking in Budapest in October 2006, he rejected the idea that the goals of the revolution had remained unrealized in 1989, arguing that 1956 should be seen as part of a European tradition of resistance to both left- and right-wing dictatorships that had eventually led to the transcendence of Europe's divisions:

> The 1956 Revolution showed that the Soviet response to freedom was oppression, murder and lies. The Revolution lit a torch of freedom; a flame that went underground to sustain opposition movements across Europe's dictatorships. A flame that surfaced again in the Prague Spring in 1968, that lit the way for the collapse of dictatorship in Greece, Portugal and Spain. It found its heirs with the foundation of Solidarność [Solidarity] in 1980, in Poland. And it inspired those who fought for freedom until the fall of the Berlin Wall in 1989. The 1956 Revolution also laid the foundations for the enlarged European Union of today. The Treaty of Rome, signed six months after the revolution, launched what is now the European Union. But it was an incomplete Union. Because just as the extreme right-wing dictatorships prevented the countries of southern Europe from joining, so the Communist dictatorship prevented so many countries from central Europe taking their rightful place in the European Community.[99]

However, it was only an international audience that saw anti-Communist resistance in this way.[100] In the region itself, anti-Communists refused to celebrate 1989 as they believed the revolution to have failed; it was only really ex-Communists who celebrated opposition to the Communist regime as a heroic story of their own ideological defeat.

CHAPTER TWO

COMPLETING THE REVOLUTION
HISTORY COMMISSIONS AND INSTITUTES OF NATIONAL MEMORY

Until the 1980s, it was not obvious to the architects of new democratic political systems that 'dealing with dictatorship' required open, public and official 'truth-telling' procedures that addressed the experience of past criminality, violence and social complicity. The end of the Nazi regime, though accompanied with punishment for its elite at the Nuremberg Trials, was not followed by wider research into its functioning, or its relationship with German society.[1] Nor did the elites who stewarded the democratic transitions in southern Europe that followed the collapse of right-wing authoritarian regimes in the mid-1970s instigate such processes: the death of General Franco in Spain, for instance, was accompanied by a 'pact of silence' in which all the new political parties agreed to limit public discussion about the suffering endured during the Spanish Civil War and the era of dictatorship for fear of threatening the peaceful transition.[2] From the 1980s onwards, however, transitional societies in Latin America, Europe and Africa increasingly utilized 'truth-telling procedures' – such as History Commissions, Truth and Reconciliation Commissions and Institutes of Memory – as a means of creating common understandings of the past, around which, it was hoped, new consensual political systems could be built. Officially constructed narratives about the evils of dictatorship would bind democratizing societies and elites to the new political regime by providing them with a convincing moral case for the rejection of the values of the previous regime. The acceptance of these new sets of stories about the criminality of recent history was often regarded as an ethical minimum for participation in the new political game.[3] Institutions and commissions charged with assisting societies in 'coming to terms' with difficult histories often had compelling rationales: they claimed to be engaged in a dignified process of reclaiming the truth about the experience of dictatorship, which had previously been hidden from public view. Yet these processes were not value-free attempts to reveal concealed episodes from a dictatorial past; they involved constructing particular historical narratives that would underpin the new political system.

Some of the political elites of central-eastern European countries also shared this concern with establishing official institutions that could help to overcome the legacies of the previous era. Most countries in the region set up commissions or institutes, viewing an official and substantive reckoning with the criminality of the Communist past as necessary for democratization. Yet none drew directly on the global examples developed during other transitions in the late twentieth century, such as the South African model of reconciliation or Latin American and Asian history commissions.[4] Rather, it was the reunited Germany's rapid dealing with the Communist past of the German Democratic Republic after 1989 that provided the model (the speed of which was in part due to West Germans' perception of their own failure to come to terms with their Nazi past sufficiently quickly after 1945). Two approaches were especially influential: first, the establishment of the Federal Commission for the Records of the State Security Service of the Former German Democratic Republic (known as the 'Gauck Office', created in 1991), which collected, preserved and made available the files of the Stasi to facilitate rehabilitations, assessments of past affiliations and the prosecution of crimes; and second, the two parliamentary investigatory commissions (created between 1992 and 1998) that were charged with examining the history of the East German SED (Socialist Unity Party) and its abuses.

The rationales for truth-telling procedures established from the 1980s onwards were shaped by the nature of late twentieth-century political transitions. Unlike earlier nineteenth- and twentieth-century cases, where popular revolutions created powerful founding myths for new political elites to draw upon, their late twentieth-century equivalents often had no moment of insurrectionary violence that could be framed as a clear, legitimate starting point for a new era. Revolutions that had swept away former elites could be constructed as heroic moments at which the involvement of 'the people' demonstrated the reality of popular discontent with the old and identification with the new. The (often semi-fictionalized) story of mass participation in revolution came to function as a powerful 'founding myth' that bolstered the legitimacy of the new regime.[5] In the late twentieth century, however, many authoritarian regimes ended with negotiated settlements between old and new elites, without recourse to popular protest. New political players were therefore faced with the question of how, in the absence of a powerful story of 'the people's revolution', they should construct a story of political change that would foster support for the transition. One response to this dilemma was the creation of History Commissions. In some cases, these were established in order to construct new histories that made the seemingly unheroic processes of transition appear momentous and appealing. In others, these procedures were envisaged as compensations for the absence of revolution: they were designed to create broader identifications with political change when countries were faced with ambiguous and partial forms of political rupture which were deemed incapable of being mythologized.

Some elites in transitional societies tried to mythologize the negotiated transition itself, celebrating the reconciliation between former adversaries and the democratic practice of discussion and compromise that the agreements themselves embodied. In South Africa, for instance, the elite settlement that brought apartheid to a close was constructed as the mythical founding event of the new political system. The architects of the post-apartheid political framework viewed the negotiated end to the former system and absence of political revenge and violence as a positive development, which needed to be underpinned through a new negotiated, shared construction of history. The Truth and Reconciliation Commission was thus conceived as a way of solidifying that compromise, by encouraging both victims and perpetrators under the previous regime to engage in a joint venture to produce a newly agreed version of how to understand what had happened under apartheid, which could in turn reinforce a reconciliation between these formerly opposed groups. For them, a social or 'dialogic' truth – a new version of history in which common ground was discovered by both sides – was as important as uncovering discrete facts about crimes under the apartheid regime.[6] The commission understood the criminality of the previous period, not merely in terms of the apartheid state's violence, but also in terms of the illegal acts of the African National Congress in its resistance; thus 'perpetrators on both sides' were expected to confess their guilt. It was hoped that through these processes new social solidarities could be forged, and the impulse for revenge subdued.[7]

In post-Communist central-eastern Europe, only a few saw the reconciliation model as attractive and advocated framing the end of Communism as a moment of the coming together of former opponents. In Romania, members of the former *nomenklatura* and post-Communist president Ion Iliescu called for 'national reconciliation' based on 'erasing the problems of the past' and providing an amnesty for those who had committed violent acts during the Romanian revolution. In Poland, reconciliation was advocated by some former opponents of the regime who believed that the negotiated settlements could provide a founding myth for the new system. These sometimes defined themselves as 'anti-anti-Communists' or 'anti-Communists with a human

face' who were committed to a Poland that rejected not only Communist practice but also the anti-Communist call for revenge. They argued that the negotiated Round Table agreements of 1989 had embodied a sufficient 'denial of
totalitarianism':[8] they had forced the Communists to abandon their attachment to a one-party state and accept the necessity of democracy. Moreover,
the agreements were themselves powerful illustrations of democratic practice
for a country in political transition: they embodied the values of dialogue and
co-operation and could be the basis for reconciliation and civilized political
discourse in the post-Communist world. Thus thinkers such as Adam
Michnik argued that the terms of the Round Table should be accepted (and
even celebrated), that groups should not look to finish the revolution through
purging the former elite, but that there should nevertheless be continued
public discussion about the legacies of the Communist past.[9]

Such voices had little influence. In Poland, for instance, those anti-
Communists who had not taken part in the Round Table talks and did not
accept the logic of compromise, did not believe that the negotiated settlement
could provide an appropriate anti-Communist mythology for a new national
memory.[10] For them, the Round Table agreements were the 'original sins' of the
new republic; they were the result of less than transparent dealings between
liberals and Communists to establish a system that benefited only their own
political needs.[11] They were concerned that a new national identity, which for
them had to be based on a firm rejection of the Communist past, had not been
established after the experience of 1989. First, they suggested, this was because
the Round Tables themselves had suppressed knowledge of the violence of the
Communist period: the memory of past conflict had had to be silenced in order
to ensure that former opponents could find common ground and that political
change could occur without bloodshed. Second, the involvement of Communists
in 'civilized negotiations' had given respectability and moral credibility to former
dictators. Third, they argued that 'the people' had been alienated from the
moment of their liberation as the process of transition had failed to involve them
in the destruction of Communism.[12] Fourth, they emphasized that the inadequacies of the settlement were maintained after 1989; even if compromises had been
necessary to ensure the initial dismantling of dictatorship, they contended, there
had been insufficient attempts to address the significant continuities in law and
political personnel once democracy had been made secure. Thus, they insisted,
the populace had neither experienced nor come to understand the collapse of
Communism as a true break with a totalitarian and criminal past, but rather as
an ambiguous mixture of ruptures and continuities.

Some elites in the region thus believed that it was necessary to 'complete
the revolution' in order to resolve what they saw as a crisis in popular

identification with the new system. What would constitute its completion was deeply contested, however. For radical anti-Communists this meant the continuation of the anti-Communist struggle and the purge of former elites (as we saw in Chapter 1). Attempts at the removal of those who served the previous system have received a lot of attention from scholars. As they have found, in most central-eastern European countries, programmes enacted to purge representatives of the former regime had little impact; they were either rejected or, in places where they were established, had their powers rapidly curtailed; rulings were enforced in very few cases.[13] More common were attempts to 'complete the revolution' by engineering fundamental shifts in the collective memory of the Communist past and the transition. Here, finishing the revolution meant the establishment of official bodies that could assist the dismantling of Communist mentalities through the state-sponsored propagation of new, liberal interpretations of the past. The latter could become the basis for a new democratic collective memory, in which the Communist regime was criminalized and liberal democracy celebrated as its political and moral inversion. This is not to argue that the desire for a new 'liberal memory' and demands for 'justice' were always mutually exclusive aspirations; indeed, some bodies were established to produce official reports that confirmed the criminality of the Communist past as a necessary prelude to the purging of former elites. Yet even in these cases actual lustration procedures rarely followed.[14] Moreover, even where legal processes were established, they were commonly reduced to being shapers of this new memory; they simply became the uncoverers and disseminators of knowledge about past episodes of violence, and their intended roles as the executors of post-revolutionary justice dropped.[15]

For those who wanted to engineer a break with the mentalities of the past, the transition needed to be narrated as a journey from criminality to liberal democracy and human rights. Moreover, it was hoped that individuals would be able to write themselves into this national journey, moving from being totalitarian subjects to liberal citizens protected by the rule of law.[16] Yet these new official discourses were being produced in environments where many perceived clear continuities between the two systems and failed to recognize the existence of a genuine political rupture in 1989. According to Jarosław Kaczyński, leader of the anti-Communist Law and Justice party: 'The new epoch in Poland which started in 1989 began in a specific way. There was no official inauguration and there was no "storming of the Bastille". And the events that followed show that this process resulted in the situation in which truth mingled with lies in people's minds.'[17] Given the absence of popular identification with the collapse of 1989, such anti-Communists argued, an alternative story that convincingly articulated the reality of meaningful change was necessary in order to bind post-Communist populations to the new political system. Thus the task for producers of new public memories was the construction of a believable popular narrative of a revolutionary rupture between dictatorship and liberal democracy, despite the absence of an actual revolution to mythologize.

Two types of institution emerged in the post-Communist landscape that sought to reconstruct collective memories in this way: History Commissions and Institutes of National Memory. The former were established to create a new account of the Communist (and sometimes Fascist) experience. History Commissions were tasked with producing a new official national narrative of the past that could assist the construction of a consensual understanding of the nature of Communism and the need for its rejection amongst post-Communist elites, and provide an official account that could be used in the state education system. Institutes of National Memory, by contrast, were established as repositories of, and regulators of access to, the files of the former secret police, but often developed both research functions (mainly producing studies on Communism based on these files) and judicial wings. Commissions and institutes were not, by and large, the product of the imme-diate transition era, when issues of past crimes and truth-telling were not at the forefront of political debate. Rather, they emerged out of later and quite different impulses. History Commissions, established in Romania, Lithuania, Estonia and Latvia, were established prior to the countries' accession to the European Union, and were usually the product of debates about how to produce liberal democratic citizens as part of their integration into western political structures and cultural norms.[18] As such, they did not seek to provide professional impartial assessments or 'balance sheets' of the recent past, but rather were set up to make the liberal democratic case for an utter rejection of a criminal dictatorial past, this being deemed necessary to become 'fully western'. Institutes of National Memory evolved more commonly out of debates about how to control access to sensitive files from the Communist period, but then developed into powerful institutions which could use the documentary remnants of previous systems to produce new accounts of the violence and illegality of former regimes into which people could re-imagine themselves as the perpetrators or victims of that criminality.

Romania's Presidential Commission

In April 2006, as a result of very specific domestic and international pressures, the Romanian state established a Presidential Commission charged with the production of a new liberal democratic account of Romania's experience of

Communism. On the one hand, this was the consequence of the election of the second anti-Communist government since 1989 – the Justice and Truth Alliance (Alianţa Dreptate şi Adevăr).[19] Its leading figures, under pressure from liberal civil society activists,[20] had promised in the election campaign in 2004 vigorous transitional justice, including lustration and potential job losses. Moreover, Traian Băsescu, who was to become president in 2005, wanted to cement his newly forged reputation as a committed anti-Communist.[21] On his assumption of the presidency, he claimed that political purging was impossible unless the Communist regime was officially declared criminal. Thus a number of initiatives focusing on the criminal aspects of the Communist past were established. These included not only the Presidential Commission, but also the new Institute for the Investigation of Communist Crimes in Romania, and the transfer of over two million files of the former security services to the Council for the Study of Securitate Archives (Consiliul National pentru Studierea Arhivelor Securitătii or CNSAS), where victims could view documents relating to them and collaborators could be identified.[22]

On the other hand, the establishment of the Presidential Commission was also part of a trend among Romanian political elites to internationalize their historical culture and align it with western norms and values. The recognition that Romanian history had to westernize itself had been central to the establishment in October 2003 of a Holocaust Commission in response to international outrage over Romania's refusal to acknowledge its role in the Shoah.[23] In early 2006, liberal Romanian elites sought to embed a new anti-Communist consensus prior to the country's accession to the European Union. Fourteen days before Romania's political and economic union with the rest of Europe, the Presidential Commission published a report which was then used as a basis for President Băsescu's official condemnation of Communism in parliament.[24] This particular historical moment, which connected anti-Communists' long-standing calls for historical justice with the occasion of Romania's return to Europe, was crucial to establishing a powerful and convincing rationale for the existence of the Presidential Commission: it allowed its members, and their presidential sponsor, to present their call for a recognition of the crimes of Communism as a necessary step to secure a westernized, modern, 'civilized' future for the nation.

The establishment of the Presidential Commission rested on the assumption that Romania needed to reject its Communist past fully in order to assure its liberal democratic future, and that the creation of a new state-sponsored official memory to which the political elite and wider population could adhere was the best way to secure it.[25] The events of 1989 were viewed by anti-Communists as an incomplete revolution; there was concern that

Communists, who still held statist and Leninist values, had maintained a hold on power, that the essential institutions of state had not been fully democratized, that corruption based on Communist-era networks was still holding economic development back, and that the true nature of liberal democracy continued to be misunderstood. It was not only the physical survival of Communists themselves, but also the resilience of Communist-era mindsets that was seen as problematic: a new liberal Romania had to be built on the complete rejection of dictatorship. A historical investigation that gave a full account of Communism's crimes, it was believed, could enable the proper establishment of a new liberal Romania, built on an anti-dictatorial consensus shared by the political elite and embedded in the population at large (an aspiration that remained largely unfulfilled, as we will see below). Such a process, it was also hoped, would be accepted by former Communists, who would subscribe to the liberal democratic viewpoint of the Presidential Commission's report, and accept the need to reject their own pasts. The central idea of the commission was the completion of a democratic revolution in collective memory which had not occurred in 1989. On 18 December 2006, President Băsescu accepted the version of history provided by his commission. In a speech before parliament, he argued that only with the condemnation of Communism by Romanian society would the country regain confidence, put away its past habits and mentalities, and the 'institutions of the rule of law [begin to] function' in a proper democratic manner. Some were sceptical about Băsescu's real purpose; after all, he had had connections to the Securitate, had been a long-standing Communist Party member and, for close to ten years, had represented the Democratic Party, the reformist faction of the National Salvation Front, the heir to the Communist Party. Nevertheless, at this moment he presented himself as the embodiment of a liberal, westernized future for Romania:

> Evoking now a period which many would wish to forget, we have spoken both of the past and of the extent to which we, people today, wish to go . . . in the assumption of the values of liberty. These values, prior even to being those of Romania or of Europe, flow from the universal, sacred value of the human person. If we now turn to the past, we do so in order to face a future in which contempt for the individual will no longer go unpunished. This symbolic moment represents the balance sheet of what we have lived through and the day in which we all ask ourselves how we want to live henceforward. We shall break free of the past more quickly, we shall make more solid progress, if we understand what hinders us from being more competitive, more courageous, more confident in our own powers. . . . Our society suffers from a generalized

lack of confidence. The institutions of state do not yet seem to pursue their real vocation, which relates to the full exercise of all civil liberties. . . . Perhaps some will ask themselves what exactly gives us the right to condemn. As President of Romanians, I could invoke the fact that I have been elected. But I think that we have a more important motive: the right to condemn gives us the obligation to make the institutions of the rule of law function within a democratic society. We cannot be allowed to compromise these institutions. They cannot be allowed to be discredited by the fact that we approach them with the habits and mentalities of our recent past.[26]

In Romania, despite the violent overthrow of the Communist government, former Communists retained powerful positions within government after 1989. Unlike other countries in central-eastern Europe, Romania had dismantled Communism through a popular uprising against the dictatorship of Nicolae Ceauşescu. The conditions that had existed elsewhere in the region for a peaceful negotiated exit from Communism did not exist here: Ceauşescu had ensured that no opposition emerged under his rule; as a consequence, there did not exist negotiating partners with whom a peaceful transition could be brokered.[27] Changes in Romania began with a popular insurrection in the provincial city of Timişoara on 16 December 1989, before spreading to Bucharest. On 22 December, faced with the storming of party headquarters in the capital, President Ceauşescu fled by helicopter, before being captured and executed. It was the only revolution in the region that resulted in widespread violent confrontation: 1,104 people were killed between 22 and 27 December 1989.[28] Yet the resultant power vacuum was not filled by opponents of Communism but rather by lower-ranking *nomenklatura*, who formed the National Salvation Front (Frontul Salvării Naţionale, or 'FSN'), a body that promised to guide Romania to its first free elections. When, on 23 January 1990, it turned itself into a political party to contest the upcoming ballot, anti-Communists withdrew their support for an organization that they now viewed as a channel to entrench the power of former party members in the new political system. As a result of this withdrawal, the transition was thenceforth primarily guided by former middle- and lower-ranking members of the Communist Party, and this control both helped their successor party to victory at the first post-Communist elections and ensured that ex-Communist interests remained embedded within state bodies.[29] More than a decade after the end of Communism, 63 per cent of the current political elite had held political positions in the Communist Party prior to 1989.[30]

For those who participated in the Presidential Commission, the completion of the revolution lay to a large degree in the reformulation of collective memory. The commission's report was envisaged as a challenge to the substantial power of former Communists to narrate the story of political change in ways that both legitimized them and impeded democratic develop- ment.[31] In other countries in the region, Communists had been forced to sit down with their former opponents, reject the former system and embrace democratic principles in order to survive. In Romania, however, the *nomen- klatura's* almost exclusive stewardship of the revolution meant that they had faced no such pressure to renounce their past. Rather, some former Communists had managed to craft an identity for themselves as heroic revo- lutionaries as part of a powerful and appealing story of the violent overthrow and execution of a dictator. In this account, the revolution was presented not so much as anti-Communist as anti-Ceauşescu; Romanians had not risen up and expressed their hatred of Communist politics per se, rather they had over- thrown a hated dictator who had failed to modernize or provide for the Romanian nation. In the immediate post-Communist period, former appa- ratchik and twice post-Communist president Ion Iliescu framed resistance and the revolution in Communist-era terms. The deposition of Ceauşescu was presented as a legitimate proletarian revolution, the end-point of a series of heroic working-class demonstrations against his dictatorship, best illustrated by the protests of the Jiu valley miners in 1977 and Braşov workers in 1986.[32] Moreover, the liberal and conservative anti-Communists who had taken part in the revolution – but then refused to support the transition process when ex- Communists came to dominate it – were attacked in the following years as 'hooligans' and 'Fascists' who had failed to support the ex-Communists' stabi- lizing stewardship of political change. The idea that it was Ceauşescu rather than Communism itself that was being rejected was made clear in the way in which the National Salvation Front dealt with the previous regime. The simu- lacra of post-revolutionary justice – the televised execution of the dictator on 25 December 1989 after his flight from the Central Committee building in Bucharest and the trials of members of his inner circle – reflected the notion that there had been a guilty elite minority who should be punished, and an innocent majority of the former *nomenklatura* who should remain untouched.[33] Iliescu also resisted any attempts to reopen the story of the revolution officially, rejecting calls for state enquiries into the deaths of those 1,104 revolutionaries and the precise role of the Communists in overseeing the transition.

For anti-Communists, this interpretation of the history of the transition undermined the construction of a liberal democracy. First, the idea of the heroic anti-Ceauşescu revolution weakened attempts at future democratiza- tion because it presented the Romanian revolution as the authentic end of a previous era, and thus political change as essentially complete.[34] Second, this account of the revolution did not itself support the idea of democratic development. Ex-Communists were not seen to reject the past on liberal democratic grounds; Communism was not reviled for its arbitrary use of violence, its lack of respect for the rule of law or the hollowness of its democratic claims, but rather because of the failure of Ceauşescu's version of Communism to modernize Romania effectively. In this account, therefore, the transition was not one from criminal dictatorship to lawful democracy, but rather a journey from a form of failed national modernization under Ceauşescu to a new form of more market-oriented modernization under the ex-Communist Iliescu. For anti-Communists, by contrast, a new liberal identity had to be built on the rejection of Communism owing to its illiberal, criminal and abusive practices, rather than on the basis of an account of poor economic stewardship that ignored the political violence and suppression of rights that had accompanied it. In addition, members of the Presidential Commission saw themselves as providing an important counterbalance to historians such as Florin Constantiniu, who produced widely read works which sought to revive the nationalism of the Ceauşescu regime, or writers such as Neagu Cosma, whose books preserved the idea of the 'good Securitate' that had helped Romania maintain its independence from both the Soviet Union and the West in the late Communist period.[35]

The Presidential Commission thus sought to reshape the collective memory of the Romanian nation in a context where attitudes towards the past and present were still contested. For its members, a new democratic society could not be created simply by ensuring sufficient space in public discourse for a plurality of memories and outlooks. Too many of these competing interpretations were still shaped, in their view, by the manipulations of the Communist regime and their ex-Communist successors. A new memory that would ensure democratic development therefore had to be imposed from above. Moreover, they assumed that it was impossible to create a shared narrative on the basis of multiple viewpoints, and that instead it was the responsibility of anti-Communists to create and promote a new liberal democratic history.[36] Indeed, the historians involved accepted that they were party to a political and moral project to provide a new account of the national past that would rationalize and underpin democratic development.[37] Anti-Communists had long dismissed calls from the political left for a Reconciliation Commission to bring together both sides in a shared re-evaluation of the past; they did not view such requests as evidence of an honest or honourable readiness to admit responsibility for the abuses of the past, but rather as an attempt by ex-Communists to avoid investigations into Communist complicity in the violence that had accompanied the

Romanian revolution.[38] According to Vladimir Tismăneanu, the head of the commission, post-Communism had been 'dominated by an absence of expiation, of penance, or of a mourning process in relation to the trauma of Communism'.[39]

Yet the commission did not reflect the broader range of anti-Communist forces in Romania either. Unlike the Holocaust Commission, which had been established three years earlier and had consisted mainly of representatives of victims' and survivors' groups, the Presidential Commission, despite claiming to give those who had suffered a new voice in post-Communist society, failed to include those who officially stood for these constituencies, with the sole exception of Ticu Dumitrescu, who represented former political prisoners.[40] Moreover, most members were picked by Tismăneanu himself, who favoured primarily liberal-minded (and humanities-trained) intellectuals. The commission's make-up was restricted in large part to those who were considered 'morally credible': its eighteen members were a mixture of anti-Communist social activists, who had long called for the condemnation of Communism, and ideologically sympathetic historians who could lend expertise (and academic legitimacy) to the endeavour.[41] Nor was the commission able to draw on a wider social input after its establishment. It was unlike other truth-telling bodies in that it had few investigative powers and thus could not subpoena perpetrators or victims. Thus it was not able to seek a range of voices or embrace clashing perspectives.[42] Rather, a new history of the abuses of Communism was to be built on the documentary legacy of the previous regime: the commission's historians were to be granted extensive access to previously unavailable archival material with a view to uncovering new data that would underline the criminality that underpinned the practice of Communism in Romania. Despite this, there was very little new research in the report eventually issued by the commission: for the most part, it simply moulded information that was already available into a liberal democratic version of history.[43] In this sense, the Presidential Commission was a political top-down 'narrative-reshaping' institution, rather than an investigative truth commission. Some thus argued that both the composition and methods of the commission undermined its aims: a restricted membership, the lack of wider social input and an overreliance on already published material would leave it struggling to forge a consensus.[44]

Although the final report published in December 2006 was a condemnation of the evils of the Communist regime, its main aim was the legitimization of liberal democratic political development. Thus, the form of that condemnation was shaped by the liberal values that its creators wished to instil in the post-Communist population. Communism was not attacked for its failure to live up to its own principles; rather, it was presented as a bleak criminal inversion of democratic rights and was used as a dark backdrop against which to contrast the legal protections of the Romanian citizenry in a westernized liberal future. The report was used to provide an account of the type of rule under which individuals would suffer without the protection of a liberal democratic state:

> The condemnation of Communism . . . is a moral, intellectual, political and social obligation. A democratic and pluralist Romanian state can and must do this. In this way, the recognition of these sad and dark pages in Romanian history in the twentieth century is indispensable for our generation, which has a right to know about the world in which their parents lived. The future of Romania depends on it knowing its past, so that it condemns the regime as the enemy of human beings.[45]

It was a relatively recent idea of democracy that shaped the report. In the mid-twentieth century, democracy's claim to be a superior political system was often based on its capacity to ensure social rights, from economic development and welfare (particularly for poorer sections of the population) to wider working-class involvement in politics. By the late twentieth century, this had been replaced by the claim that liberal democracy was the ultimate guarantor of individual rights and the rule of law.[46] Following the experience of the excessive use of state power (the Holocaust, mass terror in the Soviet Union and forced population transfer, for example), resulting in an increasing suspicion of state activism, western democracies increasingly defined their supposed superiority over other political formations in terms of the rights they ascribed to their populations. To be a democratic citizen increasingly meant being granted legal protection against the overweening power of the state, rather than being the object of the state's attempts at social improvement.[47] It was this vision of democracy – as the rule of law and thus a shield for the individual from the abusive state – that would provide the template for the Presidential Commission's liberally framed condemnation of Communism.

Thus Communism was attacked as the criminal inversion of the liberal democratic state's claims to represent judicial procedure and human rights: 'The Communists simply shattered any notion of the rule of law. The Final Report identifies the nature of abuses and its victims . . . the Communist regime represented the opposite of rule of law, an *Unrechtsstaat*.'[48] What counted in such a condemnation was the regime's criminal practices, not its ideological aims.[49] Thus, the report presented Communism as a set of repressive and disciplining institutions that sought to subjugate an independent society and committed a catalogue of abuses against Romanians. The commission's president, Vladimir Tismăneanu, argued that it was the memory of these crimes that would strengthen democratic identity: 'a genuine democracy cannot function properly in the absence of historical consciousness. . . . An authentic democratic community cannot be built on the denial of past crimes, abuses, and atrocities. The past is not another country. It cannot be wished away.'[50] Even the arguments with which the former regime had legitimized itself were reduced to an ideologically suspect cover for its criminal urges. For instance, its attempts at social levelling were dismissed as superficial pretexts for its criminal, totalitarian impulses: 'The Communist regime was of a criminal nature, in the sense that it instigated, ordered and committed crimes against humanity. It was a regime which looked to reduce the population to the condition of slaves, exploiting them pitilessly under the pretext of creating a utopian, egalitarian and free society.'[51] The report rejected the Communists' claims that they had represented a form of legitimate economic modernization. It asserted that only the institutions of capitalism and liberalism could ensure effective modernization, and hence, as the Communists had cut Romania off from this path after 1945, they had victimized Romanians by denying them the right to a productive modern society:

> The Communist regime was an anti-modern one which merely simulated modernity . . . it was a regime of foreign occupation which liquidated the Romanian elite and its institutions of democracy, its market economy and private property. All this was annihilated for forty-five years, a false turn on the path of true modernization . . . it was a giant step backwards, which led us to chronic poverty, the isolation of the country, the wasting of human and material resources, the alienation of the individual and the destruction of our traditions and national culture.[52]

Given this focus on criminality, it is not surprising that the central figures in the report were *victims* of Communist criminal practice. As the production of knowledge about dictatorship has shifted from the courtroom to the History Commission, so the main focus of anti-totalitarian histories has switched from the evils of the perpetrator on trial to the sufferings of the victim.[53] Despite the fact that victims' organizations had minimal representation and that their testimony was not sought, the Presidential Commission nevertheless justified its existence morally on the basis of its services to those who had suffered abuses under Communism. Its work, it was claimed, would ensure that victims' stories would at last be articulated, that their dignity could be restored, and that the process would publicly legitimize their experiences and make them incontestable.[54] The report also sought thoroughly to embed the idea that Romanian society as a whole had been a victim of criminal practice. First, it embraced an extremely broad definition of the term 'victim of Communism' that extended beyond those who had been deported, tortured or executed. Although some of the report's historians wished to limit its application to the 155,000 political prisoners who could be documented as having been incarcerated in Romanian political prisons and camps, they were overruled by those who wished to define Communism's victims as including an estimated two million people who had been imprisoned for more than two months for non-civilian offences before 1989. This division in interpretation was never fully resolved; the higher figure was placed in the main text, the lower in a footnote.[55] One of the commission's members, Romulus Rusan, went even further: he argued that over half the Romanian population should be considered 'victims'. Drawing upon a concept of 'class genocide', he argued that Romania's victims encompassed not only those who were persecuted on account of their social background, but also all those who suffered under forced 'ideological homogenization'.[56] Second, the commission avoided those topics that undermined the focus on victims; it dealt with neither the widespread co-optation of Romanian society by the regime after 1968 (and its importance for the stability of the system), nor with the relative absence of resistance (compared to other eastern bloc countries).[57] Third, it invoked analytical categories that sought to demonize Communism through association with the Holocaust.[58] 'Communist genocide' was an idea that emerged among the anti-Communist émigrés from the Baltics as early as the 1940s, and began to be widely used among anti-Communists in Romania from the early 1990s.[59] It was reinforced by the theory of 'class genocide' outlined in Stéphane Courtois et al's *The Black Book of Communism*.[60] The commission borrowed the term and its reworked meaning from a Romanian work of the same name by Gheorghe Boldur-Lățescu.[61] This replaced the very precise 1948 definition of genocide developed after the Holocaust as the attempt to erase all or part of a particular ethnic or social group with a much broader meaning that included not only the Communist state's political persecutions and executions but also took into account higher rates of morbidity and mortality, religious persecution, economic and environmental disasters, and cultural destruction.[62] Many anti-Communists observed that it was as a result of Soviet pressure that the 1948 international definition of genocide had excluded those forms of social cleansing practised under Communism. Thus, the report sought, on the one hand, to draw on the power of the term genocide meaning a specific form of mass killing, which immediately invoked widespread revulsion, while, on the other, widening its meaning sufficiently to make the term relevant to the Romanian context.[63] Yet – as commentators noted – this conceptual inventiveness had led to an overly broad (and hence vague) definition of both genocide and victim, which in turn had the potential to undermine later judicial procedures that required precisely drawn official categorizations that made the perpetrators and victims of Communist-era violence identifiable in legal terms.[64]

Moreover, it was a particular type of victim that was generally invoked. As Michael Humphrey has argued, those who suffered were re-objectified into new types of victims in such reports: whereas once, under Communism, they were reduced to the status of the 'justifiably persecuted' on account of their class background or political beliefs, following its collapse they were recast as the victims of human rights violations in order to legitimize a new liberal democratic order.[65] In such reports, victims were often presented not as part of a particular collective political movement for their support of which they had been persecuted, but rather were abstracted from the ideological contexts and struggles of their times, so that they were now remembered mainly for their sufferering.[66] The different visions of the world that both the victims and victimizers represented were almost entirely absent; what mattered were their symbolic roles as abusers or abused.[67]

Hence, the political reasons why certain people had been persecuted by the Communist state were not at issue; no differentiation was made between moderate democratic victims of the regime and those of the right and far right.[68] The commission was sensitive to the suggestion that this had led them to rehabilitate Fascists in the name of anti-Communism. Some members argued that far-rightists, although they deserved punishment after World War II, could nevertheless be considered victims in so far as they were not prosecuted according to a liberal conception of the rule of law but rather in Communist show trials: 'The Presidential Commission first identified victims, regardless of their political colours, for one cannot argue that one is against torture for the left while ignoring such practices when it comes to the right. The militants of the far right should have been punished on a legal basis, but this was not the case with the trials carried out by the Romanian Communist Party.'[69] Other members defended themselves by suggesting that they were following what they understood to be standard western practice when dealing with genocide: victims were identified by the way they were treated, not on account of the acceptability of their political views before their deaths. One argued that those dealing with the Shoah did not subtract Jewish victims who were also Communists from the final tally of six million, and thus those dealing with the victims of Communism should not ignore those with far-right political views judged to be obnoxious in modern political life.[70]

The report's insistence that even far-rightists could be 'victims of Communism' was understood as an attempt to re-educate all post-Communist citizens into adopting democratic identities, rather than to whitewash the history of Romanian Fascism. It asserted that these individuals were commemorated and granted respect, not as representatives of a far-right cause, but simply as victims of an anti-democratic system. As such, the commission was part of a wider series of initiatives that provided moral rehabilitation, social status and legal backing to those who were prepared to define themselves solely in terms of their suffering (rather than political identity) under the Communist regime. The Council for the Study of Securitate Archives, established in 1999 to catalogue and regulate the secret files of the former secret police, adjudicated on the granting of higher pensions to those who claimed to be victims of Communism. An Institute for the Investigation of the Communist Crimes in Romania, established in 2005, enabled those whose families had been victims of Communism to apply to initiate investigations into disappearances or deaths of family members. These processes were practical manifestations of the anti-Communist claim that Romanians had now become democratic citizens with rights that would protect them from arbitrary state power in the future.

While one aim of the report was to produce the idea of liberal democracy as the inversion of Communism, another was to promote the notion that the struggle of Romanians against totalitarianism was not yet finished; it was only with the condemnation of Communism and the acceptance of the report's anti-Communism by the political elite that the revolution would finally be complete. The idea of the continuing struggle against Communism was thus central to their work. The commissioners sought to demonstrate the presence of a tradition of resistance under Communism that anticipated the liberal democratic agenda of their report, but also asserted that its promises had been betrayed in 1989 and were yet to be fulfilled. The report constructed a history of a substantive democratic anti-Communist resistance tradition before the collapse of Communism, a task that was complicated by the fact that the actual level of protest in Romania had been far lower than in other former eastern bloc countries such as Hungary and Poland, and that the aims of those few groups and individuals who had expressed opposition did not always anticipate the mythological requirements of the post-1989 democratic state. Armed resistance in the early Communist period illustrated anti-democratic right-wing anti-Communism as much as democratic politics, while the (very limited) working-class protest in the late Communist period often called for the proper implementation of socialism rather than its demise. Thus the report needed to reshape the history of protest to the regime and refashion a diverse set of political objectives into demands for liberty, individual rights and national freedom.[71] Indeed, members of the commission often made it clear that the true extent of resistance was not important in determining the scale of attention it received in the report; rather, it was their moral duty to revive the memories of those small numbers who had fought, and to co-opt their memory to assist in the construction of a liberal democracy.[72] The report told of a long tradition of Romanian anti-Communist resistance, starting with the armed struggle in the Carpathian mountains in the late 1940s, continuing through student protests in 1956, and incorporating opposition to collec-tivization, workers' resistance in 1977 and 1987, and intellectual dissidence, before finally celebrating the popular uprising against Ceaușescu in the days before Christmas 1989.[73] Resisting groups' precise ideological aims were often ignored; what mattered was what they were fighting against: Communist dictatorship. It was deemed crucial to claim them as representatives of a democratic Romania that had survived, even during a period of totalitarian rule: 'Armed anti-Communist resistance was a struggle for liberty, also a struggle for survival, a time in which liberty and individual dignity and the Romanian nation were trampled on by the Soviets and their faithful execu-tioners, the local Communists. . . . [It] belongs to . . . a usable Romanian collective memory.'[74]

The decision not to end the report with the collapse of Communism, but rather to include an account of the revolution's aftermath, was one of the most controversial, both among commission members and the broader public.[75] This was in part because the choice to take the report beyond 1989 signalled the commissioners' desire to emphasize that the Communist period had continued after its official collapse and that 'perpetrators' had remained within the system. The report did not adopt the finale so common in other national 'resistance myths', which culminate in the heroic overthrow of the *ancien régime*. Rather, the commission's report portrayed 1989 as an unfinished revolution that had begun as a popular uprising but had been captured by middle-ranking members of the former *nomenklatura*, who had stifled authentic democratic impulses in their desire to maintain their grip on power.[76] The report thus did not focus on the revolutionaries' heroic actions in December 1989, but rather on the absence of an investigation into their deaths. This failure was given as evidence of the continued ability of ex-Communists to block investigations into the truths of 1989, and served as a symbol of the absence of justice in the post-Communist period as a whole.[77] Moreover, the commissioners – under pressure from civil-society organizations and activists such as Sorin Iliesiu[78] – continued their analysis past 1989 and framed the post-Communist period as one of continued struggle between ex-Communists and 'true revolutionary forces'. Their report celebrated those who continued the fight against former Communists even after the revolution, such as the participants in the two-month-long University Square protests in the spring of 1990.[79]

In the perceived absence of authentic change in 1989, the report presented itself as the embodiment of the possibility of a final mastering of the Communist past. For its backers, success was defined as the creation of a broader political and social consensus that Communism was a criminal regime from which Romanians were eager to escape into the arms of liberal democracy and the rule of law. Thus, the anti-Communist president Traian Băsescu presented the report to parliament as a call not only for a collective condemnation of Communism but also for 'authentic national reconciliation':

> As head of the Romanian State, I expressly and categorically condemn the Communist system in Romania. . . . Taking cognizance of the realities presented in the Report, I affirm with full responsibility: the Communist regime in Romania was illegitimate and criminal. . . . In the name of the Romanian State, I express my regret and compassion for the victims of the Communist dictatorship. In the name of the Romanian State, I ask the forgiveness of those who suffered, of their families, of all those who, in one way or another, saw their lives ruined by the abuses of dictatorship. . . . On the other hand, we must not display historical arrogance. My purpose is aimed at authentic national reconciliation, and all the more so since numerous legacies of the past continue to scar our lives.[80]

Yet even on its own terms the report had very limited success, since it failed to engender a broader consensus that Communism should be condemned. It was not able to engage the post-Communist left, and in particular the major Communist successor party, who refused to accept its findings. Although some commission members had hoped that they might sign up, and there was some indication that reformist modernizing and Europeanizing factions within the ex-Communist Social Democrats such as the Cluj Group argued for its acceptance, the content of the report made it very difficult for the ex-Communists to endorse it officially. In particular, the naming of Ion Iliescu as a Communist agent, the accusation that he and the ex-Communist National Salvation Front had attempted to hijack the revolution in December 1989 and the call for an enquiry into the suppression of the University Square protests by elements representing the former regime effectively undercut ex-Communists' claims to have played a positive role in the Romanian revolution, and instead portrayed them as barriers to liberal democratic development.[81] The report also alienated nationalists, some of whom, such as Corneliu Vadim Tudor, were named as agents too: indeed, at the moment of Băsescu's condemnation of Communism in parliament, the chamber witnessed a staged denunciation of the president by Tudor's 'Greater Romania' party.

The Commission even failed to create a consensus among other anti-Communist constituencies. This may in part have been a result of the way in which it had been established, by presidential diktat rather than as an expression of a desire for justice from below; this left it open to the charge that it was a creature of politics. Moreover, as noted above, its membership had excluded not only ex-Communists but also many representatives of victim groups: it was therefore widely perceived as representing a particular sectional interest, primarily of civil society activists, rather than a broader constituency of anti-Communist forces. Moreover, its decision to reject multiple viewpoints, and its embracing of a simple model evoking an illegal regime which for forty years had committed 'social genocide' against the majority of the Romanian population, meant that others found its conclusions one-sided and insufficiently nuanced to be convincing.[82] The report was, however, absorbed into the high-school curriculum and parts of it also served for the new high-school history textbook produced by the Institute for the Investigation of Communist Crimes in Romania.[83] Thus, in the short term at least, observers considered its impact to be limited. While it had provided Romania with an official state-sponsored liberal democratic account of its past, which widely publicized the criminality of Communism and the appeals of democratic development, it had failed to assist significantly in the forging of an elite or popular consensus over how Romania should escape that past.[84]

Producing National Memory: Poland's Institute of National Remembrance

The very different contexts in which History Commissions and Institutes of National Memory were founded shaped their claims to be providing a meaningful reckoning with dictatorship. History Commissions were often initiated at points of crisis when elites were being pressurized, often by external processes such as European integration, into the construction of new 'westernized' forms of national history-telling: thus, their claim to be producing an authentic re-evaluation of Communism lay in their contention that an explicit rewriting of history was necessary to break from the past. These commissions' reports were overt public performances in which the idea of a necessary caesura in collective memory was sold both to a western audience into whose cultural norms they were integrating, and to a domestic audience to whom they could claim to be the modernizing, Europeanizing force in their country. Institutes of National Memory, by contrast, were established at moments when control over the documentary remnants of the former Communist security services emerged as a matter of intense political debate.[85] Faced with files on citizens' lives under Communism being in the hands of institutions that still contained a large number of ex-Communists, and with the possibility of those files being used to blackmail post-Communist elites, the creation of a new 'politically clean' institution, which could regulate access to this information, was seen to be crucial for democratic development.[86] In many countries, governments introduced laws that took the files of the Communist secret police away from the security services and placed them in new state-funded institutions, which organized and regulated access to the newly assembled archive. Given their origins, Institutes of National Memory were much more committed to presenting an apolitical image of themselves as neutral custodians. Unlike History Commissions – which presented their work as a much more explicitly political intervention necessary to secure a civilized future – institutes characterized themselves as impartial arbiters of a complex and difficult past that stood above politics and that could call on the authority of the archive to arbitrate in disputes and to tame the divisive legacies of the Communist era. Like commissions, however, they craved consensus: institutes were built around the idea that it was possible to build a new, unitary, consensual history based on a scholarly account of dictatorship. However, such an apolitical self-definition should be understood as a mechanism through which these institutes established their authenticity and hence their authority in order to achieve what was in fact a moral-political project, employing the secret-service archive to reshape popular understandings of the Communist past and so embedding a new broad national liberal vision of the future.

In some post-conflict or post-authoritarian societies, such archives are feared, and are even destroyed, because of their perceived capacity to reinforce or revive memories of violence and division.[87] The founding of Institutes of National Memory rested on a different idea: they were built not only to preserve and regulate access to the voluminous records of the former secret police, but also out of a sense of confidence that these sources could be employed to create a nationally unifying account of Communism, based on rigorous and scholarly archival research, which could overcome the divided nature of post-Communist memory. In some places – such as Germany and Hungary – the institutes' main role was to control access to the files. In others, however, the judicious use of these documents was perceived as a vital tool for dealing with the taboos and unresolved political legacies of the Communist past, and as key to the process of democratization. In some countries, these new institutions, and the Communist archives they contained, were utilized as resources to construct a new 'national memory' concerning the Communist (and, to a lesser extent, the Fascist) past. In the Czech Republic, for instance, an Institute for the Study of Totalitarian Regimes (which was originally going to be called the Institute of National Memory, a name opposed by both the academic sector and sections of parliament) was established in 2007, to serve both as the guardian of secret-service archives and as a repository of knowledge about the criminality of the Communist regime which could be utilized by historians.[88] The Polish, Slovakian and Lithuanian versions had even broader visions: here, the institutes were encouraged to use the archive to confront post-Communist societies with uncomfortable material from their pasts. Moreover, these institutions were subject to political pressure from anti-Communists who recognized the archives' potential to provide evidence that might bring perpetrators to trial, or to retrieve information about a vast swathe of post-Communist citizens to support lustration laws that would exclude former collaborators from significant public offices.[89] Attempts to turn these institutions into tools of 'social and political cleansing' were limited in their effects, however: even new bodies established within these archival institutions to carry out lustration and criminal prosecutions ended up primarily as producers of new forms of democratic memory, criminalizing the Communist past in the public consciousness, rather than as executors of justice for past crimes.

The first and largest of these institutes was the Polish Institute of National Remembrance, established by the anti-Communist Solidarity Electoral Action government in 1998. It was the first new state institution to be founded in post-Communist Poland, and eventually employed over two thousand personnel in eleven branches across the country. There had been little interest in the files of the Communist security services in Poland in the immediate aftermath of the collapse. However, by the late 1990s, concerns about the possibility of 'wild lustration' – the use of illegally leaked security-service files to produce lists of suspected collaborators with the former regime – meant that an absence of control over these Communist-era records was increasingly seen as a threat to civilized and stable democratic development.[90] Thus elites looked to the creation of an institute that would gather together, organize and regulate access to a large body of material from the former Nazi and Communist security-service apparatuses. By 2009, the Institute of National Remembrance contained 88 kilometres (55 miles) of material which the former security services had collected between 22 July 1944 to 31 July 1990, including documentation from the security services of Nazi Germany and the Soviet Union. Alongside an archival role, it developed its own research wing (the Public Education Bureau – Biuro Edukacji Publicznej) and integrated into itself the Main Commission for the Prosecution of Crimes against the Polish Nation, which was responsible for investigating crimes of repression or abuses of human rights committed in Poland between 1939 and 1989. Although nominally independent of government, its president was to be appointed by a three-fifths parliamentary majority every five years, thus giving strong governments the ability to exert significant influence over the institute's strategic direction if they wished, and if the institute allowed it.[91] Indeed, in 2005–06, the radical anti-Communist Law and Justice government influenced elections for the top positions to its own advantage and established a Lustration Bureau, which used the archive to vet the Communist pasts of those standing for public office or belonging to key professions.[92]

Before 2005, the Polish Institute of National Remembrance saw its role as apolitical: it viewed itself as simply engaged in opening up a security-service archive to reveal the hidden truths of the Communist period. It rejected the radical anti-Communist claim that real democratization required the continuation of the revolution against Communists by removing representatives of the former regime from public life simply on the basis of past political affiliation (rather than through evidence of specific crimes). This was seen as a form of collective revenge, which was inconsistent with the principles of individual rights and the rule of law, and hence did not assist democratization.[93] Prominent voices within the institute thus argued against de-Communization; rather, they suggested the institute could better contribute to the building of a new democratic culture by providing access to information, and producing new knowledge, about the Communist era and the experience of Nazi occupation.[94] The institute presented itself as devoted simply to the acquisition of historical facts: 'a country does not become fully democratic until each one of its inhabitants has the possibility of knowing in an objective manner the elements of their history . . . and civil society better understand[s] the complexity of historical process'.[95] The institute would help achieve this by assembling and opening up massive new archives, housing material from the security and military organs of the Communist state, conducting new research using these collections, giving victims of the Communist state access to their files, and prosecuting particular individual crimes committed between 1944 and 1989 that had not previously been tried.

Interviews conducted for this work with prominent members of the Polish institute's Public Education Bureau revealed that they did not see themselves as engaged in a particular project of collective memory. Indeed, they viewed themselves as 'anti-political truth-tellers', involved in a process of revelation of facts that had been hidden during the Communist era and silenced for political reasons during the transition period. They rejected the idea that the revision of the Communist past was a politicized rewriting of history; rather, it was simply the 'unfreezing' of historical memory: 'The Communist system acted, one might suggest, as a historical refrigerator. It blocked and froze numerous issues, facts and conflicts by way of political control and censorship. Such censorship did not allow pertinent topics to be discussed in public.'[96] The institute also saw itself as an arbiter in historical disputes relating to the periods of Communist rule and Nazi occupation, and as a neutral body that could tame and resolve the difficult and divided memories inherited from the totalitarian past. It would counter the corrosive falsehoods embedded by Communist propaganda which still had powerful resonances, such as the idea that Martial Law (1981–83) and the suppression of Solidarity were necessary steps taken to prevent a Soviet invasion and thus protect Polish sovereignty.[97] Moreover, it would also challenge powerful myths that were central to dominant forms of Polish identity even after 1989. It frequently pointed to its work on Polish complicity in Jewish pogroms such as the Jedwabne massacre during World War II,[98] which challenged (and in fact offended) dominant post-Communist memories of Poles as innocent victims of wartime Nazi occupation. Members' claims to be neutral arbitrators who merely uncovered uncomfortable truths were underpinned to a large degree by the meanings they inscribed into the institute's massive archive of documents from the former security services that were the source of much of their scholarly and professional work. They refuted the criticism that using this type of archive as a basis for post-Communist truth-telling could not avoid being politicized, and bound to reveal a one-sided 'dark history' of terror and surveillance in which the Communist world was reduced to the relationship of victim and collaborator. Rather, they framed the archive as a font of apolitical information. On the one hand, it provided democratic access for former 'victims' of the regime who could go there to explore what the Communist-era secret police might have thought about them. On the other, it provided professional historians with access to surveillance documents that gave the most in-depth representations of Communist-era social and political phenomena – especially concerning issues such as strikes and resistance – as they were often brutally frank assessments designed for the secret police, unobscured by the ideological distortions common in material destined for Communist-era public consumption.[99] Indeed, the strength with which the institute asserted its apolitical role suggested the importance of such a formulation for its claim to authority in dealing with the country's recent past. Members of the institute realized that they were often viewed as powerful reshapers of 'national memory' and strongly contested these assertions. They argued that, even if they had helped to remould collective memory, they were nevertheless unwilling shapers of a new historical consciousness. The first director of the Public Education Bureau had sought to embrace a range of historical approaches and thus to turn his bureau into an Institute of Contemporary History.[100] Nevertheless, its members accepted that they had become key players in shaping new national attitudes to issues such as Martial Law and the involvement of Poles in the persecution of Jews in World War II.[101] However, they argued that this had only occurred because the press had constructed them as a 'Ministry of Historical Truth' that should adjudicate on sensitive historical issues, and because the civic culture that surrounded them was insufficiently strong to support a meaningful historical debate in which the presence of other competing versions of the past would turn their research from *the* authoritative argument into just one of a series of valid rival interpretations.[102]

Yet – as the institute's critics often suggested – it was a particular, partial and political project of collective remembering that it was committed to. Those who claimed the necessity of truth-telling and justice after the end of Communism often framed themselves as the only ones dedicated to a difficult reckoning with a past that former representatives of the system wished to forget. These rhetorically powerful justifications diverted attention away from the fact that they were also involved in promoting a convenient set of new (often simplified) historical myths designed to underpin particular contemporary political commitments.[103] Indeed, the institute (often implicitly) positioned itself by critiquing other ways of 'coming to terms' with the past. Although it had rejected the idea that it was appropriate to take 'revenge' on representatives of the former Communist system, it also refuted the notion that a healthy new democratic identity could be built on the celebration of the reconciliation and forgiveness that had characterized the Round Table settlements of 1989. Rather, it was motivated by the belief that a new national identity could only be built on a firm rejection of Communism, which was in turn dependent on proving to Polish society that a real revolution had taken place in 1989. It faced many obstacles in doing this. On account of the absence of 'the people' from the moment of Communism's collapse, and the real continuities of laws and political personnel between the two systems, many Poles perceived important connections between the Communist and democratic periods. Hence, many did not view the post-Communist system as a rejection of the past, but in significant ways as its extension. Many in the institute viewed this widely felt sense of continuity as the reason for citizens' inability to identify fully with the new system. Thus their work consisted of promoting the ideas that 1989 represented a revolutionary break, and that the post-1989 system was the political inversion of what had gone before.

Much of the work of the institute thus sought to attribute to Polish society a genuine anti-Communism and democratic commitment in advance of 1989, so writing 'the people' into the story of the rejection of the Communist past. According to the 1998 Parliamentary Act that established it, the institute should focus on 'the patriotic traditions of the struggle of the Polish Nation with the occupying forces of Nazism and Communism . . . the acts of citizens aimed at securing the independence of the Polish Nation and defending freedom and human dignity'.[104] Yet the experience of 1989 had not provided a symbolic moment – an equivalent of the storming of the Bastille – through which people could recognize their own commitment to overcoming Communism. Thus the institute avoided the story of the elite-level reconciliation that underpinned the transition in 1989, and instead sought to provide a heroic story of earlier popular resistance to Communism. The institute's historians insisted that this was a difficult task; the Polish population was insufficiently aware of the extent of resistance of Poles to Communism, or in part accepted the claims of the Communists before 1989 that suppression of resistance had sometimes been necessary.[105] The institute played a major role in reviving the memory of a popularly supported anti-Communist underground in the early Communist period and in trying to resuscitate a heroic memory of the Solidarity movement to demonstrate Poles' collective commitment to the end of dictatorship. Thus the past was presented as a series of popular attempts at resistance to topple the regime, and citizens were ascribed a prominent role in the liberation of their country from Communism.

The Institute of National Remembrance also sought to create the idea of revolutionary change by clarifying the distinction between Communism and Fascism, on the one hand, and liberal democracy, on the other. For it, the popularly felt sense of continuity was based on a misunderstanding about the nature of democracy and the transformations of 1989. Whereas radical anti-Communists in Poland mobilized the idea of 1989 as an incomplete revolution and the post-Communist system as the immoral and corrupt consequence of this, the institute's work assumed the necessity of narrating the idea of a clean break with a criminal past based on the rule of law in order to forge an attachment to the new democratic system. Even if there had been no symbolic moment of change, the two systems were nevertheless each other's inversion; if liberal democracy represented individual rights and the rule of law, Fascism and Communism represented the opposite of these principles. Thus, the nation's journey was charted as one from criminality and arbitrary power to the realization of a democratic state based on the rule of law and human rights. As with the work of many history commissions, this tale was to be told through victims' stories. According to the founding act of 1998 which established the institute, it should

> have regard for . . . the preservation of the memory of the magnitude of the number of victims, the scale of the loss and damage suffered by the Polish Nation in World War II and thereafter . . . the obligation to prosecute crimes against peace and humanity as well as war crimes . . . and the duty of our state to provide compensation to all persons suffering injury through the violation of their human rights by the state . . . [It is] the expression of our conviction that no unlawful action of the state against its citizens should be kept hidden or allowed to be forgotten.[106]

Thus, much of its research centred on the production of a history of Communism and Fascism as a series of crimes and infractions against human rights. It often focused on particularly bleak moments during this period (such as Stalinism and the Jewish experience of World War II), while also attempting to extend the popular conception of the era of terror beyond the 1950s to include mass surveillance and violence in the 1980s.[107] In some of their legally mandated work – such as the production of lists of victims of the Communist state – historians abandoned their wider methodological kitbag of social, political and economic explanations for violence, and simply engaged in the cataloguing of thousands of individuals who had been subjected to Communist criminality. Telling the story of those who suffered would demonstrate this inversion, graphically illustrating the suffering that Communism's failure to respect the rights of the individual had caused, and celebrating the liberal democratic state as a political system in which the legal rights and dignity of the victimized were restored.

The story of the end of Communism as a journey from criminality to legality was not only produced by historians but also by lawyers in the judicial wing of the institute – the Main Commission.[108] This had begun life in October 1944 as an investigative body founded to investigate 'German crimes' in Poland. It had existed throughout the Communist period, although it was renamed the Commission for Nazi Crimes in 1948 (in response to the foundation of the Communist German Democratic Republic). On 4 April 1991, it had then become the Main Commission for the Investigation of Crimes against the Polish Nation, and its brief was extended to incorporate investigations into Stalinist crimes before 1956, war crimes and crimes against humanity.[109] After 1998, it was integrated into the Institute for National Remembrance and its 120 prosecutors across Poland were given new powers to initiate prosecutions for those crimes (defined as 'repressions' and 'human rights violations') committed between 1939 and 1989 that contravened the law *at the time* and that had not previously been tried. The Main Commission's investigations focused on the killing of Poles, Jews and patients in psychiatric hospitals by Germans, the Ukrainian killing of Poles in Volhynia and eastern Galicia, the deportation of Polish citizens to Siberia during World War II, the torture and killing of political prisoners by the Communist security apparatus before 1956, and crimes committed during Martial Law in the 1980s. Of these cases, around three-quarters concerned the Communist period, and one-quarter World War II.[110] The institute asserted that the process of democratization and the re-establishment of the rule of law could not solely be built on *research* into past crimes, but that the *prosecution* of individual crimes was necessary too: 'One cannot mistake forgiveness with trivialization of guilt. Democracy and the rule of law cannot be built on denying responsibility and guilt.'[111]

The institute's contribution to creating a new liberal democratic collective memory proved greater than its judicial impact, however. Despite its legally mandated powers, the judicial wing of the institute, the Main Commission, did not aggressively pursue a policy of legal action; this was in part because many of the crimes had been committed in the distant past and so were difficult to prosecute successfully.[112] Yet, more importantly, it was believed that a policy of pursuing lawsuits would undermine the powerful symbolism of the institution. The director of the Main Commission stressed that as a body it represented the antithesis of dictatorship through its commitment to the recovery of the rule of law. As such, the number of prosecutions was not a gauge of success; in fact, it publicized, and thereby stressed, the very restricted ways in which it was seeking to bring those responsible for Communist crimes to trial. This 'self-limiting' form of activity illustrated the superiority of democratic justice: it would not prosecute on the basis of collective justice (as the Communists had done), nor would it prosecute those activities that were considered illegal after 1989 but not before (retroactive justice). Thus many injudicious features of the Communist regime, such as class law (on account of which those from undesirable backgrounds were discriminated against in education and the workplace), would not be subject to tribunals since they had been legal at the time. The low level of its prosecutions was not taken as a sign of failure, however; the work of the Main Commission was a vital adjunct in the liberal reshaping of national memory. On the one hand, in exercising significant judicial restraint, it became the embodiment of a new post-Communist order in which the rule of law triumphed over a world of totalitarian criminality and arbitrary justice. On the other hand, the fact that few cases were tried meant that the Institute's resources were, in effect, being used to research past crimes and thus helping in other ways to situate mass criminality and barbarity at the heart of knowledge reclamation about the eras of Communist rule and Nazi occupation.

Indeed, the best known of the Institute's investigations placed the lawyers of the Main Commission alongside its historians in a scholarly investigation: both sets of professionals were charged with producing accounts of one of the most controversial crimes of the German occupation – the massacre of the Jewish population at Jedwabne on 10 July 1941. In response to Jan Gross's *Neighbors*, which had created a widespread and virulent debate about the role of Poles in World War II because it had implicated Polish nationals as collaborators in this atrocity, the institute instigated official investigations and commissioned parallel enquiries from both its historians and prosecutors. Both confirmed Polish involvement: the historians' account focused on the evolution of German policy towards Jews in the region and the story of how Poles became complicit perpetrators; the Main Commission carried out judicial investigations which attempted to identify individual perpetrators and give a more exact estimation of the number of victims, in part by exhuming mass graves.[113] The findings proved extremely divisive: although many accepted the results, a significant group of right-wingers contested them in parliament, suggesting that the number of victims had been overestimated and criticizing the institute for betraying its function in that it had shamed Polish society and weakened national identity.[114] This controversy was important for the institute, in part because it bolstered its neutral self-image: the shrillness of the right's response, combined with its assertions that the building of a new national identity required an examination of both the glorious and ignominious aspects of the national past, allowed the institution to frame itself as a scholarly centre that stood beyond politics. Yet the incident also revealed the ways in which it was committed to a particular paternalist historical vision, attempting to use the power of elite scholarly research to forge and embed a consensual, healing and unifying understanding of the past onto a nation divided by different interpretations of history. Moreover, the episode demonstrated how the institute was committed to an explicitly national and liberal historical vision in which Communism and Fascism could be understood merely through reference to the crimes that had occurred under these systems, that the social categories of perpetrator and victim were sufficiently encompassing, and that the link between a small number of perpetrators and victims, and the nation as criminal or victim, was obvious and historically correct. Indeed, the very notion of balance could only exist within this totalitarian paradigm; faced with the fallout from the

Jedwabne controversy, the institute's response was to focus on incidents where Poles had been victims rather than perpetrators in order to bolster a unified, patriotic national identity.

The institute did not only seek to shape a new democratic memory from above; it was able to use its massive archive to assist in the creation of processes through which ordinary citizens could re-imagine their own personal histories. This archive contained large amounts of information on the relationships of citizens with the state before 1989, which could be used to pressurize individuals to re-remember their Communist past in criminal terms, even if they had not seen their former lives in this way before. Various processes were constructed either to encourage or, in some cases, to force citizens to declare whether they had been victims, resisters or perpetrators. The validity of these declarations would be checked in the archive, and might then lead to the acquisition of privileges, reprieve from punishment, or exclusion from public service.

This power to force people to reconsider the way they understood their own pasts was powerfully illustrated in Poland in 2007, when the Law and Justice government came to power promising a much more radical policy of de-Communization. For the Law and Justice government, reckoning with the past did not mean simply the production of an anti-Communist public memory that could rally society to support the post-Communist system; it also meant completing the work of 1989 by revealing those remnants of the former regime whose continued presence was both a moral affront to the new political system and responsible for the maintenance of corrupt former *nomenklatura* networks in the economic and political spheres.[115] In a speech given after his inauguration as president of Poland in December 2005, Lech Kaczyński declared, 'Poland absolutely needs to establish a moral order, and this moral order also means our efforts to deal with the burden of the past by rejecting it. . . . This can be achieved by political screening. Vetting must be carried out with all determination.'[116] The new Law and Justice government gained significant influence over the Institute of National Remembrance. A new leadership rejected the self-limiting vision that it had held until 2005, and instead tried to employ it to continue the 'unfinished revolution'. To this end, a Lustration Bureau was established within the institute in March 2007. It worked with a new lustration law that massively expanded the scope of a previous law of 1997, which had only enforced the vetting of 27,000 'senior office holders' (such as ministers and members of parliament). From March 2007, it was estimated that around 700,000 people in positions of 'public trust' – such as teachers, academics, lawyers, police and diplomats – would be screened.[117] (In the event, only 140,000 vetting declarations were filed based on the new law.)[118] The definition of what constituted inappropriate behaviour was broadened too: 'regular contact' with the Communist security services was now enough to constitute collaboration.[119] Although the institute's archive had previously been used for vetting (by the Office of the Spokesman of Public Interest), far fewer people had been investigated, and the work had not involved the institute itself. From 2007, however, the institute would become part of a project to use the secret-service archive to investigate whether public servants had been 'secret informers' under the Communist regime to a far greater degree than ever before.[120] According to the head of the new bureau, its work was 'delayed compensation' for the inadequacies of the system changes of 1989.[121] The institute also ran cultural projects to target former 'perpetrators'. Historians were charged with identifying major players in regional Communist security services and organizing photographic exhibitions of local 'collaborators' which were displayed in town squares across Poland,[122] while the younger generation was encouraged to unearth sites of former Communist terror in their localities. However, the constitutional court eventually diluted the power of the new lustration law in May 2007, ruling that its definition of collaboration was too broad and that the absence of a right of appeal was unconstitutional.[123]

Through these lustration procedures, those who had had significant contact with the Communist security services were pressured to revise the way in which they publicly presented their activities under Communism.[124] Individuals who had worked with the former security services could avoid sanctions if they were prepared to admit to their role under the previous regime and define themselves as collaborators. Individuals had to declare whether they had been full-time employees of the security service or secret informers. If they admitted their complicity, no further investigation took place, while all those who answered in the negative were further investigated via the institute's archive.[125] Legal punishment was not administered primarily on the basis of past collaboration, but rather because of lying on the vetting form: depending on the seriousness of the falsehood, individuals could be excluded from public office for between three and ten years.[126] If a person declared that he or she had been a collaborator on the lustration form, there would be no further investigation, since it was deemed sufficient that the person concerned had made a public declaration of past activities.[127] This process was considered adequate as it was expected that further informal punishment would be likely to be meted out by the public: those who stood for election would not be voted for, while others would be shamed.[128] The mechanism was not therefore designed in the first place to punish people for past misdemeanours but rather to encourage individuals to conform to new understandings of past behaviour deemed appropriate by post-Communist political elites: the readiness of the individual to accept society's new categorization of their past actions as that of a 'collaborator' was considered more significant than the actions themselves.[129]

The archives of Institutes of National Memory were not only used to pressure individuals into re-imagining themselves through totalitarian categories (such as perpetrator) to avoid punishment; files could also be used to encourage individuals to define themselves as victims or resisters in order to receive greater rights or social privileges. In Poland, individuals needed to enquire officially whether they had been 'victims of surveillance', and be defined as such by the institute, in order to obtain access to their own Communist-era files (before the new lustration law of 2007 ended this restriction). Other institutes in central eastern Europe offered the possibility of social and financial advantages if individuals were prepared to ascribe certain totalitarian identities to themselves, provided such identities were subsequently confirmed by their archives. In Romania, individuals could apply to the Council for the Study of Securitate Archives to be recognized as a victim and be awarded a special pension or granted the status of 'revolutionary' for taking part in the overthrow of the Ceauşescu regime. If such recognition was granted, individuals might be awarded free commercial space and tax breaks on their businesses and personal incomes. In Lithuania, the Genocide and Resistance Research Centre could ascribe post-Communist citizens legal identities as volunteer fighters, freedom fighters or victims of the Communist and Fascist systems, depending on the findings of a monthly commission which considered individual submissions and eyewitness accounts. These bodies therefore not only helped construct new histories that invoked the analytical categories of victim, perpetrator and resister, they also managed processes through which post-Communist citizens were encouraged, or even pressurized, to imagine their past lives in such terms.

Conclusion

Many post-Communist elites viewed the 1989 settlements as unfinished and looked to 'complete the revolution' in the decades that followed. Although some radical anti-Communists saw the removal of former 'collaborators' from public office as central to this task, judicial approaches were of relatively little significance in the two decades after the collapse of Communism. More common were the attempts to remould collective memories that were carried out by History Commissions and Institutes of National Memory. The rationales behind these bodies differed significantly. History Commissions emerged in anticipation of post-Communist countries' accession to the European Union, and hence regarded themselves as explicitly political interventions that were essential to the modernization and westernization of their nations' historical consciousness prior to their encounter with Europe's cultural and historical norms. Institutes of National Memory, by contrast, presented themselves as apolitical institutions which both regulated access to the voluminous files of the former security services and employed them to arbitrate in disputes in order to forge a more cohesive post-Communist culture, whose political fissures were often based on divided memories of the past. Despite these differences in rhetorical self-justifications, however, the different bodies' aims were in fact quite similar: both viewed the completion of the revolution in terms of providing a new liberal collective memory that would bind a post-Communist population to democratic development. They did not, by and large, see the struggle against Communism as something that still needed to be fought, as radical anti-Communists did; rather, their approaches embodied the idea that post-Communist populations needed to be shown that they had already escaped from a criminal past and that this realization would help them to identify fully with a post-Communist present based on the rule of law and human rights. This moderate liberal model of dealing with the past was sometimes put under strain, however: both the Romanian Presidential Commission and Polish Institute of National Remembrance were pressurized by more radical anti-Communists to contribute to a historical culture in which former perpetrators could be more aggressively pursued. For the most part, however, they remained close to their more limited and less explicitly politicized visions.

Some critics noted that, although they were propagating an essentially liberal history of their nation's escape from a criminal world into the arms of a liberal democratic system, they used methods that might be considered illiberal. These were not initiatives fundamentally concerned with the democratic pluralization of memory, rather they were moral-political projects that had at their core the notion that the legacies of Communism could be best overcome through a powerful institution forging a unitary interpretation of the past from above. For them, democratic remembrance did not mean the nurturing of a culture that encouraged multiple competing accounts of historical experience. This was because, they argued, too many of these alternative versions were based on historical falsehoods and misshapen memories derived from the experience of Communism. Hence, methods that enabled the collection of 'plural memories', such as oral testimonies gathered at Truth Commissions elsewhere in the world, were rejected. These approaches embodied the idea that a new liberal memory had to be created from above, by state institutions, on the basis of files put together by the previous regime. Indeed, the archives of the former security services were an ideal instrument though which to engender this revolution in collective memory. They allowed History Commissions and Institutes of National Memory to authenticate themselves as apolitical explorers in search of the truths that the Communists had once tried to repress, while simultaneously providing them with powerful, credible sources that reduced the Communist past to an account of its criminality, and could be used to pressurize post-Communist citizens to re-imagine themselves as collaborators or victims of the previous regime. Yet – as the Romanian Presidential Commission demonstrated – it was far from clear that top-down approaches were capable of engendering a new elite or popular consensus over how the Communist past should be overcome.

CHAPTER THREE

CRIMINALIZING COMMUNISM?
HISTORY AT TERROR SITES AND IN STATUE PARKS AND NATIONAL MUSEUMS

The widespread public exhibition of the dictatorial past in central-eastern Europe after the collapse of Communism was a novelty in the history of Europe's gradual process of democratization in the second half of the twentieth century. The newly democratic systems that followed the collapse of Fascist regimes at the end of World War II and right-wing authoritarian regimes in southern Europe in the 1970s did not at first explore the recent past in museums or memorial sites to any significant degree.[1] After 1989, a few museums sympathetic to the Communist past emerged, notably sites that idealized dictators[2] or displayed nostalgia for aspects of everyday life under Communism.[3] For the most part, however, the left played an insignificant role in the construction of a new museum and memorial landscape. Rather, it was anti-Communist groups consisting of former political prisoners, dissidents and exiles who founded the vast majority of sites that dealt with the Communist past.

Those groups who moulded the post-Communist memorial landscape were often concerned about Communism's residual power: they were alarmed that the former regime's supporters had survived the collapse of 1989 and feared their continued influence within the machinery of the state and ability to perpetuate a (now modified) form of leftist ideology. Moreover, since the post-Communist political system proved incapable of providing judicial compensation for the victims of Communism by prosecuting former perpetrators or excluding them from public office, many anti-Communists instead sought to target the unresolved legacies of Communism in the cultural sphere. They envisaged memorials and museums as spaces where the former system could be put on 'cultural trial' and condemned. Moreover, these sites sought to instrumentalize stories of individual suffering in order to construct a new, broader 'imagined community' of national victims of Communism, whose status as heroic martyrs who had stoically endured the trials of dictatorship imbued them with a moral force that could be galvanized in the continuing struggle against the remnants of Communism in the present. The 'cultural trial of Communism' took place at sites of terror where the political condemnation of Communism could be made historically credible: these locations allowed their founders to present themselves as uncovering powerful direct evidence of the former regime's violence and criminality, which could be linked to the ways in which the country as a whole had been victimized. Thus, many of these memorial museums were placed in political prisons: the Sighet Memorial was located at the site of one of Romania's most important political jails of the early Communist era; the Museum of Genocide Victims at the former prison at the KGB headquarters in Vilnius, Lithuania; the Museum of Communism in the former KGB cells in Tartu, Estonia. Alternatively, they might be placed in former secret-police headquarters, such as the Stasi Museum in 'House 1' of the former Communist Ministry for State Security building in Berlin, or the House of Terror in the former headquarters of the Arrow Cross and Communist state security services in Budapest, Hungary. Some were also situated in former political camps, such as the Vojna Memorial at the site of the 1950s hard labour camp for Communist political prisoners at Příbram, now in the Czech Republic, or the Gulag Museum at the site of the political Perm 36 camp in Russia.[4]

After 1989, the choice of space in which the Communist past was exhibited was crucial for those seeking to condemn it. Founders of new memorial sites feared not only the residual power of Communism but were also afraid of the attraction that objects belonging to the pre-1989 era might still hold. They were troubled by the possibility that monumental public sculptures, or even the everyday household products of Communist consumer societies, might still inspire an inappropriate nostalgia for existence under the previous regime. They were concerned that the physical remnants of Communism should be displayed in places where their power could be contained. Alongside sites of terror, Communist-era objects were hence displayed in statue parks such as Szoborpark ('Statue Park') in Hungary and Grūtas Park in Lithuania. These were located in marginal spaces where the power of monumental objects could be deadened and their political irrelevance confirmed. By contrast, sites such as national history museums, where exhibition spaces could not be so easily politicized and which were thus considered insufficient to demonize Communism effectively, were found to be much more difficult to find ways of acceptably displaying the Communist past.

Sites of Terror

For many of the founders of anti-Communist 'sites of terror', Communism had not been defeated in 1989; its ideological carriers had survived and retained the capacity to reproduce their leftist ideology in the present. As such, these sites were regarded as playing a crucial role in the ongoing anti-Communist struggle, as places where the Communist past could be contained and repackaged in such a way that its appeal would be destroyed. One such was the House of Terror, located at 60 Andrássy Boulevard in Budapest at a site that had formerly served as the headquarters for the security services of the Hungarian Fascists – the Arrow Cross – in the autumn of 1944, and then for their Communist equivalent between 1945 and 1956. The House of Terror occupied an important city-centre location on the main route leading to Heroes Square, and cost over $20 million to construct. It was established by an anti-Communist conservative government – Fidesz – and was opened in the midst of its campaign for re-election in 2002. Its director, Mária Schmidt, was a supporter of the party, and Fidesz's leader, Viktor Orbán, often used the location for political speeches. Schmidt, who was a historian, frequently echoed the dominant anti-Communist claims that conservative politics in the post-Communist period meant the continued struggle against Communists who had not merely survived 1989 but had failed sufficiently to renounce their violent and criminal pasts:

> The Hungarian Socialist Party is a successor party. The party made this deci-
> sion itself upon its formation. The other option would have been to choose
> to dissolve the united party, and set up the Socialist Party following the tradi-
> tion of the Social Democrats . . . [The new Socialist Party] unquestionably
> admits its historical heritage, including Kun [leader of the 1919 Communist
> dictatorship in Hungary], Rákosi . . . and Kádár's retaliation [i.e. the retribu-
> tion on Hungarian society following the 1956 Uprising]. It is difficult to
> co-operate with such a successor party, as even a debate requires some kind
> of a common base, a political and ethical minimum: for example . . . the
> party leaders . . . refuse to apologize on behalf of quislings.[5]

Prime Minister Orbán opened the museum in the midst of the election campaign on the eve of the Memorial Day for the Victims of Communist Dictatorships on 24 February 2002. He presented the House of Terror as an institution where the violence of both right and left could be condemned; the context, however, suggested that the museum was intended as a coded warning to the Hungarian electorate not to let the Communist successor party back into power: 'We have locked the two terrors in the same building, and they are good company for each other as neither of them would have been able to survive long without the support of foreign military force. . . . At the very last minute, before it could return, we slammed the door on the sick twentieth century.'[6] Following the failure of Hungarian voters to 'slam the door' on the past when they anyway elected the 'Communist successor party', in 2003 Orbán framed the institution as 'ethical compensation' for the failure to oust 'former perpetrators':

> Since 1990, when we regained our freedom, we have been struggling with the past. Our facing up to history has been full of failures, ambivalent compensation, failed trials of those who took part in the crushing of the anti-Soviet uprising in 1956, the ridiculing of 'vetting'. The only honest part of facing up to our past is this House. A year ago, we felt that . . . the House of Terror was our living pain. Today, an increasing number of us feel increasingly strongly that this is also our living conscience.[7]

At some sites this idea was developed further. Their founders asserted that their memorial museums offered not only moral compensation for an incomplete revolution but were also substitutes for the absence of justice for the victims of Communism. Given the failure of the judicial sphere in aiding a proper reckoning with the past, it was necessary for the producers of culture to assume the role of condemning and 'convicting' the former regime. Their memorial museums would thus serve as 'cultural courtrooms'. One place that embodied this approach was the Sighet Memorial for the Victims of Communism and the Resistance, founded in 1993 at Sighetu Marmației in Maramureș County on the border with Ukraine, which was the site of the most prominent political prison of the early Communist period in Romania (see Figure 3). It had been built as a jail in 1897 under the Austro-Hungarian Empire, used as a holding centre and transportation hub for Jews being taken to concentration camps under the Hungarian occupation during World War II, and under the Communists became a prison for some of Romania's most prominent politicians, journalists, and military and religious figures between 1950 and 1955. Its remote location meant that politicians and intellectuals could be isolated from their former communities, that prisoners could be deported without fuss to the Soviet Union and that Soviet advisors could easily travel across the border to the prison. The site, which lay in ruins after the collapse of Communism, was taken over by the Civic Academy Foundation (a body led by two human rights activists and dissidents from the late Communist era, Ana Blandiana and Romulus Rusan) with a view to creating a memorial. The foundation's wider ambition was to contribute to the building of a new 'civil society' committed to open discussion and democratic values, and effectively inoculated against a return to authoritarianism. For Blandiana and Rusan, this process was hindered by the absence of an official condemnation of the crimes of Communism due to the ingenious ways in which Communists had managed to survive the 1989 revolution: 'double speak [was] the fundamental method of Communism. Communists know how to reposition themselves and mobilize promptly in critical situations. They suddenly turn from Bolsheviks/Mensheviks [into] . . . Social Democrats . . . they forget that they were themselves the preferred victims of Stalin.'[8] Moreover, 'the West' was not helping their cause by refusing to place left-wing tyranny on a par with Fascism. According to Rusan: 'It appeared to us, at a certain time, that the West did not want to learn the truth about Communism' and that '[they] dissociate the two types of totalitarianism[,] pleading, in reality, for the minimization of Communism and an amnesty for its crimes'.[9] In the absence of a real judicial process, a 'cultural trial' was regarded as necessary. The onus was on 'civil society', unsupported by the state, to keep the memory of Communism's crimes alive.[10] Blandiana conceived the Sighet Memorial itself as a form of substitute justice, a place where citizens could be given close encounters with irrefutable evidence of the previous system's criminality: 'When justice does not succeed in being a form of memory, memory itself can be a form of justice.'[11]

Sites of terror were places where these essentially politicized condemnatory accounts could be made historically credible. There, Communism could no longer be understood as a failed project of modernization or social levelling; rather, they were places where Communism could be condemned as criminal.[12] These locations enabled curators to put Communism on trial by re-creating the world of the courtroom, with the imprisoned as the prosecution and the political system that created these prisons in the first place as the accused. Sites were selected for their power to evoke a criminal past and build up a case for the prosecution: Sighet was chosen in part because it was here that many of the violent practices used by Romanian Communists had first been developed;[13] at Vojna, political prisoners had been forced into uranium mining; the House of Terror site had been used by both the Fascist Arrow Cross and Communist security services to imprison and eliminate their opponents.

These memorial spaces helped their founders to construct the idea of 'the victims of Communism'. Here, people's lives could be reduced to their suffering, which was now instrumentalized and turned back against the individual's former persecutors. In such a setting, the complexity of lives could be forgotten; they simply became brutalized objects of the ousted regime, to be held up as evidence for the post-Communist prosecution. The House of Terror was opened on the eve of the anniversary of the execution of Imre Nagy, the leader of the government during the 1956 Uprising, and his fate plays a significant role in the museum itself. The presentation of his life to a post-Communist audience illustrates the process by which individuals became defined by their experience of victimization alone. Nagy was one of the central figures of twentieth-century Hungarian history: as an illegal Communist he had fled to Moscow where he had been involved (as a spy) in the Stalinist purges in the 1930s. He had returned to Hungary after World War II and became the Communist minister for agriculture. He was appointed as a reformist prime minister in 1953 after the death of Stalin, was proclaimed leader of the government during the 1956 revolution and was executed for his role in it in 1958. In 1989, his reburial – this time as a national hero – was the main symbolic act that delegimitized the Communist regime and prefigured its collapse. As such, Nagy could not be ignored by the House of Terror. However, his complex life had the potential to illustrate a range of stories: his complicity with Stalinism, his later ideological commitment to reforming Communism in the national interest, his role as the awkward resister in 1956 and as the victim of a show trial in 1958. Yet, in the House of Terror, his life, and in particular his globally known role as the leader of the 1956 Uprising, was obliterated. He does not appear in the subterranean cavern-like chamber in which the 1956 revolt is represented, at least in part because his presence would have had the capacity to illustrate the role that reformist Communists had played in resisting the system in their struggle to institute a new form of democratic socialism. Rather, at a site devoted to the instrumentalization of suffering, his story is reduced to his sham trial in 1958, simply in order to condemn and convict the previous regime; thus Nagy became a historically under-contextualized symbol of the criminality and arbitrary justice of Communism.[14]

These terror sites did not seek simply to commemorate particular individuals who had suffered. They were also designed to portray the entire post-Communist nation as having been victimized, and to suggest that it had stoically endured at the hands of foreign dictatorships and their traitorous local henchmen. They also encouraged their indigenous audiences to identify with these scripts and imagine themselves as national martyrs. In some cases, these processes were very explicit: the House of Terror, for example, created an online database where individuals could write an account of their sufferings under dictatorship, and name those whom they believed to have persecuted them. Through such techniques, these museums concerned themselves principally with the creation of a new 'imagined community' of national martyrs, whose voices provided a moral force that could be called upon in the ongoing struggle to banish the remnants of Communism from their countries. The power to make their stories of a victimized nation credible rested first and foremost on their claims to be providing direct encounters with the realities of the terror embodied by their sites. Yet these locations often proved problematic in that they had complicated pasts and had borne witness to other forms of suffering, including the Holocaust. The institutions themselves, however, were concerned with the 'production of a selective authenticity', invoking the past horrors of the site to make their morally powerful invocations of victimization under Communism credible, while simultaneously restricting the site's potential to speak about other victims' histories that might drown out Communism's victims' appeals to national martyrdom.

Nevertheless there was a problem: many of these terror sites had witnessed multiple atrocities against different ethnic groups under various regimes. The Sighet Memorial was located on a site that had been used as a jail under the Austro-Hungarian Empire from 1897, then under the Romanian state in the interwar period, then by the Hungarian state after 1941 and then again by the Romanian Communists after World War II. Moreover, it was located in what had been one of the most ethnically diverse regions of Europe until World War II. In the early twentieth century, the town of Sighetu Marmaţiei was dominated by Hungarians and had one of the largest Jewish communities in the region; indeed, it was the birthplace of Elie Wiesel, the Holocaust survivor and Nobel Laureate. During World War II, the Sighet penitentiary became a transportation centre for Transylvanian Jews being taken to Auschwitz.[15] Many other Communist memorial museums similarly contained multiple histories of suffering: the Museum of Genocide Victims in Vilnius had previously been used by the Gestapo during World War II, and had been the site of the persecution of Poles, Germans and Jews alongside Lithuanians;[16] the House of Terror in Budapest, prior to its use as the Communist security service headquarters, had been used by Hungarian Fascists in the autumn of 1944. Yet the accounts that these institutions now produced for the most part identified the story of the nation's suffering with the victimization of its dominant ethnic group under Communism, while the loss of minorities prior to the Communist period was often viewed as a competing story of victimization that needed to be downplayed. This complex history of multiple forms of persecution was not considered because the institutions behind the memorial sites saw themselves as representing the interests of a post-Communist nation now far less ethnically diverse and more closely congruent with its dominant ethnic group.[17]

The latent histories of these buildings – particularly those that alluded to Fascism and the Holocaust – were potentially threatening to the new museums' versions of the past. Curators believed that reviving the memory of Fascist-era violence had the potential to undermine the power of the story of national suffering under Communism that they wished to place at the centre of a new post-Communist history. Accounts of Holocaust victims, for instance, had the capacity both to drown out the appeals of Communism's victims and, indeed, to destabilize their message further by redirecting the viewers' thoughts to the roles that the Soviets and local Communists had played as liberators of the region from Fascism. Moreover, these alternative histories were also ideologically threatening as they had the capacity to undermine the sites' appearance of providing a direct, unmediated encounter with the horrors of Communism. This was particularly the case as these locations no longer bore direct witness to the crimes committed there: they had not seen violence for decades, and Communist regimes had effectively erased any signs of former criminality. The Sighet prison had only been used for political prisoners between 1950 and 1955, had then become a common jail, and was abandoned in 1970. After the collapse of Communism it had to be renovated from ruins. The House of Terror building had been part of the Ministry of Foreign Trade since 1956, and prison camps such as the one at Vojna (now in the Czech Republic) had been almost entirely destroyed. This not only meant that there was often an absence of direct evidence to display to the visitor, it also required that these sites be extensively excavated or rebuilt before being shown to the public. The existence of alternative histories for the sites thus had the potential to reveal that curators were not merely showing the sites as they were, but had made an ideological choice about which version of the prisons' pasts they were to reconstruct. Thus, curators were often concerned that their sites would not be viewed as authentic revelations of the horrors committed at that location, but rather as sites that had been designed and created, thereby losing their power to shock. The displays within these museums were therefore concerned with the 'production of authenticity': how to make the visitor feel they were experiencing them *as they really were*, and to divert attention away from other realities that could have been re-created. The construction of the terror site, no matter how real and horrific the experiences it had witnessed, required artifice. Most crucially, it often had to deal with the site's associations with Fascism and the Holocaust. Some sought to incorporate the location's Fascist past only in so far as it could be used to make its attack on Communism appear more powerful and convincing; where it threatened the authenticity of the reconstruction of the Communist terror, however, it was excluded or marginalized.

In the following sections, I will address how two sites – the Sighet Memorial and the House of Terror – dealt with the problems posed by the necessity of reconstruction and the alternative pasts of the buildings in their museum-courtrooms dedicated to the Communist past.

Sighet Memorial

At the Sighet Memorial (see Figure 3), the memory of Fascism was invoked only in so far as it could be used to reinforce a narrative that emphasized the persecution of national martyrs under Communism. On the one hand, it incorporated the atmosphere and forms of representation common to Holocaust memorials across the world in order to tap into a widely recognized iconography of suffering that would demonize Communism by association. On the other, it excluded the particular Holocaust histories that the site had witnessed. Many founders of these terror and prison museums had visited Holocaust sites and claimed to have drawn inspiration from them. Ana Blandiana, for example, was motivated to found Sighet after a visit to Auschwitz, which she said had led her to question the absence of Communist equivalents of concentration-camp memorials, and had inspired her use of museal techniques to attack Communism.[18] Many terror sites drew upon an internationally recognized visual iconography of genocide derived from mainly western sites devoted to remembering the Holocaust, which included the creation of banks of prisoners' photographs taken by the prison authorities, walls of victims' names and spaces in which to reflect on suffering.[19] The Sighet Memorial replicates these familiar devices: the visitor first enters a hallway that leads into the main prison, which is filled with hundreds of photographs of prisoners taken by the prison authorities on their entry to Sighet. Outside, a non-denominational space of meditation situated in a circular building sunk into the earth is available to visitors for reflection. It is surrounded on three sides by walls inscribed with thousands of names of those who were victimized under the Communist regime; here, families can identify their relatives who may have perished. Banks of victims' photographs provide a powerful visual demonstration of the capacity of the former regime – whether Fascist or Communist – to inflict mass terror on a large body of people. The memorial was also conceived as a space where the memory of those victimized could be restored and the victims once more humanized.[20] The walls on which are inscribed long lists of names reflect the democratizing society's commitment to the recovery of human rights; they demonstrate that it took seriously the individuality of victims, by naming them and providing spaces for their individual histories to be dwelt upon.[21]

Other sites also drew on Holocaust imagery to demonize Communism. The Vojna site (near Příbram, south of Prague) had been a prisoner-of-war camp for German soldiers in 1945 and was used as a military barracks between 1960 and 1989. It was reconstructed as a hard labour camp, which was the form it took between 1949 and 1960 when the Communists' political prisoners worked in nearby uranium mines. Here, the rebuilders of the political prison camp borrowed imagery from Auschwitz that had not been present at the site itself: a board proclaiming *'Praci k svobode'* – the direct translation of the sign above the entrance to Auschwitz, *'Arbeit Macht Frei'* – was hung above the camp entrance, next to a new 'control tower' that had been designed to resemble the 'fist of the proletariat'. The absence of verisimilitude was deemed unimportant; what mattered was that the sign was able to tap into the power of globally recognizable imagery drawn from the Holocaust in order to alert visitors to the continuities between Fascist persecution and that of Communists after the war.[22]

Although sites devoted to Communist terror utilized symbols commonly associated with the Holocaust, they often refused to make connections with their buildings' own links to Holocaust history. The Sighet Memorial at no point makes it clear to the visitor that the location had been used as a transportation centre for Jews being deported to Auschwitz. It should be noted that some considered Sighetu Marmaţiei to be an inappropriate location for the commemoration of the Holocaust in post-Communist Romania, since it was under Hungarian control at the time. The region had been given to the Hungarian state by Germany and Italy as part of the Second Vienna Award of 1940, an agreement that lasted until 1944. To place a post-Communist Romanian memorial to Holocaust victims at a location where the Romanian state clearly had had no complicity in events might provoke charges that the political elite was using another state's participation in genocide to avoid questions of Holocaust collaboration in areas that *had* been under its jurisdiction such as Moldavia.[23] However, the complete absence of information about the site's connection to the Holocaust suggested that curators understood all too well the power that such an alternative history had to undermine their appeal to the suffering of the victims of Communism. The museum thus reconstructed only the Communist-era prison.

There was only one particular form of criminality and suffering that the Sighet Memorial was designed to emphasize: the martyrdom of the nation under Communism. In order to shore up the connection between the site and its victims, the memorial did not merely reconstruct the spaces of imprisonment but looked for direct physical proof of the presence and suffering of Communist-era national 'martyrs'. To this end, the founders turned to forensic archaeologists to discover the bones of prominent figures who had died within the prison and whose remains had been scattered in the town's 'Cemetery of the Poor'. Archaeological excavation appeared to offer the possibility of providing the visitor with solid, irrefutable evidence of the violence and illegality of the Communist regime, and powerfully link the site with the suffering of the nation. Excavations were conducted in July and November 2006.[24] They were initially conceived as general site surveys of the 'Cemetery of the Poor', although it was clear that the archaeological team wanted to find the bones of the two most important Romanian 'martyrs' who had died in the prison: former head of the right-wing National Liberal party Gheorghe Brătianu, and leader of the interwar National Peasant Party Iuliu Maniu (who had had an iron support implanted in his leg, and whose remains, it was hoped, could thus easily be identified without DNA testing).[25] The excavation echoed the aim of the memorial on the site of the former prison, which in its main exhibition framed the martyrs' deaths as symbols of the suppression of the nation – despite the fact that both Brătianu and Maniu had probably died of natural causes. The ninety-year-old Brătianu, it was reported, had been denied medicine after he refused to renounce his belief in a future union of Romania and Bessarabia, a region that had become part of Romania in 1918 but was occupied by the Soviets in 1940/41 and incorporated into the Soviet Union in 1944. His death was thus used to evoke not merely the callousness of the Communists but also the spirit of those who had martyred themselves for the territorial integrity of the Romanian nation.

Forensic disciplines had the potential to provide powerful legal proofs of the criminality of Communist regimes, and bolster these memorial institutions' claims to be providing bona fide 'cultural trials' of Communism. Forensic archaeology had emerged, as part of a broader movement within democratizing societies, as a discipline designed to collect evidence to enable the prosecution of past crimes of dictatorships in places such as Latin America, Africa, post-Communist Europe (including the former Yugoslavia) and Iraq. Its methodologies were often shaped by the requirements of judicial processes: forensic scientists treated historical mass graves as crime scenes, and conceptualized remains as evidence through which criminal responsibility could be attributed.[26] Even where prosecution was not possible, forensic archaeology had the capacity to provide a rhetorically powerful scientific account of the illegality of dictatorship. The Sighet Memorial sought to draw on this power. The excavation was initiated by the Institute for the Investigation of Communist Crimes in Romania,[27] a body established in December 2005 by the Justice and Truth Alliance, which had come to power claiming to be the first post-Communist government to provide justice for the victims of Communism. The institute aimed to bring the previous system's crimes to broader public attention and, where possible, to prosecute them.[28] Its director, who was a trained archaeologist, established a department devoted to uncovering the remains of mass graves.[29]

The excavations, however, revealed the problems of re-creating sites of terror, decades after they had last been used for such purposes and any physical traces had deliberately been erased. Archaeologists were forced to rely on multiple (and often contradictory) accounts by former prison guards to locate possible graves, and found themselves excavating a site where the remains of many individuals were mixed together. They discovered bones 'buried without respect': bodies faced west (which often denoted suicide) and had been placed outside the formal Christian graveyard. They also uncovered the remains of children buried in the 1980s; some surmised that these were orphans, born as a result of Ceaușescu's anti-abortion policies, who had perished living on the streets.[30] The bones of the political prisoners could not be found.

Yet not only was the absence of politically significant remains deemed unproblematic, but the very failure to uncover them was used to bolster the ideology that lay behind the museum. After 1989, Romania's inability to unearth the bones of its 'national martyrs', particularly those killed during the revolution of 1989, was used by anti-Communists to illustrate the incompleteness of the political transition and to inspire a continuing anti-Communist struggle in the present. Unlike elsewhere in central-eastern Europe, the fall of Communism in Romania was particularly violent: an estimated 1,104 revolutionaries died. Moreover, hundreds of their bodies went missing, probably destroyed by the Securitate. As in many other countries in the region, however, Communists survived in large numbers within the political system; more than a decade after the end of Communism, 63 per cent of the current political elite had held positions in the Communist Party prior to 1989.[31] Former Communists often blocked investigations into the disappearances of the revolutionary dead.[32] Thus, for anti-Communists, the absence of victims' bodies represented not merely the extreme inhumanity of the security services but also the continuing power of ex-Communists to block a reckoning with this difficult past. Memorials were established in places where no evidence could possibly be retrieved, such as rubbish dumps and sewers, where the ashes of the bodies of the revolutionaries were supposed to have been deposited by the Securitate.[33] Ceremonial processes were organized to accord victims, whose bodies were lost, proper funerary rites. In 1993, for example, citizens from Timișoara marched on Bucharest with urns to visit the site of the sewer where the remains of their city's revolutionaries were thought to have been scattered; there they gathered dust in the hope that a few 'molecules of the ashes of the heroes' would be among them. Anti-Communist groups saw in their commemoration of lost bodies a respectful acknowledgement of the victims of Communism, which the post-1989 political elite had otherwise failed to produce.

The idea of absent remains became central to the memorial at Sighet. Rather than marginalize the Cemetery of the Poor because no bones had been found there, this very absence was incorporated into visitors' experience by presenting the site as a protected space in which the nation could shield its martyrs' lost bones from the power of ex-Communists. Its memorial landscaping reflected the idea that the 'martyrs' remains' were present but, due to the perfidy of the Communists (who tried to hide their bones among those of the poor) and a lack of post-Communist political will, they could not be found. Curators sought to invoke the ideas of both presence and absence – that the bones were there, brutalized, yet undiscovered – a tension that enabled them to narrate new histories in a number of ways: 'According to local legend, it was here that the fifty-two dead from the political prison were secretly buried at night. The graves could not be identified among the thousands of [other] graves . . . [so] for the celebration of the sacrifice of these victims, a landscape project was developed in 1999. On the 14,000 sq m (16,744 sq yards) of the cemetery, the outline of the country was drawn.'[34] Trees and bushes were planted in the shape of the borders of Romania around the areas where the remains most likely lay (see Figure 4).

The site articulated the idea that the bones still needed to be guarded, enveloped in an 'organic Romania' that represented the power of a newly risen anti-Communist nation to protect them from further violation. According to the memorial guide book, the vegetal map 'through growth . . . will become an . . . amphitheatre, in the inside of which the country will remain like a "glade". The idea is that, in this way, the country keeps its martyrs in its arms and mourns them through the repeated generations of vegetation.'[35] The notion that the bones could be called upon in the continued struggle of the nation against Communism was embedded in the cemetery's landscaping and iconography. In Orthodox Christian beliefs in the region, the absence of a proper burial is not only calamitous for the soul of the dead person but also for the living; the dead have the potential to return to punish those who have denied them proper funerary rights. Indeed, in the county of Maramureş (where Sighetu Marmaţiei is located), peasant culture emphasizes communication between the dead and the living; at funerals, 'lamenters attempt to convince the deceased not to depart'[36] while living relatives use laments to invite the return of the dead (though they do not expect these pleas to be answered).[37] The memorial framed itself as a special site that could invoke victims' remains to help in the construction of the new nation. On the northern edge of the vegetal outline of Romania, at the exact location of Sighetu Marmației on the map, an altar was placed at which masses were held annually to commemorate the martyrs and to call upon their memory in the name of the continued anti-Communist struggle. Moreover, in an appeal to the supposed supernatural force of prominent victims such as Maniu, Brătianu and Daniel Ciugureanu, grave markers were installed and inscribed with exhortations to the dead.[38] A marker for Ciugureanu – who had been an advocate for the unification of Romania with the Bessarabian lands prior to their eventual absorption into the Soviet Union after World War II – reads:

> This wooden cross is made to mark the symbolic place of the unidentified grave of the great national fighter killed in the Communist prison. . . . In this earth the souls of the most powerful and famous are working for the country now. . . . Dante's inferno [i.e. the Communist system] is going down to hell – the noble souls are going to paradise . . . the bones of the martyrs of Romania have melted away but the myths of the heroes rise from here, and prayers are rising from the servants of our people.[39]

Thus, even where bones could not be found they could still be invoked to support this new historical narrative. A dearth of remains did not mean an absence of evidence but rather illustrated the residual power of Communism to block the truth about the past, and reinforced the necessity of calling upon the lost remains in the name of a resurrected anti-Communist nation.

The House of Terror, Budapest

The House of Terror (see Figures 5 and 6) could not easily reconstruct the spaces where dictatorships had formerly inflicted violence on their enemies. The traces of the building's past as a political prison were erased in 1956 when it was converted into offices for a company devoted to foreign trade. The new museum's curators could not find plans from that era either of its upper floors or its basement where the prison cells were located. Thus, although the House of Terror constantly invoked the power of the building in which it was placed, it could not, unlike its sister sites elsewhere, recreate authentic spaces in which terror had occurred. Instead, it used modern museal techniques to dramatize the experience of terror by using a combination of artefacts, reproductions, and artistic and musical installations.[40] It was not designed by a museologist but rather by Attila Ferenczfy Kovács, a Hungarian film-set designer who took his cues from the gloomy interior spaces of the Moscow metro. He went to extraordinary lengths to reanimate the world of the victim; the experience of those Hungarians deported to Siberia was recreated by constructing a swimming pool-sized chamber, its floor entirely covered with a carpet-map of Siberia illustrating the camps to which their countrymen were sent, and its walls mocked up as the sides of cattle trucks, with televisions as windows, showing the Russian landscape flying by – 'a snowy, icy, cold, freezing view symbolizing the endless spaces of Russia and Siberia' – in order to evoke the experience of being deported.[41] Even the rebuilt water-torture cells and places of execution in the basement were designed, rather than authentically reconstructed, spaces. The House of Terror sought to endow these spaces with power, not by giving the visitor a direct encounter with the evidence of terror (which it did not have), but rather through the staged replication of the horrific experience of victimization. The museum recreated the horror of being a political prisoner being taken down to the cells: the visitor was transported to the basement in a lift that descended at such a slow pace that the journey lasted over three minutes. During this descent he or she would face a large video screen showing a former political prisoner, who had to clean the cells after executions, laconically recounting the gruesome horrors perpetrated there. The visitor was then left in the empty cells, surrounded by strategically placed objects of torture and execution collected from other sites and invented graffiti on the walls, which sought to invoke the horrors and hopelessness of the prisoners' plights.

The inability to reconstruct authentically also gave the museum greater freedom, since it was not tied to exhibiting the particular functions of rooms where political violence had been planned or executed. Rather, it saw itself as a 'narrative museum' whose role was to provide a clear account of the Fascist and Communist experience in Hungary, in which the objects on display would be carefully selected (or made) to fit the exact historical interpretation it wished to establish. 'Narrative museums' emerged in the 1990s, partly as a reaction against institutions that celebrated and festishized the individual object to such a degree that the creation of wider narratives or meanings within collections was inhibited; this new type of approach was widely embraced by museums devoted to the histories of suppressed peoples, where authentic objects for display were difficult to recover.[42] In the House of Terror objects were also subjugated to narrative: items from the Communist past were never presented as being of interest in themselves, but were there to support a particular historical account that ran across the entire museum. Visitors were not able to browse and select individual pieces to view at random; rather, there were set routes to follow, which ensured that they encountered items in particular situations that supported and emphasized the specifics of the narrative that the museum wished to establish. In this way, objects were denied the possibility of multiple or ambiguous meanings. Items were carefully placed in a sequence that led the visitor – perhaps best conceived of as a member of a jury – to conclude that Communism should be convicted as a criminal regime.[43]

An analysis of the House of Terror must therefore include an exploration of how the narrative of Hungarian history was constructed, and how objects were instrumentalized to make this storyline appear authentic. Unlike the Sighet Memorial, the House of Terror did not shy away from its building's associations with Fascist terror. On approaching the museum, the visitor spots the blade walls protruding horizontally from its top floor, into which the Fascist Arrow Cross emblem and the Communist star, alongside the word terror, have been carved (see Figure 5). When the sun is at its zenith these cut-out spaces cast a shadow on the road below: a reference to Arthur Koestler's novel about totalitarianism *Darkness at Noon*. In the entrance hall, there are two freestanding memorial tablets commemorating the victims of both systems. The visitor thus expects a memorial to the victims of both totalitarian systems. However, inside, Fascism is employed only in so far as it has the capacity to demonize Communism by association; where the power of the story of Fascism and the Holocaust might drown out the central focus on Communist-era suffering, these histories are neutered or erased.[44]

As such, only two rooms are devoted to the victims of the 'Hungarian Nazis'. The museum's first substantive room on terror highlights Jewish suffering: it features a table set for Hungary's Arrow Cross leader Ferenc Szálasi's 'last supper'. Behind him the image of a flowing Danube is projected onto a wall, while the sound of bodies splashing into the river is repeated every minute. The museum alerts the visitor to the fact that this is a reference to the Arrow Cross's execution of Hungarian Jews on the Danube embankment in autumn 1944.[45] Yet the foregrounding of some aspects of Jewish suffering serves to conceal something far more important: the vast majority of the approximately 600,000 Hungarian Jewish victims of the Holocaust died prior to the Arrow Cross coming to power.[46] One curator argued that this should not be seen as a deliberate exclusion: the museum was only there to tell the history of the building in which it was housed, and it had not been used as a site of terror until after the majority of Jews had been killed.[47] Besides which, Budapest had a separate Holocaust museum which dealt with that subject in depth.[48] However, critics of the museum wondered how it was possible to deal with Jewish suffering in Hungary without a full account of the Holocaust.

Moreover, stories of Jewish survival in the Budapest ghetto are foregrounded and followed in the next room (about the deportations of Hungarians captured by the advancing Soviet troops in 1944–45) with displays of religious items from Jewish citizens who were taken to the Gulag at their moment of supposed 'liberation' from Fascism by the Red Army.[49] The decision to display objects belonging to Jews deported to Siberia in 1945, rather than to Jews sent to Auschwitz in 1944, conveyed an important point: if even Jews were sent to the Gulag, there could be no group in Hungary that could view itself as really having been liberated by the Red Army in autumn 1944. Jews feature one more time, as henchmen of the Communist security services, in the room devoted to Péter Gábor, the (Jewish) head of the Communist ÁVH (State Defence Authority). Here, the story is told of Jewish complicity in the terrors of Communism as part of the regime's security services, and Jews' subsequent persecution by the state when their usefulness was at an end. As a panel in the museum reports, 'His [Stalin's] most faithful disciple, Mátyás Rákosi, did not hesitate to throw to the wolves the ÁVH's henchmen of Jewish origin, who had for years obediently carried out his inhumane orders.'[50] Through these narratives, the capacity of the story of the Holocaust to undermine the power of the suffering of the victims of Communism is contained. The full extent of Jewish suffering is sidelined, the capacity of the Communist state to persecute Jews is presented as equally significant, and Jews' status as archetypal victims is compromised by the insinuation of their complicity with Communist totalitarianism.[51] The final room of the museum – the Hall of Victims – is covered in crosses but contains no Jewish iconography, likewise suggesting that Jewish victimhood is not a central concern of the museum.

The memory of Fascism was deployed, however, where it had the capacity to demonize Communism. The linking hall between the exhibitions on the war period and the Communist state is called 'Changing Rooms'. Two mannequins with Arrow Cross and Communist uniforms are placed back to back on a revolving podium. The text that adorns the walls of the hall – a statement from Communist leader Rákosi that 'Unfortunately sometimes we let Fascists into the party' – makes the meaning even clearer: many of those who had victimized Hungary as Fascist Arrow Cross members subsequently slipped into new uniforms and continued their persecution of the nation in the guise of Communists.[52] Such people did exist – the revolutionary anti-elitism of both movements appealed to some members of the working class – but the rapidly expanding Communist Party consisted of many other groups too, such as those on the left radicalized by the experience of Fascism, or public-service workers who needed to maintain careers. Their stories, however, could not demonize Communism as much as those of party members who had pasts as perpetrators of Fascist crimes.

The House of Terror was a politicized institution from the very moment of its establishment. It was opened during an election campaign, used as a backdrop to it, and was supported by the conservative elite who wished to place the suffering and endurance of 'Hungarian patriots' at the centre of a new collective memory. According to one of its greatest supporters, the leader of Fidesz, Viktor Orbán:

> There is a huge force in this building, the force of the victims, those humiliated, their relatives and those who sympathize with them – the force of the nation. This is a museum, instead of retaliation, repayment or revenge. An agreement can be reached with history in this way as well. Many people may feel that what happened in this House calls for retaliation. However, after the collapse of Socialism, in the last moments of the twentieth century, those who suffered from violence had the strength to say no to retaliation. There was a need for self-restraint and dignity, that is, the self-restraint and dignity of the victims, the humiliated, those who lost their parents, brothers or sisters, or children – the survivors. Their sacrifice and restraint made it possible to regain the nation's independence and citizens' freedom without the loss of a single life, without a single violent action. Respect, recognition and thanks for this.[53]

Following the election of the former Communists in April 2002, Orbán declared, in another speech given outside the House of Terror, that the museum would preserve a true version of history against the ascendant socialists who were sure to undermine it. Sustaining a focus on the suffering Hungarian nation – rather than Jewish victimization – was deemed necessary in order to protect 'true Hungarians' from predatory international forces:

> We will not allow them [i.e. the Hungarian Socialist Party] to re-christen, and to rearrange the House of Terror museum which has been criticized for focusing on the actions of the Communist regime while allegedly ignoring the deeds of the Hungarian Fascists, including the mass murder and deportation of Hungarian Jewry during the Holocaust. Because we are strong enough, we will not allow them to sell Hungary's arable land to foreigners and dispossess Hungarian farmers, no matter how cunning [the] methods they will use to do so. We will not allow them, because we are strong enough, to destroy the status law on preferential treatment granted by Hungary to ethnic Hungarians from neighbouring states. We will not allow them, we

will not permit them, to take away from families what they have gained for themselves in recent years.[54]

The House of Terror did not merely seek to criminalize Fascism and Communism and to restore memory to victims by its location at a site of execution and imprisonment. More than this, it used the idea of the 'narrative museum' to provide a very precise account of who should be considered the true perpetrators and real victims of recent history. Genuine Hungarians could not be Communist perpetrators; rather, according to the museum's narrative, the Communist Party consisted of former Hungarian Nazis (whose support for the subordination of Hungarian interests to those of Nazi Germany meant that they could not be true patriots) who changed their political spots after 1945, and Jews who turned to radical left-wing politics after the war. Moreover, this narrative established that Jews, unlike patriotic ethnic Hungarians, could no longer claim to be pure victims: even if they had been persecuted before 1945 (and the museum downplays the degree to which that was the case), they had undermined their claims to victimhood by coming back as Communists to 'take their revenge' on their victimizers. It was only the eternal Hungarian ethnic nation, untouched by collaboration and which had stoically endured the pains of Fascism and Communism, that now had the right to control the future of the country.[55] The moral voice of a victimized nation could finally be heard and invoked in the continuing struggle against those former dictators who had remained within the system after 1989 and whose movement's crimes had not been sufficiently addressed.

Sites of terror were places where these accusatory, condemnatory histories of Communism could be made authentic and convincing; they provided encounters with the horrors of the Communist period, closed down other non-criminal readings of the pre-1989 period and framed the nation as Communist martyr. Yet some of these sites also had the capacity to undermine these narratives; they had multiple histories which were connected with the suffering of other groups, notably Jews under Nazi occupation. These sites drew on Fascism in so far as it could demonize Communism by association, but removed it from sight whenever the power of its memory threatened to undermine the anti-Communist accounts they sought to establish.

The Statue Park

The statue park emerged alongside the site of terror as an alternative – albeit much less frequently used – location for the public display of Communism.

After the collapse of Communism, two such parks were founded in central-eastern Europe: Szoborpark (Statue Park) in Budapest, in Hungary founded in 1992 (see Figure 7), and Grūtas Park (often called 'Stalinworld') in Druskininkai, southern Lithuania (see Figure 8).[56] These locations provided a resting place for monuments and memorials from the previous regime which, rather than being destroyed, were removed from the urban spaces they formerly occupied and deposited in open-air venues for public viewing.[57] Both were created after the bodies responsible for the fate of Communist statuary and the like asked private consortia to present ideas for their display. In 1991, Hungary adopted legislation – as was the case in many other parts of central-eastern Europe – that gave local authorities the choice of what to do with Communist memorials in their region, hence Budapest's municipal government became responsible for removing statues and settling their subsequent fate.[58] In Lithuania, by contrast, the process started much later, in 1998, when many Communist-era statues had already been long removed and placed in storage. Here, it was the national parliament that was responsible for dealing with these monuments. In both cases, private entrepreneurs were then chosen – supported by funds from both government and the European Union – to implement designs and run the sites.

Both parks emerged from political debates over fears concerning the residual power of Communist-era statuary. In Hungary, the peaceful nature of the transition to democracy in the summer of 1989 had meant that most Communist monuments had remained intact. In 1991, faced with increasingly violent assaults on these Communist-era objects, the Budapest municipal assembly was forced to consider their future. As Maya Nadkarni has argued, the assembly was faced with polls showing that the majority of residents did not want to see them destroyed. This was interpreted as evidence for Hungarians' accommodation with the regime during the years of 'goulash Communism' (1968–89), when many had grown fond of these statues either because of, or despite, their political meaning. The public's continuing sympathetic attitudes towards these statues after 1989 were therefore feared to be evidence of the unwanted appeal of Communism in the present.[59] A statue park was a way of preserving these objects, as popular sentiment demanded, while removing them from prominent locations where they functioned as problematic symbols of popular accommodation with the former regime.

In Lithuania, by contrast, when the issue was debated in parliament in 1998, most Communist-era statues had already been dismantled and stored in warehouses. As in Hungary, there was significant support – 63 per cent of people in a poll taken in June 1999[60] – for their preservation. Yet, unlike in Hungary, there was significant opposition to the creation of a statue park, particularly from conservatives who saw the preservation of statues as an insult to the victims of Communism, and the statues themselves as dangerous carriers of an ideology that was still not fully dead.[61] For them, the monuments should not have been preserved in any environment; their power could not be sufficiently neutered by their installation in walled parks far from the prominent city centre locations in which they once stood. According to a letter addressed to the secretary general of the United Nations, signed by representatives of political prisoner and deportee associations and the Lithuanian independence movement Sajūdis, 'We demand that the exhibition of Communist leaders and their henchmen in Grūtas forest be eradicated and the sculptures melted down or broken up. It is also essential to destroy all the other dismantled and yet to be dismantled Communist monuments. . . . This exhibition is a hidden time bomb of Communist ideology.'[62] These groups feared that the statues would elicit feelings of nostalgia rather than oppression, and allow visitors to live out the 'good old days'.[63] After the park opened in 2001, debates over the legitimacy of displaying Communist statuary erupted as part of wider discussions about whether Communist symbols should, as with their Nazi-era equivalents,[64] be forbidden in public spaces across Europe, and whether such prohibition should include museum and memorial sites too. Representatives of the conservative Homeland Union frequently argued that Grūtas Park should be included in any such ban.[65]

Those who designed and ran Grūtas and Szoborpark rejected these 'primitive' calls for the destruction of Communist-era statuary, arguing that the campaigns represented a continuation of totalitarian mentalities in that they reproduced the Communists' own previous violent attempts to destroy public memorials after World War II. For them, these parks were superior 'civilized' democratic responses to dictatorship. Viliumas Malinauskas, the private entrepreneur whose plan for the Lithuanian statues triumphed in the tendering process in 1998, argued that his park represented a proper attempt to come to terms with the past in line with advanced and sophisticated democratic practice: 'It was a cruel, violent history, [but] it is our history . . . To destroy the figures would be to destroy that part of history, that's why they were saved, collected and now are presented here [in a] civilized evaluation of history. . . . more than one million suffered [under] the Stalin regime, we do not have the right to forget such numbers and such victims.'[66] Ákos Eleőd, the architect of the Budapest site, wanted a 'counter-propaganda park' that neither demonized nor celebrated the memorials contained within; this humane approach would demonstrate that the 'totalitarian' mindset of the Communist era had been overcome. Yet the way in which these objects were presented in the parks suggested that another form of destruction was necessary before they could be acceptably exhibited. A refusal to engage with the holdings as objects of political power, the brutal and bleak landscape they constructed around them, and the permission they gave to their audience to ridicule and belittle their objects, all suggested that the parks' founders also still feared a residual ideological attraction in these objects, and they designed their sites as places where the allure of these statues could be obliterated.

These parks emerged out of fears that such objects represented the accommodation that society had made with the ousted regime, or that they still embodied the possibility of a real ideological communication between the fallen regime and the post-Communist population. As such, the statues were now placed in settings that made such a reading impossible. These objects were now arranged, as at sites of terror, to represent a world in which Communism was simply a criminal system that victimized the nation and its people. Despite the fact that many of these statues (and almost all in the case of Grūtas) were created in the late Communist era, they were placed in a setting that evoked the violence and criminality of the earlier Stalinist period. Grūtas was designed to resemble a 1940s or 1950s Gulag: the site itself, a drained swamp filled with birch trees, was chosen for its 'Siberian ambiance'. Walkways were surrounded by high barbed-wire fencing, while guards in towers watched over the statues. Moreover, its founder, Viliumas Malinauskas, wanted to install tracks and a replica cattle wagon that would have taken visitors on a mock journey to Siberia to view these statues. He was restrained from doing so after protests from the Ministry of Culture; instead, he placed a cattle truck bearing the following inscription by the entrance: 'This is a Soviet relic, a horrific symbol that takes our memory back to the 1940s and 1950s. During this period the repressive Soviet regime was carrying out a massive genocide against the Lithuanian nation.' As one Lithuanian observer commented, Grūtas presents itself as a jail in which those responsible for the terrors of Communism can now be imprisoned: 'In some sense, Grūtas is a gulag upside down where the Marxist-Leninist state, visually objectified through museified party propaganda, is held captive as a punishment for the many crimes it committed against its own people.'[67]

The objects in Budapest's Szoborpark were dangerous in that their very survival was taken as evidence of an unfortunate absence of iconoclasm, which in turn could be regarded as proof of a popular accommodation between state and society under so-called 'goulash Communism' in the 1970s and 1980s. Thus, the statues were placed in settings in which they could only be understood as propaganda for a violent, brutal regime. Regardless of when they were made, all objects were presented as symbols of the earlier terrors of the Stalinist period: the park was opened with an 'ironic' 1950s-style party rally, promoted itself with images of 1950s monumentalist sculpture, and was given the full name of the 'One Sentence on Tyranny Statue Park' – a reference to Gyula Illyes's 1950 poem on the excesses of Stalinism. Moreover, its centre-piece was not an authentic surviving statue at all, but rather a replica of 'Stalin's Boots', the remnants of the Stalin statue from Felvonulási Square that had been destroyed by revolutionaries in the Uprising of 1956.[68] Indeed, the central position given to a replica of part of a destroyed statue within the park's memorial landscape suggested that the authentic Communist statues on display were not doing all the ideological work the park required. 'Stalin's Boots' was necessary to indicate to visitors that Hungarians were capable of attacking symbols of Communist power, since the memorial landscape was otherwise filled with 'authentic', unmolested objects that might suggest that for most of the Communist period they had done quite the reverse.

These parks did not merely provide a totalitarian setting; statues were arranged to suggest the Gulag, turning objects that had been created to glorify the Communist regime into ones that illustrated a criminal world inhabited by victims and perpetrators. Decisions regarding the layout of the statues within these parks provided curators with ample room to create new historical meanings and narratives with their collections. At Grūtas, these objects were arranged in two walks or 'avenues': one representing perpetrators (Lenin Street), and the other victims (Melnikaite Street). Such a division was crucial for the capacity of the park to contain the power of the statues; arranged in this way, they could no longer be interpreted as a siren song for the ideals of Communism, but were only able to evoke a world in which the imposition and endurance of violence and suffering were the be-all and end-all. Figures of Communist 'perpetrators', who worked to destroy independent Lithuanian statehood and its traditions, were lined up along the first forested walkway, watched over by prison camp lookout towers. Alongside major figures of Soviet Communism such as Lenin were placed their 'Lithuanian henchmen' who had been responsible for the wartime and postwar purges of Lithuanian national-ists and had engaged in acts of violence against national culture, and hence were considered responsible for the 'genocide' of the Lithuanian nation. Along the second forested avenue, statues that were originally created to glorify Communist heroes and martyrs were now made to illustrate victim-hood under the Soviet state. To achieve this reversal in meaning, it was neces-sary to ignore the political context of the statues' creation and focus on the nature of the death of the individual depicted. For this reason, all sculptures at Grūtas were accompanied by in-depth biographical details about their subjects, but rarely by information about the sculptures' creators or the polit-ical environment in which they had been produced; to do so would have undermined the ideological intentions of the site.[69] To turn statues of Communist heroes into representations of victims of Communism, curators chose sculptures of individuals whose biographies could be used to illustrate the violence of the Communist experience, such as Lithuanian Communists who perished in the Stalinist purges of the late 1930s, and young, politically committed, leftist women who were killed by nationalist partisans and became 'martyrs for Communism'. They simply ignored the fact that partisan statues were created to commemorate Communist martyrs who had given their lives to defeat so-called 'reactionary Lithuanian nationalism'. With the provision of more historical context, they might instead have been considered 'perpetrators'. At Grūtas, however, their monuments merely reflected the conflict that the Soviets had brought to the Baltics, and the brutal violence that had created victims on all sides. The female partisans were presented as innocents caught up in a struggle beyond their control which pitted Lithuanian against Lithuanian. Here, a historically decontextualized and ideologically empty account was created in which Communism was simply a regime that created victims by forcing Lithuanians to kill each other, regardless of the ideology that produced this violence.

While these parks arranged their objects in order to demonize Communism through the re-creation of terror and the Gulag, they simultaneously attempted to denude them of all political significance or emotional power so that they could not speak (politically at least) to a new generation. Powerful and aesthetically intriguing statues that had once been employed to inspire local populations to support the Communist state could no longer be allowed to move or affect the viewer. Unlike many sites of terror, these parks were located far from seats of power, in remote, often inhospitable, locations, 'adrift in a suburban wasteland'[70] on the outskirts of Budapest or in a mosquito-infested drained swamp in a southern Lithuanian forest in an area of former anti-Communist partisan activity. One ethnographer found that many visitors to Grūtas experienced feelings of power over a system that had once controlled them:[71] here was a marginal site that neutered the statues it presented, removed their pedestals, brought them to ground level, denied them a monumental setting, and encouraged visitors to interact and pose for photographs with them (see Figure 8). Viewers were being directed to treat the monuments not as powerful icons of a former age but as objects open to ridicule. Likewise, at Szoborpark, visitors were encouraged to view the statues as kitsch rather than as art, to deny them reverence and to treat them as objects of entertainment. Indeed, both parks opened with ironic events that ridiculed their collections. Grūtas opened on April Fool's Day. Both also surrounded their objects with Communist kitsch: Grūtas wished to evoke aspects of everyday life under Communism, and established a Soviet-style restaurant with 'nostalgia' dishes and a children's playground full of antiquated Communist-era slides and swings. Szoborpark sold reproduction Communist objects and albums such as *The Best of Communism*. As Paul Williams has argued, these sites allow visitors to 'practice irreverence in public'; they do not force them to address their own relationships with the Communist past.[72]

Szoborpark also denuded these objects of power by denying them a political or historical meaning that could speak across 1989. As such, it was very different from sites of terror and Holocaust memorials, where objects were assigned a political purpose: excavated graves, remodelled gas chambers, the shoes of victims and abandoned prison cells were all used to point to the inhumanity and criminality of past regimes, and to provide a 'lesson for future generations'. By contrast, the park's curators refused to demonize their objects openly as remnants of a totalitarian ideology: information about the statues themselves usually extended little beyond the names of their creators, dates of production and former sites of display. Virtually no information was given about their ideological content, their intended appeal or purpose; nor, most crucially, did the park take issue with the messages – of the necessity of Soviet power, or the class or anti-Fascist struggle, for instance – that these statues had been created to convey. Addressing these messages was resisted on the grounds that such engagement opened up the possibility that Communism was still worthy of debate, or that it could elicit quarrels inspired by objects (such as monuments to antifascist Spanish Civil War fighters) that had enduring political resonances for some visitors. The implicit pointlessness of taking these objects seriously suggested that their consignment to the dustbin of history was self-evident. They were displayed as an undifferentiated mass of monumental sculpture. Objects that were capable of carrying very different meanings – such as monuments to Spanish Civil War International Brigadiers and to those who suppressed the 1956 Uprising – were placed alongside each other in the same section entitled the 'Unending Promenade of Workers' Movement Groups'. No attempt was made to distinguish morally between the different forms of antifascist struggle represented; the statues could be lumped together because they had all once been used to justify a dictatorship that had now crumbled.[73] They were being framed as 'dead objects' belonging to a distant, amorphous past that had no conceivable link to the present or contemporary politics. Indeed, leftist critics of Szoborpark suggested that the project was an attempt to remove the Communist period from Hungarian history and to reject the idea that there were continuities across 1989 that were worthy of consideration.

In addition, the parks used the very fact of their preservation of Communist objects (perhaps paradoxically) to establish an unbridgeable distance between the present and the dead Communist past. While some felt the preservation of such remnants had the potential to revive political passions for the former regime, for others these parks presented the very fact of their display as an argument against Communism and as a paean to democracy. For the latter, to be able to exhibit and initiate discussion through these statues was a reflection of the wonders of democracy. According to Ákos Eleőd: 'This park is about Dictatorship – but in the very same moment when it becomes utterable, describable and possible, then this park is suddenly about Democracy! Only democracy can give us the chance to think freely about dictatorships (or democracy even ... or anything).' He also stated in his original proposal for the park, 'There is pleasure in participating in the *absence* of book burning.'[74] Thus, the contrast with autocracy was made: whereas the Communist takeover had been violent and had involved the destruction of the symbols of the past, democracies had the civility and self-confidence necessary to preserve even a hated history. The absence of crude iconoclasm supported the idea that an enlightened, 'western' approach to history was now possible.[75] Hence, the preservationist instinct, which curators presented as emerging out of an appropriate respect for recent history, was in fact being used to distance the Communist past from the present: the very existence of the park asserted the effortless moral superiority of the post-Communist present over the recent past.[76]

The statue park was thus centrally concerned with the containment of the power of Communism. Unlike sites of terror, however, it used a combination of the re-politicization of its objects – as symbols of criminality and violence – and their de-politicization – displaying them irreverently and refusing to attribute to them a history or politics that might speak across 1989. The parks drew criticism from both right and left based on very different understandings of the meanings of these objects and their new settings. For representatives of the anti-Communist right, the impossibility of containing the power of these objects – even at quarantine sites in marginal locations designed to evoke the criminality of Communism – meant that they should be denied public display. For those on the liberal-left, however, the critique was different: the sites were not a celebration of democracy but rather a manifestation of the desire to deny Communism's impact on national culture, and to remove it from the account of national history.[77] According to István Rév, a history professor and director of the Open Society Archives in Budapest, the statue park 'removed the visible signs of our past, and . . . made it easier to think that we had nothing to do with Communism. . . . We cannot deny that they are part of our history. Rather than target a statue, we should deal with the decades of dictatorship.'[78]

Communism in the National History Museum

Whereas Communism was widely exhibited at specialist locations after 1989, it had far less presence at national history museums. Many of these institutions, some of which held large collections of Communist artefacts dating from the Communist period which had been displayed before the transitions, chose to remove such objects from the public gaze rather than remake them for a post-Communist audience. Only a few – such as the Peasant Museum in Bucharest, the National Museum in Budapest and the War Museum in Riga – attempted to deal with Communism in new ways. While the statue park and the terror site provided answers to problems of display by providing locations in which Communist ideology might be convincingly demonized, ideologically deadened and presented as an aberration from national history, the national history museum had the troubling potential to do the exact opposite: curators feared their spaces might normalize the Communist past as part of a natural teleology of national development, or provide their Communist-era objects with a power that they did not wish to give them. Thus, these three national institutions that did tackle Communist material – in Bucharest, Budapest and Riga – drew on the methods of the statue park and terror site to contain the power of their objects.

All three had been Communist-era national history museums; hence a central problem for the curators was how to deal with both spaces and objects in their collections that had once been used to legitimize dictatorship. Bucharest's Peasant Museum was created in 1990 in what had been the building of the History Museum of the Communist Party and Revolutionary and Democratic Movement of Romania; in its new guise, it soon became the most visited history-themed institution in the city.[79] According to the minister of culture, who supported the establishment of the new institution, an ethnographic museum representing the traditions of rural Romania was appropriate in such a building as 'it seemed symbolically useful to exorcize the ghosts of a fake museum [i.e. the Communist-era one]'.[80] Like curators at sites of terror and statue parks, those at the Peasant Museum were frightened of the remaining power of Communism; in this case, the power was perceived as residing in the building itself and the older Communist objects it still contained. Its first director, Horia Bernea, fearing the ideological ghosts of the past, brought in Orthodox priests to remove them in spring 1991: 'we needed to clean the space not only of fake walls and fake objects, but also of the bad spirits. . . . he [Horia Bernea] brought in some prelates who came to sprinkle holy water . . . . when they found themselves in front of that famous sculpture of the heads of Marx, Engels and Lenin . . . . they drenched, flooded it with water as if this would destroy it.'[81] In 1997, the museum hosted *The Plague*, an exhibition on the effects of Communist ideology and collectivization on the Romanian peasant. This was unusual; nearly all Romanian historical institutions had removed Communist-era materials after 1989 and had thenceforth refused to exhibit them. The Romanian National History Museum (opened on Ceauşescu's initiative in 1972) was one of these; its curators claimed that the previous period was so controversial, and its interpretations so distorted, that more time had to pass before related materials could be displayed again.[82] According to this view, the past had to lose its political significance before it could be exhibited. Only one other site – Bucharest's National Military Museum – displayed the Communist past; here, an institution that held close ties to former Communists after 1989 simply continued to exhibit 'national Communist' accounts of Romanian history, first established under Ceauşescu in the 1970s.[83] The Peasant Museum, by contrast, considered it vital that the suffering inflicted on peasants during the period of collectivization be publicly displayed. Yet the objects were still seen as problematic and threatening and hence were placed in a marginal location within the museum, in a basement next to the toilets. Moreover, like the statue parks, the museum sought to mute the power of the items it displayed. In other exhibitions, objects were allowed to dominate the spaces around them; in this cramped basement space filled with busts of famous Communists and Marxist propaganda, by contrast, what was stressed was the objects' ugliness and incapacity to inspire. According to the museum's director: 'here we absolutely needed a political bias. As we couldn't exhibit the lies of the regime, we tried to exhibit its ugliness.'[84]

The fear that surrounded the power of Communist objects was also an issue in Budapest's National Museum and Riga's War Museum, where curators wanted to use collections inherited from their Communist-era predecessors to provide a less politicized account of recent history that dealt with everyday life as much as the experience of terror or repression.[85] Riga's War Museum – which had previously been the Museum of the Soviet Revolution – had kept most of its pre-1991 material, and wanted to redeploy it to illustrate domestic interiors and the everyday experience of Communism at home, school and work.[86] Budapest's National Museum brought in new material in 1996[87] and mocked up the offices of an agricultural collective and late Communist-era domestic settings alongside Communist-era art and tableaux of the 1956 Uprising. Yet these spaces differed from the rest of the museum, where items were displayed as objects of beauty or scientific interest, since here their apparently benign ordinariness failed to delegitimise Communism sufficiently. In both museums these exhibits drew upon the iconography of sites of terror: all objects were displayed within models of prisons or cages. Budapest's

National Museum included mock-ups of cells and secret-police headquarters alongside the everyday 'prisons'; the central display bay contained a reconstruction of the cell of the 1956 revolutionary leader Imre Nagy prior to his execution, in which was placed the smoking jacket and pince-nez he had worn while incarcerated. The form in which these objects were displayed embodied the tension between the need to depoliticize objects that had once been the source of Communist propaganda and the simultaneous requirement to demonize them so as to deny them ideological power in the present.

The museums also worked to set Communism apart by ascribing it a different relationship to historical time. Both the Riga and Budapest institutions were history museums: curators sought to present Communism as an aberration from their country's past, but were doing so in the context of institutions that were devoted to presenting a linear account of the chronological development of the nation-state.[88] They therefore had to find ways of displaying Communism as a historical phenomenon while simultaneously denying it a place in their national history. First, the institutions physically divided their exhibitions on Communism (and often on the periods of German occupation and Fascism) from the rest of the museum. In Riga's War Museum, for instance, at the beginning of the material relating to the period of Soviet and German occupation, visitors have to squeeze around a gate blocking a railway crossing and then pass over train tracks, where their ears are assaulted by a soundtrack suggesting the fast approach of a locomotive representing the deportation of Latvians to the Gulag. Visitors are left in no doubt that they are crossing the 'frontier between independent Latvia and occupied Latvia,'[89] and in the process descending into a separate historical universe. Hungary's National Museum takes this idea one step further, forcing the visitor to anticipate the return to 'proper' national development in 1989 before the exhibition has even begun. Displays relating to Communism are hidden away in cubicles at the side of a main corridor that are invisible to visitors entering the exhibition, whose gaze is directed towards the wall at the far end where a large-scale photographic reproduction of Imre Nagy's reburial in June 1989 is displayed; for most Hungarians, this is the moment that represents the fall of Communism. Thus, on entering the exhibition, the visitor first sees its end; the Communist period is erased and the visitor anticipates the return to national history before the 'aberrant era' has even been explored.[90] In Riga, too, the end of Communism is prefigured: the walls of cages that condemn the objects they display start to fall away in the period of 'national reawakening' in the 1980s, and disappear with the achievement of full independence. These museums present Communism as an aberration within national history, both by borrowing the iconography of the terror site and by forcing the visitor to anticipate the return to 'normal' national history even before the 'historical deviation' has begun.

The Peasant Museum in Bucharest is, by contrast, an ethnographic museum. Here, in a reversal of the strategy of the standard national history museum, the curators provide the visitor with no conception of linear time in the main body of the building. Their institution was dedicated to the idea of a timeless, traditional rural life. Thus, displays provide little sense of historical developments in the life of the Romanian peasant. The museum only diverged from this approach in its representation of peasants' experience of Communism in the *Plague* exhibition: the violent process of collectivization of Romanian farms by the Communists was the only moment where peasant life was ascribed a place in the chronological development of the modern world. Here, Communism was shown to be an aberration, not by removing it from history, as was the case in the national history museums in Riga and Budapest, but rather by representing it as a moment when the imagined timeless existence of the Romanian peasant came face to face with the violence of modern Romanian history.[91]

Conclusion

This chapter has highlighted the importance of place in determining the type of historical narrative memorials and museums are able to relate. After World War II, both liberal democratic and Communist regimes sought to demonstrate their superiority to the dictatorships that had preceded them by highlighting the victims of their predecessors. Sites of terror, concentration camps, burnt-out villages and former political prisons were effective locations at which to build powerful reminders of the barbarous and criminal nature of those previous political systems. Since the 1970s, the prison has increasingly become the location par excellence for the memorialization of past dictatorships' violence across the globe. Among the best known are the Tuol Sleng Genocide Museum in Phnom Penh, Cambodia, which was the former Khymer Rouge Security Prison 21 (S-21); the Robben Island Museum in South Africa, the former jail of the African National Congress' anti-apartheid leaders; and the Escuela de Mecánica de la Armada (Naval Mechanics School), a clandestine detention centre in Argentina, where many of the so-called 'disappeared' were tortured. The Shiite-led Iraqi regime reconstructed part of Abu Ghraib prison to tell the story of Saddam Hussein's crimes against his citizens.[92] These sites give the visitor a visceral encounter with the horrors of a previous era which are being used by new political movements or regimes to frame their accounts of the recent past.

The comparison with post-apartheid South Africa is particularly pertinent here, as it illustrates the very different historical narratives it is possible to construct in settings of historical violence. In South Africa, the legacies of the apartheid past are addressed at two very different sites of former terror: the Robben Island Museum, where many of the most prominent anti-apartheid activists, including Nelson Mandela, were imprisoned from the 1960s onwards, and former British-run concentration camps during the Anglo-Boer War of 1899–1902, where over 28,000 Boers (mostly women and children) and 14,000 black Africans died.[93] The Robben Island curators refuted the necessity of demonizing those responsible for apartheid and, though acknowledging the suffering that their site represented, did not seek to dwell on stories of persecution and victimization. Rather, they aligned themselves with the narratives of reconciliation advocated by a new post-apartheid political elite, and sought to tell the story of a difficult past that had been overcome. The narrative of struggle is most powerfully experienced in Nelson Mandela's cell, where his ability to lead his nation out of a violent, discriminatory past is stressed in preference to his experience of persecution. According to Ahmed Kathrada, the chairman of The Future of Robben Island Committee, who had also been imprisoned there:

> we will not want Robben Island to be a monument to our hardship and suffering. We would want it to be a monument reflecting the triumph of the human spirit against the forces of evil, a triumph of freedom and human dignity over repression and humiliation; a triumph of wisdom and largeness of spirit against small minds and pettiness; a triumph of courage and determination over human frailty and weakness; a triumph of non-racialism over bigotry and intolerance; a triumph of the new South Africa over the old.[94]

Although the Robben Island Museum became much better known internationally, it is striking that a greater proportion of heritage funding in the immediate post-apartheid period actually went to preserve Anglo-Boer War concentration-camp sites rather than locations devoted to the anti-apartheid struggle.[95] After the collapse of apartheid, new political elites, who had already set up a Truth and Reconciliation Commission, looked to historical memories that could bond former enemies together. Sites devoted to the anti-apartheid struggle were often deemed problematic: they were threatening to the white minority and seen as divisive. Former Anglo-Boer War concentration camp sites at first seemed problematic too: they were regarded by many as being complicit in the construction of apartheid after 1948, since they had previously een used by a dominant Afrikaaner elite to narrate the story of the victimization of the Boer race at the hands of outsiders. The sites had helped the architects of apartheid to invoke the memory of the threat of racial anni-hilation, and had thus provided cultural justifications for the necessity of remaining separate and superior to other ethnic groups in South Africa.[96] Moreover, prior to the collapse of apartheid, the African National Congress opposition had usually viewed the Anglo-Boer War as an inter-European struggle of little interest to black South Africans. Despite this, however, they were turned into sites of inter-ethnic reconciliation: newly refurbished, they now admitted to the level of black South African victimization at the camps during the Anglo-Boer War, and became *lieux de mémoire* for the story of shared white and black South Africans' suffering at the hands of the British. The sites could thus be used to assert that groups that had been enemies during apartheid also had a common history based on suffering and anti-imperialism.

South African memorial sites embraced the spirit of reconciliation promoted by the architects of the post-apartheid system. In post-Communist central-eastern Europe, by contrast, curators of memorial sites refused to highlight the forms of mass terror other than that of Communism that the region had experienced and the sites themselves had witnessed, and used them more narrowly to remind the remaining ex-Communist elites of the crimes of the old regime. South African curators differed in that they accepted the logic of the negotiated transition, celebrated its peaceful nature, and sought to embed the value of reconciliation and the notion that hatreds had been overcome in their presentation of the past. Robben Island prison became a symbol of the 'indestructibility of the spirit of resistance against colonializa-tion, injustice and oppression' and of the overcoming of the evils of the previous political system.[97] For the founders of post-Communist prison and camp museums, by contrast, the past had not been overcome. The revolutions of 1989 were left unfinished; justice for the victims of the system had not yet been achieved. Thus, these sites were envisaged as places where Communists could be accused of, and tried for, their crimes. They were not devoted to overcoming older conflicts and divisions with a new message of reconcilia-tion; instead, they embodied the ideology of the continued struggle against an enemy that had survived and refused to be defeated.

CHAPTER FOUR

CONTAINING FASCISM
ANTI-COMMUNISM IN THE AGE OF HOLOCAUST MEMORY[1]

Alongside Ethiopia, central-eastern Europe is the only part of the globe that has experienced Fascism as well as Communism. In the 1930s, many eastern European elites had looked to the authoritarian right to provide solutions to both the economic and political pressures that followed the crisis of the Great Depression and the continued fear of Soviet expansionism. Hungary, Romania, Croatia and Slovakia all saw the rapid growth of ultra-nationalist and quasi-Fascist movements in the late 1930s. Even where Fascists themselves had less direct influence on political life, the threat of radicalism from both left and right often pushed conservative elites to abandon the liberal constitutionalism that had been established in the wake of World War I and replace it with anti-parliamentary military-authoritarian political systems. By the late 1930s, Hungary, Bulgaria and Romania had adopted racial measures inspired by Nazi Germany's Nuremberg Laws (although during World War II regimes in Hungary and Slovakia attempted to limit the effects of German pressures to carry out their genocidal policies). After the rapid Nazi wartime advance across the region in 1941, Hungarian irredentists and Slovak and Croat nationalists, who wanted independent states, sought alliances with Nazi Germany to realize their ambitions. In Slovakia and Croatia, collaborationist regimes emerged; the Hungarian and Romanian governments formed alliances with Germany and fought alongside them on the eastern front; while Poland, the Czech lands and the Baltic States were placed under varying forms of German administration. The impact of Fascist ideology under German occupation varied widely across the region, but among some groups and in some areas the human devastation was immense. Around two-thirds of all Jews exterminated in the Holocaust were eastern European, mainly from Hungary, Romania, Poland and Lithuania. In addition, around three million non-Jewish Poles and almost 1.75 million Yugoslavs were killed during the war.

Despite the immense scale of the devastation brought to the region by Fascist ideology and Nazi territorial ambitions, it was not seen as obvious to the creators of a new democratic public memory in the immediate post-1989 period that the new political system should address the horrors of the Fascist era as well as those of the Communist. This was partly owing to the fact that Communist regimes had formerly legitimized themselves through appeals to anti-Fascist ideology: they had claimed to be the protectors of the nation and the working class from the return of Fascism. Hence, in the immediate post-Communist period, stories of Nazi atrocities or resistance to Fascism were far too closely associated with the Communists' manipulative use of history after World War II. Neither was the memory of the Holocaust viewed as especially significant. The Communists had not sought to remember it: although they placed Fascism at the centre of their commemorative tradition, they referred to the suffering of the nation, or of the working class under Fascism, but beyond that seldom focused on a particular ethnic or religious group. Hence, Jewish suffering was usually subsumed within the wider category of the horrors of Fascism.[2] Moreover, Jewish communities decimated in the Holocaust found their numbers further depleted by emigration to Israel before, during and after the Communist period; hence they did not exist in sufficient numbers after 1989 to draw particular attention to their history as a group.

Moreover, following the collapse of dictatorship, in some countries aspects of the Fascist experience could even be commemorated in the name of anti-Communism. Those who had fought the Soviets 'in advance' during World War II were celebrated; in some cases, this meant the commemoration of virulent anti-Communists on the far right (such as Marshall Antonescu in Romania) or those soldiers who had fought on the eastern front alongside Nazi Germany to, as they saw it, 'protect Europe from Bolshevism'.[3] Indeed, the Nazi puppet states set up during World War II in Croatia and Slovakia represented those countries' first moments of independent statehood before being reabsorbed into Yugoslavia and Czechoslovakia respectively after the war. Hence, after the re-establishment of their independence following the collapse of Communism, their earlier experiences of Fascism were understood in ambiguous terms: no matter what horrors had occurred, the period was nevertheless remembered by nationalists as an important moment that foreshadowed their later achievement of sovereignty.

It was from outside the region itself that the exclusion of the horrors of Fascism from new national memories was most commonly noted, and powerfully challenged. There were some domestic groups – leftist and minority associations in particular – that objected too, making critical connections between the marginalization of the memory of Fascism and the rise of a post-Communist far right.[4] However, for the most part, the pressure to remember the region's 'other deviation' from liberal democratic development came from external sources; as such, the region came to terms with a Fascist past that had largely been reconstructed for it abroad, and hence in a form that did not always fit easily alongside local experiences or traditions of memory. Of greatest importance here were the preparations of many central-eastern countries for accession to the European Union on the one hand, and the election of Vladimir Putin to the Russian presidency in 2000, on the other. By the 1990s, remembering the Holocaust was considered a vital part of 'being European' by many western European political elites. The Jewish genocide was conceived as an absolute moral evil against which to define those values – tolerance and diversity – that were seen as essential characteristics of modern western civilization.[5] This was particularly the case in the European Union: as the integrative effects of the fear of Communism fell away after the end of the Cold War, so its elites increasingly presented the Union as emerging out of the horrors of genocide and as an insurance against them occurring again.[6] Thus, from western institutions came an insistence that former Communist bloc nations place the Holocaust at the centre of the region's new collective memory as part of 'a return to Europe'.[7] From post-Communist Russia, by contrast, came a revival of Soviet-era anti-Fascist memory. Under the Putin presidency, the heroic role of the Soviet Red Army in saving Europe from the horrors of Fascism was positioned at the heart of a newly assertive national identity whose paradigms it sought to export to the rest of the continent.[8] These pressures to re-remember the past according to norms that emerged outside national cultures not only produced international disagreements over appropriate forms of civic remembrance but also fed into domestic debates about the relationship of the region with its 'former masters' to the east or its future political partners to the west. The European Union (and NATO) insisted on commitments to particular forms of Holocaust remembrance as part of joining their elite western clubs. The preparedness of a national culture to adopt these discourses was often taken as an important sign of its readiness to westernize itself.[9] Russia's post-Soviet discourse, though not as influential on a region that was trying to escape its geopolitical grasp, could nevertheless make bilateral relations difficult when elites of the smaller central-eastern European nations explicitly challenged it: forces from within Russia launched a 'cyberwar' on Estonia following its relocation of Tallinn's monument to Soviet liberators from a prominent city-centre location to a military cemetery in 2007.

By the late 1990s, most central-eastern European political elites were very responsive to western demands that they should construct politically appropriate memories of Fascism. As part of their accession to the EU, many central-eastern European states incorporated the trappings of western Holocaust memory, establishing memorial days and educational programmes. The Baltic States established History Commissions to reassess the way in which Fascism (alongside Communism) should be understood prior to their 'return to Europe'.[10] In Romania, following the international outrage that met President Ion Iliescu's assertion that his country had not been complicit in the Holocaust, a History Commission was established under Elie Wiesel to investigate the nation's involvement. These initiatives, although justified in terms of reforming local memories and erasing Communist mentalities, were often as much directed at an international as a domestic audience, with the aim of demonstrating the westernizing impulses of their post-Communist culture.[11] In some cases, it was the international nature of the funding for local projects about the Fascist past that resulted in significant pressures to conform to western norms: for instance, a scheme to establish a Jewish history museum in Warsaw failed for a long time to raise sufficient capital from North American sources, primarily because it did not deal in sufficient depth with the phenomenon of Polish anti-Semitism, which its North American sponsors wanted to see stressed – the museum itself preferred to celebrate Poland as the cradle of Jewish culture in Europe rather than to dwell solely on the historical divisions between Jewish and ethnic Polish communities.[12] In addition, post-Communist elites attempted to control (and in some cases suppress) local memorial projects relating to Fascism that were deemed to be violations of the norms of global Holocaust memory. Estonia's Forbidden Structures Act (2007), for example, was an attempt to protect the country's international reputation by controlling inappropriate local forms of the memory propagated by Estonian nationalists, who wanted to celebrate their struggle for national freedom alongside German armies.[13]

Many anti-Communists viewed this form of memory, which was dominated by the Holocaust, as having been imposed on the region; a feeling that was not assuaged by western Europe's perceived failure to reciprocate the gesture by incorporating the story of Communism's crimes into a common form of European remembrance. It seemed that western Europeans continued to view the constant re-invoking of only the horror of Nazism as central to the maintenance of a civilized modern European identity, since it illustrated the possibility of such evil occurring at the heart of European culture and at the apogee of economic development. Communism, by contrast, had taken root only in Europe's eastern borderlands and thus for westerners could more easily be dismissed as a phenomenon of backwardness and hence was not considered to be an acute problem of European civilization.[14] Indeed, critics of the ways in which Holocaust memory was treated often noted that it was one of the few remaining manifestations of Eurocentrism that western liberalism tolerated: it required the assertion that the Nazi genocide was morally worse than other genocides perpetrated elsewhere in the world, not only because of its scale but also owing to the fact that it occurred at the heart of an advanced (and hence 'superior') European civilization.[15] Anti-Communist politicians were particularly strong critics of what they perceived as a blanket western insistence on the uniqueness of the Holocaust (they were less attuned to the contestations over the validity of foregrounding Holocaust memory that also occurred in western European countries).[16] The European Parliament, after the entry of central-eastern European MEPs in 2004 and 2007, became an important space where the continent's divided conceptions of the past were revealed. Nationalist Polish and Baltic representatives were at the forefront of critiquing the European Union's unequal estimations of the evils of Nazism and Communism, and argued for the necessity of including equal recognition for the victims of left-wing ideology.[17] Indeed, the achievement of European Union entry freed foreign policy-making elites, particularly in the Baltics and Poland, from subservience to western models of remembrance and enabled them to assert much more confidently the differences of central-eastern European experiences in World War II. Nevertheless, they did not primarily call for a respectful tolerance for the plurality of European historical experiences and memories, but rather they aped the western insistence on the necessity of a unified European memory, albeit now with central-eastern European experiences added.[18] On 2 April 2009, the European Parliament adopted a resolution on 'European conscience and totalitarianism', the form of which clearly reflected these new political pressures. It incorporated the historical experience of those new member states from the former Communist bloc, calling for an equal recognition of victims of all totalitarian regimes, not just Fascist states. Simultaneously, however, it downplayed their importance: it reasserted the EU's commitment to the idea that the Holocaust was unique, a position that implied that the Shoah held more profound moral lessons for modern Europeans than the crimes of Communism.

Central-eastern European elites were also confronted with new historical discourses on Fascism emanating from post-Communist Russia. Following his election as Russian president in 2000, Vladimir Putin orchestrated a revival of the Brezhnev-era commemoration of the Soviet Union's 'heroic struggle' to save Europe from Fascism in the 'Great Patriotic War', and reanimated the notion that Stalin and the Red Army were the great liberators of twentieth-century European history.[19] Anatoly Khazanov argued that this was due to the fact that Putin and his generation were the 'children of defeat': '[For Putin], the greatest catastrophe of the twentieth century was not the two World Wars, not the Holocaust and Gulag, but the disintegration of the Soviet Union.'[20] These heroic memories from the Soviet period were viewed as vital underpinnings for the revival of a proud, assertive post-Communist Russian identity. Since the perestroika period in the late 1980s, Russian liberals had been arguing that remembering the criminality and violence of the Soviet experience was a necessary step in the process of moving away from an authoritarian past and ensuring democratization. This approach was rejected under Putin. The new Russian president viewed such an interpretation as perverse and shameful to the Russian people, and considered the constant invocation of a past built on victimization as a further humiliation for a nation that had recently lost an empire and its superpower status. Moreover, this approach to remembrance was too closely associated with the imposition of liberal western philosophies in the 1990s, which Russian elites increasingly blamed for the economic collapse and political corruption of the immediate post-Communist period. Thus, no official monuments to the repressed were built in the first decades of post-Communism; indeed, the only serious attempts to do so were begun before the collapse of Communism, under Khrushchev in 1961 and Gorbachev in 1988.[21] Under post-Communist President Boris Yeltsin (1991–9), the idea of Russians as a nation of liberators was promoted, and central-eastern European states continued to be viewed as grateful recipients of Soviet forces; at the Great Patriotic War Memorial in Victory Park in Moscow (planned since 1957 and finally opened in 1995), the suffering of central-eastern European nations under Fascism was emphasized at the 'Tragedy of Peoples' exhibit as a way of justifying the necessity of Soviet intervention. Within this memorial culture, the Holocaust was not entirely absent, but Jewish contributions to the victory over Fascism were stressed to a far greater extent than Jewish victimhood.[22] Nevertheless, under his presidency, the state did accept a measure of responsibility for investigating the negative impacts of the old regime's domination of its eastern borderlands. Yeltsin himself apologized for the Soviet intervention in Hungary in 1956, and Poles secured an acknowledgement from the Russian government in 1995 that the massacre of Polish officers and members of the intelligentsia at Katyn in 1940 had been the responsibility of the Soviet NKVD, not the German Wehrmacht.[23] Putin, on the other hand, only viewed Russia as a successor state to the Soviet Union in so far as he could draw on the heroic memory of Russians as liberators of Europe in 1945. In contrast to

President Yeltsin, he treated the Soviet Union as a distant memory when it came to discussing the atrocities it had committed in the region.[24] It was only after the plane crash in March 2010 that killed eighty-seven high-ranking members of the Polish political and military elite (including the President of Poland, Lech Kaczyński, and the President of the Institute of National Remembrance, Janusz Kurtyka) as they travelled to a commemoration ceremony for the seventieth anniversary of Katyn, that Russian efforts to release official documentation on the atrocity into Polish hands were stepped up.

Central-eastern European elites were divided in their reactions to the dominant anti-Fascist discourses revived under Putin. Some left-wing politicians aligned themselves with these interpretations. Ferenc Gyurcsány, socialist prime minister of Hungary (2002–8), often spoke of the role that the Soviets had played in liberating the country from German occupation and its indigenous Fascist Arrow Cross regime in late 1944.[25] Aleksander Kwaśniewski, the former Communist who became president of Poland between 1995 and 2005, was more ambivalent. He was critical of the post-Soviet refusal to address those unexplored aspects of history that threatened to complicate post-Communist Russia's anti-Fascist narrative, such as the Soviet Union's support for the Nazi invasion of Poland in September 1939, and the absence of sufficient recognition that the Polish Home Army had also made a contribution to the defeat of Nazism.[26] Despite these objections, he was prepared to see the Red Army as liberators, and accepted the invitation of the Russian state to the international sixtieth Victory Day celebration in Moscow in 2005 (an event that some of Poland's neighbours refused to attend). In doing so, these ex-Communist politicians refuted the idea that they were reviving the anti-Fascism of the Communist period, in which the presentation of the Soviets as liberators had been fundamental to Communist states' strategies of legitimization. Rather, they were aligning themselves with the norms of modern western European approaches to history in which it was acceptable, following the end of the Cold War, to commemorate the major role that the Soviets had played in freeing Europe from Nazism.[27] Thus those who still refused to acknowledge the Soviet role in the victory over Fascism, and who wished to fight anti-Communist battles, were characterized as backward-looking. The left's readiness to embrace the idea of the Soviets as liberators was in fact illustrative of its own escape from a totalitarian past in which nationalists were still stuck. Indeed, many anti-Communists could only view this post-Communist Russian anti-Fascist memory as the revival of the rhetoric of Soviet-era imperialism. For them, it was evidence of a newly assertive post-Communist Russia seeking to retain influence over those areas it had liberated in 1945 through new neocolonial strategies. This was particularly the case for nationalists in those new states, such as Latvia and Estonia, that had been part of the Soviet Union and had retained large numbers of Russian-speaking Soviet-era migrants in their countries. For them, the fresh promotion of the discourse of Soviet liberation had a deleterious effect on social cohesion between Soviet-era settlers and the dominant culture, since it encouraged the former to see the Soviet Union's involvement in the region as unproblematic and hence not reconsider their own complicity as colonialists in the Soviet imperial project.

The understanding of Fascism in central-eastern Europe was thus shaped through the interaction between international and local forces: between Russian and western pressures that, on the one hand, forced local elites to reshape their memorial cultures, and, on the other, local cultures that attempted to resist, remould or, in some cases, incorporate aspects of these transnational historical narratives. The remainder of this chapter will focus on one region where the pressures from post-Communist Russian elites and the European Union to remake national history were particularly strong: the Baltic States. In particular, it will focus on three 'sites of memory' where the debates over how to remember Fascism were felt especially intensely. The first – Lithuania's Museum of Genocide Victims, sited in a former NKVD-KGB prison – illustrated the early post-Communist impulse to purge Fascism from the memorial and museum landscape and to promote the memory of the victims of Communism as a corrective to one-sided western accounts. The remaining two sites – the occupation museums of Estonia and Latvia – reflected the later desire to incorporate the Communist *and* Fascist experiences into a national history and so contribute to a broader European memory that reflected both of the continent's great terrors of the twentieth century. They also revealed the way in which international norms were remade for a domestic audience: the memory of Fascism could only be incorporated into these sites' representations of the past in so far as they did not disturb their basic anti-Communist paradigms or feed into revived Russian historical agendas.

Erasing Fascism in the Baltics

In the late 1980s, nationalist opposition movements in the Baltics constructed new semi-public histories that were to provide the foundation for official narratives after independence in 1991. These rejected Soviet versions of the past, which had emphasized the role that Baltic peoples and parliaments had played in voluntarily inviting the Soviet Union into the region in 1940, the depth of the suffering under the Nazi occupation which followed, and then the role of the Red Army as liberator of the Baltics in 1944–45. Against the background of perestroika, glasnost and Gorbachev's criticisms of Stalinist historiography, younger reform-minded Baltic historians, encouraged by revelations about the secret protocols of the Molotov-Ribbentrop Pact, created new histories that explored the Baltic States' forced incorporation into the USSR and presented the Soviets as occupiers. This provided a historical narrative that underpinned their contemporary struggle for independence.[28] At the centre of this new history was the idea of the 'Soviet genocide', a term that had been used by diaspora historians since the 1940s to describe the Stalinist-era repression and deportation of Baltic peoples, but which was now taken up by nationalist historians and politicians in the region. Oral histories of deportees and research by new organizations such as the 'Commission for Research into Stalinist Crimes committed in Lithuania' or 'Memento: The Association for the Illegally Repressed in Estonia' played a large role in constructing new public histories that de-legitimized the Soviet Union as an unwanted, brutal dictatorship.[29] Only in the late 1990s did public interest in Stalinist repressions decline, although groups such as Nuremberg-2 in Lithuania continued to campaign to keep former injustices visible in the public arena.[30]

Before the late 1990s, by contrast, the story of suffering under Nazi occupation was of much less importance in the public histories of the newly independent Baltic States.[31] This absence was in part the result of the Soviet regime's use of Fascist crimes to legitimize its own power. For many, talk of 'Nazi atrocities' was still associated with Soviet propaganda, and there was thus little appetite for any further uncovering of Fascist atrocities. This post-Communist silence was also due to the fact that some of these crimes – in particular the Holocaust – had not received much attention during the Soviet period. In Latvia, for instance, despite Jewish communities' efforts to promote Holocaust memory and organize regular commemorative events at sites of Jewish killings such as Rumbula, there was insufficient political space to challenge the regime's silence before the perestroika period. The term 'Holocaust' was first used in Latvia only in 1988.[32] In Lithuania in the late 1980s, the nationalist opposition movement Sajūdis did try to promote the memory of the Holocaust alongside Soviet crimes and to forge links and common historical understandings with the Jewish community. Lithuanian Jews also used the greater political space afforded by perestroika to commemorate the victims of the Panieri killings and the Vilnius Ghetto,[33] and to reopen, in 1989, the Vilnius Jewish Museum, closed by the Soviets in 1949. In 1990, the latter institution established a permanent exhibition on the Holocaust called *Catastrophe*.[34] After independence, some governments made efforts to support Holocaust memory officially. In 1994, the date of 23 September was declared National Memorial Day for the Genocide of the Lithuanian Jews, while a state-sponsored Holocaust Victims' Remembrance Day was instituted in Latvia.[35] Yet despite these initiatives 'from above', there remained a very low level of general social awareness of the suffering of Jews. Immediately after independence, the story of Nazi terror was often drowned out by new nationalist histories that focused exclusively on Communist crimes, viewed the period of Nazi occupation as less severe than the Soviet one, and valued anti-Communism much more highly than anti-Fascism.

These new national histories that foregrounded Stalinist crimes had a powerful influence on the new museum and memorial landscape in the early 1990s. First, they meant that the history of the recent past was as commonly displayed at sites of former violence and incarceration as it was in purpose-built museums. Second, they meant that it was spaces of former Communist terror and imprisonment, rather than Fascist sites, that were most often restored and presented to the public. One such was the Lithuanian Museum of Genocide Victims, founded by the Ministry of Culture and the Union of Political Prisoners and Deportees.[36] Here, the term 'genocide' referred both to the deaths and sufferings of those Lithuanians who were deported in 1940–41 and in the postwar purges by the Soviets, and to the attempt of the Soviet Union to destroy Lithuanian nationalists' idea of the Lithuanian nation.[37] It was located at what had been the site of the NKVD-KGB republican headquarters in Vilnius; the cells of the former security-service prison were opened to the public on 14 August 1992.[38] In 1997, the museum became part of the state-financed Research Centre of Genocide and Resistance of the Inhabitants of Lithuania. It aimed to place the suffering of the nation under Communism at the centre of local memory and, in addition, sought to address a western audience who refused to accord Communist victims the same respect as those who had been victimized under Fascist regimes:

the political prisoners [who initiated the project which led to the museum] . . . of course it was important for them to show to the world that Communism was as bad as Fascism. . . . Communism isn't condemned by everybody in public opinion . . . in [western] Europe Communism is little considered, and it was very difficult for them even to get support from Europe for projects concerning Communism. It doesn't seem so important to them . . . mainly because, in World War II, Great Britain and the United States were together with Russia, so, you know, they were against Fascism, so they don't want to.[39]

It inhabited a former administrative building and political prison in Vilnius which had not only been used by Soviet security forces in 1940–41 and 1944–91,[40] but had also been run by the Gestapo as a prison between 1941 and 1944, had hosted prisoners of multiple nationalities and had served as a barracks for the Vilnius Extraordinary Detachment, responsible for the annihilation of Jews in the district in 1942–43. The building itself potentially threatened the story that the museum wished to tell, as it had witnessed forms of suffering that extended far beyond that of Lithuanians under Communism. However, it was only the Soviet-era prison that was renovated, excavated and displayed. In 2000, a Communist-era execution cell was opened in the basement. From 2002, exhibits dealing with the two periods of Soviet occupation were developed on the upper floors.[41] The prison building's alternative histories did not feature in the displays: the remnants of the Gestapo prison, where Jewish and Communist victims were interrogated and tortured, were ignored, and its historical displays also omitted the period of German occupation (1941–44) while covering the Soviet occupations (1940–41 and 1944–91). The absence of any recognition that this had also been a Gestapo prison was not seen as a deliberate exclusion of one part of the building's history. Rather, it was argued that the experience of Fascism could be more appropriately dealt with at a separate site such as the city's Jewish Museum or at another Fascist-era prison.[42]

Despite assertions that it was not necessary to deal with the site's associations with Fascism, the active strategies employed to justify their absence suggested that the museum understood the potential of such associations to undermine its ideological message. Such sites draw their power from the presentation of their buildings as authentic places of terror which 'speak for themselves' about past evils and give the visitor a direct encounter with these earlier horrors.[43] The exclusion of Fascism threatened to undermine this, as it revealed the ideological interventions of the curators. In Vilnius, this marginalization was framed simply as a question of the museum's inability to reconstruct the cells 'objectively'. One staff member deployed arguments about the availability of information, in particular stressing the absence of evidence for the Fascist use of the prison because the Communists had destroyed it.[44] Initially, however, it was clear that there was just as significant an absence of evidence for the Communist use of the prison: it had not been used as a site of torture and execution since the 1950s,[45] and the Communists hid their crimes very effectively. Yet the implications of these absences were presented differently in each case. The lack of evidence of Communist-era suffering was used to illustrate the evil ability of the Soviets to cover up their crimes, and the capacity of post-Communist reconstructions to uncover (and thwart) their suppression of the 'historical truth'.[46] In the case of Fascism, the paucity of evidence was used as a justification for the absence of any attempt at historical reconstruction. This can be illustrated with reference to two rooms in the Vilnius museum: the reconstructed Soviet-era execution chamber[47] (see Figure 9) and a cell containing graffiti from the period of Nazi occupation. The decision to restore the execution cell, and to make it the centrepiece of the museum, was, of course, an ideological choice informed by an approach that placed suffering under the Soviets above Nazi-era crimes. Since the power of displays at museums is in part determined by an audience's perception of them as objective and balanced, curators needed to demonstrate that their interventions at these sites were merely the value-free bringing to light of crimes, the evidence for which was already embedded in the buildings. In Vilnius, the idea that they had made an ideological choice to excavate and renovate the Soviet prison, but not the Nazi jail, needed to be sidelined. To this end, the display of the execution cell was concerned as much with the process of discovery as it was with the actual history of the cell itself. Focusing on the uncovering diverted attention away from the initial choice of *what* to uncover, and enabled the museum to frame its work as the objective revelation of a 'true, hidden past'. First, it stressed that there was little evidence for the existence of the cell: it was marked as a kitchen on KGB plans; few warders were told of its existence and no surviving prisoners ever knew of it (as any who might have been taken there would not have lived to bear witness to its existence).[48] Eventually, a possible site was identified by General Jurgis Jurgelis (a director of the State Security Department), who had garnered the information from eyewitness reports of former KGB workers. Yet the paucity of evidence was not used to explore the problems inherent in restoring sites of terror. Rather, it was employed to justify the legitimacy of the project. Focusing on the process of overcoming the former regime's ingenious ability to cover up its crimes enabled curators to present Communists as the devious destroyers of historical fact and thus the post-Communist museum as recovering the truth against all odds. Moreover, this narrative presented the cell, not the curators, as the active agent in the process; it established a notion of hidden crimes that were merely waiting to be uncovered. Thus curators had not actively chosen to unearth the Soviet execution cell; it had merely presented itself for excavation. Second, the exhibition was designed to demonstrate the objectivity of the process through which this past had been uncovered in order to confirm to the viewer that this was a simple case of stripping bare Communism's hidden crimes through archaeology. For this reason, the execution chamber was not reconstructed to appear as it might have looked in the 1950s, in a fashion similar to the rest of the building where prison cells were filled with narrow beds and the accoutrements of a Stalinist-era prison. Rather, it was presented as a present-day archaeological dig in progress, with the scientific tools of archaeology laid out for the visitor to observe. A glass floor was placed a foot above ground level, on which visitors could stand to look at the dug earth below, where objects such as a pair of glasses and a small piece of barbed wire were placed as if they had just been uncovered there. Visitors were directed towards the remnants of bullets holes in the wall and a newly excavated drain where, it was claimed, blood from the executed victims would have flowed away. The display appeared to freeze the moment of revelation, when the violence and brutality of the Communist system were first revealed by archaeologists.

In fact, the chamber was artifice masquerading as naturalism. The objects scattered on its floor had not been found there, but rather were collected from the mass-grave site on the outskirts of the city and professionally arranged to mimic the popularly understood representation of an archaeological dig. Moreover, the form of the display was as much about concealment as it was about revelation: its power lay in its capacity to distract the viewer from the notion that it had been an ideological choice to excavate, reconstruct and display the Communist prison but not the Fascist-era jail. The appeal to the moment of scientific discovery assured viewers that they were gaining an unmediated experience of terror; visitors were simply being provided with the evidence of atrocity which Communists had tried to hide and the museum uncovered and left untouched. An awareness of the choice that had been made to reconstruct one apparatus of terror but not another would have had the capacity to erase the sense of authenticity that made the museum's stories of martyrdom so powerful. Thus, forensic archaeology played a central role in the creation of new anti-Communist histories; it provided a powerful sense of unmediated revelation of criminality and terror which could be utilized to tell the stories of national suffering that were at the heart of their new visions for national identity, while justifying the exclusion of those other stories that threatened the ascendancy of these accounts in post-Communist collective memory.

Whereas the paucity of evidence and the difficulties involved in reconstruction were used to add power to the presentation of 'hidden' Communist crimes, it was the same lack of physical proof of Fascist terror that was used to justify its marginalization in the museum. The evidence presented for Fascist crimes was minimal and confusing. The only remaining sign of the building's use as a Gestapo prison appeared in a cell, otherwise unadorned and without explanatory texts, that contained the almost unrecognizable (and easily missed) graffiti of a swastika and the name and date (1943) of imprisonment of a Polish partisan. Those taking guided tours were shown the swastika as illustrating not only the space's Nazi-era use, but also the impossibility of reconstructing it. It was used as a springboard to talk about the insufficient physical evidence of Fascism and the lack of objects from the German occupation around which to construct an exhibition. Thus the inadequate evidence of Fascism was used to rationalize the impossibility of proper historical reconstruction, whereas insufficient evidence of Communist crimes was employed to justify the necessity of further research to uncover the truth. Hence the choice to reconstruct one experience, but not another, was framed as a question of the historian's proper and objective use of evidence in each case.

The erasure of the Fascist past was also a feature of the museum's engagement with the archaeological excavation of the Tuskulėnai estate on the outskirts of Vilnius. At the end of 1993, Lithuania's national security service discovered documents relating to NKVD-KGB executions in the Vilnius prison, which suggested that remains had been buried in a mass grave at Tuskulėnai.[49] In January 1994, the Lithuanian president Algirdas Brazauskas (an ex-Communist) established a national committee to oversee the investigation of the executions and the Tuskulėnai site. This then appointed professionals from Vilnius University's Institute of Forensic Medicine, who carried out excavations between 1994 and 1996, and again in 2003.[50] At least initially, they sought to discover only the remains of those national heroes who had resisted, or who had been victimized by, Communists, specifically the Catholic bishop of Telšiai, Vincentas Borisevičius, who had opposed the Soviet occupation, and a member of the armed resistance in Vilnius whose relatives in North America wanted to find his remains. The prospective discovery of the 'martyrs' remains' promised to link the prison-museum with the suffering of the Lithuanian nation under Communism. As it became clear that the Tuskulėnai site did indeed contain a mass grave, it quickly became framed as a site of national martyrdom, with the General Procurator's Office launching a criminal lawsuit against the perpetrators which pointed to the location as evidence of the 'genocide of the Lithuanian people'.[51]

Yet the discoveries themselves did not easily support a simple anti-Communist account of the recent past. In fact, the excavations revealed remains that had the potential to support different – and potentially threatening – histories. The Tuskulėnai excavations in Vilnius were unusual in that they focused on the identification of victims. Often forensic work at mass graves accepted the impossibility of individual identification and settled instead to prove the existence of the atrocity and, on occasion, the methods and identities of the perpetrators.[52] Indeed, for the prosecution of crimes against humanity and war crimes, personal identification of victims was not necessarily the central issue. Forensic scientists needed to establish only that people had been killed because they belonged to a particular targeted group.[53] The Tuskulėnai excavations, by contrast, were able to recover the identity of specific victims; a dig that had begun as a search for two individuals eventually led to the unearthing and forensic examination of the remains of 724 bodies, from which around fifty individuals were identified.[54] This was done partly because they *could*: the Lithuanian secret service had obtained a KGB register listing the names of the majority of those executed in Vilnius in between 1944 and 1947, providing precise information about sex, age and stature, and often including a photograph of the victim.[55] Families whose lost relatives appeared on the list might then provide further photographic documentation and bodily samples which allowed the forensic scientists to use techniques such as skull-photo superimposition and DNA testing to identify individuals.[56]

Yet the discovery of detailed NKVD-KGB records proved double-edged. On the one hand, they provided irrefutable proof of Soviet complicity and enabled some families to recover their relatives' remains. On the other, they revealed that the grave contained the bones of individuals from a much wider range of national and ideological backgrounds than was initially supposed. Alongside 206 Lithuanian participants in the postwar anti-Soviet resistance, documents listed 32 soldiers and supporters of the Polish Home Army, 80 members of the Lithuanian police (under German control) who had collaborated with Nazis and their subordinate officers, or worked as supervisors of prisons and concentration camps, and 257 people of different national backgrounds sentenced for crimes against civilians and participation in crimes connected to the Holocaust.[57] (It should be noted that there is good reason to doubt the validity of some of the accusations made in the records: Soviet authorities regularly categorized their enemies as Nazi collaborators or as being complicit in the killing of Jews, even where the evidence was slim or non-existent.)

At the Tuskulėnai grave, the identification process polluted the category of 'Lithuanian victims of Communism' that the site was initially supposed to support. The bodies of Polish, German and Lithuanian Holocaust perpetrators proved the most problematic. First, their existence demonstrated that the site had not only witnessed Lithuanian suffering: the victims in the mass grave were multinational, while their biographies alluded to other tragedies and historical events whose scale might have the power to overshadow any appeal to Lithuanian national martyrdom. Second, the remains did not simply document Communist criminality; they also demonstrated the role the

Soviets had played in bringing an end to Fascism and the Holocaust in the region. Third, the category of 'victims of Communism' could no longer be equated simply with 'heroes' who had fought for an independent Lithuania: this grouping now included Holocaust perpetrators alongside anti-Communist resistance fighters and, most problematically of all, those Lithuanians who were both fighters for an independent Lithuanian nation and perpetrators of the ethnic cleansing of Jews and Poles. It is therefore not surprising that some observers rejected the all-inclusive category of 'victims of Communism' and started to classify the bones into those belonging to either morally worthy or morally unworthy victims. They could not understand how the Soviets could have placed such an ethically confusing jumble of remains in one grave, and rebuked the Soviet security forces for not having anticipated the requirements of post-Communist Lithuanian nationalism in advance: 'It is as if the NKVD made this "cocktail" and jigsaw for our generation with the intention of puzzling us. Completely innocent people and fighters for an independent and democratic Lithuania are mixed up with those who participated in the Holocaust.'[58] The Genocide and Resistance Research Centre would have liked to have separated them out; indeed, DNA technology made it theoretically possible to divide up co-mingled skeletal remains.[59] However, at Tuskulėnai it was practically impossible: '[Our opinion] of the war criminals and Nazi collaborators [who were buried there] is unfavourable, but there was no question of separating out the remains as the bodies had been disfigured by lime and some other chemicals and so the identification of them was impossible.'[60]

Whereas the co-mingling of bones could not be resolved through the techniques of forensic archaeology, their troubling and destabilizing associations were tackled through a process of memorialization, which erased the multinational associations of the site and its relationship with the Holocaust. This process should be read in the context of a wider attempt to remould the Vilnius cityscape as a Lithuanian space in the post-Communist period. The city had had been part of the Russian empire between 1795 and World War I, part of Poland between 1922 and 1939, and then part of the Soviet Union from 1944 to 1991. It had been dominated by Poles and Jews before World War II (in the 1930s, there were only a few thousand Lithuanians in a city of 200,000).[61] It was only after the Holocaust and deportation of Polish communities in World War II and its aftermath that it became dominated by ethnic Lithuanians. The city was made the capital of an independent Lithuania for the first time in 1991. At this time other memorial projects also attempted to nationalize the city's historical spaces. One of the most important of these was the reconstruction of the Lower Palace of the

Lithuanian Grand Dukes, a structure that was built before the Polish dominance of the city and that had been torn down by the tsarist state in 1801,
sixteen years after Vilnius had been incorporated into the Russian Empire.[62]
The history of its construction, destruction and reconstruction was used to
tell the story of a city once dominated by Lithuanian culture that had been
destroyed under Russian (and then Soviet) rule, and that could only be
revived after 1991. Yet this narrative required the forgetting of certain aspects
of Vilnius's multi-ethnic past: Lithuanians had been only a small minority
even when the palace was first erected under the Grand Duchy of Lithuania,
a multi-ethnic empire whose official languages were Old Ruthenian and
Belarussian, Latin and Polish (not Lithuanian), and whose chief religion was
eastern Orthodoxy.[63]

   In this broader attempt to build a new Lithuanian identity, based on
national victimization, there was little room for the appreciation of the sufferings of other groups. The cleansing of the city's Polish communities was
forgotten, in part because it was done by the Soviets, who in effect thereby
created the foundations for an ethnically Lithuanian Vilnius.[64] There was
some attempt to recover aspects of Jewish culture,[65] although the Holocaust
(in which 93 per cent of Lithuanian Jews were killed) was not extensively
commemorated: a small museum was founded in 1991,[66] but Nazi mass-grave
sites such as the Panieri Woods were not excavated (on the other hand, a mass
grave of Napoleon's army who died on the retreat from Moscow in 1812
received substantial attention).[67] Some believed that Holocaust remembrance
in western Europe and North America drowned out an appropriate recognition of Lithuanian suffering under the Communist terror, or had the potential
to exonerate the Soviets as 'liberators' of the Baltics from Fascism. Only in
the late 1990s did it become common to accord weight to Nazi persecution
alongside Soviet crimes. Even then, however, this new approach was often
adopted grudgingly and regarded as a foreign imposition associated with integration into European political and cultural norms, rather than as a domestic
imperative.[68]

   The form of memorialization chosen for the mass-grave site stripped out the
multi-ethnic character of the remains and did not seek to deal with the difficulties of their associations with the Holocaust. Regardless of the national,
political or religious affiliations of the victims found in the mass graves, their
bones were accorded a central place at the new memorial site opened in 2004.
They were placed within a columbarium, a structure sunk into an earth mound
near the site of the mass grave (see Figure 10). Here, the bones were stored in
hundreds of marked boxes, placed in recesses in a circular wall that ran around
a central chamber, where wreaths and other dedications could be left for the

dead contained there (see Figure 11). The columbarium functioned addition-
ally as a storage facility from which bones could be retrieved when families
made requests to identify relatives. The choice of repository, which had been a
popular form for the burial of Lithuanian Catholics prior to World
War II, effectively presented all the remains as representatives of Lithuanian
suffering alone.[69] The entrance was surrounded by the double cross of St Vytis
(see Figure 10), symbol of the destruction (and rebirth) of the Lithuanian
nation. As part of the national revival in the nineteenth century, St Vytis on
horseback came to represent the soon-to-be-liberated nation chasing the
intruder from its borders; for this reason, the saint's image was deemed subver-
sive under Soviet rule and banned.[70] Moreover, the power of these remains was
invoked annually on 14 June by political elites,[71] when the site was used for the
Day of Mourning of Hope, a commemoration of the Soviet repression of
Lithuanians.[72] Yet, for many, these bones should not have been invoked in the
name of post-Communist nationalism: the presence of Germans, Poles and
Lithuanians complicit in the Holocaust – whose co-mingled remains could not
be separated from other bones within the columbarium – meant that Fascists
were being commemorated in the name of anti-Communism. Hence this
particular memorial site was viewed as inappropriate. While the columbarium's
supporters claimed that 'death equalized the victims' and that they were being
commemorated not for their lives but for the criminal nature of their demise,[73]
others protested. Emmanuel Zingeris, director of the Vilna Gaon Jewish State
Museum, declined to attend the opening ceremony, and the local Catholic
church would not become involved in the project.[74] Thus one aspect of Baltic
memorialization has been the dominance of anti-Communism and the erasure
of the memory of the Nazi occupation, even at historical locations that would
have appeared initially to demand its inclusion.

Incorporating Fascism

Yet not all the sites that dealt with the Soviet period marginalized the history
of Fascism. The capitals of Latvia and Estonia, the main sites that dealt with
the history of these nations in the twentieth century, adopted a comparative
approach which addressed the experience of the respective nations under *both*
Soviets and Nazis. Riga's Museum of the Occupation of Latvia and Tallinn's
Museum of Occupations of Estonia structured their historical accounts, as their
names suggested, around the classification of Nazi and Soviet rule as a continuous period of 'occupation' of the nation by rightist and leftist dictatorships. The
pressure to incorporate the Nazi genocide into these museums came for the most
part from international, not domestic, sources.

By the mid-1990s, western European commentators and political elites were increasingly critical of dominant Baltic representations of Fascism. In the immediate post-independence period, veteran associations for those who had fought alongside the Nazis as part of the German military, or in Waffen-SS units to 'protect the nation against Bolshevism', and had thus chosen the German occupiers as 'the lesser evil', were given public space to articulate their anti-Communist memories. By the late 1990s, however, these groups began to be viewed as an international liability by Baltic political elites, and they met with governmental attempts to silence them.[75] In 1998, faced with international criticism, the Latvian government withdrew its support for the annual anniversary celebrations of the Latvian Legion.[76] In 2002, the Estonian government objected to the public display of a privately funded memorial depicting an Estonian soldier in a Waffen-SS uniform in Pärnu. An inscription dedicated the monument 'To all Estonian soldiers who fell in World War II to liberate their homeland and to free Europe 1940–45'. It was taken from its original location following government protests, removed again, after two weeks of public display, from the village of Lihula in 2004 (despite violent popular protests against its removal), and was unveiled in the grounds of the privately funded, small-scale Museum of the Struggle for Estonia's Liberation in the village of Lagedi outside Tallinn in 2005.[77] For the Estonian government, the dismantling of the statue was a necessity in order to preserve the country's democratic reputation. In 2004, Estonia's foreign minister, Kristiina Ojuland, argued that

> Estonia, as a small country that shares common European values and is building its future as a NATO and European Union member, will not, in its approach to the past, rely on the memories of those, who view the past as linked to World War II German uniforms, which the democratic world identifies with Nazism. In today's global environment, Estonia must not isolate itself from the international community and damage its reputation. Local inappropriate actions can often result in very serious and far reaching international consequences.[78]

Increasingly, the Estonian government looked to control politically problematic local memorialization projects. In February 2007, the Estonian parliament passed the Forbidden Structures Act. This enabled the state to refuse permission for, or to remove, memorials that might incite 'violations of public order', thereby allowing central government both to take down Soviet-era monuments considered offensive in an independent Estonia, and to dismantle memorials whose representation of Fascism was seen as politically provocative.[79]

While western elites were critical of the revival of the story of the struggle alongside Nazi Germany, they nevertheless began to encourage the Baltic countries to remember Fascism in a different form as part of their integration into western political and economic structures. As part of the negotiations to join NATO and the European Union, it was often made clear to prospective entrants that 'becoming western' meant the placement of the victims of the Holocaust at the centre of national memory. On 24 April 2000, the US told the Baltic States that 'NATO aspirants need to do more to better prepare themselves for membership. . . . For the Baltic states this means hard work – not just words but concrete action on complex domestic issues like dealing with the history of the Holocaust.'[80] There had been very little promotion of Holocaust memory 'from below' by the remaining small Jewish communities in the Baltics after independence.[81] Baltic political elites thus looked to find an acceptable way of presenting their histories to an international audience.[82] Commissions were created in Estonia, Latvia and Lithuania in 1998 to investigate the crimes of the Nazi regime alongside those of the Soviet. In order to ensure a revision of recent approaches to history, the Estonian, Latvian and Lithuanian commissions chose international representatives.[83] These bodies were shaped mostly by the demands of the western political community, rather than a domestic audience. They sought to demonstrate to the west that the Baltic States' historical cultures would now recognize the Holocaust as an important part of national remembrance, and simultaneously convince western Europeans of the importance of ascribing equal weight to the Communist terror in the building of a common European appreciation of the past.[84] They also encouraged new domestic memorial cultures, which were west-facing and incorporated the terrors of both Communism and Fascism into their accounts of recent national history.

The Estonian Museum of Occupations, which was opened in 2003, was a product of this new approach (see Figure 12). It too was funded from abroad, in this case by the donations of an Estonian American exile, Olga Kistler-Ritso. Its director, Heiki Ahonen, had been a dissident and victim of the Soviet Gulag, but he nevertheless considered it important to consider both periods of occupation. This focus was in truth largely decided by Estonian academics who were increasingly receptive to calls to represent the double terror in national memory.[85] The museum's inclusion of both occupations reflected broader shifts in mainstream historical memory in the Baltics in those ten years before its foundation, from an almost exclusive focus on Soviet occupation and terror in the early independence period to an emphasis on the effects of both Nazi and Soviet occupation by the late 1990s.[86] It deployed the rhetoric of equality of victimhood at the beginning of its displays, where it appeared to be according equal weight to the sufferings caused by Fascism and Communism. The gateway to the Tallinn museum, framed by two trains adorned with a swastika and a red star respectively (representing the deportation and killing brought by both systems) (see Figure 13), set up expectations of a substantial exploration of the different destructive capabilities of the two systems. In fact, dissimilarties between the two occupations were ignored in favour of an approach that absorbed all those who had suffered into a national martyrology and did not draw attention to their relative merits as victims.

Riga's Museum of Occupation was founded earlier, in 1993, at a time when it was not fashionable to tell the story of the dual terrors in Latvia (see Figure 14). Its agenda was initially shaped by diaspora rather than indigenous perspectives; the Latvian state was at first ambivalent about a museum that included both occupations, and in its first decade it was funded for the most part by donations from Latvian diaspora social organizations and private individuals from North America.[87] Dr Paulis Lazda, an American Latvian history professor who left the Baltics with his parents in 1944 and lived in the United States from 1950 onwards, was the 'author of the concept'[88] of the museum (as well as being one of its ten founding members). Having lived most of his life in a country where Holocaust memory had become an important part of national remembrance, he insisted on the necessity of a comparative approach, despite some unease about the inclusion of Nazism and the Holocaust from both the public and his collaborators within the institution. According to Lazda:

> that was a demand I made of people who were joining the effort [that they accept the 'double occupation' concept]. There was a natural and strong push to make it a 'museum of Soviet repression' and these were good, fine people who had suffered this and that, and the memory of the Nazis was not as strong, but I said that it could not be otherwise. And my colleagues generally agreed. That was something I insisted upon . . . there were differences . . . they argued in the quantitative sense, but I said, no, we should consider the qualitative aspect as well, in other words, the three or so years of Nazi occupation was relatively short, well, I said, that's true, and that is in some ways an ongoing debate in the museum. But there is not a really meaningful opposition to the occupation concept.[89]

Since its opening in 1993, the museum has presented itself as a counterbalance to restrictive accounts of totalitarian violence that concentrate on one terror to the exclusion of the other. Indeed, the museum appeared to be according equal worth to the sufferings caused by Fascism and Communism;

its introductory panel, encountered as one walked up the stairs to the main exhibition, stated: 'During the periods of Soviet and German occupation, Latvia lost 550,000 people, or more than a third of its population. This is the number who were murdered, killed in battle, sentenced, deported, scattered as refugees, and who disappeared without a trace.' Moreover, the institution viewed itself as a channel for transnational communication between eastern Europe and the west, which would facilitate the education of both halves of the continent about each other's particular memories of victimization. It saw itself as pioneering an approach that would lead to a common European memory that could incorporate the suffering caused by dictatorships of both the right and the left. According to Valters Nollendorfs, the deputy director of the museum: 'East Europeans must now come to terms with the Holocaust and everything connected with it. West Europeans must get to grips with the Gulag. That's the only way both sides can come to an understanding.'[90] Indeed, as the Baltic States were increasingly pressurized to incorporate the Holocaust into their memorial landscape in the late 1990s, so the museum developed the idea of taking its message of the double terror to the west: from 1998, travelling exhibitions to western Europe and North America were organized.[91] Despite being a privately funded museum that initially attempted to challenge restrictive aspects of Baltic memory, from the late 1990s it increasingly found itself in tune with a Latvian political elite that embraced the idea of the 'double genocide' under both Nazis and Soviets, and became a site for official state visits.[92]

While these museums responded to western calls to place the horrors of Fascism in their memorial culture, they nevertheless rejected the common western conception of the Holocaust as a uniquely terrible tragedy incomparable to any other atrocity. Instead, they looked to incorporate Fascism into their basic anti-Communist paradigm. Despite western pressures, these institutions remained fundamentally anti-Communist in their outlook. Thus, those aspects of the Nazi occupation period that could be used to attack Communism were played up in the Riga and Tallinn occupation museums. Others threatening this anti-Communist reading of recent history were marginalized or 'contained'. Two versions of the story of the Baltics' experience of Fascism were particularly threatening: first, stories of the horrors of German occupation that could have justified attraction to the Communist state and evoked sympathy for the idea of the Soviet Union as the liberator of the Baltics; second, the potential for the memories of victims of Fascism to drown out the appeals of those who suffered under Communism. These museums illustrated the ways in which an increasingly globalized Holocaust memory was 'domesticated' to suit different contexts, interacting with local historical norms and becoming refined by local political imperatives.

Fear of the power of the horrors of Fascism to overshadow the anti-Communist account was in part a hangover from the period of Soviet rule. From the late 1950s, Soviet historians, influenced by a number of well-publicized war-crimes trials, turned their attention to publishing works on Nazi atrocities in the region.[93] During the same period, sites of Fascist crimes were opened to the public and increasingly became established as excursion destinations for Baltic schoolchildren: the Ninth Fort (Kaunas), the site of the killing of 45,000 Jews and Soviet prisoners of war, was opened as a museum in 1958; Salaspils concentration camp near Riga, the location for medical experiments on, and the murder of, European Jews, Russian prisoners of war and Roma, became a memorial site in 1968. Such locations were used to illustrate the depth of suffering caused by the Nazi occupation (although the specificity of Jewish persecution at these sites was not highlighted; a memorial tablet to the thirty thousand Jews who died at the Ninth Fort was constructed only in 1991). They had thus been employed to demonstrate the role that Soviets had played both as liberators and continued protectors of the region from foreign and indigenous sources of Fascism, and hence to bolster Communist claims about the legitimacy and appropriateness of the incorporation of the Baltics into the Soviet Union.

However, the fear of displaying Fascism was also part of a contemporary struggle, this time with post-Communist Russian elites over the meaning of the recent past. Curators feared that, in responding to new western pressures and agreeing to present the story of Fascism in their museums, they might provide support to a narrative of the Soviets as liberators of the region from Fascism, an idea that was being revived among Russian elites in the late 1990s. In the perestroika period in the late 1980s, it had initially appeared that the pro-Soviet Baltic liberation narrative had been fatally undermined: the exis-tence of the secret protocols of the Molotov-Ribbentrop Pact, which laid out plans for the forced incorporation of the Baltics into Nazi Germany and the Soviet Union, was finally revealed by the Soviet authorities.[94] Although the 'liberation idea' never really disappeared in Russia after the collapse of Communism, it was reinvigorated with the ascent of Vladimir Putin to the Russian presidency in 2000. As stated above, Putin revived the Brezhnev-era focus on the Great Patriotic War and viewed the story of the Soviet victory over Nazism as fundamental to rebuilding a sense of national pride after the political and economic woes of the 1990s. Hence, important elements of the liberation narrative were retained or revived: it became common for members of the Russian political elite to state that the Soviets had been invited into the

Baltics in 1940, and to dwell longer on their roles as liberators of the Baltics in 1944 than as an occupying force that remained.[95] The Russian Foreign Ministry attacked occupation museums in Estonia, Latvia and Georgia for equating Communism with Fascism and demonizing Soviets solely as brutal occupiers in their exhibitions.[96] While Russians might admit that repression was a regrettable part of postwar Soviet life, they nonetheless saw it as offensive to conclude that this had been directed at particular national groups. Rather, post-Communist Russian elites saw these historical memories as attempts to justify the marginalization of their Russian-speaking minorities, many members of whom had been denied full citizenship in post-Communist Estonia and Latvia.[97] Thus, in the first two decades after the end of Communism, Russian elites refused to apologize for the incorporation of the Baltic States into the Soviet Union, and maintained that the region had voluntarily associated itself with the USSR in 1940. For many in the Baltics, this rhetoric marked the continuation of an imperialist rhetoric aimed at justifying Russian neocolonial interference in the region.

Staff in the Estonian and Latvian occupation museums thought that many in their remaining Soviet-era settler populations still believed in the former 'colonial' rhetoric of Soviets as liberators of the Baltics from Fascism.[98] One curator in Riga commented that 'they [the Soviet-era immigrant population] don't like the word "occupation" and don't think that our [museum's] history is correct. . . . They think that it was not occupation, that we wanted to be incorporated into the Soviet Union at the beginning of World War II and there were no solutions other than to make an alliance against Nazism.'[99] This continuing fear of older anti-Fascist narratives can be seen in the debates over the removal of Soviet memorials and statues, most notably the 'Liberation' monument in Riga and the Soviet 'Bronze Soldier' in Tallinn (see Figure 15). The Tallinn monument, which depicts an ethnic Estonian member of the 'liberating' Red Army grieving his fallen colleagues, was erected in 1947 and survived the collapse of Communism as a relatively uncontested place of mourning.[100] Yet, after 2004, possibly in response to the forced removal of monuments to Estonians who had fought alongside the German army, it was frequently vandalized. Prime minister Andrus Ansip, among many others, argued for the relocation of the statue from Tönismägi Square to a less prominent location, possibly a military cemetery or memorial park, and also for the remains of twelve Red Army soldiers under the monument to be reburied at one of these sites.[101]

Concerns over residual anti-Fascism were confirmed by the strength of the response to this proposal from Russian nationalists in both Estonia and Russia, and from the Russian state itself. The Russian foreign minister referred to the proposed removal as a blasphemy against those who had defeated Nazi Germany, thus confirming that important Russians still saw Soviet intervention in the region more in terms of liberation rather than occupation.[102] Moscow's mayor, Yuri Luzhkov, called for a boycott of Estonian goods.[103] After the riots that followed the decision to remove the 'Bronze Soldier', a cyber-attack was launched against Estonia – one of the most internet-dependent countries in the world – which shut down government and business websites for short periods. The most sustained attack came on 9 May 2007, Victory Day in post-Communist Russia. Estonian Russian nationalists such as Dmitri Klenski, leader of the Constitution Party, co-opted the statue as a symbol of Russian identity in Estonia and presented the attempt to remove it as a revival of Fascism there and continued evidence of human-rights violations against the Russian minority.[104] However, it should be noted that other representatives of the Russian community in Estonia suggested alternative plans that aimed to subvert the ethnic divisiveness of this debate: Sergei Ivanov of the Reform Party recommended a monument that would commemorate the victimization of both ethnic Russians and Estonians in Estonia during World War II.[105] Indeed, some left-wing Estonians – particularly those who fought with the Red Army – also interpreted the statue not as a colonial monument but as one dedicated to all those, including Estonians, who fought to end Fascism, and argued that it should be left alone.[106] Yet debates over the statue appeared to confirm the imagined power of a residual anti-Fascist narrative for certain sections of the population; some of the advocates for its removal suggested that if it could not be destroyed, then its power might be neutralized by removing it to a site, such as the Museum of Occupations, where it could not be interpreted as a valid monument that legitimized the Soviet 'liberation'.[107] At the end of April 2007, the statue was moved to a military cemetery for the Estonian defence forces.[108]

These occupation museums were caught between the pressures of two international 'memory cultures'. They responded to western demands to incorporate the horrors of Fascism into their memorial culture in order to 'become European', yet sought to achieve this in a way that would not confirm the validity of contemporary Russian narratives, which still presented their Communist predecessors as welcomed liberators of the Baltics from the evils of Nazi occupation. This post-Soviet Russian account undermined the Baltic States' basic historical account of themselves as independent nations that had been occupied, annexed and denied their national freedom by both Soviet and Nazi forces. In response, dominant nationalist voices in the Baltics articulated a complicated version of the past, which included Fascism but retained an overall anti-Communist and anti-Soviet focus. Where the memory of Fascism had the capacity to undermine this version of history, it was edited out or framed in very particular ways. On the other hand, Fascism was placed in the foreground of new national histories where it had the potential to confirm the anti-Communist script.

Thus the Holocaust was included in a new Baltic memorial culture, but in such a way that it did not undermine the basic focus on the victimization of the nation under Communism. Two stories were particularly threatening to this anti-Communist national paradigm: first, that some among the local population had been Holocaust perpetrators; and second, that the focus on Holocaust victims might drown out the appeal to the victims of Communism. Although transnational forms of Holocaust remembrance were adopted in the Baltics, such as Holocaust Day on 27 January, they did not always concentrate solely on Jewish suffering but were instead remodelled to address local historical concerns. On 27 January 2007, for instance, Andrus Ansip, the Estonian prime minister from the libertarian-conservative Reform Party, used the horrors of the Holocaust as a springboard to talk about wider forms of suffering in his country:

> Today on International Holocaust Remembrance Day we bow our heads in honour of its innocent victims. . . . The understanding that no crime against humanity should ever be forgotten is self-evident to all of us – Estonia too suffered during and after the Second World War under totalitarian regimes and we paid for this with our independence. Their crimes will never expire and their perpetrators cannot be justified. Our thoughts are with all of the victims of the Holocaust.[109]

The presentation of the Holocaust at the Riga Museum reflected some of these conflicting pressures. Educating Latvians towards a greater Holocaust awareness was a fundamental aim of the museum; it was reported that some Latvian visitors were surprised to discover displays about the Holocaust and Nazism at a museum of occupation, as the latter term was for them almost exclusively connected with the Soviet presence and Communist crimes.[110] In the museum itself, Latvia's experience of the Holocaust was described in depth: the story of 70,000 Latvian Jews (and 25,000 Jews from elsewhere)[111] who were exterminated was well documented, and presented both elements of Nazi persecution from above and also the mixed, complex nature of the response of non-Jewish Latvians. It showed cases of assistance to Jews, but also stressed the passivity of the majority of the population and the role of Latvian extremist groups such as the Arājs Commando in the killings.[112]

Both of these museums incorporated the story of the atrocities of German occupation, including the Holocaust, but only in such a way that it would not drown out the story of the victimization of the nation under Communism. The Riga Museum, for instance, placed its account of the Holocaust outside the story of the Latvian nation. The narrative was presented in a separate set of panels, and was clearly divided off from the main material about the German occupation. Here, it was asserted that for the Latvian nation the experience of occupation had been far less severe under the Nazis than it was under the Soviets: businesses were allowed to flourish, property was returned to farmers and a certain degree of cultural autonomy was granted. Such a (relatively) positive narrative was only possible through the complete exclusion of the Holocaust from the national story. This placing of the Jewish experience outside the mainstream also allowed the museum to present Communist demographic policies as a worse form of ethnic cleansing than Nazi programmes: thus the resettling of 800,000 Soviet citizens in Latvia was presented as a greater tragedy than the Nazi Ostplan which had envisaged bringing in 'only' 164,000 Germans over twenty-five years.

However, Jewish suffering was not always placed outside national history. Where it could be deployed as evidence of the Stalinist terror, it was incorporated. In the panels on the Soviet occupations of 1940–41 and 1944–91 in the Riga museum, the persecution of Jews was not related as a separate narrative but rather absorbed into the national story. In the course of the Soviet deportations of June 1941, for example, a far higher proportion of Jewish Latvians (compared to non-Jewish Latvians) were affected.[113] In the display, however, the Jewish and non-Jewish deportees were conflated to produce a single national figure and the particularity of the Jewish experience was ignored. The absence of the story of Jewish deportation under the first Soviet occupation meant that the museum provided no refutation to the historically inaccurate yet still commonly held prejudice that Jews in league with the Soviet authorities were responsible for the deportation of ethnic Latvians.[114] Hence, it was made to appear that Jews suffered as a minority whose experiences stood apart from the nations under the Nazi occupation, an interpretation that assisted in the presentation of Latvia's encounter with Fascism as being less severe than their experience of Communism. Elsewhere in the museum, however, Jewish persecution was co-opted into a story of national suffering, where it helped to emphasize the nation's victimization under Communism.

Estonia's Museum of Occupations' presentation of history reflected the country's very different experience of the Holocaust between 1941 and 1944. Here, 'only' 943 Estonian Jews were killed, and there was no real collaboration between members of the local population and the death squads (as there had been in the Arājs Commando in Latvia or the Hamann Commando in Lithuania). The memory of the Holocaust played an even smaller role in its memorial landscape than in the other Baltic States; there were virtually no memorials, and no former ghettos (as existed in Riga and Vilnius) to remind the local population of the absence of a Jewish community.[115] For the Museum of Occupations, the Holocaust was thus a discourse imposed from the outside which had little relevance to the Estonian setting; to foreground the Shoah was a politically correct but historically inaccurate nod to stifling international conventions, which prohibited exhibiting more relevant, and intriguing, complexities within Estonian national history. Indeed, the museum's director, Heiki Ahonen, argued that Holocaust museums in the west treated the subject with such a degree of 'religious reverence' that it forced the visitor to suspend critical thought:

> In Holocaust museums you are told that you should not speak loudly, you should not make any noise, you have to behave in a certain way. [It's] what I call a 'church atmosphere', which, I believe, doesn't support learning. You are just made to act in a certain way. . . . Holocaust museums tend to have a dark and oppressive atmosphere, so you are dragged into some kind of environment where there should be no doubts . . . from my point of view, it doesn't provoke any thinking. It's all clear. It's all set. And I believe that especially the younger generation doesn't want that. They tend to try to question things and find answers by themselves. You know: you type in something into the internet and you get thousands of answers, then you have a choice. I believe that if people are given a choice, they usually make the right choice; at least this is what we want.[116]

Thus, Ahonen claimed that he wanted a light, open museum that dealt with both forms of twentieth-century totalitarian occupation and avoided the darkened atmosphere and 'closed questions' of Holocaust sites. To this end, the museum scattered across the exhibition space a diverse range of objects such as telephone boxes, suitcases and prison cell doors, designed to set off memories and provoke debate, rather than guide the viewer to fixed answers.[117] Yet the Holocaust was almost entirely absent in the section on the German occupation period and, despite the museum's emphasis on the inclusion of striking objects from the three periods of occupation, there was virtually nothing connected with Jewish suffering. When asked about this absence, Ahonen pointed to the impropriety of importing a western style of history that was of much less significance to Estonia:

we were visited by a director of the Washington Holocaust Museum and she asked . . . some specific questions . . . 'what is there here about the Holocaust?', and I said almost nothing because it didn't basically happen here physically [i.e. the apparatus of the Holocaust was on a much smaller scale in Estonia] and I said because, yes, Estonia had Jewish refugees, nearly all [of whom] were killed, but a few survived . . . but Estonia never had a Jewish question and we just simply don't have any physical items from these people who were killed. . . . we are never going to do what's done with some [former] concentration camps; let's say they built a new crematorium and said that it is original.[118]

A number of arguments were thus advanced to justify the museum's very brief treatment of the Holocaust. First, that it was not really an omission; rather, the number of Estonian Jews killed was relatively small compared to the 70,000 Latvian and 225,000 or more Lithuanian Jews[119] who died, and the 122,000 Estonians who suffered repression under the Stalinist terror.[120] Such a conclusion, however, was dependent on conceptualizing these events in national, rather than more broadly European, terms. While the extermination of Jews involved far fewer individuals in Estonia than elsewhere, the country nevertheless played a significant role in the wider European system of extermination established by the Nazis. Around 15,000 Jews were deported to Estonia, particularly from Lithuania and Poland, and it is estimated that 8,500 Jews died in Estonian camps in total.[121]

Second, it was argued that, given the relatively small numbers of Jewish victims involved, the foregrounding of the Holocaust story would be the result of politicized and distorting pressure from the international community to conform to artificially prescribed and (in an Estonian setting) empty Holocaust norms, rather than based on a historian's objective consideration of the local importance of these events. According to this view, nations needed to be allowed to tell their own stories, and the specificity of those national accounts should be respected. It was thus locally inappropriate to give undue weight or space to the Holocaust.

If the experience of Fascism was to be included, it was also vital that it should not be able to support the idea of the Soviet Union as the liberator of the Baltics. Thus, these museums did not provide space for the discussion of the potential appeal of Communism as an ideological reaction against Fascism. Rather, they favoured a narrative of one brutal occupation followed by an even more brutal one. Ideology could be presented only in so far as it evidenced the evils of each system: in the Riga museum, for instance, the racial ideology of Nazism and class-based principles of Communism were described in depth in so far as they explained the reasons for the terrors of both systems. However, no displays explored how each system defined itself in relation to the other, how each presented itself as the negation of the evils of the other, or how this ideological battle impacted on the worldviews of citizens in the Baltic States. Rather, history was tightly contained in a framework in which the Soviet presence after 1944 meant merely the continuation of foreign occupation, the ongoing absence of sovereignty, the renewed oppression of the nation and the citizen as the victim of yet another external power.

To maintain the idea that Latvians, for instance, were simply victims of foreign occupiers, it was necessary to exclude accounts of political radicalization. Where Latvians had supported or resisted these systems, they were never described as doing so on the basis of left- or right-wing convictions. Rather, they were only ever presented as Latvian citizens trying to defend their occupied nation in the best possible way. Under Nazi occupation, this usually meant a limited accommodation with the occupier in so far as it was part of a greater struggle against Communist domination; under Communism, it meant resistance to the Soviet destroyers of the nation. Ordinary citizens were very seldom seen as having been politicized by any ideology other than Latvian nationalism. Thus, battles during World War II in which Latvians fought for both Nazi Germany and the Soviet Union were always presented as evidence of national tragedy – 'Latvian fighting against Latvian'. The possibility of Latvian soldiers fighting for different ideologies was never considered.[122]

The story of Fascism was also threatening in so far as it could provide potentially sympathetic narratives of those radicalized to Communism by the experience of Nazi occupation and terror. It was therefore necessary to close down the idea that some social groups might have felt themselves liberated by the Soviets. In the Tallinn Museum of Occupations, even death-camp survivors were shown to have rejected the idea of Soviet liberation. A film presented the point at which inmates were 'liberated' by the Red Army from the Klooga labour camp, the site of the largest massacre of Jews in Estonia during World War II. When asked by a Soviet soldier whether she was grateful to have been liberated from the Fascists, one survivor replied that her husband had been in Russia (it is not clear how he got there) and had not been heard from.[123] Thus, even Fascism's victims were co-opted to corroborate an anti-Communist script: their experiences confirmed that suffering caused by the Soviets could be placed on a par with Nazi crimes and that, even for those who narrowly escaped death, the arrival of the Red Army in 1944 could not represent an unambiguous liberation as their relatives might have been deported to the Soviet Union. Both museums then began their accounts of the Communist period with stories of partisan resistance to the new regime. It was thus apparently the fear of the continuing power of the liberation idea, and the lack of certainty that the notion of occupation was sufficiently embedded in post-Communist society, that led some curators to avoid displaying any ambiguities in the response to the arrival of the Soviets in 1944.[124]

While the horrors of Fascism were played down where they had the potential to drown out the anti-Communist story, they were played up in those instances where they could provide ballast for it. The story of the experience of Fascism under the German occupation could be shown in a museum of 'occupation' of the nation because it made Communism appear worse. Given the chronological reach of these museums, from 1940 to 1991, Fascism only appeared as a short interlude between the two Soviet occupations of 1940–41 and of 1944–91, whose far greater impact on the nation in this framework was obvious. Moreover, Fascism was used to demonize Communism by association. Although both systems were condemned both for their criminality and their suppression of the Baltic nations, Communism's status as the great evil in the history of the Baltic States was emphasized by the assertion that not even the experience of Fascism could match it. The Soviet occupation of 1940–41, which preceded the arrival of the Nazis, was depicted as the first attempt by outside forces to destroy the nation. The Riga museum, for example, focused on the subjugation of national culture and deportations of Latvian nationals to the Gulag. Both museums displayed evidence of their citizens enthusiastically welcoming Nazi troops. It was assumed that support for the Germans did not need to be excused or attributed to particular 'collaborationist' social groups. Rather, these images were employed to support a narrative in which the first Soviet occupation had been so terrible that entire Baltic populations were forced to turn to the Nazis for protection. This evidence of support was thus being used to illustrate anti-Communism, not collaboration. The German occupation was then presented as far less brutal: the Tallinn museum narrated how the Nazis allowed the national flag to hang publicly (alongside the swastika); the Riga museum drew attention to the greater, albeit limited, forms of cultural expression allowed under the German occupation.[125] Although Fascism and Communism were both condemned, it was clear that aspects of the German occupation could be revived in so far as they facilitated the presentation of the struggle against Communism. Thus, those who fought with Nazi Germany against the Bolsheviks were celebrated as patriots and heroes in the Tallinn museum. A film recounted the German occupation primarily through the eyes of those who fought with the Nazis, and stressed the desire to force the Soviets out in 1941 and prevent their return in 1944. These fighters were lionized for defending their land from the 'Bolshevik avalanche'. Later, an enthusiastic narrator revealed that three times more men than called for volunteered themselves for military service in 1944, to prevent a second Soviet occupation that would 'imperil the nation'. Whereas in western Europe, alliances with Nazism – whether ideological or merely strategic – tend to be condemned as collaboration, sensitive and sympathetic stories were told in the Baltic States which helped to frame the German alliance as a tactical necessity born of limited choices to save the nation in constrained circumstances from the greater Soviet evil.[126]

Conclusion

In their construction of new national histories, these museums were caught between two powerful anti-Fascist framings of the recent European past. On the one hand, Communist-era rhetoric – which presented the Soviets as the liberators of the Baltics from Fascism – was deemed to be still influential among both Soviet-era settlers in their countries and in contemporary Russia. On the other, the museums were faced with a new, powerful Holocaust-centred anti-Fascist narrative that was an important part of western European (and official European Union) memory. Hence, the eastern and western demands for the incorporation of Fascism into national memory could only be met in so far as they did not unsettle the fundamental anti-Communist paradigm. Holocaust memory was absorbed into public history as a necessary consequence of accession into the western cultural sphere, but was not accorded sufficient historical weight to risk undermining the story of those ethnic Balts who had suffered as citizens of the Soviet Union. Revived Russian memories of Fascism, and the role of the Soviets as the liberators of Europe from its horrors, were almost entirely rejected. Placed at the geographical intersection between Europe's competing traditions of memory, these museums primarily saw themselves as defenders of a dominant memory of the suffering of Baltic peoples in the 'Soviet genocide', rather than as ideally situated to facilitate a reconciliation between the different ways of viewing the past across the continent. Only Riga's Museum of the Occupation of Latvia considered the idea that it might play a part in such a reconciliation, viewing itself as a bridge between the different historical perspectives of the western and eastern halves of Europe. However, no museum sought to bridge the gulf in perception between dominant memories among ethnic Balts and Russian-speakers within their own countries. The curators themselves admitted that their institutions represented the construction of a new dominant set of Baltic memories that their countries' minorities could not identify with. Very few ethnic Russians visited these sites, and those who did often experienced feelings of alienation and guilt as they identified themselves with the demonized 'occupiers'.[127] In the face of the maintenance of Communist-era rhetoric of Soviets as liberators of the Baltics from Fascism, which these nationalist producers of memory could view only as part of the neocolonial strategies of Moscow's elites, the propagation of national histories of Baltic suffering was deemed a necessary assertion of independence and difference.

CHAPTER FIVE

REMAKING THE AUTOBIOGRAPHY
COMMUNISTS AND THEIR PASTS

James: Is it difficult to talk about being a party member today?

Tomáš: Of course it is. They make me out to be a criminal, but I wasn't a criminal, I was sure about the ideals. . . . In every church, the heretic is the greatest enemy. The heretics are burned, their families and their pasts are destroyed.

In the post-Communist period, some former party members, such as the former Slovak partisan Tomáš, found their life stories difficult to talk about. Faced with a new political world in which they might be demonized as criminals, ex-Communists had to consider how they wanted to come to terms with their past lives: some defended their actions or resorted to silence, while others began to consider the extent to which they should create new autobiographies that were both morally and politically acceptable for a new political age, in which they atoned for their mistakes, criticized themselves for having supported dictatorship or justified their choices as morally defensible when considered in a historical context.[1] Yet the process of working through their pasts was not simply a matter of accounting for what they had done under dictatorship; it was matter of revising the very stories that had once been the core of many individuals' identities under Communism.

The emphasis that Communist states placed not only on belief in their project, but also on constructing the correct autobiographies to signal ideological commitment, had meant that individuals had learnt to conceptualize their life histories in profoundly ideological terms. Communist states, aiming to promote those social groups in whose interests they came to power, required a range of information about their citizens in order to judge who should be elevated and who excluded. Communist citizens themselves were expected to produce public curricula vitae to enter university, when applying for employment, in annual workplace reviews or when joining the party. Through repeated engagement with these procedures, individuals learnt how to write their own experiences to fit the template of the anti-Fascist and class struggle if they wished to ensure social mobility or avoid discrimination. Many central-eastern European Communist states awarded privileges – better housing, educational and workplace opportunities, pensions, and so on – to those whose pasts fitted these historical templates, or to those who used this framework to narrate their lives.[2] The willingness to revise the meaning of one's history was often just as important to the regime as one's actual past. Hence, even those who came from prewar elites, or had fought alongside Nazi Germany, might be able at certain points to ensure their professional survival in the Communist system if they were prepared to attack their own family as oppressors or Fascists, and demonstrate publicly the extent to which they had rejected them.[3]

For many during the Communist period itself, these procedures created what were considered to be essentially invented and inauthentic public narratives. However, for party members, especially those born in the interwar period who joined after the war and who are the focus of the interviews conducted for this work, these were not hollow fabrications but meaningful self-fashionings. These autobiographical exercises shaped how they viewed the very function of telling their life story and critically informed how they thought about themselves and their backgrounds. Their young lives were marked by a particularly intense encounter with these procedures: before the 1960s, Communist states saw these techniques as essential to the absorption of individuals' identities into the Communist ideological orbit, and to the creation of the ideal socialist citizen. Writing the right autobiography in an age of Communist mass mobilization in the 1940s and 1950s in central-eastern Europe was experienced as an intensely political and meaningful act, through which supporters of the regime interwove their personal experiences with official narratives to produce life stories that confirmed them as true believers in the transformatory potential of the socialist project.[4] Research has begun to suggest that by the late Communist period, however, these procedures were increasingly routinized and hollowed out of real meaning; even for those who still believed in the system, the production of autobiographical texts privileged form over content, and did not signal the interweaving of personal and public to the same degree as it had for older generations.[5] This chapter is based on the life testimonies of twenty-nine party members who lived through this earlier period: nine from Poland, seven from Czechoslovakia and thirteen from Hungary. They were all born between 1918 and 1942, and the vast majority joined the party before the shocks of the 1956 Uprising in Hungary, the Prague Spring in 1968 in Czechoslovakia or the anti-Semitic purges of the party in 1968 in Poland.

After 1989, it was not only Communist ideology but also the Communist autobiography based on class and anti-Fascist struggle, that became the object of political contestation.[6] In this new environment, it was unclear whether such life stories had real democratic content, if they articulated the narrator's genuine beliefs in the 'progressive struggle', or whether they should simply be regarded as an invention that confirmed that the individual had supported dictatorship and was thus complicit in its violent, anti-democratic methods. Some anti-Communists sought to attack former anti-Fascist fighters, not on account of what they had once done, but for the ways in which they had been advantaged by their autobiographies under Communism. This phenomenon was particularly noticeable in the way in which those eastern European nationals who had joined the International Brigades and fought against Fascism in the Spanish Civil War were dealt with by post-Communist parliaments.[7] After 1989, their privileged status during the Communist period was weighed against their actual struggle against Franco's right-wing dictatorship in the 1930s.[8] In Poland, for instance, the first post-Communist parliament voted to strip veterans of their special pensions; the first post-Communist president, Lech Wałęsa, argued that the struggles of Spain had nothing to do with the fight for Polish independence, and that Poland had its own tradition of anti-Nazi resistance – embodied by the Home Army – which should be celebrated instead.[9] In many countries, monuments to Spanish veterans built by Communist regimes were removed.[10] Yet the ex-Communist left did try in some places to revive the status of the anti-Fascist biography; after their victory in the 1993 election, the Polish Democratic Left Alliance restored the pensions of those Polish 'Brigadiers' who had 'fought for democracy' as part of a wider European struggle against dictatorship.[11] In Spain itself – partly in response to the demoted reputations of anti-Fascist fighters in the east of the continent – all International Brigadiers were granted honorary citizenship in 1996.[12] Other countries were caught between anti-Fascism's association with Communist dictatorship, on the one hand, and late twentieth-century forms of remembrance for the victims of Fascism and the Holocaust, whose memory had become considered a vital part of a European democratic education, on the other. The parliament of the newly unified Germany, for instance, adopted a compromise between these two positions: it severely reduced (but did not eliminate) state pensions for the Spanish veterans, and reclassified them as 'victims of Fascism' who received 'compensation payments', rather than as 'anti-fascist resisters' in receipt of 'honorary pensions'.[13]

After 1989, former Communists who were socialized in the postwar period often questioned whether their Communist-era autobiographies – which might articulate their beliefs in the anti-Nazi struggle or social levelling – still had democratic content. Some accepted that the Communist life story was the biography of a collaborator. Writing a 'democratic autobiography' after 1989 therefore required a purging of the ideological story of the previous era, and a search for new ways of understanding and recounting a life. The erasure of the older autobiography was central to the process of demonstrating that he or she had redeemed him or herself. For others, the process was more difficult. Their life stories simultaneously evoked their very real struggles against Fascism and class inequality of the 1940s, and their later complicity with dictatorship: for them, 'coming to terms' with the past lay in determining what was salvageable from their past narratives when reframing them for a post-Communist liberal democratic society. Thus, for party members who had joined in the 1940s and 1950s, 'coming to terms' with their pasts was not merely a reckoning with their actions, but also with the conceptualizations of their lives that had been written into the Communist autobiographies through which they had once understood their place in the world.[14]

Writing the Communist Autobiography

After the Communist takeovers in central-eastern Europe in the late 1940s, the new regimes sought to legitimize their rule by presenting themselves as the strongest possible expression of anti-Fascist and class-based politics, framing themselves as the true inheritors of the struggle against both Fascism and the iniquitous economic systems of the interwar era. Indeed, in this worldview, these fights were in fact one and the same.[15] Fascism was understood as the expression of bourgeois class interests, an extreme form of capitalism that relied on coercive power to protect the interests of bourgeois elites from the threat of working-class unrest. The liberal capitalist states of western Europe were viewed as remnants of Fascism after 1945. In this framework, Communist states saw themselves as providing protection for central-eastern European nations from both counter-revolutionary right-wing forces at home and the bourgeois Fascist systems that had survived the war in the west. Communist states in central-eastern Europe represented their ascent to power as the victorious outcome of these struggles, and sought to discriminate in favour of those classes who embodied the continued fight against Fascism. In the immediate postwar period, therefore, discovering who could be relied upon to take up these struggles was imperative. Communist regimes became intensely biographical: they set up systems to uncover the true histories of their subjects, and used this information to judge individuals' standpoint in relation to the anti-Fascist and class struggles. Citizens were forced to detail their life histories according to Communist templates in the curricula vitae they prepared. Successfully 'writing oneself into' politically appropriate histories, or learning to craft one's past to fit the stylistic conventions expected of Communist citizens, became a key skill that could help the individual secure employment or higher education, or simply avoid discrimination and punishment.

Yet anti-Fascist and class-based politics predated the Communist takeovers in the region, extended far beyond the Communist movement, and had been capable of mobilizing much broader social constituencies in the immediate aftermath of World War II in central-eastern Europe. The 'anti-Fascist idea' had emerged as a concept across Europe in the mid-1930s in response to the rise of Nazism. Many who opposed the rise of Hitler put aside other (seemingly less significant) political differences and defined themselves simply as anti-Fascists. Immediately after 1945, many central-eastern European states were ruled by progressive anti-Fascist popular front governments, which consisted of peasant and moderate leftist parties alongside the Communists, all committed to a redistributive politics (often through nationalization) and to preventing the return of right-wing extremism to the region.[16] Thus, many liberals, leftists and even moderate conservatives had, in the immediate aftermath of the war, seen themselves as progressive anti-Fascists, and the Red Army as the liberators of central-eastern Europe from Nazism.[17]

It was only from the late 1940s onwards, after Communist regimes began to instrumentalize this rhetoric to justify their ever more dominant hold on political power, that many began to abandon such viewpoints. Increasingly, Communists presented the Red Army and their local supporters – partisans in the case of Hungary and Czechoslovakia, the People's Army in the case of Poland – as the sole, heroic liberators who paved the way for an anti-Fascist politics. The memory of other non-Communist anti-Nazi fighters in the region, such as the Home Army in Poland, was repressed. Thus, many non-Communists remember how they became alienated from ideas that, immediately after the war, had provided them with a way of understanding the world and an argument for progressive change. One Hungarian social democrat, Csaba, remembered that many people had been proud to celebrate the Soviets' role in the freeing of the region from Fascism in 1945; he himself had once viewed the 'liberation' as a prelude to the building of a more socially equitable Hungary. However, as Communists started to claim that they were the only true representatives of progressive anti-Fascist politics, and used the idea to legitimize their ever more dictatorial approach to rule, Csaba remembered his rejection of an idea that he had once held dear:[18] 'Loads of people used to say "liberation".... But in France there is an idea of liberation that remained after the war. Here there isn't, because they [the Communists] changed the street names to Liberation Boulevard and Liberation Square. They don't say this word "liberation" now, because now it is connected with the Russians and the occupation.'[19]

While anti-Fascist and progressive identities were never simply the creations of the Communist state, the autobiographies that Communist subjects had to write in order to declare their fealty to anti-Fascism and the class struggle certainly were. Individuals had to learn the categories and stylistic conventions by which to describe themselves and their pasts. Jerzy was a government minister in the 1970s who began his career doing youth work on an industrial site in the Polish town of Nowa Huta outside Kraków. He described how he had constructed his background in order to appear as ideologically accepable as possible and thereby gain promotion within the party. He realized that his family could have been classified according to a number of different Communist definitions. Nevertheless, he found a way of packaging his background in a politically advantageous format and described himself as coming from 'working peasant' stock.[20] Speaking from the perspective of post-Communism, he presented these choices as part of a game of self-refashioning in which he deftly placed himself on the right side of the class struggle:

James: How did the Communist state in Warsaw classify your family?

Jerzy: It is very important! The classification was very important....
Working man, peasant, working intelligentsia: my family could have belonged to any of these groups! [*laughs*] ... I became a political apparatchik, a functionary, so, me, personally, I was strongly linked to the 'intelligentsia' class ... [this classification] was better than being a 'peasant', because a peasant could have either one hundred hectares or only one hectare, and the peasant who had one hundred hectares was deemed to be a kulak[21] and he was liquidated....
[But] father and mother were ... working class, but in a village, [so they were] 'working peasants'. ... But of course I must say that I manipulated my biography. Those classifications, that background, 'poor peasant' and later this one of 'working peasant' – of course, because of my work, it was a necessity [to use it] in the party [*laughs*]. ... I am aware how that dogma changed me – out of necessity.[22]

He also had to learn to explain away his autobiographical liabilities and, if possible, turn them to his advantage. The fact that his father emigrated might have been viewed dimly by the state (relatives abroad were seen as a source of potential ideological contamination, or as evidence of a family's antipathy towards the regime). However, he constructed the story of his father's departure in such a way as to emphasize his humble working-class origins and to attack 'bourgeois' Poland. Despite the emigration, his family was therefore placed on the correct side of the class struggle:

> If I wanted – and I did want – to be in the stream of political life, I would have to join the party. And there was some hesitating and some difficulties because in those days, anybody who had been abroad was not considered trustworthy and my father was abroad in France [for ten years]. I dealt with it in this way. [I said] that my father was a worker in *bourgeois* Poland before the war and as an unemployed man he went abroad to France and when he saw he had prospects in Poland, he came back.

Though Jerzy presented his Communist-era autobiographical reformulation as evidence of a system in which everyone was gainfully manipulating their pasts, others presented their encounter with these processes as more profound experiences through which they had both made sense of their own lives and explained their commitment to the movement to themselves. Thus for some, these autobiographical procedures very effectively bound individuals' sense of their own history to the regime's legitimizing historical stories; personal accounts of their heroic wartime sacrifices, or their suffering and lack of opportunity as part of poor, disadvantaged families, became intertwined with the narrative of how they came to support the Communist state. Therefore these procedures were immensely effective at getting individuals to connect their own family stories with the regime's postwar political project. Most common was the conversion narrative, which applicants frequently had to reproduce as part of their attempt to join the party, and to reiterate at party functions during the 1940s and 1950s.[23] Individuals did not need to come from the right class or political background; rather, they needed to show that they had grasped the incontrovertible truth behind the Communists' historical paradigms and were able to narrate their own journey from political ignorance to revelation. Even testimonies collected in the post-Communist period contained remnants of these narrative forms: personal and family stories were still related as teleological accounts in which everything in the individual's pre-Communist life anticipated their eventual belief in the Communist project. Mátyás, a Hungarian Jewish respondent from Budapest, presented his life as apolitical

1 Soviet tank stolen from an open-air historical exhibition in Budapest in October 2006 during the demonstrations which accompanied the fiftieth anniversary of the Hungarian Uprising. The right-wing protestors saw themselves as the true successors to the revolutionaries of 1956, and sought to recreate aspects of the Uprising on the streets of the capital.

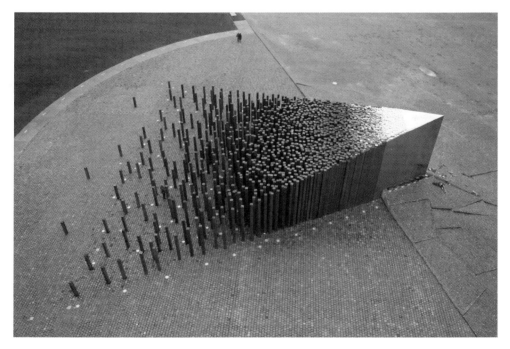

2 'Central Monument of the 1956 Hungarian Revolution and War of Independence', Felvonulási Square, Budapest, unveiled 2006. Located at the site of a former Stalin statue destroyed by revolutionaries in 1956.

3 Main prison hall, The Memorial of the Victims of Communism and of the Resistance, Sighetu Marmației, Romania.

4 Cemetery of the Poor, The Memorial of the Victims of Communism and of the Resistance, Sighetu Marmației, Romania. Note the trees and bushes planted in the shape of Romania's borders.

5 House of Terror, Budapest, Hungary. Exterior from Andrássy Boulevard. Note the symbols of the Fascist Arrow Cross, and the Communists, on the blade walls. When the sun is at its highest point, the word 'Terror' is spelled out in shadow on the pavement below: a reference to Arthur Koestler's novel about totalitarianism, *Darkness at Noon*.

6 Main Atrium, House of Terror, Budapest, Hungary. A Soviet T34 tank stranded in 'oil' is placed beneath a wall of photographs of Hungarians who were executed or imprisoned as enemies of the regime. The juxtaposition presents the Communist dictatorship as one imposed from the outside, and Hungarians as those who suffered under it. It also suggests a now defunct system being judged 'from above' by its victims, re-inforcing the idea of the museum as a 'cultural courtroom'.

7 Statue Park, Budapest, Hungary.

8 Grūtas Park ('Stalinworld'), Druskininkai, Lithuania. Note that the statues are deprived of their power by being at ground level, and 'watched' from guard towers, as if incarcerated within a fir-forested 'Siberian prison camp'.

9 Excavated Execution Chamber, Museum of Genocide Victims, Vilnius, Lithuania. Note the raised glass platform above the dug earth, from where visitors can inspect the scattered objects placed there to resemble the excavated results of an archaeological dig.

10 Columbarium Exterior. Tuskulėnai Mass Grave, Vilnius, Lithuania. The entrance is framed by the double cross of Vytis, the saint whose image is used as part of the national emblem of Lithuania.

11 Columbarium Interior. Repository for Bones from the Tuskulėnai Mass Grave, Vilnius, Lithuania. (Photograph courtesy of Prof. Dr. Rimantas Jankauskas)

12 Museum of Occupations, Tallinn, Estonia. Opened in 2003 in a building specifically designed for the purpose. (Author's Photograph)

13 Gateway to the exhibition at the Occupations Museum, Tallinn, Estonia. Note the models of trains, symbolising the deportation of Estonians. Locomotives adorned with Nazi and Soviet symbols are placed side by side, denoting the idea of the 'double occupation'.

14 Museum of the Occupation of Latvia, Riga. Between 1970 and 1991, this building housed the Communist 'Memorial Museum to the Latvian Red Riflemen'. It was leased to the Museum of Occupations by the Latvian state in 1991.

15 'Bronze Soldier' Monument, Tallinn, Estonia. This Soviet-era 'Monument to the Liberators of Tallinn' was unveiled in the central Tőnismägi Square in 1947, and was removed and 'exiled' to the Cemetery for the Estonian Defence Forces in April 2007.

16 Hungarian Propaganda Poster, 1944: 'Do you want to be taken to Siberia too? Never! Then fight and work for victory!' Note the bodies of women and children by the side of the railtracks. Courtesy of the Hungarian National Museum Poster Collection, Magyar Nemzeti Múzeum, Budapest.

until a very specific moment in January 1945: following the deaths of family members in the Holocaust, which had been brought to a halt by the arrival of the Red Army, he spotted Communists tearing down Fascist signs in the centre of the city. At this moment, his political identity was formed: the world was suddenly revealed to be divided between reactionary Fascists, on the one hand, and Communist anti-Fascists, on the other. Mátyás emphasized the stark choice available to him and his enthusiasm to join the anti-Fascist side. From a post-Communist perspective, he related the story in terms of regret – that he had been forced to live such a political life – but nevertheless presented his entry into this newly politicized postwar world in terms familiar from Communist 'conversion' autobiographies. His entire prior life story built to the moment at which the bipolar world was starkly exposed and the obligation to commit politically to the correct side was revealed:

> Now it's a terribly politicized society and in the last forty to fifty years the community where I have lived . . . everything and everyone has been politicized. This is an abnormal society. Now in my childhood it wasn't like this, the war brought it . . . in normal circumstances a family doesn't talk about politics but about sport, food, where the boys are, women, cards. . . . Now we were faced with a directly life-threatening situation from 1943–44, and already, in this non-political and also non-politicized family, politics was becoming the main topic of conversation . . . so [we were discussing] how the eastern front was moving . . . the family, as they were not Communists, they were afraid of the Russians, but at the same time they hoped for their victory. . . . I remember 19 March and then the Szálasi putsch [the Fascist Arrow Cross takeover] on 15 October really well. I don't just remember the events, I remember the psychological effects too. . . . we were *liberated* on 12–13 February. . . . I was already politicized and in the spring of 1945 I joined MADISz [the youth wing of the Communist Party] of my own free will – nobody invited me. I wanted to, and that moment when I decided to join was based on a very simple experience. I read in a newspaper in Buda that MADISz were tearing down the signs from Hitler Square and Mussolini Square.[24] And then I thought, that's the place for me! And slowly life got back to normal, and I would have just become a normal student and I would have had a normal life, and I wouldn't have got closer to the Communist movement. Does a fifteen-year-old boy search for a political movement, if he lives in normal circumstances, if he doesn't live through a war and if his father hasn't died in that war?[25]

Tomáš, from southern Slovakia, portrayed his conversion as a rejection of his parents' politics. They had been 'petty-bourgeois shopkeepers' whose economic suffering, under Béla Kun's Communist Republic of Councils,[26] had given rise to a firm anti-Communism that had remained with them for the rest of their lives. Tomáš's radicalization and rejection of his parents' beliefs came in reaction to the Nazi occupation of the Czech lands, the growth of the right-wing Slovak collaborationist state, and his belief that only the Communists were strong enough to overcome these developments. The focus of the early part of his autobiography was the moment of his realization that the world had been divided into two political camps, and that he had to choose sides. All other details existed in relation to this: information about family, education and social life was moulded around the moment when this 'truth' was finally revealed. His conversion story started at the point at which an independent Slovakia (as a Nazi satellite state) was established in 1939, and focused on how his headmaster and Slovak teachers at school had turned from supporters of Masaryk's united democratic Czechoslovakia into Slovak nationalist Fascists who wanted to expel the Czech teachers and his Jewish classmates:

> Going back, I remember we were taken to this one classroom and our headmaster was telling us about the death of Masaryk [in 1937] . . . and he was crying. That he was crying in front of small boys was a greater shock for us than the death of Masaryk itself, because of the authority of the head-master. And in only two years he changed into a leader of the Hlinka Guard [a paramilitary organization that supported the Slovak collaborationist state] and he wore the black shirt. He walked around in the uniform and he 'siegheiled'. . . . The Czech teachers were forced to leave the new Slovak state – *we* didn't care what nationality a teacher was. As I was an active pupil at school I organized goodbye parties for the teachers, and after a month I saw my classmates change into young Hlinka guardsmen who wanted to put the Czechs six feet under and send the Jews to Palestine. It was that that made us radicals. . . . we used to beat up the Fascists at school [*laughing*]. And when Russians were liberating Slovakia, I had a list of these people and my headmaster was on it. . . . he was taken to Siberia and he never came back.[27]

Tomáš then gave an account of how he had used his wartime anti-Fascist credentials in order to gain privileges under the Communist regime. He had been a Communist partisan fighter in the Slovak Uprising against the collaborationist Slovak regime, and in the first decades of the Communist system had 'allowed' himself to be turned into a Communist-era 'hero' for gain. By his late twenties, he was the head of an institute in Prague:

James: Can you tell me about the process you had to go through to join the party?

Tomáš: I was a member of the movement of fighters against the Nazis so it was an honour. I was in the newspapers. Many people were telling me how wonderful I was. And only afterwards the disillusionment came.

James: Did it help you as you'd been part of the anti-Nazi partisans . . .?

Tomáš: Yes. It helped me [in]to the grave! [*laughs*] . . . We had to prove our past [i.e. that they were real partisans] all the time in the 1950s. . . . The Czechs who had fought with the British [in World War II], they were suspected of being Fascists, they were imprisoned. Those [anti-Fascists] who had fought in the Spanish war against Franco were suspected and they were put in prison. Because they were suspected of being agents of a foreign secret service. But *my* past was 'confirmed' in 1947 – that I really had been the member of partisan groups – then in the '50s I was 'confirmed' again, but in the '60s I became an enemy of the country, then again an enemy after the Russian invasion [in 1968]. But they could never deny that I really was there [i.e. a real partisan]. The people from the place where I was born always confirmed that I was on the right side. We had to fill in this form (*dotaznik*) all the time [about our pasts]. And over it was written that if the statements were not correct you could be punished. . . . And decades after the victory of the Communists in 1948 the fact that some people didn't tell the truth about their lives kept coming up. I saw it in Bohemia when many Nazi collaborators joined the Communist Party. They joined the party just for their careers. They hated those of us who knew it. They told me just after 1948, 'Tomáš, we don't want you. Why? You remember too much.'

Those who had joined the party in the 1940s and 1950s learnt to construct Communist autobiographies, and indeed used this framework to make sense of their lives. These life stories were the result of both powerful personal experiences *and* political ideology; they were often based on very real experiences of Fascism, poverty or lack of opportunity, but their form was moulded by Communist ideology and manipulated to advance their careers within the system. The fact that these stories became perceived by their narrators simultaneously as 'genuine' invocations of life-changing experiences *and* as politicized manipulations for personal gain was to lead former party members to struggle with their own autobiographies for much of their lives.

Life stories collected by the oral historian after 1989 can be used to explore both how individuals are shaped by the past, and how the meanings of their experiences are remoulded into new forms to serve the needs of the present. While this testimony provides evidence of how people learnt to turn their life experiences into powerful Communist autobiographies in the postwar period, it is also clearly shaped by the values of the post-1989 era: former party members needed to remould their stories for post-Communism. Yet these oral histories also reveal how the values of the past leach into the present: even when creating life stories in a liberal democratic context, these former Communists continued to understand the autobiographical exercise in political terms, just as they had been socialized into doing in their youth: stories of family, career and public life were still moulded into ideologically laden accounts which served to explain their relationship with the current political system. Whereas once they had created autobiographies that signalled the level of their commitment to the socialist project, now their narratives indicated their political relationship with the post-Communist political and economic system.

Their very relationship with their previous Communist autobiographies was central to recasting their life stories for a liberal democratic age. For most respondents, their autobiographies now had to anticipate their later commitment to democracy. Thus many suggested that they only held to Communist autobiographies at those moments when the stories were capable of sustaining democratic ideals and the possibility of reforming the socialist system along more democratic lines; if that belief was broken, their former anti-Fascist autobiographies had to be discarded. For some, their life stories were not merely accounts of their commitment to, and then disillusionment with, the democratic potential of Communism; they were also accounts of an often painful and drawn-out process of coming to terms with the Communist autobiographies they had not only written in public but also believed in and once used as a set of stories through which to understand their lives.

Central to writing a 'democratic autobiography' after 1989 was the process of coming to terms with the anti-Fascist stories that the former party members had written into their Communist autobiographies. While most had perceived themselves as combatants in the fight against capitalism in the name of the working class in the 1940s and 1950s, coming to terms with the ways in which the story of the class struggle had marked their lives was not an imperative in post-Communist life stories. This may in part be because class rhetoric often declined in the later years of Communist regimes, and thus former party members simply did not routinely have to practise the creation of a meaningful 'class-based life story' from the 1960s onwards.[28] Yet it may also be because the story of 'coming to terms' with anti-Fascism gave this generation of party members the opportunity to define themselves as democratic according to the values of the post-1989 world, which still valued the fight against Nazism as a modern, relevant and civilized way of recalling the past. Some believed, especially following the defeat of reform socialist movements after 1956 in Hungary, and 1968 in Czechoslovakia, that anti-Fascism had been denuded of any democratic content: their life stories became an account of how their earlier anti-Fascist autobiographies had been purged and of their attempts to find other ways of understanding, and narrating, their lives.[29] These stories will be explored in the first section below. For others, the re-evaluation of their anti-Fascist autobiographies was more complex: they been socialized into seeing anti-Fascist narratives as appropriate in the 1940s, had then rejected the anti-Fascist content of their life stories after their disillusion-ment with the system, but revived it again after 1989. This too was part of the production of a 'democratic autobiography': they showed how they had purged their anti-Fascist autobiographies in the late Communist period when it represented an inauthentic legitimization for dictatorship, but reclaimed its content again in the post-Communist period to combat what they saw as the rise of anti-democratic nationalist right-wing forces in their society. This will be explored in the second section below. Finally, there were those who never eradicated their anti-Fascist autobiographies at all: for them, the Communist project was either more democratic (in terms of its progres-sive politics and aspirations to social equality) than the market-driven liberalism of post-Communism, or had remained a necessary bulwark against the return of Fascism to the region until the 1980s. Hence, they held to their earlier Communist autobiographies as a form of political resistance against the post-Communist present. This phenomenon will be explored in the last section.

Purging the Communist Autobiography

Some former party members' autobiographies developed into accounts of their growing realization not only of the illegitimate nature of Communist power, but also of the increasingly inauthentic claims that Communist regimes made to represent a progressive, anti-Fascist struggle. They saw the set of politicized stories through which they had come to make political sense of their world as having become corrupted by Communist regimes that were now incapable of reform or democratization. Their production of a Communist autobiography was increasingly viewed as a sign of complicity with what had turned into an illegitimate dictatorship, and for them their 'personal democratization' required the elimination of their earlier anti-Fascist selves, and the stories that had underpinned them.

Those who purged themselves of their Communist autobiographies often remembered a particular moment at which their questioning of the legitimacy of the state's use of progressive, anti-Fascist rhetoric started. This was often an instance when anti-Fascist rhetoric was employed to purge colleagues, eliminate enemies in show trials or justify excessive violence. Tomáš recalled that by 1949 he had begun to question the authenticity of the anti-Fascist story that had first provoked his politicization and by which his political worldview had been framed. He recalled attending the trial of the leaders of a military unit that had refused to lay down its arms after the capitulation of the rest of the German forces in Czechoslovakia. Just as his earlier autobiography had contained a conversion narrative that pinpointed a particular experience through which the truth about Communism was finally revealed, so his life story, built for the needs of post-Communism, isolated a key moment when his faith in the class and anti-Fascist struggles began to fall away:

> In 1949, when I was twenty-two, I got a pass for the trials of the six generals of the Nazi Scherner's army who were the last intact German army in Czechoslovakia. And it was a terrible shock for me because it wasn't a trial, it was a farce. I thought . . . they will have the right to defend themselves objectively. . . . There were judges who were calling them rude words, that they were 'Fascists'. The generals were crying, they were sentenced to death long before the judgement was revealed. It was so terrible that all the audience was shocked. I didn't dare to talk about my reaction with even my closest friends, that it wasn't a trial but a farce that equalled the way in which Fascists had treated their enemies in court.

The Hungarian Alajos had never been a party member but described himself as a 'reform socialist'. Like Tomáš, he recalled the symbolic moment when his conversion away from anti-Fascism began, and he started to understand that this ideology was increasingly empty of meaningful progressive content and was being used solely as a tool of power. He spoke of the clashes that occurred between reformists and Stalinists in his Marxist-Leninist seminars at university. He highlighted the Stalinists' need to invent new 'inauthentically Fascist' enemies and to present the conflict between Fascists and anti-Fascists in ever sharper terms in order to justify their own power:

> So I was talking about these classes in Marxism-Leninism: there was this huge auditorium, and the man who spoke couldn't see the back where we

were playing cards. They were such primitive lectures . . . but one wouldn't argue with them. It happened once in a Marxist-Leninist exam that the examiners weren't quite sure whether I was right or not . . . and the question was 'What do you think – is America becoming more Fascist?' . . . and I had just read in the party paper that the American High Court actually ruled against segregation, and it was the first time they ruled against Southern segregated states, and I said, no, I don't believe it's getting more Fascist, I mean, I've just read in the papers that there was a decision in favour of blacks, so whoever says that is ridiculous. Because, you see, one of the Stalinist tenets was that the class war was getting sharper all the time, so if you had reformist thinking, you immediately challenged that view. And you'd say, 'It can't be true, because if there really was class war, there would be a revolution, there would be war, so it can't be true!'[30]

Yet early encounters with these inauthentic ideological expressions were not presented as immediately engendering a crisis in anti-Fascist worldviews. Rather, these respondents emphasized that in the early Communist period anti-Fascism was still capable of generating an authentic democratic impulse: it remained an ideology that could motivate genuine resistance against the dictatorial excesses of Stalinism. From a post-Communist perspective, therefore, it was not necessarily to be taken as a sign of having been complicit with a now discredited system. From 1953 in Hungary, and from the early 1960s in Czechoslovakia, reformist elements within the elite became increasingly influential and opened up the possibility of democratization of the system. Reformist-minded socialists often claimed that they had been the real anti-Fascists who had fought to defeat dictatorship in 1945, and had presented the Stalinist state as inauthentic and as having betrayed the democratic ideals of anti-Fascism by having re-established dictatorial rule. These forces often turned anti-Fascist language back against the state as a means of critiquing it. Alajos remembered using anti-Fascist rhetoric in this way in his protests in 1956. He had seen himself as part of the anti-Fascist tradition that had struggled against Nazism and 'reaction' in the immediate postwar period; he believed that this gave him the right to resist Stalinism. He had found himself involved in the demonstration that followed the reburial of László Rajk on 6 October 1956. Rajk, a former Communist interior minister, was found guilty of Trotskyism and espionage at a show trial in the summer of 1949. Although the charges against him were fabricated, he was later executed; his death became a symbol for the perversions of Stalinism and his reburial thus became a magnet for reform Communists. Alajos recalled transforming old anti-Fascist slogans and a well-known anti-Fascist poem into attacks on Stalinists:

On 6 October 1956, you had the Rajk reburial. . . . when I was coming out after the speeches . . . I saw a little group with a flag and they were beckoning me to join in. I joined them, and then I found somebody . . . a bloke I knew from the Széchenyi library, who said, 'Somebody told me there's going to be a demonstration.' 'Where are you going to?' 'Oh, we're going to Hősök Tere [Heroes' Square], and then to the Batthyány Örökmécses.' This is a flame in memory of Lajos Batthyány who was the prime minister of Hungary in 1849, and was executed.[31] This is a kind of place where people go, sort of a 'Martyrs' Corner'. All right, so I joined the group. It wasn't particularly political, but we started producing slogans together. . . . between 1945 and 1948, the Communist Party slogan was: 'We're not going to stop halfway. Let reaction perish!' So we adapted this slogan, instead of saying 'reaction' saying 'Stalinism', so 'We are not going to stop halfway. Let Stalinism perish!' And then we shouted over and over, two hundred people, as we marched with this flag, and people looked at us, and they didn't understand what was going on. . . . I read out a poem by Atilla József,[32] which was anti-Fascist, rather anti-German, and was a patriotic poem ending with the words, 'So that we shouldn't be a German colony,' but I read, 'So we shouldn't be a foreign colony.'

Before the reformists' final breaks with the Communist Party after 1956 and 1968, progressive and anti-Fascist language was employed as much to justify resistance to Stalinist dictatorship as it was to identify oneself with the system. In Hungary, those reformist Communists who participated in the 1956 Uprising viewed their involvement as an attempt not to destroy Communism but rather to replace a corrupted Stalinist dictatorship with a democratic socialist state that would hold to authentic anti-Fascist ideals. Benedek produced revolutionary leaflets in Russian and distributed them to the first wave of Soviet tanks as they arrived in Budapest. Worried that the soldiers might view the insurgents as Fascists intent on destroying Communism, he sought to reclaim anti-Fascism for the revolutionaries by explaining to the Russians that they were sincere anti-Fascists who merely wanted a more humane form of socialism. His involvement in the Uprising revealed the extent to which he had continued to view the world in anti-Fascist terms until 1956: he regarded those other revolutionaries who fought against the power structure not to reform socialism but rather to restore capitalism as 'unrealistic' Fascists rather than fellow insurgents:

The '56 revolution was just about which of the left-wing options we take. There was no one, except for a few unrealistic people, who was dreaming of restoring capitalism, but the revolution was always just about which of the various possibilities of socialism we should adopt. . . . We decided that we would try to explain to the Russian soldiers who we were; that we were anti-Fascists, that we were not Fascists trying to re-establish capitalism or Nazism or anything like that. So we wrote a one-page leaflet in Russian and took it to the university printing press, where I had a printer friend, and he printed it for me, and then with other friends in my circle we went around the whole of Budapest and climbed up on the tanks and handed the soldiers these leaflets. It said that we wanted democratic socialism, not capitalism, and we wanted equality between nations, friendship with the Russian nation on the basis of equality . . . . this was the first day of the revolution . . . so the leaflet was quite a mild document if you like. We didn't dream of leaving the Warsaw Pact.[33]

In Hungary in 1956 and in Czechoslovakia in 1968, the intervention of Soviet tanks to repress these revolts effectively ended reform Communists' attempts to democratize the system and enable a limited political pluralism. Many became alienated from the party and the Communist state, and as a consequence eventually abandoned their Communist autobiographical selves. They no longer viewed the world as divided between Fascist reactionaries, on the one hand, and anti-Fascist progressives, on the other. The collapse of their ideological worldview also precipitated a crisis in the way they conceptualized their own pasts: they began a long process of purging anti-Fascism from their private autobiographies. They were faced with a new official public discourse in which those who had struggled in 1956 and 1968 were now attacked as 'rightists', 'opportunists', 'agents of Fascism' or 'counter-revolutionaries'; in this context, official anti-Fascism no longer had any appeal for them. The defeat of 1956 convinced many that socialism could not be reformed within the geopolitical environment of the Cold War, hence they did not want to cling onto anti-Fascism as an ideology of resistance to the excesses of dictatorship.

In November 1956 in the immediate aftermath of the Hungarian Uprising the newly reconstituted Communist Party under János Kádár characterized the revolt's suppression by Soviet tanks as the 'second liberation of Hungary'. According to this view, the heroic efforts of the Red Army to free Hungary of Fascism in 1944–45 had been replayed on the nation's streets in the autumn of 1956.[34] The Uprising's participants – including those reform Communists who fought for a democratic socialism – were attacked as Fascist counter-revolutionaries intent on returning Hungary to the semi-feudalism of the interwar period. After the defeat of the Uprising, the Communist Party did not exclude former members automatically on the basis of their involvement, but did if they were not prepared to condemn their part in the revolt. The party made them a 'redeeming offer': those who had participated in the newly christened 'counter-revolution' could be forgiven for supporting what they had naïvely believed to be a movement to reform socialism, so long as they now accepted that the revolution had in fact been the work of Fascists who had manipulated and controlled the entire event behind the scenes.[35] Thus many who had viewed their involvement as the expression of a genuine anti-Fascist reform socialist movement were being asked to redefine themselves as dupes of Fascists and to accept that their challenge to authoritarian Communism had been inauthentic. Many, such as Mátyás, rejected this 'redeeming offer':[36]

James: Did you think of rejoining the party?

Mátyás: After 1956, it wasn't any kind of temptation at all, because by 4 November 1956 the situation had been resolved morally; we were only really thinking about whether to stay in Hungary or to emigrate. But not to join the party was, for my wife and my friends, a completely clear moral imperative; we had no doubts about it . . . there were many who joined and many who didn't. Some joined because they thought it was a counter-revolution, or because they wanted to be in with the convinced Communists. And some thought that they had to join the party because there was no other possibility of ensuring their survival . . . . it really pulled apart our community where I lived, us young Budapest left-wing intellectuals. Still, there were those who up until 1956 had not been party members, and in 1957 everyone joined the party, because at that point the party had collapsed, and they thought that here was the opportunity to join and make their careers.

In Czechoslovakia, the democratizing reform movement within the party began later – in the early 1960s – and culminated in the so-called 'Prague Spring' of 1968. Unlike in Hungary, the Stalinist leadership in Czechoslovakia tarred its reformist opponents as 'counter-revolutionaries' even before the suppression of the democratic reform movement by Soviet troops in August 1968. Indeed, from June of that year, it invoked the term in an attempt to invite Soviet intervention.[37] It continued to be used to attack reformists until the collapse of Communism in 1989.[38] Unlike in Hungary, the Czechoslovak party did not disintegrate; hence, those who had been involved in the reform movement remained members and were forced to submit themselves to screening processes, which eventually led to large-scale purges. By the end of 1969, it had been decided that the cleansing of the party would take place by means of an interview process (*pohovory*) in which individuals would be asked to explain their political views and their past actions.[39] Involvement in the reform movement was not always enough to earn expulsion; if individuals were prepared to renounce their involvement and welcome the Soviet intervention, it was sometimes possible to remain in the party.[40] Nevertheless, many quit before the purge had even begun, while others were expelled despite having renounced their actions in the Prague Spring as counter-revolutionary.[41] Reformists who left, or were expelled from, the movement presented this moment as the beginning of the purge of their Communist autobiographies; their previous life stories now seemed to legitimize dictatorship. Olga recalled her refusal to identify with a new anti-Fascist script, in which the arrival of the Russians was seen as part of a tradition of Soviet intervention in the region, which had defeated Nazism in 1945, 'Hungarian Fascists' in 1956 and now Czechoslovak 'counter-revolutionaries' in 1968:

> When they were doing the screening interviews [after 1968] the first question was whether you agreed that the Russians should have come. And I said no, it was a mistake, they shouldn't have come here. I could have played stupid and not said anything – because my family had a good working-class background – and then possibly they would have let me continue in my job. . . . [A] very important figure in the party told me openly that I was doing so well, and my background was so good, that if I hadn't been so open they would have been very happy to [keep me] . . . but I simply disagreed [with the Soviet intervention]. It was necessary to say 'yes'. It makes me angry even today, makes me really despair. . . . Excuse me [*becomes very emotional at this point*] . . . it's just memories. I don't watch TV or read the newspapers on the anniversaries.[42]

The end of Olga's career as a prominent journalist in 1969 also signalled an end to the significance of her 'performance' of anti-Fascism in public. Once demoted to menial work, she could afford to reject the post-1968 Czechoslovak state's interpretation of the reform movement as a counter-revolution since it could make no further practical difference to her life. She chose to maintain her position publicly by expressing her disagreement with the Soviet intervention on yearly workplace curricula vitae, but simultaneously realized that protest was meaningless and had no impact:

> It was impossible to get out of it [filling out a yearly curriculum vitae], it was horrible. As an example – there was a question, 'What was your understanding of "Victorious February" in '48?' I didn't have any problems with this – I could write that I was a child. And so I could deal with it unproblematically . . . and

then there was a question of your understanding of events in Hungary in '56. . . . And in '56 I said I had a small child and I was a housewife . . . but for the invasion in '68 another question appeared . . . and then I had to write that I disagreed [with what had happened]. I had been excluded from the Communist Party, and nobody else wanted to spend ten years working night shifts, nobody wanted to do the kind of job I had to do, so it was of no importance [what I wrote on my CV].

In Poland, some of the older generation of Communists were purged from the party in 1968 in a quite distinct process.[43] During World War II, Poland, unlike Hungary or Czechoslovakia, had its own powerful non-Communist anti-Nazi resistance movement, the Home Army. Thus, there were two competing anti-Nazi traditions in the country. In the early Communist period, the assertion that the Communist state was the true manifestation of the anti-Fascist struggle therefore required not only the celebration of the Red Army (alongside the Soviet-supported Polish People's Army) as the liberators of the country from Fascism; it also necessitated the repression of the memory of the Home Army since it had a substantial and potentially threatening claim to the mantle of the anti-Nazi struggle. Like Hungary, Poland experienced political and economic unrest in 1956; however, it was effectively managed by the local Communist Party and did not lead to armed Soviet intervention. Unlike in Hungary, where anti-Fascism was redefined to stigmatize the participants in the 1956 uprising as Fascist counter-revolutionaries, the Polish elite responded by starting a process of redefining anti-Fascism in much broader terms, in order to establish a greater degree of popular legitimacy as a national, less Soviet-dominated regime in the late 1950s and 1960s. As part of this redefinition, Communist elites led by Władysław Gomułka reconceptualized the anti-Fascist struggle as being waged by the 'Polish people' and not simply by Communist forces. The main state anti-Fascist veterans' association, the Union of Fighters for Freedom and Democracy, began to allow Home Army members who wanted to accommodate themselves to the regime to join (as long as they were prepared to deny any involvement in anti-Soviet activity after the war).[44] For those Communist Party members who, in the immediate postwar period, had joined the party, which they viewed as a form of protection against both the return of Nazism and right-wing Polish nationalism, this ideological shift was especially difficult to deal with. Andrzej was from a non-Communist left-wing Jewish family and lost his father in the Holocaust. He presented his decision to join the party not only as a result of gratitude to the Communist liberators of Jews from Fascism but also because he feared the revival of anti-Semitism from the Polish right, represented by the National

Democratic Party (the so-called 'Endecs'), before World War II. His political development had been shaped not only by the impact of the Nazi occupation in Poland but also by his experiences of anti-Semitism as a scout within the Home Army: thus, the party became his protector both from German Nazism and indigenous anti-Semitic traditions. While many Poles who had fought with the Home Army were alienated from the Communist movement, which had demonized them as enemies of the state, Andrzej was attracted to the youth organization of the party:[45]

James: Can you tell me more about what attracted you to the Communist youth movement?

Andrzej: There were a couple of reasons. Under the occupation, the Nazi occupation, I was a scout. It was an underground scouting union – very patriotic, sometimes nationalistic. And I had a bad experience with this scouting union, because in time they learned about my [Jewish] origins – not from me, but from somebody else; and the commander of our unit assured me that I could stay and nobody would denounce me . . . but nevertheless they also started to explain to me that it was a Polish patriotic organization and it did not want to have a Jew among its members. . . . I was thirteen at the time, and it was a very humiliating experience for me, because it came not from enemies, but from my own folk. So after the war when the scout organization was rebuilt in Poland. . . . I did not want to go there anymore, but at the same time I wanted to belong somewhere. . . . I had a very democratic approach to life. I joined the Union of Socialist Youth. I was a son of the Warsaw intelligentsia. They were the sons of Łódź workers. It was obvious for me that we were now together and we had the same ideals.[46]

Andrzej then charted his growing disillusionment with the Communist state's anti-Fascism, leading to his final 'moment of conversion' in 1968. He had in fact lost his faith in the Communist project after 1956 and the suppression of reform socialism in the Hungarian Uprising, but had been too afraid to hand in his party card and so remained a 'passive member' until 1968. During the 1960s, he was increasingly concerned about the nationalist direction of the party, especially the way in which it was trying to reconcile itself with the Home Army, whose nationalist traditions were gaining increasing acceptance amongst party elites. Increasingly, the younger nationalist wing of the party sought to cement its rise to influence by attacking the older postwar elite as Jewish and anti-national; this culminated in 1968 with anti-Semitic purges. A new form of anti-Fascist rhetoric was mobilized to support this position: in the wake of the Arab-Israeli War of summer 1967, Polish Communist propaganda equated Israeli aggression with that of Nazi Germany and presented Polish Jews as Zionists who supported these 'Fascistic' policies.[47] Moreover, Jews were deemed to be anti-Polish as – it was argued – they gave credence to western 'Fascistic' propaganda by claiming that the Poles had assisted the Nazis in the Holocaust.[48] As Andrzej saw it, the nationalism and anti-Semitism that he had joined the party to escape now began to play a major role in its activities. In March 1968, following the demonstration against the regime that sparked off anti-Semitic purges within the party and the large-scale emigration of Jews to Israel, Andrzej finally decided to leave:

> In the autumn of 1956 I understood that I did not want to be a part of this party anymore . . . but I didn't have enough courage at this time to leave it. I didn't take on any party duties for the next eleven years, and I felt distanced from them. I could do this because under Władysław Gomułka, a good citizen was simply someone who never shouted and was obedient and passive. After 1956, Poland was no longer a totalitarian country and nobody demanded any political enthusiasm from you. It was only in March 1968 that I handed in my party card with a short note. . . . when I saw the strength of anti-Semitic opinion in the party, the purges and the nationalist direction of the country, I thought the party capable of anything. So from 1968 I had absolutely no illusions . . . the anti-Semitic campaign was a terrible experience for all of us, both the Jews and non-Jews in the intelligentsia, and many of my friends left Poland . . . . my brother and many of my friends also went to Israel . . . . they were dispersed all over the world and when we said farewell to them we were told that we would never see them again.

It is worth noting that many *were* attracted to this nationalist redefinition of anti-Fascism to include those 'Polish patriots' who had fought Nazism as part of the Home Army.[49] Interviewees who joined the party from the late 1960s remembered the importance of this reconceptualization of its meaning, which allowed them to reconcile their Polish patriotism with membership of the party. Krzysztof, for instance, had been brought up in a family with Home Army traditions. In the 1960s he was part of the youth wing of the party that was seeking to create a new nationalist form of Communism in place of the internationalist anti-Fascist traditions of the older postwar elites who still drew inspiration from the Russian Revolution and the Spanish Civil War, rather than the Polish struggle against Nazism in World War II. Although he acknowledged and regretted the fact that in 1968 this nationalist re-orientation had led to an anti-Semitic campaign which forced many Jews to leave the party, he nevertheless had considered the cleansing of anti-national Communists as necessary for the future growth of the movement:

I started studying in 1963 – that was a period when we fought for the control of the Union of Socialist Youth in the university in Warsaw. We had quite a large following among those people who came from the scouting union which had played a very important role in the Polish underground [during World War II]. . . . [In the 1950s] I was a scout for three years in a unit that was commanded by two guys who came from the 'Grey Ranks' (*Szare Szeregi*) [which had close connections to the underground and Home Army]. So we were under the spell of this Home Army tradition. [In the late 1950s] I remember going to summer camp and standing on the platform of Warsaw's Eastern Station and suddenly we saw a youth group marching who had these bright red scarves. They belonged to the 'Walterowcy' [named after General Walter of the Spanish Civil War and dedicated to ideologically pure Marxism and internationalist anti-Fascism]. We saw them as a kind of a Trojan horse in the youth movement . . . many of them came from old prewar Communist families and had grown up in the tradition of the 'Spanish war' and thought that the biggest threat came from Polish nationalism. . . . These Walterowcy had a very different image of Poland to mine; they saw the Russian Revolution and the fight against Fascism in the Spanish war in a very romantic way. . . . Most of them had a better situation than we had, they were part of the establishment. For me [the 1960s] meant a struggle with the establishment. So that was the reason I got involved. The anti-Semitic campaign [which was used as pretext by the regime to purge the older anti-Fascist generation in 1968] was something that was unacceptable for me; some of them were my good friends . . . so of course this [struggle] was, for my generation, one of the most important formative experiences.[50]

Individuals who left the party in 1956 or 1968 did not only recall these points of turmoil when they came to doubt the socialist state's capacity to enable a progressive politics; they also related them as moments when their former Communist autobiographies were thrown into crisis. In particular, they were faced with an inauthentic official anti-Fascist script with which they now refused to identify in public. Many began to question whether they could even retain personal stories of struggle and liberation given the power of any invocation of anti-Fascism to support a system they now considered degraded. Some thus began a systematic reassessment of their memories to discover which could be considered authentic and real, and which were bogus later inventions shaped by their support for a political system they now thought illegitimate. The change in the public narrative struck a blow to Mátyás's private understanding of anti-Fascism after the 1956 Uprising; no longer able to give his support to the state, after having seen left-wing colleagues violently treated, and even executed, for 'Fascist', 'counter-revolutionary' activities, he began to question whether the anti-Fascist framing of his life up until this point had been a sham. Despite having been saved from extermination as a Jew by the Red Army in early 1945, he wondered whether he had in fact been liberated by their arrival. The experience of a bastardized official anti-Fascist narrative after 1956 therefore provoked many to abandon anti-Fascist stories, even in private settings:

James: Did you use this word 'liberation'?

Mátyás: Naturally, absolutely. It was an everyday saying that 1945 was a liberation. There wasn't another word other than liberation for it in 1944–45.

James: How have you used the word 'liberation' since the collapse of Communism?

Mátyás: Already [in 1956] it became a confusing word as the consequence of the so-called 'liberation' was the destruction of the 1956 revolution. . . . When the propaganda started on 4 November 1956 that the destruction of the revolution was the 'second liberation of Hungary' – and I'm not exaggerating here – from that second onwards I didn't consider 1945 a liberation anymore. Because in that second, in 1956, we woke up to the fact that the Soviets were attacking the city and we didn't feel that they were liberating troops anymore. I wasn't disgusted with myself that I had called the arrival of the Red Army in 1945 a liberation, but [after 1956] I didn't use it anymore. It is complicated. Or it is very simple. Probably both. At Christmas 1944, when the Russians came and saved me and my mother's lives, was it not a liberation? What the hell was it, if it wasn't a liberation? That's all. I don't have anything more to say about it.

Many who abandoned the idea that Communism could be reformed after the experiences of 1956 and 1968 also dropped their anti-Fascist stories. As long as they believed that a more democratic form of socialism was possible, they had kept their anti-Fascist identities as these had provided a language through which they could critique the Communist state on its own terms and inspire constituencies within the party to try to reform it. Tomáš, for example, narrated his increasing disillusionment with political life from the late 1950s onwards alongside his attempt to purge his autobiography of its Communist credentials, which had previously facilitated a very successful career. Following his removal from an important management post for being too vocal about Khrushchev's revelations of Stalin's crimes, in 1961 he became a so-called 'half-citizen', confined to working in construction as a lorry driver. He was rehabilitated, but then, following the Prague Spring, which he had supported, he refused to sign a document stating that he approved of the crushing of the reform movement. He presented his subsequent life as an attempt to come to terms with the ideological commitments of his younger Communist self. At this point, in the late 1960s, he was attracted to the 'anti-political' movements of late Communist Czechoslovakia, which advocated withdrawing from political life and merely living by non-Communist values in the private sphere without threatening the state. He attempted to depoliticize himself, a process that distanced him from many of his former reform Communist friends:

> There were my friends who had the same life as me, who were in Dubček's government [i.e. reform Communists who supported 'socialism with a human face' in 1968] and today we don't understand each other at all, because they aren't able to overcome their pasts . . . they still say it was good when we [the reform Communists] were in power. I have problems with them. I don't go [to meet them] anymore because I don't understand them. I am not a Communist any more, but I'm not an anti-Communist. I am a *non-Communist*; it is more serious, an anti-Communist thinks in the same ideological way as a Communist. . . . I am liberated of Communist ideology and I am sure of it. . . . I don't understand them [i.e. my former Communist friends] and when the discussion ends we realize we are [back] at the beginning. There is no sense in it. So I have lost many of my friends. We have nothing to say to each other. It's very hard to bear . . . they still feel they have to uphold the ideology. I won't do it. . . . Arthur Koestler said it in 1944 when he announced at a conference in Paris that he was leaving the Communist movement. He said that everyone who had once been captured by an ideology and came to be disillusioned with it could be categorized into two camps. One who then joins the [. . .] ideology [opposed] to the one he formerly believed in, [such as] those who join the anti-Communists. And then the other type who [. . .] tries and struggles for the rest of his life to settle his disillusionment with his younger self. It is not just the Communist movement but all ideological movements; when the ideology crashes, they look for help from a new ideology. Not to look for a new ideology

requires self-reflection and very great effort, and it's really only a very small minority [who can do it].

Tomáš's autobiography as a heroic anti-Fascist partisan had helped him advance his career in the early Communist period. He now realized that he was implicated in allowing his own life story to be used to legitimize a state he had since turned against. Hence he rejected it: 'decorations are important only when you are going up in your career! As soon as you start going down all these decorations are bad for you. I heard from the security services [after 1989] that people said I had rejected my own biography.' Now excluded, and increasingly at odds ideologically with the regime, he wanted to destroy that part of his autobiography that had formerly been instrumental in his success. He did not want to hide his past as a partisan of the Slovak Uprising completely; instead, he sought a way of telling it that undermined the heroic Communist narrative of anti-Fascist struggle. He therefore recast the fight as a tragedy in which the partisans had been 'cannon fodder' for the Germans and in which his brother had been seriously wounded. He ridiculed those Communist leaders who traded on their partisan status, such as Gustáv Husák, undermining their claims to have been heroes of the Slovak Uprising in fighting against the German-supported regime. The partisans were no longer to be seen as heroic figures whose struggle eventually led to the creation of an anti-Fascist Communist state: they were tragic figures who had been poorly equipped, brutalized during the war, and had subsequently become the 'playthings of politics'. Tomáš's new version of events was thus an attempt to undermine the heroic version of history that he had previously been complicit in propagating, and that had been used to justify an illegitimate regime.[51] He was now able to relate his own personal past in a non-Communist fashion:

> The front was approaching; we were all evacuated, all over Slovakia. My brother was twenty so he had to join the partisan army. We met later in a hospital. He was badly wounded: we had fought against very experienced Germans troops and we had had only two days of training. We didn't know how to shoot. We didn't know how to clean our weapons. We were fighting against professionals. We were fighting two SS divisions badly decimated by war. And many of them were badly wounded . . . but they were used to fighting the partisans. They laughed at us. We were cannon fodder for their guns. My brother was disabled for the rest of his life. He was put at the front and shot to pieces. And ever since those Fascist trials [in 1949] I have had a completely different opinion about people's roles in the [Slovak] Uprising. In fact, I realized when I entered the army school, that we were the

absurd playthings of politics. They [the Communist regime] liked us [i.e. the partisans] because they could weep over our memory. But the partisans who left their units were later considered deserters and they suffered for it [i.e. under the Communist regime]. But one of the leaders who was in the Slovak Uprising – Gustáv Husák – hid himself with his friend who was a priest. He was warm, he was provided with meals and he was safe. He never suffered.

Although all the above respondents charted the purging of anti-Fascist language both from their personal and political lives, some were nevertheless prepared to use it in public curricula vitae in the late Communist period in order to preserve their careers. Here, the Hungarian Ágota, who had been a teacher, describes how she kept referring to the Communist liberation of Hungary from Fascism in order to keep her job:

James: When did the use of the word 'liberation' change?

Ágota: For me, after 1956 it slowly began to change, because my husband in 1955 had already been chucked out [of the party] . . . myself, I was already calling it an occupation (*megszállás*).

James: Did you use it after 1956?

Ágota: In teaching absolutely, if I wanted to keep my job. It was that kind of word, like 'table' or 'drink' – it was a word that meant that here the Russians had defeated the Germans. But for me the word no longer had any political content – this is still true today.[52]

For such individuals, the continued use of politically degraded anti-Fascist terminology in public was neither a compromise nor a betrayal of their older political struggles. They did not view these historical revisions as morally problematic because they saw themselves as politically disengaged. Moreover, because it had become meaningless, the idea of the anti-Fascist struggle and liberation could be publicly stated without implying that one was in league with the state or accepted its version of the past. It was simply the banal iteration of politically empty terms.

Thus, for some ex-Communists, 'coming to terms' with their pasts meant ridding themselves of the stories they had used to make sense of their lives in the 1940s and '50s. They had clung to their Communist autobiographies only as long as they were seen to represent the victory over Nazism and the chance to build a more progressive society. As soon as the anti-Fascist idea was stripped of its democratic content and came to represent the ideology of a degraded dictatorship, an anti-Fascist autobiography became the mark of a collaborator. For these ex-Communists, the post-Communist life could not draw upon 'anti-Fascist' narratives: a 'democratic autobiography' now required them to rid their life stories of an ideological framework that had once structured the way they had understood their lives.

Remaking a Democratic Communist Autobiography?

Zdeněk: It was thanks to our generation that the regime collapsed. . . . It was our generation that tried to criticize first; we demanded changes while other people compromised themselves. . . . After '68, when I was thrown out of the economic institute, I went to about thirty-five companies where I applied for jobs that would have been appropriate for my level of education. It was hopeless. . . . You can't blame a child for his behaviour [i.e. when he joined the party as a young man]. . . . I would feel guilty if, at the moment when I started to understand things, I continued to behave badly. . . . The young generation haven't lived all that – they have problems understanding it. I know families where children were saying to their parents, 'How could you join such a party? How could you do that?' But of course they already know what we didn't know.[53]

Not all of those who removed themselves from the Communist movement gave up on their old autobiographies in order to 'become democratic': they thought that anti-Fascism could be reclaimed from its dictatorial associations and remade for a liberal democratic era.[54] Like Czech left-wing economist Zdeněk, they said they represented an alternative political tradition of struggle which 'demanded changes', while others 'compromised themselves'; hence they could claim a major contribution to the eventual collapse of the regime. Anti-Fascism for them represented a democratic tradition of struggle against dictatorships of both the right (in 1945) and the left (in 1956 and 1968), which anticipated the collapse in 1989. Thus their anti-Fascism allowed them to show themselves to have been democrats 'in advance'. The impetus for reframing anti-Fascism in this positive way was often explained as the need to educate a younger generation who had only been brought up on anti-Communism, and did not understand the importance of the struggle against Fascism to the eventual realization of democracy in their country.

These respondents presented the most complex evolution of their autobiographies. Following their disillusionment with Communism in 1956 and 1968, they had erased anti-Fascism from their life stories as it appeared to legitimize an unwanted state; once Communism had collapsed, however, it was revived and deployed politically to show the importance of anti-Fascism to the development of democracy. They did not produce one 'true' account of their lives, but rather reflected on the multiple ways in which they had constructed their autobiographies in different political environments. This was particularly the case in Hungary, where reform socialists had purged their anti-Fascist stories in the wake of the 1956 Uprising, when they were seen as legitimizing dictatorship, but revived them after 1989 as they sought to explain the left's contribution to the growth of democracy in twentieth-century Hungary.[55] This case will be considered below.

After the suppression of the 1956 Uprising, many Hungarian reform Communists left the party and rejected all aspects of their political autobiographies. Some turned towards a private life and 'tamed' their political pasts, wanting neither to politicize their children through the memory of anti-Fascism and resistance, nor to allow their political pasts to impact on their careers.[56] Autobiographies told both in public and private during the late Communist period were often designed to insulate individuals and their families from politics, and to ensure a prosperous apolitical life. Any manipulation of the past was acceptable as long as it protected the private sphere. Some former Communists chose to silence, or depoliticize, their life stories in the private sphere while continuing to display fealty to the anti-Fascist idea in public in order to safeguard their careers or avoid discrimination.[57] Thus, their relationship to the liberation in 1945, or to the 'authentic anti-Fascist struggle' in 1956, was hidden from the younger generation.

Károly had set up a new reformed socialist party in his locality in October 1956, had contact with Imre Nagy, the leader of the government during the Uprising, been imprisoned, faced execution and had been spared. Despite this earlier revolutionary life, he maintained silence about 1956 whenever possible: he claimed to have talked about it only once in the entire late Communist period. His children were aware that their father had been under political surveillance. Not wanting to radicalize them, however, Károly refrained from telling them about what had happened to him until the late 1980s. In fact, he only admitted involvement in official workplace reviews, which had required him to outline his life story, and where the omission of his participation in the Uprising might have been discovered and left him open to dismissal:

James: Did you talk later with your family or friends about 1956?
Károly: There was a classmate of mine with whom I had graduated and we
          were on especially good terms, and in 1963 – by that time I was

already thirty-seven – we went out for a two-day walking holiday, and there I told him everything. He listened with dismay – he was the first [I told]. . . . Otherwise I never really brought it up.

No, it was an interesting thing, at just about the time when the system changed [in 1989], my children reproached me that they had never known anything about what had happened to me; it was not a subject we had discussed at home. When I was set free from the prison, for years a car stood outside my home every night . . . even with this going on we never talked about it, but they were small children. Even much later it wasn't a subject for discussion – even when things settled down [in the 1970s] – my children always knew there was something, but it was not a subject for discussion. Then in 1987–88, when they were already adults, and had families, then they asked what was what.[58]

However, after 1989, some Hungarian ex-Communists revived these memories when they were faced with newly dominant right-wing 'anti-anti-Fascist voices' which dismissed the importance of all aspects of the anti-Fascist experience – including the liberation of Hungary from Fascism – because it was associated with an ideology that had been used to legitimize Communist rule.[59] For anti-Communists, leftist ideology could only be associated with dictatorship and the suppression of democratic movements such as the 1956 Uprising.[60] Jenő, who had been a party member between 1947 and 1956, remembered the way in which all anti-Fascist experiences were delegitimized after 1989. Here, he discusses the difficulties of acknowledging the role that the Soviet army and the Hungarian left had played in ending Fascism in Hungary:

James: Is it difficult to speak about the [Red Army] 'liberation' today?

Jenő: Today it is much more difficult, because society violently denies that it was a liberation and attacks the idea. I naturally approve of the fact that it is no longer obligatory to call 1945 a liberation, as it was under the Communist regime. But saying 'liberation' shouldn't be forbidden, or made almost impossible to say. Here it is a real problem, because the Jews and the left-wingers felt it was a liberation as the arrival of the Russians and their driving out of the Germans made life much easier, because danger to one's life or the danger of losing one's freedom ended. [But] a large part of the population didn't experience it like that.[61]

He was also shocked to discover that what he had seen as a legitimate reform socialist struggle against Stalinism in 1956 was now attacked by the post-Communist right:

James: Are there debates about 1956 today?

Jenő: Of course, there are debates again. But now we are not primarily debating whether it was a counter-revolution: they [i.e. right-wingers] want to falsify other things. Before 1989, the Kádár system presented it as a counter-revolution – now the right describes the revolution in just about the same way, but for them this is not a negative but rather a positive sign. They say it was an anti-Bolshevik, anti-socialist revolution and everyone wanted to go back to before 1945, to the [semi-feudal] Horthy era. . . . They say that we called ourselves reform Communists, and they say that we weren't really on the side of the revolution, we really remained true Communists and we only wanted to change things just a bit in the interests of the Communist system. According to them, we didn't have a role in the revolution, we merely ascribed ourselves a leading revolutionary role.

Hungarian reform Communists were faced with the charge that they had, in essence, collaborated with the system; their acts of resistance were viewed as unimportant tinkerings at the margins, and as ideologically suspect. The post-Communist right, who viewed Communism per se as illegitimate (rather than just its Stalinist variant) and the Communist government as an occupying power, argued that only those who attempted to end left-wing rule and eject the Soviet presence were real revolutionaries. Thus, the role of reform Communists in the Hungarian Uprising was denigrated, and only those on the right who wanted to destroy Communism wholesale were deemed to be authentic revolutionaries whose memory was worthy of commemoration after 1989. These ex-party members thus revived their stories of liberation and the 1956 revolution in order to present themselves as democrats who had fought against dictatorships all their lives. They saw themselves as the harbingers of democracy: they had opposed Fascism in 1945, resisted Stalinism in 1956 and refused to support a corrupted Communist state after 1956. To make these personal accounts believable, some respondents recognized the need for a new type of anti-Fascist language that did not remind other Hungarians of Communist propaganda, but rather evoked sympathy for the personal suffering of Jews and those on the left. In reviving the story of his 'liberation', which he had suppressed during the Kádár era for fear of echoing a degraded anti-Fascist script, one respondent no longer characterized Soviet troops as 'liberators' but rather as 'life-savers':

James: Do you remember when you heard that the Russian army was getting close to Budapest?

Mátyás: We were overjoyed. It's absolutely clear. There wasn't any type of ideology or political requirement [to say], 'The liberators came', but today this has become a worn-out phrase, so now one can say, 'The life-savers came'. If somebody is drowning in water, if somebody throws them a life-ring, then you don't think about the ideological basis on which they threw it to you; it's that simple. The Arrow Cross wanted to wipe us out, they wanted to slaughter us; the Russians came, they saved our lives.

Károly had refused to speak about his involvement in the 1956 Uprising in the late Communist period; he now revived its memory in order to establish that it was he and his kind, not his right-wing critics, who were the real revolutionaries who had striven for the change that anticipated the arrival of liberal democracy in 1989. He argued that whereas he had struggled (and suffered in prison in 1957) to reform the socialist system, conservatives such as Cardinal Mindszenty should be remembered as having fought in 1956 with the aim of restoring the 'reactionary', less democratic, semi-feudal Hungary of the prewar era, but with the consequence of having scared Moscow into military intervention:

On 23 October, when the revolution broke out in Budapest, then with my friend and one other person, we went to party headquarters. . . . There was a very broad political palette on display – from Imre Nagy to the extreme right – but right to the end I was on the left of the revolution. I still believed in socialism, but it didn't have to be done in the way it was being done, it could have been reformed. Ours was the biggest, most threatening form of resistance and, interestingly, those who attacked [the system] from within were always the most dangerous. We got information about how to set up a new left-wing party, and in only an hour and a half we started our discussions. We were in a rather optimistic mood . . . in the afternoon we received a working-class delegation from Miskolc [a city in northeastern Hungary] and we went and saw Imre Nagy with them. That was an alarming meeting, because the old man was clearly uninformed and incapable of doing anything. . . . It was 1 November when we went back to our town and set up a new party organization.

. . . We were shocked by Mindszenty's speech;[62] even today I have a very poor opinion of him. Certainly his trial was illegal, but I considered him to be a habitual, consistent reactionary – much more than just a conservative – who hurt us [i.e. the revolutionaries] a lot in 1956. Of course, even without him the revolution would have come to an end, but he really harmed the movement. . . .

We were sharply anti-Soviet, and when suddenly the Soviets came back . . . on 4 November, at dawn, I was woken at my flat and some civilian police with sub-machine guns appeared. At that time, I didn't know that the Russians had come back; they came in and they took me away. I believed at that time that extreme right-wing elements had come [to my flat] because the revolution had become divided politically, because there were those who were strongly anti-Communist. Because I stood on a socialist platform, they didn't like it. Only when I was inside the police station did it turn out that this was not the case; rather, the old regime had come back and they wanted to execute me. The leader of our county informed my wife that they would execute me, and then, after I had sat there for a bit, they transferred me to prison and my time inside began.[63]

Thus, after 1989, some ex-party members tried to 'democratize their autobiographies', not by purging them of anti-Fascism but rather by reviving the anti-Fascist framings they had abandoned in the late Communist period. They wanted to show that anti-Fascism had been an ideology that fostered resistance to the Communist regime as much as it inspired collaboration with it. For them, there was a genuine left-wing anti-Fascist tradition, distinct from the corruptions of Stalinism and Kádárism, which had consistently fought for a more democratic Hungary.

Clinging On to the Communist Autobiography

For some, the Communist life story had never gone away. Even after 1989, they still reproduced it in the form in which they had initially constructed it in the 1940s and 1950s. Despite the ideological challenges of 1956 and 1968, and the collapse of Communism, they still 'clung on': the maintenance of their earlier autobiography was an expression of resistance to the values of the post-Communist world. These were former party members who refused to accept newly dominant liberal democratic discourses in which Communism was presented as an aberration from the nation's journey to freedom and democracy, or as a fundamentally anti-democratic, criminal idea. Rather, they still viewed Communism as central to the country's progressive and democratic development. They believed either that Communism was a necessary stage in the expansion of democracy in central-eastern Europe, or that Communism still contained within it the potential to be more democratic than the form of liberal democracy and market economy that emerged after 1989. Like all the respondents above, they believed that they had to produce an autobiography that celebrated democracy; however, they contended that the continued championing of Communist-era values and stories was essential to that appreciation. They still believed that their class-based, anti-Fascist stories were a powerful form of democratic expression that could be used to critique the historical misunderstandings or the anti-democratic features of the post-1989 world.

Judit, a Hungarian Jewish woman from Budapest, continued to frame her life in anti-Fascist terms after 1989. She had suffered under the German occupation and then Arrow Cross rule; her mother's family had been deported to Auschwitz and their home had been confiscated. She had celebrated the role that the Red Army had played in liberating Hungary, saving her and her remaining relatives from deportation, and had joined the party immediately after the war at thirteen (having lied about her age). She had left it in 1954, but had wanted to rejoin after 1956, ultimately deciding against doing so in the light of her domestic responsibilities and her inability to play an active role. Her husband rejoined, however, and remained an engaged member until the 1980s. After 1989, she continued to refer to the arrival of the Red Army in 1945 as an anti-Fascist liberation, and criticized those in contemporary Hungary who saw it only as an occupation:

the only thing, in my mind, was that the Russians were Communists and they gave us freedom, I thought it is my duty to be attached to them . . . without my parents' knowledge, I joined the Communist Party, despite the fact that I was thirteen, and I said that I was sixteen. . . . I was very enthusiastic, because it was freedom for us that the Russians came. Absolutely, freedom. I love it [the Soviet liberation monument on Gellért Hill, Budapest]. . . . it was a stupid thing to remove the Red Army soldiers [after 1989][64] because they now say it was not a 'liberation'. . . . Now they say it was an occupation, but for the Jews it was absolutely a liberation.[65]

Judit accepted the arrival of liberal democracy in Hungary, but rejected the common post-1989 view that Communism had been a 'historical detour' or aberration from the natural course of liberal democratic development. For her, Communism had provided a necessary protection against reactionary conservative anti-Semitic forces, at least in the decades following World War II. She accepted the state's claim that the Communists were the strongest defenders of the region against the return of Fascism, and was prepared to deploy her own autobiography to prove that this was the case.

Unlike others who had abandoned the party after 1956, she accepted the state's assertion that the Uprising's suppression was a necessity. Indeed, she continued to present the Uprising as a counter-revolutionary anti-Semitic movement that had to be put down by Soviet troops. She rejected the idea that it had been a brave attempt to democratize socialism or to attain liberal democracy, and ridiculed those who claimed to be its heroes now:

James: So before 1956, were you often afraid?

Judit: I don't remember [being afraid]. But on 23 October '56, the first day [of the Uprising] my mother was working near the Stalin statue and she came home by foot. On the first day she was attacked on the street as a Jew. There came a group and they spat on my mother, saying, 'You ugly Jew!' And after that we were glad we were living near to the Russian embassy, on Bajza Utca, and that Russian tanks were there, because an anti-Semitic movement was taking shape underground. . . . We felt more secure with the Russians. But that is an absolutely Jewish point of view. Absolutely. I don't know whether the others felt the same but . . . it was rumoured that the Fascists were moving against the Jews again. . . . But a lot of Jews left the country [in the emigration during and after the 1956 Uprising], not only because of Communism, but also because they were afraid that 'something' could begin again.

James: Most people say the opposite about the Russian tanks.

Judit: Yes, I can imagine. I know. It is my personal view.

James: So can you remember what you thought when the Russian tanks came in?

Judit: It's a difficult question to answer. My feeling was that we were more secure, but I don't know how to explain it after so many years.

James: What did you say about '56 itself?

Judit: You know, nowadays, people say that they were heroes in '56, when I know for certain that they were nothing, they had nothing to do with '56. It was the very same thing that after the war, in Hungary, loads of people claimed to be partisans. But during the war there weren't really any. And it is the very same thing. Nowadays they are saying they are heroes of '56, when there were not so many of them.

Judit held on to her anti-Fascist autobiography because she had seen Communism as a necessary stage in the country's historical development after the experience of Fascism, though she thought it had now rightfully been replaced with liberal democracy because Fascism was no longer a threat. Others, however, saw 1989 as representing the illegitimate imposition of a liberal, capitalist system, and it was in this context that their autobiographies remained dominated by the stories that had justified Communist rule. They thus refused to reform their life stories to accommodate themselves to the demands of a liberal democratic system. Olga was one such respondent. She came from a poor mining family and considered her own upward mobility – she had become a journalist and writer – to be the result of living under a socialist system. She viewed the collapse of Communism as signalling an end to working-class social mobility and hence as a 'betrayal of the proletariat'. She believed that capitalism had not been popularly desired in 1989 but rather imposed from the 'west'; hence, it was an illegitimate revolution. Although she was glad that the hardline regime that had controlled Czechoslovakia since 1968 had ended, she nonetheless saw the immediate adoption of capitalism and liberalism as an unsupported imposition:

It's nonsense talking about 'Communism', it was *socialism* and it represented hope for humanity; it meant that children would have the opportunities that I had [i.e. to transcend their backgrounds]. In 1989, nobody wanted the restitution of the capitalist system. We have witnessed the 'downfall of the proletariat'. . . . My relatives, they are all suffering again. In our newspaper I read some analysis saying if some child is very smart but from a working family then he has no chance, no possibility of getting a good job, a good position, because his parents do not have connections, do not know people. Today it's one of the most important things to have connections. It's called social capital. These simple people, poor people they don't have it. . . . Some of these [working] people are really primitive, some of them have a very high natural intelligence but they had the bad luck to be born into certain families in which they had no support.

She thus refused to alter her autobiography as so many others had done. Asked about her family at the start of the interview, she immediately wrote herself into a narrative common to many Communist countries: she was a member of an oppressed class who found personal liberation and cultural uplift under the Communist state:

James: And can you tell me when and where you were born?
Olga: 1935. In Ostrava. It was the steel heart of the republic. It was the most important town . . . there were mines and steel factories.

James: And can you tell me something about your family background?

Olga: My grandparents knew how to read and write, they had a lot of children, lived in a miners' baracks. That's where I lived when I was young, with eight to twelve people living in one room. . . . My mother's sisters were hospital cleaners . . . one of them eventually became head nurse. This was possible only during socialism. They worked well and they got the qualification and that was why it was possible.

Asked about her family life, she used the opportunity to relate the moment of her anti-Fascist awakening, aged only seven and a half, when she witnessed her parents' reluctance to provide aid for German troops at Stalingrad. She then gave an account of her liberation by Soviet troops, an experience that was later confirmed in its meaning for her in a Soviet propaganda film. Even after 1989, the way in which she recounted her early experiences was still fused with early Communist-era anti-Fascist narratives:

James: So can you tell me a little bit about your experiences with your family?

Olga: I remember Stalingrad. I was seven and a half years old and . . . there were people collecting underwear for the German army in our miners' colony. I felt the tension between my parents and this man [who was collecting]. It's interesting that a little child can feel the tension between two people, even if they are speaking normal words like 'good morning' . . . my parents looked at each other and my mum wanted to say something but my father signalled to her not to say anything in front of me. . . .

It was spring, the end of April [in 1945, i.e. the point of libera-tion] . . . very sunny . . . there was a Russian soldier walking . . . he was really like Gagarin . . . he was smiling, it was like a film . . . . we didn't have much . . . [but] the houses had gardens and there were people coming in and bringing him flowers . . . lots of flowers, narcissi. . . . In our house in one room, there were eight Russian soldiers. They were really very polite and nice people. And they bought me red shoes as a present. . . . *At Dawn, It's Quiet Here*:[66] it's the title of a very famous Russian film [in which] the young Russian women who are fighting in the war are all beautiful . . . but in reality all the female Russian soldiers were not nice women at all. And once I saw my father – they looked like witches, these women – and he felt embarrassed. He just smiled at them, but it was

> an embarrassed smile . . . they probably didn't have the time to take
> care of themselves . . . but that is the only negative thing I can say
> about Russian soldiers.

For both Judit and Olga, the anti-Fascist autobiographies into which they had
been socialized during the early Communist period remained pertinent to
their post-1989 political standpoints: they refused to rid their autobiographies
of anti-Fascism because they were unwilling to categorize the Communist
past as an aberration or as criminal. For Olga, anti-Fascism still meant the
possibility of social equality and opportunity superior to what was offered
under liberal democracy and capitalism; for Judit, anti-Fascism represented
protection from persecution, with the Communist anti-Fascist state a necessary stage in her country's democratic development.

Conclusion

Those who joined the Communist parties of central-eastern Europe were socialized both to consider the world in terms of the anti-Fascist and class struggles,
and to see their autobiographies as important sites where these political beliefs
should be expressed. Family stories were crafted to illustrate the victory of the
working class over Fascism and its agents, the bourgeoisie. Yet these autobiographies were also the product of a particular era. It was only those who joined the
party in the 1940s and 1950s who were drawn wholeheartedly into these
processes, absorbed the state's claim to represent these struggles and experienced
Fascism at sufficiently close hand to find the appeal to construct their entire life
stories around the concept of anti-Fascism meaningful and convincing. By the
mid-1960s, anti-Fascism as a mobilizing idea that could create a powerful bond
between state and party members was in decline. In Czechoslovakia, for instance,
a 1965 internal government report raised the concern that the younger generation, who had never experienced the struggle against Fascism or 'the consequent
class war', were 'politically handicapped'.[67] Indeed, from the late 1960s an attempt
to raise the profile of anti-Fascism attested to this crisis in historical legitimization: many regimes in the region began to authorize the publication of the
memoirs of old anti-Fascist combatants as a 'fighting instrument' with which to
inspire a new generation who had not lived through Fascism.[68] As a result, those
interviewees who had joined the party after 1968 did not need to 'come to terms'
with their Communist-era autobiographies as those from the postwar generation
did.[69] Often, they had not been pressurized to identify their own stories with
those of the state's anti-Fascist or class-based public histories; and even when
they were, these procedures were often regarded as ideologically empty iterations

of Communist formulas, rather than as a significant interweaving of private and public selves. Such interviewees did not need to remove parts from, or reformulate, their histories.

Jarosław, for example, came from minor nobility in southern Poland who had lost most of their property by the time of the Communist period. He had joined the Polish Workers' Party in the mid-1960s. The emphatic anti-Fascist and class-based ideology of the postwar period was gone, and therefore as a prospective party member he did not need to write himself into these older stories in order to be fully accepted within the party: as such, his upper-class 'patriotic' background was no longer a hindrance. He presented his journey into the party not as a process of autobiographical transformation, as the postwar generation had done, but rather as the story of the Communist state relaxing its autobiographical demands and accepting individuals with a wide range of backgrounds who were not forced to deny their own pasts and adopt a Communist persona. When asked about his family, he simply related the story of their decline and their proud resistance against the Russians in the nineteenth century, and the Communist state's acceptance of a biography it would earlier have found deeply problematic:

James: Can you tell me something about your family background?

Jarosław: My father's family were minor nobility in the nineteenth century and had land and property. One of my grandfathers, with his sons, went to the forest to participate in the January Uprising against the Russians in 1863 . . . . the town's authorities were going to confiscate their property so he handed over the deeds to a French teacher of ours who wouldn't give them back when my grandfather returned from exile [from Siberia] . . . . soon after he died, but one of the sons survived. He returned and started to work in construction and got enough money to buy a small farm, not very far from the old property, so they had perhaps about seven or eight hectares of land. . . . On my mother's side it was a different story . . . they had family property somewhere close to Kraków and lost it simply through debts . . . . there was no dramatic story, at least that I remember. But one of my mother's cousins, in the 1970s, had her wedding at Wawel Cathedral [in Kraków] and placed all our old family heraldic symbols on the door . . . you had to prove your nobility and show all the certificates of the family . . . it was completely ridiculous. We needed swords but of course we didn't have any at home, but they wanted a great performance in the cathedral, because they had been part of the nobility . . . . you know that was the time [the 1970s] when we turned to our national roots, and for the first time the people with noble origins started to look through genealogical books and put their heraldic symbols on the walls.[70]

Unlike Jarosław, those who joined the Communist Party in the immediate postwar period had created Communist life stories that were considered 'biographies of collaboration' after 1989. 'Coming to terms' with the past required a rethinking of the anti-Fascist stories through which they had learnt to make sense of their earlier lives. Just as in the 1940s, when they wrote teleological stories in which all the relationships and events of their early life were channelled into a linear narrative that ended with their involvement with the Communist Party, so after 1989 they wrote stories in which their lives anticipated their attachment to liberal democratic ideals. For some ex-party members, anti-Fascism was a degraded idea that had been used to legitimize dictatorship; thus, the story of becoming democratic required a compelling account of how they had erased the way they had formerly understood their lives. For others, anti-Fascism had provided a language of resistance against the excesses of both Fascism and Communism; for them, it could be revived, relieved of its associations with dictatorship, and be used to support the idea that the anti-Fascist left had made the largest contribution to the democratic struggles of central-eastern Europe against the tyrannies of both right and left. Whereas once they had written life stories in which they were anti-Fascist fighters for the Communist system, they were now anti-dictatorial fighters whose struggles anticipated the arrival of democracy in 1989.

CHAPTER SIX

VICTIMS' STORIES

The stories of those individuals and groups who were victimized and excluded under Communist regimes took centre stage in post-Communist central-eastern Europe. For some, the late 1980s marked the moment when the stories of the oppressed could finally be recovered after years of public silence. The collection of these life stories was seen as providing a direct link to the realities of life under Communism; a growing fascination with biography, combined with a suspicion of public narratives, led to a valorization of the individual story of suffering as a means of gaining access to previously hidden truths about the Communist past.[1] Oral historians were often at the forefront of this movement, producing many accounts of deportees, Gulag survivors and female victims of Communism.[2] This culture that foregrounded and commemorated victimhood under Communism was rapidly contested, however. For others, the growth and power of the victim's story was not so much the telling of previously repressed histories, but rather a product of new political imperatives in which democratizing, westernizing societies encouraged their citizens to re-imagine themselves as victims of a fallen dictatorship. Critics claimed it was not merely those who had been seriously persecuted who claimed victim status, but also large swathes of society who had had more complex relationships with Communist regimes.[3] Some who held this view identified the emergence of such victim stories as indicative of a lamentable failure of society to come to terms with the complex compromises that individuals had been forced to make with the previous regime. Rather than acknowledging their varied roles as bystanders, collaborators and the persecuted, individuals were said to be seeking to present themselves only as victims. Others, however, viewed this post-hoc reframing of experiences as a healthy process, through which people were encouraged to see themselves as having lived under a criminal system that victimized individuals by denying them rights; through the construction of new life stories as victims, citizens democratized themselves and hence distanced themselves from the values of dictatorship.[4]

Although nationalists encouraged post-Communist citizens to view themselves as national martyrs under Communism, and new liberal voices promoted the notion that citizens had now been rescued from a situation in which they had been victimized by a criminal regime that had deprived them of democratic rights, post-Communist life stories of those who lived through the Communist period suggested that many did not embrace the identity of 'victim of Communism'. This was true even for those who had suffered, or were discriminated against, on account of their class or political background; although there were many who wanted to bear witness to the punishment and exclusion they had experienced, equally there were many who did not and who sought to downplay what they had lived through. The question of whether to draw on personal stories of marginalization under Communism was for many a political issue, related both to their relationship to the Communist state before 1989, and to their attitude to the dominant 'victim culture' that emerged after the collapse of Communism. Some did not want their lives reduced to that of victim of Communist criminality; others sought to align their experiences to dominant anti-Communist accounts of the past.

The decision to recall one's own exclusion or victimization under the Communist state was not simply a matter of the individual's willingness to confirm accounts of Communist violence and criminality; these stories were part of much wider biographical frameworks within which individuals understood their lives. Those who embraced the 'victim's story' were mainly from nationalist and Catholic backgrounds: they testified to their sufferings after 1989 in order to assert that they were the ones who had assumed the heroic role of preserving national values in a time of foreign occupation, who had refused to collaborate and who had been victimized as a consequence. For them, making their suffering public in this way was evidence of their resilience in this mission. Moreover, far more ambiguous experiences of Communism were incorporated into these frameworks; even stories of social mobility and professional success were seen as evidence of victimization.[5] Others rejected the adoption of victimhood because, although they themselves might have suffered, they viewed the recollection of suffering as a politicized and contrived activity that allowed the teller to gloss over more complex relationships that they or others had had with the Communist state. They disliked the way in which victims' stories had been hijacked by the right, and did not want their own lives reduced to accounts of anti-Communist martyrdom. They often composed themselves as 'anti-victims': i.e. those who had suffered and been marginalized, but refused to see themselves as victims either before or after 1989. Their autobiographies were built around this refusal to identify with dominant narratives.[6]

The Anti-Communist Life Story

The life stories of many who came from anti-Communist families focused on experiences that illustrated their victimization under Communism. Despite having autobiographies that demonstrated the complexity of their lives under the former system – experiences of social mobility, periods of discrimination and moments of resistance – their post-Communist identities were bound up with framing all of these as part of their suffering, and many life stories began from this starting point. The dominance of the story of the victim of Communism after 1989 meant that these narratives were often seen as uncontroversial and self-evident by their narrators, and requiring no further explanation or justification. István, who came from a family of noble origins who had lost their wealth prior to the Communist period, began his life story as follows:

James: And could you tell me something about your family background?

István: Well, we were class enemies. No, I mean, I have a title. We have had a title going back to the sixteenth century. But my father had no estate. He actually worked for his living. My mother ran a dress shop. In '51, there were deportations, *I don't have to explain it to you* [my emphasis]. I wanted to avoid being deported and it seemed a better idea to go off on my own accord to work on a socialist construction site as an unskilled labourer, which I did for two years and a bit .... nobody asked too many questions if one turned up and said one wanted to work here. So one could get lost in socialist construction. I was actually doing a junior technician's job. Calculating angles and radiuses and marking out railway lines and things like that. But technically I remained an unskilled labourer paid 2.08 forints an hour. That was nice [*laughs*]. [We] tried to find some way of going, not quite underground, but getting out of sight of the authorities, and this was somewhere where it was possible. . . . It was quite obvious that I was going to be deported. I was a class enemy. Anyone who was titled was ipso facto a class enemy. Very easy. If you know your Communist ideology. So I've nothing more to add to it. The basic point is that being a class enemy in Communist society was the equivalent of being a Jew in Nazi Germany. You were a second-class citizen. You could be treated like dirt. Okay, we weren't actually gassed. [In autumn 1953] I was called up and the next two years I was doing my national service.

In '55, I was arrested. Basically they had taken two years to get round to it, and I should never have been in the air force. I should have been in the labour corps. Because at the time of my call-up, my papers said here is an unskilled labourer working on a socialist construction site, and somehow [I] looked like a basically reliable person. I was interrogated and there was the usual offer that if I was willing to co-operate they would drop the case. I would return to my unit and be demobbed and then all I had to do was to work as an informer as and when instructed. So they had a deadline, because if I accepted, everything had to look normal – I had to get back to the unit on time and so on. And I didn't accept the offer so then I was brought up to the Fő utca prison[7] and then tried, given two years, and deprived of my staggeringly high rank of corporal. And then spent from November '55 to the end of October '56 in various prisons, well, mainly camps, actually. Why didn't I accept their offers [to work as an informer]? Well, it's not the sort of offer one accepts. Period. One doesn't work for them. And particularly when it's put in terms of 'owing to your background you will find it easy to gain the confidence of people whom we ask you to find out about'. Hardly the sort of role one plays. And it was easy for me, I was a single young man; much more difficult for somebody who has a wife and children and a job.[8]

Many of those who came from nationalist or Catholic anti-Communist families did not merely present themselves as witnesses to, or victims of, the violent criminality of the Communist period, but also ascribed to their persecution a wider purpose. They had suffered not just because of their backgrounds but because they had refused to 'give in' to the Communist state. They saw themselves as representatives of the nation, who had a historic mission to preserve national values within their families from contamination by left-wing ideology until Communism eventually collapsed. In their post-Communist accounts, they claimed that they had been marginalized precisely because they refused to collaborate or to demonstrate any form of ideological allegiance to the Communist state. Their victimization thus confirmed their fortitude and resilience, and was proof of their determination to ensure that national values endured during a period of occupation by a foreign ideology and its local 'traitorous left-wing collaborators'.[9]

Nationalist anti-Communists related their autobiographies after 1989 because the latter were viewed as *the* space where the stories of the nation had been preserved in the face of a Communist culture that had attempted to destroy them.[10] Family stories, related in private settings, had been constructed as places where traditions were maintained, to be passed on to a new generation.[11] Thus, after 1989, nationalists still had a reason to produce these personal accounts, which combined their ancestors' fates with the destiny of the nation. Stories were told of relatives who had fought for national freedom or suffered under foreign occupation. Józef, for instance, started his family's story with their involvement in 'Polish resistance' during World War II, detailing his parents' involvement in the nationalist Home Army who had fought against both the Nazis and Bolsheviks for Poland. He connected his family's history of struggle against foreign occupiers to their refusal to collaborate under the Communist regime:

James: Tell me about your family.

Józef: Well, my mother is a Polish teacher and my father is an engineer. During the war, which is very important in Poland, my parents were fighting in the Home Army for Polish independence. My father was a soldier with the Home Army and he took part in the Warsaw Uprising. My mother was a member of the 'Grey Ranks' . . . and they participated in the Warsaw Uprising . . . . until 1956 I was surrounded by this atmosphere of fear, which I remember at the time. For example, as a child I once saw a woman in the street who was selling cheese, a village woman, you know, a simple woman who was selling cheese in the street and I saw a police officer taking her off the street and I was absolutely sure that this was the end of that woman's life, that she would be taken somewhere and killed. And that was my idea of what the authorities did to people, so I remember at that time I had a strong feeling that the authorities that ruled this country were completely alien to me, that I had nothing to do with them. . . . We cannot say that my father's career was an easy one but it was mainly just the fact that he was never a member of the Communist Party and that he once fought with the Home Army.[12]

Through telling stories in private and familial settings, a different vision of the nation and political organization could be transmitted and maintained. In the face of the requirement for all Communist citizens to present their life histories publicly as part of longer-term accounts of class and anti-Fascist struggles (see Chapter 5), nationalists often composed autobiographies at home that wrote their own experiences of endurance and victimization under the Communist state into broader family tales, which drew upon their ancestors' earlier attempts to represent the nation in the face of occupation or left-wing radicalism. While Communist public narratives encouraged individuals to rethink their family's experience within politically appropriate templates, anti-Communist life stories were constructed along similar lines as an 'autobiographical defence'. Thus, even those nationalists who were deeply opposed to the Communist state and sought to withdraw from its ideological realm were shaped by the early Communist state's politicization of the autobiography: they produced life stories in private that integrated their family history into the anti-Communist struggle, thus echoing – but simultaneously reversing – the formulas that they had been taught to produce in public Communist-era curricula vitae. These narratives often documented distant forebears who had fought to preserve traditions and values in the face of hostile regimes in a manner that mirrored the tellers' own later struggles under Communism. Bálint began his life story with an extended account of his family's patriotic past, in which his heroic and victimized ancestors anticipated the dilemmas that conservatives living under Communism would face, and provided moral exemplars for their instruction:

James: Could you tell me something about your family background?

Bálint: Well, we are an ancient Hungarian family, our ancestors came from the Adriatic coast . . . and my family was pushed up to the north of Bratislava, and that was the – so to say – border between the Turkish-ruled area and the Austro-Hungarian part, and around that border there were always clashes between Turkish military patrols, little groups of Turkish soldiers, and on the other side the Austro-Hungarian kingdom, and my ancestors took part in those fights, trying to hinder the Turks' progress to Vienna. And for their dedication some members of the family were granted special rights. . . . Let me start with an ancestor of ours who fought in 1809 in the Battle of Győr on the side of the Austro-Hungarian monarchy against Napoleon . . . . forty years later, in 1849, he fought on the side of the Hungarians against the Austrians . . . . then, it was in '49 [i.e. *1849*] or '50 that he was arrested, sentenced and, in '62, he was pardoned and had his property returned. So he was the first one. . . . Well, my grandfather was a ministerial counsellor in the Ministry of Finance after World War I and [he was] declared an enemy of the people [under the Béla Kun Communist Republic], and was arrested and imprisoned in the cellar of the Hungarian parliament, waiting to be executed. His ministerial aide managed through friends of his to make sure my grandfather could escape. ... I was fourteen when he died, but he was never prepared to relate anything about the circumstances of his escape .... so being arrested [and] political resistance, it is, so to say, endemic in our family .... in 1950, I was arrested, having worked for the United Nations, on the charge of having spied for them ... the United Nations was considered as a cover for Anglo-American imperialism. The public prosecutor argued for the death penalty. With God's help I was given only a life sentence, and I spent six years and three months in a political prison for the regime's greatest enemies. So I just wanted to characterize the attitude of our family through, I should say, through 150 years. That [we were] always on the side of the nation and never inspired by personal interests. Always in favour of the country, of the nation. We were never involved in politics at all. My generation, my parents' generation, no one, political involvement was something strange. Irrespective of the political tendency – National Socialism or Communism or whatever – we were patriots and Christians. Our conviction was that we were not experts in the field of politics, and if you are not experts in the field of something then you should not deal with it.[13]

Conservatives' attempts to preserve national traditions, in the face of what they regarded as an alien anti-national Bolshevik ideology, was central to their post-Communist life stories. They recalled how they had sought to retire from the public sphere after the Communist takeovers of the late 1940s, to withdraw into private settings and to remove from their lives any temptation to collaborate with what they perceived as a foreign occupying regime. The assertion that they had been victims of, and had not engaged with, or been contaminated by, the Communist regime was far more important for them than it was for any other interviewees. To assimilate in any way was to betray their mission to preserve national values. Thus, their stories often make manifest an obsession with defining the line between private life and public engagement. Their accounts constantly assess the proper distance that individuals should maintain between themselves and the regime, and continuously consider whether their own actions constituted collaboration. Bronisław, who came from a family of intellectuals, started his life narrative by outlining the decision that his parents had made to remain in the less developed 'Poland B'[14] (i.e. to renounce their professional ambitions by not attempting to work in the major cultural or political centres) so as not to be pressurized into 'unconditionally surrendering' to the regime in order to succeed. His own first political experiences as part of a Catholic intellectuals' club in the late 1950s was again interpreted in this light: the extent to which the club might compromise its values in order to ensure its survival but without losing its identity and thus becoming 'collaborationist' was a central question for him as a young man:

> My parents always felt that one should keep a certain distance, that you cannot just push yourself forward and forget your identity. Also you know their Catholicism would prevent them from absolute *unconditional surrender* to this [regime]. You know, before the war there was a saying that you couldn't be an honest man and not be leftist . . . so many intellectuals were in their ways leftist, and then after the war many of them unconditionally joined the new world order . . . . to tell you the truth, even among the right-wing nation- alistic groups there were many who unconditionally went over and collabo- rated very actively with the new regime . . . . it was after six years of war and people were tremendously tired and wanted to rebuild the country . . . and the Soviet system had this tremendously skilful machinery of sucking in people and enslaving them mentally. My parents never yielded to that, so they never really forged a great career during the socialist period. [This was also] because they were never motivated to be at the centre – in Warsaw or in Kraków – they always had that mission of organizing cultural life in what we called 'Poland B' . . . . they were running an orphanage and they had to quit because they were giving the kids a Catholic education; we all went to church, there were prayers, morning, evening and so on. . . . [When I was at univer- sity] we were always discussing how far we could compromise. . . . How far our Catholic club could say yes to the Communists. Where the limit lay. That was the period when I started to become aware of this continuous question of how far we collaborate or demonstrate our obedience to the regime without losing our identity. One of my very good friends resigned from the club because he said we were going too far, we surrendered too much of what we were, so he decided, well, he came from a very old gentry family and was a very adamant fellow in his thinking.[15]

The question of collaboration was crucial because, in many central-eastern European countries, individuals were faced with a Communist system that attempted to integrate its ideological enemies as much as persecute them. Many were given opportunities to succeed within the system if they were prepared to adopt its values, at least in public. This was not just limited to favoured social groups: even the old intelligentsia and middle classes of central Europe were able to integrate themselves and achieve a degree of social mobility if they wished, even during the Stalinist period.[16] Rapidly industrializing systems (in the case of Hungary and Poland), with elites decimated by the war (in the case of Poland) or with working-class communities who did not heed the call to social advancement (in the case of Czechoslovakia), often required the expertise and skills of many who were from the 'wrong' class or political background.[17] Thus, accounts of the early Communist period, even by 'enemies of the regime', were often a mixture of persecution and integration. Jan was from a Polish aristocratic family that had been dispossessed of its Ukrainian estates in the Russian Revolution and then of its Warsaw palaces after 1948; his father had been a military officer before the war; he had family connections to the right-wing National Democrats.[18] His account of social mobility in the early Communist period reflects the often contradictory mix of opportunity and persecution that even some of the severest class enemies experienced. The family was forced to give up its palaces, not simply as a matter of course, but as part of a bargain that allowed Jan and his eight siblings to go to university. Although he could not attend his institution of choice, he ended up completing a degree and eventually had a successful career in foreign trade:

> My maternal grandparents had a palace next to Warsaw University . . . my uncle agreed at the time that it could be used by the state and he could retain two apartments . . . . this was what gave my younger brothers and sisters the possibility to go to better schools than they were attending, and after to go to higher-education establishments. . . . [But] it was '49 when I first tried to get to university, and I experienced the system of 'class revenge' where workers were considered better . . . . there were not only class considerations; my father was an army officer before the war and so his children were considered unsafe. . . . You became a second- or third-rank citizen. That was so terrible for people who had risked their life fighting the Nazis in the Polish underground. Anyway, this was the way that children were classified . . . not only because my father belonged to the army of the government-in-exile, but also because on my mother's side the family had the title of princes, so you can imagine that the Communists were absolutely against us. . . . I knew that they would not allow me to study political subjects at university so I decided to study architecture. They told me after the examination: you cannot study in Warsaw, you can go to Białystok – which was closer to where my parents lived anyway.[19]

Yet such advancement was threatening because it required the erasure of former national identities and traditions that resided within the autobiography. In order to progress within the system, individuals were expected to write their own life stories into class-conscious or anti-Fascist historical templates, in which they emphasized politically appropriate roots or attacked those family members who came from the wrong backgrounds.[20] Some historians have termed this type of system a 'biocracy':[21] one in which an individual's chances of succeeding are determined by his or her ability or readiness to construct a politically acceptable public autobiography. These were constructed in curricula vitae at the point of university entrance or when making job applications. Individuals manipulated information about their family or undertook political tasks in order to produce an appropriate version of their life story that would ensure their suitability for advancement in the eyes of the state. Integration was threatening for anti-Communists not merely because it involved working for the Communist regime, but also because it forced the individual through processes that were designed to erase older identities and ways of thinking.

In Hungary, this usually meant the politically correct rewriting of one's class background, and demonstrating that one saw the past in 'class' rather than 'national' terms. Flóra described the way in which she had to reject her bourgeois identity publicly in order to attend tertiary education: she was forced to work in a paprika factory to demonstrate that she was 'free from contempt for physical labour' before applying to a university. Such procedures were designed to provide biographically suspect individuals with sufficient class-consciousness:

James: And could you tell me something about your family background?

Flóra: Well, my father was a watchmaker and jeweller in this small town. Before the war he had at least one helper to assist him, but after the war he had none. Nevertheless, because of this particular trade, that's why we were called bourgeois. . . . I managed to end up with a very good mark at the end [of middle school], and I was expected to continue and go into the local grammar school. But that coincided in Hungary with the period when children were judged on whom their parents were, what their affiliations were, what strata of society they were associated with, and my family was labelled 'bourgeois' and 'clerical', and with this double burden I was barred from entering grammar school. In fact, I couldn't enter any kind of education after the age of fourteen, and I was absolutely devastated – so was my family. My family tried to do everything, whatever they could. I went and attended private classes with teachers who were first class but couldn't teach any longer because they weren't appropriate for the Communist regime. That went on for about a year, then my family was told that if I did physical labour – let's say [for] two, three, maybe even four years – maybe there was going to be some redemption and then I could go to secondary school. So I tried to work in all sorts of places, but not being used to it, it was pretty daunting. I was working in a paprika mill in my home town, because my home town is very famous for its paprika . . . and I became very ill, and somehow that coincided with a slight relaxation of the rules, and I was told, when I recuperated, that I could continue. . . . Although I came top of my class, I was advised that I had to be very careful when I applied to university, because I might not get into university with this background at all. And therefore I didn't apply for a place in Budapest, because I was absolutely certain that I wouldn't get in, and judging by what happened to some of my contemporaries, who were in a similar position to myself, that was a very wise move. But I applied for a place at the University of Szeged, and I was called for an interview, and, yes, I was accepted. So, in 1954, I went up to university in Szeged, studying Hungarian language, literature and history.[22]

In Poland, by contrast, class background was much less important as 'former elites' were much less of a threat than in Hungary: 77 per cent of the professional, government and business class had been killed during World War II.[23] Reforming class identities was therefore less significant: 'There was no class segregation . . . . if one declared that he or she supported the values of the system it didn't matter whether they were from the aristocracy or from the bourgeoisie; the only important thing was whether one declared oneself to be supporting the values of the system and joined Communist youth organizations.'[24] Rather, Polish respondents much more commonly had to hide their former political activities, particularly as members of right-wing parties or the Home Army. Thus, Jan, the aristocrat we met above, did not seek to disguise his family's wealth but needed to cover up his family's political affiliations: 'I never admitted to being in the Home Army underground . . . I would have immediately become an enemy.' Thus, the avoidance of discrimination or the pursuit of ambition led to individuals' erasure of their own pasts, at least in public; integration threatened the maintenance of national traditions and memory.

Many anti-Communists did find educational and professional success within the Communist system, particularly in the later decades of Communist rule. However, in post-Communist testimony, they needed to demonstrate how their engagement had not led to an erasure of their values or to a dilution of the memory of those national traditions that they had tasked themselves with preserving. To suggest that they had 'given in' ideologically, in order to advance their own interests, would have marked them out as collaborators. Rather, they needed to show that they were still victims, regardless of the success they appeared to have achieved. Hungarian Erzsébet's family was Catholic, conservative and connected with the previous regime; her father had held a high-ranking post in the Ministry of Education until he was sacked for refusing to join the Hungarian Workers' Party. Erzsébet related the story of her social mobility as one of victimization:

Erzsébet: I tr[ied] to gain good points in other directions which didn't conflict with my conscience, like, for example, to hope for university entrance, if you came from a so-called middle-class family, that was out of the question. It didn't matter how well you had done in your exams, or generally in your schooling, to become a university student was almost impossible. So to assist the possibility I did First Aid courses, which at that time was considered as preparation against imperialist attack. And it was taken as a political good point. For me, it was part of the preparation for university as I was heading for medical school anyway. So it was an easy way of gaining so-called political good points without actually being political. And so I became an instructor in First Aid and that was definitely counted. When I finished school with a gold medal, that alone would not have allowed me university entry, [but] if you added my First Aid courses, and the fact that my father had just lost his job and so I became a working-class girl.

James: So how did that work?

Erzsébet: Simply because the questionnaire for university entry, among other personal details, asked for your father's occupation, and in all honesty I could write down 'labourer'. They didn't ask who he was, just who he is. So immediately I became a member of the proletariat [*laughs*]. And with good results at school, First Aid, I got the largest university scholarship, not just a university place.[25]

Like many conservative respondents, Erzsébet's story was often paradoxical: no matter how much success she achieved, her self-identity remained that of victim. She began her narrative by highlighting the complete exclusion she was bound to suffer, claiming that it was impossible for her to go to university as a member of the former middle class. However, her narrative quickly undercut this initial assertion; she described not only how she got to university, but how she obtained the largest scholarship in her year. The victim identity was crucial as it helped her refute the accusation that she had collaborated. She began her story by explaining that she was forced into making compromises because otherwise she was doomed to exclusion. As a victim, she was relieving herself of ethical responsibility for her own actions. The remainder of her narrative reinforced this point: her account was an attempt to explain how the concessions she had made did not taint her ('didn't conflict with my conscience'). For example, it was important for her to maintain a distinction between morally acceptable and unacceptable forms of compromise. Despite the fact that she decided to take on 'anti-imperialist' 'First Aid' work and admitted that this helped her, she emphasized that it was not a political decision but 'an easy way of gaining so-called political good points without actually being political'. It was true that this type of social activity did not require individuals to carry out explicitly political work on behalf of the regime. Respondents knew, however, that it was a method of demonstrating loyalty towards the system. Erzsébet therefore needed to assert that it was a natural choice as she was 'heading for medical school anyway'. Even when involved in clearly politicized activities, she tried to deny that she had been tainted. Only as an apolitical victim, forced by virtue of her excluded position to make compromises with the state, could she find an identity that made her experience of success morally manageable.

Communist states gave opportunities to many well-educated anti-Communists, especially in the late Communist period. Jan, despite coming from an aristocratic family, enjoyed a successful career as a foreign trade representative and travelled around the world. He presented his success not as evidence of his eventual accommodation with the system, but rather as a simple apolitical expression of his professional expertise. He argued that his professional training had anticipated his capacity to serve an independent Poland after 1989: he had not collaborated with Communists but rather had been working for an independent nation in advance of its inevitable arrival:

> I did my duty for the good of the economy . . . any government in power needs foreign trade representatives . . . . it was a necessity, for the survival of the country. It let us be less dominated by Russia as it made our economy more independent. . . . It was impossible to live without having this hope that one day the system would crumble and [that] people with skills and knowledge would be needed in a 'liberated Poland', which turned out to be true. [After 1989] I was immediately taken on by the Ministry of Foreign Trade because of the professional knowledge [I gained in the Communist

period]. It's comparable to my father thinking that even under the Russian occupation somebody who learns military skills will one day be able to make themselves useful to the independent country.

Others argued that they had succeeded without 'giving in' ideologically: the Communist state had required their skills, and they had provided them, but only because the state had accepted that they were necessary, and had not required them to become politically or morally compromised. Bálint came from an 'ancient Hungarian' upper-middle-class anti-Communist family, had been imprisoned for five years on trumped-up charges of spying in the 1950s and had been released in 1956; from the early 1960s, he increasingly made a successful career for himself in foreign trade in south-east Asia:

> So I was, so to say, *accepted as I was, without any hope of being changed* [my emphasis]. And I was considered, from a professional point of view, with respect to transportation and shipping, to have a good name. I mean, internationally. I published lots of scientific articles in different languages . . . . there was a monopoly company for international transportation called Masved, where I was a member of the board of directors, and I was made the representative of the company in Bombay. At that time we had a foreign trade turnover with India of 300,000 tonnes . . . so we then had to have a trade representative there as we had a very advantageous trade agreement at that [time] with India, which we don't have now. But owing to the volume, the company had to have someone on the spot, and there were very few people in our company who knew English and could correspond in English and deal with the different shipping companies in English, so I was put in charge and we were in Bombay for five years and three months.

Surprisingly, perhaps, many nationalist anti-Communists refused to use their experiences of public resistance to demonstrate their anti-Communism after 1989. Despite the fact that they usually had autobiographies that evidenced moments of opposition, they were unwilling to testify to them or to ascribe them significance.[26] After 1989, they argued that it would have been inappropriate to engage in resistance activities against the Communist state. The public expression of opposition required a dialogue between resister and regime, and thus had the potential to contaminate the individual ideologically.[27] They rejected the idea that anti-Communism required heroic opposition; rather, the true anti-Communist should merely 'endure' the system, withdraw into the private sphere, protect national traditions and refuse all forms of engagement, even opposition. Bálint revealed why he had not become involved in the 1956 Hungarian Uprising after being released from prison: he believed the revolutionaries to be 'collaborators', and considered it important that the regime should not regard him as a threat:[28]

No close relatives were involved [in the 1956 Uprising] . . . we did not have any direct contact with those who were actively involved . . . no one in our family is of a revolutionary type. I mean, we are not fond of extremes. And certainly not in the field of politics. But we are, I mean, as a family, we seem to be rather balanced types of people in every respect. . . . We were not happy with those who took part . . . we always tried to find the reasons, the motivations, why they were ready to give in, to collaborate or even to be active. . . . no one took any leading position in the party . . . . [we were not like] those scientists whose rank depended more on their membership of the party than actual scientific achievement, because the party tried to promote their comrades, not necessarily on the basis of brilliant knowledge and scientific achievement, but owing to the fact that he or she was a member of the party. We didn't have people like that in our family, no one chose to join anything, not even a trade union. [This meant that] the system was not so kind towards us, on the one hand, but, on the other, [it meant] that we were not put under such heavy pressure, which would force us to 'give in'. So it was perhaps a fortunate situation that we were considered people who would never give in; we would never go against them openly or plead against them, loudly carrying posters and banners in the streets. We simply disliked them and did not believe them. That's all. So we were not dangerous for them. . . . We were patriots and Christians . . . they [participants in the '56 Uprising] were those who had compromised themselves, they had reservations about the system but basically accepted it. Well, in my case, well, I think I was really lucky because in spite of that I was known as one [who had] no sympathy with the system whatsoever, I did not speak out [about it]. I mean, if I was asked, I told them; well, this is my opinion. But I never made my anti-Communist views public. I never entered into dialogue with them; it was a bad situation, but I kept calm. But I was sure never to leave any hopes with those Communists that I might change my mind in favour of their [system].

In fact, many nationalists and committed anti-Communists did find themselves involved in protest. However, they did not build this into a story of heroic resistance against a hated state that anticipated the collapse in 1989; rather, it was usually presented as a pointless act that had the potential to compromise the individual with the state, which in any case could not be changed. Hence they argued that although they found themselves resisting, they were never really combatants. Bronisław played a prominent role in the nationalist, Catholic wing of the Solidarity movement, yet he declined to make resistance a central part of his identity. Here, he relates how he had given speeches in church during the Solidarity period; like many, he did not write this into a heroic narrative of overcoming Communism, but rather wanted to illustrate the minor status of what he had done and to insist that he was not a real resister:

> [my dissent began] only during the period of Solidarity . . . before that I was not especially active in challenging the Communist regime. . . . I was the first chairman of the Solidarity unit in my workplace . . . and after Solidarity became illegal, I became a member of the underground committee. . . . that sounds so tremendous, 'underground'! . . . but, well, we didn't regard it as a very dangerous job . . . we were organizing lectures in churches for young people all over Poland. . . . I was asked to give a speech on Gandhi because at that time [Richard] Attenborough's film was screened and people were fascinated by his use of non-violent methods, so I was . . . invited to speak on Gandhi in those church lectures . . . once I was supposed to speak in Katowice but they detained me at Katowice railway station and I could not deliver the lecture. . . . I was kept for some hours at the police headquarters . . . [but] I do not have much claim to being a 'combatant' [*laughs*] . . . I am not a combatant really.

The Hungarian Dezső found himself involved in street fighting with Communist vigilantes in the early 1950s, but now represented his participation as pointless and shaming:

> Now the story involves hooliganism . . . we were fairly drunk and then on 1 May, which is a day of vigilance for Communists, Imre started to throw bricks at lamps, and we did this because we knew the Communist vigilantes were there, and three of them from two different sides of the street started to rush towards us, and three of us, you know, went in four different directions. . . . So it wasn't bravado, it wasn't a sort of conscious heroic opposition to the regime. In a sense one was ashamed of it, it didn't really matter somehow . . . I certainly didn't feel that I was fighting the Communists, I didn't feel that at all. And had you asked me at any point, I would have said that no, no, no, I'm an observer.[29]

Rather, what was required was the quiet articulation of values in private, in a context and manner untouched by the Communist state. The only acceptable forms of resistance were those the state could not perceive and that could thus not be considered as engagement, as the Hungarian Irén explains: 'I think we only had *silent weapons* [my emphasis] – not to do this or that or not to participate at certain events. For instance, when we saw ... public flower displays in the shape of red stars, we decided not to cross that park where they were planted any more. Just such small things, but in our family we did not really go against the system or resist or anything, no.'[30]

Nationalist, anti-Communist respondents saw their role as the protectors of pre-Communist traditions within the home. The domestic sphere was the place where the values of the victimized nation endured. Ryszard, who was born into a peasant family in a village near Kraków before becoming an agronomist in Warsaw, referred to this space as a 'little Poland': 'In my life I had a kind of "passive fighting", not active ... it was very important to have my own sphere of liberty in the home, to have good contacts with the church and organize a *"little Poland in our family"* [my emphasis] ... for me it was not the done thing to fight with Communists.'[31]

It was the articulation of national values and stories from the pre-Communist era that was seen as protecting the individual from being integrated mentally into the Communist project. Many respondents remembered telling family stories as a way of communicating other forms of history that would keep alternative, anti-Communist, views of the world alive. The Polish aristocrat Jan described how traditions of patriotic story-telling within the family helped to construct the necessary 'fortress' against the persuasive claims of the regime:

James: Were there traditions that you tried to maintain?

Jan: Well in the first place belonging to the Catholic Church was something fundamental. . . . at home we heard all about the members of the family who had died for the patriotic traditions of independence ... that *built a fortress around you* [my emphasis]. There were actually things that could make inroads into your outlook ... when you watched the [Communists'] social revolution, you had to admit that making 100 per cent of the Polish population literate ... you had to admit that it was something to be approved of.

Nationalist anti-Communists narrated their autobiographies in the post-Communist period in such a way as to transmit those national traditions and stories that they believed had been marginalized during the Communist period. They presented themselves as having preserved these traditions in the private sphere in a period of occupation, ready to pass them on to the next generation after 1989. Their victimization was proof that they had faithfully served the

nation during a period of foreign rule, enduring persecution in order to maintain the nation's values in the face of an integrative (and often persuasive)
Communist state. To have collaborated or 'given in' was considered threatening
because, as they testified, the former regime was especially effective at pressur-
izing people to forget their own pasts and family traditions as it incorporated
them and offered them opportunities. Assimilation into, or engagement with, the
Communist system could thus be accompanied by the loss of 'proper' national
memory. If they found themselves socially mobile or in active opposition during
the Communist period, then they needed to demonstrate how this had not
morally compromised them or impinged on the values they maintained within
their families or communities. Nevertheless, while they protested that their
victimization convincingly demonstrated that they had stayed outside the ideological orbit of the Communist state, their very conception of the purpose of
autobiographical story-telling suggests that this was not the case. The forms their
life stories took after 1989 were marked by their encounters with the politicized
structure of autobiography in the 1940s and 1950s; the Communist state's earlier
insistence that they relate their lives in terms of the class and anti-Fascist struggle
in order to demonstrate their fealty had persuaded them that autobiography was
a way to express one's relationship to the dominant political power. Hence under
Communism they had written anti-Communist family histories as a form of
defence against the regime and, after 1989, reproduced these private accounts of
victimhood to demonstrate that they had preserved national traditions to pass on
to a now reconstituted anti-Communist nation.

Anti-Anti-Communist Stories

> When I was still in prison, I swore two things to myself: first, I would never
> join a veterans' organization that hands out medals for service in the struggle
> against Communism; second, I would never seek revenge . . . [but] we can
> only forgive the wrongs that have been done to us, while it is not in our
> power to forgive the wrongs done to others. We can try to persuade others
> to do likewise, but people have the right to demand justice.
>
> Adam Michnik, in conversation with Václav Havel, 1991[32]

Anti-Communist and nationalist forms of witnessing the Communist past,
although powerful after 1989, did not go uncontested: many who suffered
exclusion and punishment under Communist rule refused to subscribe to histories that pegged them as martyrs for national values, and tried to find other ways
of narrating the meaning of their marginalization and victimization. Many of
those who had suffered on account of their social class or political beliefs did not

want to turn themselves into victims. Yet they were aware that, as representatives of classes and political traditions that were demonized in Communist ideology, they were widely expected after 1989 to narrate their lives in this way. After the collapse of Communism, they were faced with liberal and nationalist accounts in which they were presented as victims of the Communist state. Thus, in composing their experiences of Communism, they not only had to contend with the complex lives they had lived before 1989 but also with the dominant expectations of the post-Communist period that they would relate their experiences in terms of persecution and suffering. What emerged were accounts in which the whole structure of the life story was deployed to disprove the victim identity they were supposed to adopt. For them, the 'victim story' was not rooted in experience but rather was an identity adopted by many post-Communist citizens to reconcile themselves to the compromises and accommodations they had formerly made. Some argued it was an identity only taken on by those who felt humiliated by the compromises they had chosen to make under the previous system, and was an attempt to absolve themselves of the moral degradation they experienced for so doing. Others suggested that the victim identity was a convenient gloss, adopted only after 1989, that allowed individuals to deflect attention away from the ways in which they had engaged with, and succeeded under, an essentially integrative political system. Post-Communist citizens with these pasts and attitudes might best be described as 'anti-anti-Communists': they had neither identified themselves with the Communist project before 1989, nor did they like the way in which anti-Communists tried to take their revenge by criminalizing the system and pursuing its perpetrators after 1989. Although they had suffered, they were not prepared to testify publicly in ways that could bolster political agendas with which they did not identify. Indeed, their whole lives were presented as an escape from a victim identity; they demonstrated how, despite the marginalization they had faced on account of their backgrounds, they had refused to view themselves as anti-Communist martyrs either before or after 1989. They fully admitted the ways in which they had chosen to engage with, and contribute to, the system, despite their experiences of exclusion. They were determined not to produce life stories after 1989 that reinforced radical anti-Communist or common western liberal perspectives that they were simply 'history's victims'.

Many who came from socially or politically undesirable backgrounds refused to re-imagine themselves as victims in the post-Communist period. Anna had married into a liberal anti-Communist middle-class family in Hungary just after World War II. She and her husband presented themselves as having 'done a deal' with the Communist state in which they would be tolerated despite their class and political backgrounds if they did not oppose the system. They would be allowed limited educational and workplace opportunities as long as they confined themselves to narrow professional ambitions and remained politically inactive:

James: How did the Communist regime describe your social position?
Anna: We were a borderline case. We weren't 'enemies of the people'; they tolerated us.[33]

Likewise, Csaba presented himself as having entered into what he saw as an unspoken agreement with the Communist state: in return for being tolerated as a member of the 'old bourgeoisie', he would refrain from public dissent.[34] As an artist, this required him to desist from making explicitly political statements in his creative work, and instead to take up the role of the technically proficient craftsman. He did consider these restrictions to be a form of victimization, but nevertheless accepted the 'bargain' as a reasonable, rational way to behave under a state that he neither supported nor opposed, and under whose rule he just wanted to 'get by'. Unlike the nationalists quoted above, he did not see minor acts of compromise with Communist power, or small displays of loyalty that ensured his professional status, as morally degrading or as forms of collaboration:

James: Were there things in your past which you wanted to keep secret from the Communists?
Csaba: Of course, I didn't brag about going to a church school, but of course they knew, because they knew everything about everyone, but I did not make myself conspicuous. They made me feel that if I stayed quiet and I behaved myself, then things would be alright. They would tolerate me. In a sense, this attested to their tolerant treatment of me, but despite this, I had to stay silent. I trained as a painter, an artist, but I was not used for propaganda and it was not a career where a person had to say a lot, but rather get on with his craft. It wasn't really difficult to always play the craftsman. I didn't take part in the life of the party, nor did I take part in any sort of movement, but there were obligatory things. The 1 May parade was compulsory during my university years.

Yet those who came from socially demonized classes were aware that after 1989 there was a strong expectation that they should construct themselves as victims of a criminal regime. They had come from communities stigmatized by the Communists, where stories of persecution were common and many had personal experiences of suffering that could have been turned into such an account. These respondents therefore produced very self-reflexive forms of autobiography: they showed how they could be understood as victims, but constantly undercut this expectation by showing how their experiences – even when these illustrated intense suffering – had not led them to adopt such an identity. Edit was one such person; she had grown up in a wealthy banking family, but wanted to show that she had identified with the project of economic modernization that the Communists had begun after the war. At the same time she realized that, given her background, she would be expected to present herself as a victim of the system. Her life story therefore related her engagement while simultaneously parodying the victim story that contemporaries might have expected her to tell. Edit started her autobiography with the demonization that her family – who were Jewish – experienced at the hands of the Communists:

> Edit: I learnt German, French, English, art appreciation and went to the best school in Budapest, and the idea was I would go to a finishing school in Switzerland. We had a cook and a maid. But my husband's family had a cook and two maids!
>
> James: So how did the Communists describe your family?
>
> Edit: Very badly . . . capitalists.[35]

Yet this did not develop into an autobiography of victimhood. She realized that by portraying herself as a victim she would undermine her earlier progressive ideological commitments. Edit disliked the Hungarian Workers' Party, but identified with its anti-Fascist rhetoric and considered it less anti-Semitic than other postwar political groups. She was on the liberal left and identified with the postwar effort to modernize rapidly in order to create a more equitable society, and to keep right-wing 'reactionary' politics from returning; hence she always tried to undercut (often with humour) the idea that she had simply been a victim of Communism. She wanted to present herself as someone who had contributed to the building of a progressive social system, and thus demonstrated how her skills had made her necessary for the new economy despite her official demonization. Moreover, 'being needed' provided her with an identity with which she was comfortable:

> James: So how did the Communist state describe you?
>
> Edit: Me? They had very few people who could speak three languages. They needed them. And I had a very good job, because my boss couldn't speak any [other languages], only Hungarian, so I was needed.

Even when she was persecuted, she did not take refuge in the identity of a victim, but rather found ways to reconcile her suffering with the sense of being needed. Edit was imprisoned in 1955 for following her husband in his attempt to cross the border to get to the west. Instead of using the experience to bear witness to her exclusion and persecution as a politically unreliable 'class enemy', she described the prison as a 'marvellous bed and breakfast'. She was able to manipulate the prison authorities, who 'needed' her:

> We were in that marvellous bed and breakfast place [*laughs*], and the military commander says, 'Is there anybody who can cook for thirty people?' and I said, 'I can cook for thirty people.' 'Alright, you come with us.' And I said, 'Before I start cooking I want a shower.' You had only so much water a day for washing. They said, 'Alright, there is a shower in here, you can have a shower.' And I said to the soldier, I said to him, 'Would you be so kind and go to the cell where I came from and bring down my husband's shirts and I will wash them while I have a shower?' They accepted that. So we were clean. And I cooked. I think nobody could eat the food I cooked [*laughs*]. Because I was brought up as a princess. I didn't have to do anything because I had servants. Then the head of that institution came down and said, 'I see that you can type and you have shorthand and you are a secretary.' And I said, 'I used to be, but lately I've become a cook.' And he said, 'You shan't be a cook any longer because I need a secretary and you come up and you work for me.' So I worked for a week as his secretary, and on perhaps the third day he said to me, 'I have deported your husband.' I said, 'You wouldn't do that to me – deport my husband to another prison and not even give me the chance to say goodbye to him.' 'Yes, I deported him.' And I was taken back to my cell and my husband was sitting there. They gave us a cell for the two of us as a reward because I was a good secretary.

Through such descriptions of her interactions with authority figures, Edit revealed her own particular construction of Communist power. For her, the prison was not a symbol of oppression but a space in which she was needed as a cook and secretary. Whereas some would have seen such activities inside prison as a form of collaboration, for Edit they were a way she could be of use to the state in return for occasional rewards. She rejected the notion that she was a victim. She employed the cliché of the unpredictable totalitarian state, common in conservative testimony, reporting the commander's comment that he had arbitrarily deported her husband. However, she then undermined this trope of the 'victim narrative' by revealing that she had in fact been rewarded for her labours with a conjugal cell. For

Edit, co-operating was not a form of moral compromise. Rather, it was a legitimate kind of behaviour in a society that she believed still needed her, even while it persecuted her.

For anti-anti-Communists, the victim story was not merely rejected as an inappropriate way to understand their own lives; it was also seen as an invalid form appropriated by those who wanted to hide their complex relationships with the Communist state for fear that these might be seen as kinds of collaboration or moral compromise. Urszula rejected the stories of victims and perpetrators she encountered after 1989, despite her own experience of professional marginalization and ideological enmity she felt for the former system. She had been brought up in a wealthy Polish Catholic landowning family, as a young girl had fought with the Home Army against both the Germans and the 'Bolsheviks', had been excluded from a research career on account of her background and beliefs, and as a consequence had been forced to take impermanent jobs in schools. However, she consciously reflected on the fact that she could have presented herself as a victim after 1989 but chose not to do so. She considered that those who did were 'taking revenge' on the previous system: 'From the very beginning [i.e. from the 1940s], I was against the system, but nevertheless I first of all considered . . . how I could help . . . how I could engage . . . and that's why after 1989 I didn't say I had suffered, and [I didn't] become some big anti-Communist who wanted to take revenge on the system.'[36]

For the Czech Jiří, the identity of victim was not an objective description of suffering, but rather an identity that some had chosen in order to make sense of the difficulties they had faced and the choices they had made. A computer engineer who had become part of the dissident movement in the mid-1970s and had signed Charter 77, one of the founding texts of the Czechoslovak democratic opposition, he was forced to leave a number of jobs; his career effectively stalled in the mid-1970s and he was never allowed to progress into management positions. Nonetheless, he did not want to conceive of his life as one of discrimination and persecution. In his view, it was only those who had chosen to collaborate with the system, and felt dishonoured on account of that decision, who now presented themselves as victims in order to hide the shame of their capitulation. Indeed, for him, the widespread appeal of the victim identity was a symptom of the fact that so many in late Communist Czechoslovakia had assimilated themselves into the system and felt morally compromised as a result. He presented the case of his brother-in-law, who had joined the party to ensure an education for his children and had felt ashamed for doing so, and thus began to view himself as a victim of the regime despite having been part of it. According to Jiří, his brother-in-law now viewed the

Communist world as divided into perpetrators – those Communists who had forced him to join the party – and victims – a group of people such as himself who had to compromise themselves morally in order to survive. Indeed, his brother-in-law had called for lustration to make sure the line between 'bad' and 'good' Communists (such as himself) was made clear. Jiří, by contrast, rejected the idea of any such purge precisely because it allowed many to hide the complexities of their lives behind the label of 'victim':[37]

> This anti-Communism after '89, I am deeply convinced, was really based on humiliation. Because if you felt yourself humiliated by the system, then of course you wanted to punish the people who ran the system. . . . My brother-in-law joined the party because he wanted to be vice-director of a research institution and he wanted to alleviate the situation of his son who was clever but was not disciplined. My family didn't care [that he had joined the party], but he had a problem with it, he was really ashamed [*laughing*]. It was really funny, after I signed Charter 77 and I refused to join the party a number of times, several times, I said, 'Well, if I have to be a party member to be a boss then I won't be a boss.' . . . But after the 1989 revolution, my brother-in-law was very angry that we as dissidents didn't punish Communists [*laughing*]. You see, he saw himself as having been humiliated, he wanted to take revenge, he saw himself as a victim of the regime. [He didn't consider] that he could have made other choices, no, [he had determined] that it was not his decision, he believed he was forced, he was ashamed, he couldn't have decided otherwise . . . so he said that we, as dissidents, should punish those Communists [who had forced him], so he started to instruct me into how I should fight against Communism! . . . And we quarrelled terribly! [*Laughs uproariously*] I can tell you about a particularly nice discussion . . . . after the revolution he started up a private business. He was a very good architect and . . . really earned a lot of money in construction . . . and so after I asked him, 'So should we prohibit former Communists from running businesses?' And he started to think, and he said, 'Yes!' And my sister said, 'No. You should prohibit the bad Communists, not the decent ones like my husband!' That's really what they said! [*Laughing heartily*] . . . So the general approach is the system forced us to do something and not that we were responsible. You see in Iraq at Abu Ghraib that the soldiers also say that they were following orders.[38]

Both Jiří and Urszula presented their lives as attempts to avoid assuming the mantle of victimhood despite experiencing marginalization. Indeed, the whole structure of their life stories was a refutation of the necessity of resorting to victimhood as an identity, even in the most trying circumstances. They had both seen others inscribe a victim identity upon themselves because they felt they had been humiliated by the system: thus, their own life accounts were stories of how the individual could avoid being shamed by the system by engaging 'honestly' with it. Jiří's life story began with the experience of his father who had been forced to join the party in 1948 and had spent the rest of his life unable to come to terms with the choice he had made. He claimed to have learnt at an early age that one should only engage with the system on one's own terms, and even resist where necessary:

> As a member of the civil service my father was forced to join the party and he was always angry about that . . . . he needed to do it for his career . . . my father was ill and he had three children and he did not really want to be sent to the uranium mines [as a political prisoner] . . . so he signed the application . . . . he was always very disgruntled and never came to terms with it . . . . it was one of the reasons why I signed Charter 77, because I didn't want to be as discontented as my father.

Jiří had a reasonable career as a computer programmer, beginning in the early 1970s, but emphasized that he had refused party entry and hence had not been promoted. He had not been particularly political before 1968 but had turned against the system after the experience of the Soviet invasion following the Prague Spring. Despite repeated approaches from the party, he refused to join and had signed Charter 77, the first public joint declaration of Czechoslovak dissidence, in order to avoid the moral crisis his father had experienced. He was demoted soon after. He presented himself as morally free of the system, as 'living in truth', and hence not degraded by his experiences: 'I didn't feel the need to conceal political views and therefore I and other dissidents did not feel humiliated by the regime. We were living, but of course we knew we couldn't be bosses, we knew that we wouldn't get passports, and we wouldn't be able to go abroad, but we had free communication, so therefore I felt no hate with this Communist environment.'

Urszula also wanted to tell her story of trying to live 'honestly' within the system, and saw those who had defined themselves as victims under Communism as disguising their true roles from themselves. She believed that dividing society between party members, on the one hand, and victims, on the other, obscured more important divisions between those who made their choices for moral or immoral reasons. In this way, she was able to keep many friends who had joined the party for what she considered the right reasons:

Of course I had friends who were engaged in the system and sometimes I was open with them about my attitudes . . . all of them knew that I was against the system. I still have these friends now . . . because this is not the most important criterion for me, whether someone was in the party or not. For me, the question of how you treated people was more important than whether one was or was not in the party . . . . sometimes people joined the party for pragmatic reasons, and not only in their own interests . . . a director of the hospital [joined] because there was important work to do . . . or sometimes it was a very pragmatic thing, and you find out that he or she agreed to join the party for the opportunity to forge a professional career. It's not so easy to judge people like this.

She illustrated this moral code through stories from her own life. She had wanted to engage with the system in such a way that she did not have to be 'dishonest'. She presented her early life as a tale of disillusionment in which she lost her belief that she could live morally within the system. As a young woman, excluded from a proper career, she had found an honourable engagement impossible and had joined a 'Suicide Club' in the early 1950s. Its members constantly considered whether, given the impossibility of living a virtuous life under a political system that forced people to hide their real backgrounds and ideological commitments, it was better to commit suicide:

[Our discussions were about] whether it were possible to live dishonestly in this system or it were better to be honest and commit suicide . . . . we had lectures about suicide from a sociological, a psychological, and from a legal point of view . . . and then there was a discussion about whether we should commit group suicide or not. And one of our chemist colleagues managed to get poison for us to drink. Two people from this club committed suicide and they left a letter that our discussion, our consideration of this matter, lasted too long and they had no money to live, they had no job, and we found them in the attic where we had this meeting. It was a real problem because I wanted to live honestly and I didn't see any possibility of doing so under this system, and I didn't want to go to jail and to be destroyed there.

However, in later years Urszula discovered ways of engaging 'honestly' by accommodating herself at the margins and engaging with the system where she could. Her decision not to deny her past to the state – that she had been educated by nuns and that her family used to be substantial landowners – meant that her career had been curtailed, but also that she had engaged honestly: 'And after some time it was already clear that I could work on the margins quietly but there was no chance to get anything more. I couldn't be, for example, leader of the university or get any better post like director of the institute or anything like that.' Jiří and Urszula were typical of many of those who had been opposed to what they considered an illegitimate regime and had been excluded from pursuing their careers, yet nevertheless rejected the identity of victim of the system. For both of them, assuming the mantle of victimhood was about disguising the true nature of one's engagement with the system. Each argued that they had attempted to live an honest life – Urszula through finding ways to engage despite her marginalization, and Jiří through refusing to engage. They had not been humiliated by the regime and thus, they argued, had not needed to adopt a victim identity.

Conclusion

The question of the moral and political choices that an individual makes, in the face of intense pressure to produce politically appropriate autobiographies, was a significant theme in two works by dissident Czech authors: Jiří Grušaʾs *The Questionnaire* and Milan Kunderaʾs *Slowness*.[39] In the context of 1970s Czechoslovakia, following the crackdown after the Prague Spring and the re-emergence of a culture that insisted upon politically appropriate autobiographies,[40] Grušaʾs work explored the tensions between the official stories that the Czechoslovak Communist citizen was expected to tell, and the unofficial tales that existed within communities across the nation. From the perspective of exile in France after the collapse of Communism, Kunderaʾs novel *Slowness* dealt, among other things, with the way in which eastern Europeans 'performed' politically appropriate versions of their autobiographies in front of westerners when relating their experiences under the Communist system.

Grušaʾs work suggests the existence of a 'true autobiography' behind the historical fabrications that a Communist citizen was expected to produce. His main protagonist, Jan Chrysostom Kepka, is requested to fill in the questionnaire that all citizens had to complete as part of any job application; on being asked to give an account of his life, he rejects the official formulas and instead produces a story that celebrates the diverse life paths his family has taken, and the ways in which they have survived various regimes and occupations. It is a novel that shows the importance of maintaining an independent autobiography based on family and community memories as a means of resistance against a co-opting power. Kundera, by contrast, presents autobiography as performance, exploring how individuals show different aspects of themselves, and frame the meanings of their lives in various ways, according to their audience at the time. In particular, he examines how those who lived complex lives under Communism now react to globalized liberal discourses that see life under Communism – as life under any non-democratic system – in terms only of suffering, victimhood and exclusion from the dominant path of liberal democratic development. The novel itself is set at an entomology conference in France, and one of its main characters is a former Czech dissident, Cechoripsky, who was expelled from his academic post following his involvement in the 1968 Prague Spring, and resumes his career only after 1989. He experiences the power of the western totalitarian narrative at first hand: he struggles to assert his presence to westerners at the conference, and only becomes recognizable to them when he describes himself as a victim who suffered in the wake of the purges that followed the Prague Spring. However, he simultaneously realizes just how uncomfortable he is with this; he privately recalls how his time in a labour camp was actually more enjoyable than his experience at the conference, and later rebukes a western scientist for describing the east as a concentration camp. Cechoripsky cannot decide whether to become a victim of Communism or not: he performs totalitarianism to a western public, but rebukes himself for betraying his much more complex past which cannot be reduced to a simple story of victimization and suffering.[41]

For the generation interviewed for this project, these autobiographical pressures existed under both Communism and post-Communism and shaped the ways in which they wrote and rewrote personal accounts of their lives. Many conservative and Catholic opponents of the regime framed their lives as victims of Communism, even when their autobiographies contained information that suggested much more complex pasts. For them, telling stories of their own victimization was important in itself. They had conceptualized Communist power as a form of foreign occupation, or at least as occupation by a foreign 'eastern' ideology. They were the ones who had refused to give in, and who had experienced discrimination on the margins of Communist society in order to preserve national values from contamination by external forces. They had told stories of their own suffering and endurance during the Communist period in order to signal their separateness from the regime and to insulate their values from contamination by Communist ideology, and continued to tell these 'martyr narratives' after 1989 in order to assert their heroic role as the defenders of values that could now form the basis of a newly revived post-Communist nation. Yet, after 1989, this powerful post-Communist national martyr narrative in turn begot the 'anti-victim story'; many of those who had suffered discrimination wanted to reject the notion that they had simply been victims, even when pressurized to present their lives in such terms. Despite their antipathy towards the Communist regime, they had not regarded it primarily as a foreign occupation, but rather as a mixed experience of progressive politics and discriminatory (and sometimes violent) dictatorship. Thus, they presented their lives as a search for an honest engagement with the progressive, modernizing aspects of the regime, and did not consider that their participation turned them into traitorous collaborators. After 1989, faced with powerful nationalist and western narratives that tried to reduce their life stories to mere accounts of victimization, they rebelled: they refused to emphasize marginalization in their autobiographies, instead presenting their lives as a continual refusal to adopt the identity of 'victim of Communism', no matter what they had endured. They coped with Communism by refusing to accept the persecution they had suffered as being central to their identity. For them, 'becoming a victim' was the real sign that one had 'given in' to the regime.

CHAPTER SEVEN

THE AFTERLIFE OF ATROCITY
REMEMBERING RED ARMY
RAPE AFTER 1989[1]

It was not just the memory of victims of Communist regimes that was revived in 1989 in central-eastern Europe: the experiences of those who had suffered under the Red Army occupation of central-eastern Europe at the end of World War II were also highlighted. In particular, the mass rapes committed by the Red Army in 1944 and 1945 became an object of interest for various political and professional groups who sought to revive the story of the millions of women whose experiences, they claimed, had previously been hidden. The number of victims is hard to determine accurately. Conservative estimates suggest that almost two million German women were raped.[2] The capital cities of the Axis powers were particularly targeted – some suggest that 110,000 women in Berlin, 87,000 in Vienna, and 50,000 in Budapest were violated, although the real figures might be much higher.[3] Women in the remainder of Hungary and East Germany, alongside those in eastern Prussia, Transylvania, Slovakia and north-eastern Yugoslavia, also suffered in large numbers.[4]

In the first few years after the war, in some areas such as East Germany and Yugoslavia, women could publicly articulate the ways in which they had suffered under the Red Army occupation. Indeed, in Germany, rape was widely discussed within families, in public and at political meetings.[5] By contrast, in other places, such as Hungary, the experience of rape was very quickly silenced at a public level.[6] After 1949, however, Communist states everywhere made the discussion of Red Army atrocities a taboo subject. This silence was not absolute: some political and cultural historians have recently begun to excavate the marginal ways in which rape could be addressed in the Communist German Democratic Republic, Yugoslavia and Hungary.[7] For the most part, however, remembering Soviet atrocities was not compatible with state-sponsored images of the Red Army as the heroic liberators of the region from Fascism. These silences were not only maintained in the Communist east; in the immediate aftermath of World War II, faced with their own soldiers' fraternization, use of prostitutes and rape, the Allied powers also failed to draw attention to Red Army atrocities.[8] Moreover, by the 1950s, Austrian and West German women were pressurized to suppress their stories of sexual contact with Red Army troops: they 'were not supposed to have a history'.[9] Although rape often functioned as a metaphor for the brutalization of the German nation in postwar conservative discourse, little attention was paid to the stories of those who had actually suffered sexual violence.[10]

Sexual brutality on the eastern front was also hidden from public view in the Soviet Union. Red Army soldiers themselves were initially complicit in the suppression of such knowledge: the private correspondence of Soviet troops, written for the consumption of friends and families back home, often boasted of incidents of looting and forced acquisition, but was absolutely silent on the question of sexual contact between Red Army troops and civilian populations.[11] Moreover, the few Soviet writers and journalists who recorded the scale of the atrocities were unable to report what they had witnessed when they returned to the Soviet Union.[12] Testimony on the subject of rape grew very difficult for historians to obtain: sexual atrocities on the eastern front had become a non-issue. In later reflections on the subject, sexual encounters were often not recalled as brutal acts. Boris Slutsky, the Russian poet who travelled with the Red Army suggested in his memoir *Things That Happened* that in many cases Red Army soldiers engaged in consensual intercourse with 'affectionate' eastern European women: 'Hungarian women loved the Russians in their turn, and along with the dark fear that parted the knees of matrons and mothers of families, there was also the affectionate nature of young women and the desperate tenderness of the women soldiers, who gave themselves to the men who had killed their husbands.'[13] After the collapse of the Soviet Union, there was no national debate about the behaviour of Soviet troops; President Putin, in reviving the memory of the Red Army as heroic liberators of Europe, did not reflect on the atrocities they had committed in their drive to Berlin.[14] Moreover, at a social level, ex-Soviet citizens' persisting pride in the Red Army for defeating Fascism meant that such war crimes continued to be denied. One documentary-maker found that many ex-Red Army soldiers still refused to accept that rapes had occurred at all, admitting only to consensual sexual relations or claiming that eastern European women deliberately used sex to spread diseases in order to weaken the fighting capabilities of the Red Army.[15]

After 1989, a wide range of groups sought to bring the story of the rapes committed by the Red Army into the public arena. Their revival of these memories was framed in very particular terms: they were breaking the political, social and personal taboos that had surrounded the experiences of 1945, bringing rape to the centre of public culture, and providing women with a social space in which to articulate suffering that they had had to keep to themselves for forty years. Some were not only interested in recovering knowledge about rape itself, but also hoped that their projects would lead to forms of social healing, personal liberation and new societal attitudes towards rape in wartime. Feminist historians and film-makers in Hungary and Germany, often prompted by the contemporary debates surrounding the mass rapes that accompanied the wars of Yugoslav succession, presented their recovery of women's stories from 1945 not only as breaking a politically motivated silence, but also as addressing the broader refusal of their culture to take gender-based victimization in war seriously. Thus, their works not only recovered experiences from 1945 itself but used them to encourage greater awareness of the suffering of women in conflicts generally.[16] New nationalist historians, particularly in Hungary and Czechoslovakia, presented the breaking of taboos primarily in political terms – as the overcoming of Communist-era enforced silence – and used the memory of atrocities to frame a new national identity based on the brutalization of the nation at the hands of the Soviets. For others, the exploration of women's experiences was motivated by a concern to address the traumatic psychological effects of wartime rape. Indeed, the first published work on the subject in Hungary was a personal account of violation by a woman who subsequently became a child psychologist, and who presented her own rape as a traumatic and psychologically damaging event that she had eventually overcome.[17] In the former East Germany, mental-health professionals looked to recover the 'unspoken secret' of World War II in order to analyse the effects of wartime sexual violence on women, and to develop psychological approaches to help sufferers overcome wartime traumas later in life.[18] Moreover, the two works that did the most to publicize the memory of the brutalization of German women – Antony Beevor's *Berlin: The Downfall 1945* (2002) and the republished diary (and later film adaptation) *A Woman in Berlin* – were presented as ending long-held taboos, and were frequently promoted alongside interviews with women who claimed to have been liberated by their appearance to speak publicly about their experiences.[19] Although these various individuals and groups had very different motivations for reviving the memory of Red Army rape, they all framed their work in similar terms: they were engaged in a modern, civilized, and heroic process of overcoming repressed memories within cultures which, for a variety of psychological, cultural and political reasons, had silenced a difficult past.

Despite these powerful claims regarding the beneficial effects of the recovery of stories of women's victimization, some were sceptical that their revival was a necessary or helpful part of mastering a traumatic past. This was particularly the case in Germany, where liberal-left observers were critical of the increasing tendency, observable from the early 1990s onwards, to present the violation of German women either as part of a universal story of the victimization of women in wartime, or through the emotive accounts of individual tragedies. For them, these memories needed to be firmly rooted in their problematic historical setting. Decontextualized representations, they argued, ignored the basic point that women could not simply be reduced to victims and Soviets to perpetrators: sexual atrocities were carried out by those who had also liberated concentration camps and brought an end to Fascism, and were inflicted upon women who belonged to the 'perpetrator' nation. Here, a simplistic notion of good and evil would not do.[20] Moreover, for them, these new historically ungrounded representations of sexual violence ignored the problematic postwar episodes in which memories of German victimization in World War II were revived. The rescue of the story of women's rape could not simply be packaged as the uncovering of an untold past: it fed into a conservative tradition of history-making that made considerable use of German suffering at the end of the war – through the stories of expellees from the east, or victims of aerial bombing – in order to frame ordinary Germans as the victims of Nazism.[21] Thus, the process of witnessing rape, left-wing observers believed, often allowed their narrators to evade debates about ordinary Germans' complicity in Nazism before the arrival of the Red Army, and showed an inappropriate foregrounding of their own suffering in the face of a much greater atrocity: the Holocaust.[22] The question of whether it was possible to testify to German suffering and simultaneously sustain a sufficient reverence for the victims of the Holocaust thus continued to be a central and contested question for German culture in the post-Cold War period.

This chapter will focus on the victims and witnesses of the Red Army occupation of central-eastern Europe, many of whom experienced directly the sexual violence of the troops in 1944–45, and then lived through over four decades of enforced silence. After 1989, did these victims and witnesses want to relate their experiences? Did the recovery of the public memory of Red Army rape, and its new depiction as a traumatic event, give them room to articulate what they had seen or been subjected to? It will focus on one case study – the Hungarian experience of rape in Budapest in 1944–45 – to explore these issues in depth.[23] During the Soviet occupation of Hungary's capital at the end of World War II, it is estimated that around one in ten women were raped by soldiers from the Red Army.[24] The women of Budapest suffered in large numbers partly because the city was defended, and therefore subject to a drawn-out siege, and the civilian population was not evacuated. Moreover,

Hungary's alliance with the Axis powers meant that the besieging Soviet army saw Budapest as enemy territory, and its women as more legitimate targets than those in regions perceived to be sympathetic to the Allied cause.[25] For some Hungarian women, 1989 represented the moment when they could finally tell the story of their brutalization at the hands of the Red Army. They presented rape as one of the defining horrors of World War II, and placed the suffering they had faced as young women in 1945 at the forefront of their life stories. Yet for others, witnessing these events was far more complex: they had experienced, and now remembered, sexual violence in very different forms from the stories articulated by newly dominant anti-Communist voices after 1989. Some denied that rapes had occurred, or refuted the idea that Soviet soldiers were sexual aggressors. Many refused to testify to trauma or suffering, or used their experiences of sexual contact with the Soviets to articulate very different ideas about the meaning of Fascism, 'liberation' and the Red Army. The post-1989 public space was not simply an arena in which repressed memories of traumatic events could return.[26]

Rape Stories: Victimization and Trauma

James: So, can you tell me more about your experiences of Soviet troops?

Erzsébet: Frightening, definitely for a few months. My father was already in the capital and my mother and four children stayed in Komarom.[27] I well remember mother dressing me as an old lady, just to make sure than no one would attempt . . . to take advantage of me, although I was only nine years old. But with good reason, because my best friend, her mother didn't do it, and the child was grabbed and when she didn't let her go, they shot her in her mother's arms, because the Soviet army officer took a fancy to her. . . . So these are dramatic experiences and very dramatic memories.[28]

Stories such as Erzsébet's are typical of much of the post-Communist representation of the Red Army.[29] In these accounts, soldiers would molest any type of woman, whatever her status, age, condition or appeal: hence even a nine-year-old girl would have had to protect herself. The social expectation that an individual's encounters with the Red Army would inevitably have been violent meant that where women were not themselves violated, they needed to account for this absence. They told stories in which they were almost raped but escaped through unusual circumstances, ingenious strategies or just luck:

There were three of us who were fourteen and fifteen years old. We were dug into the coal in the cellar, so that only our noses stuck out. Moreover, we were doing this for a week, when the procession of Russians came in every night. My mother and the mother of the other small girls smeared our faces with coal, and let their hair down to make themselves look like old women. And then they sat on us, to hide us.[30]

Yet in showing that rape could be avoided, such stories detracted from the theme of inevitable violence. Stories of escape were therefore frequently juxtaposed both with reiterations that rape was unavoidable and with further accounts of those for whom similar strategies failed:

There was a well-known thing that everybody painted themselves black, and dressed up in all sorts of headscarves . . . to appear much older than they were. But, I should say, this didn't affect them, because we heard that this [i.e. rape] happened to sixty- or seventy-year-old women also, if the mood took them, because they were drinking together and they didn't know what they were doing.[31]

These respondents' underlying claim was that all Hungarian women were victims, regardless of whether they themselves had been violated. Rape was an endemic, everyday threat from which nobody could escape. Many historians have seen the outpouring of these narratives as the authentic and objective recollection of events previously repressed. Decades after the event, Hungarian women have finally been able to 'come to terms' with the shame they felt at having been raped and are now able to speak about it. The best-known post-Communist account of rape, Alaine Polcz's wartime memoir *Asszony a Fronton* ('Woman at the Front', translated into English as *A Wartime Memoir*), was promoted as the story of a traumatized victim of rape who had overcome tragedy, found happiness and could now tell her story.[32] In addition, these accounts have been presented as post-Communist 'truth-telling': women, freed from public censorship, were now able to relate their brutal experiences at the hands of the Red Army.

It is certainly the case that the collapse of Communism has afforded both women and men a first opportunity to talk openly about rape. Immediately after the war, Hungarians could not publicly articulate their experiences at the hands of the Red Army. At a political level, even before the Communist takeover in 1948, there was no free discussion of these atrocities. No public commission was set up to collect women's stories, as had been the case after other conflicts.[33] By early 1945, the press in Hungary was controlled by the

Soviet-dominated Allied Control Commission, which did not allow stories of atrocities to be printed. At a social level too, there was very little discussion of rape: unlike in other cities that suffered such as Berlin, women did not take pride in publicly recounting the stories of what had happened to them, neither did they keep records of their experiences.[34] The fear of being stigmatized meant many rape victims chose to hide their suffering for many years.[35] The Communist regime maintained a public silence over the issue for more than four decades: stories of mass rape were not compatible with the state-sponsored image of the Red Army as liberators of Hungary from Fascism.

While the end of Communist censorship allowed the issue of rape to be aired, the historian must examine the political forces that have pushed victim stories into public prominence, rather than simply accepting the phenomenon as post-Communist 'truth-telling'. The popularity of such stories was not the result of a post-Communist feminist movement. Rather, victim stories were shaped mainly by the agendas of Hungarian nationalism. Indeed, it was only those women who came from nationalist, conservative and strongly anti-Communist backgrounds who foregrounded the sexual brutality of the Red Army and presented themselves as terrified victims of mass atrocity.

Nationalists understood that stories of violation bolstered their version of Hungary's Fascist and Communist past and sought to bring them into the public domain. Narratives of victimization under Red Army occupation were employed to underline and foreshadow the suffering of the Hungarian people under the later Communist regime. Moreover, stories of Soviet atrocities, including rape, had the effect of diverting attention away from Hungary's experience of, and involvement in, Fascism and the Holocaust.

Stories that connected personal experiences of Soviet rape with the general brutalization and subjugation of the Hungarian nation under Communism could be powerfully resuscitated after 1989, in part because they were a revival of the way in which the atrocity had been understood at the time of the Communist takeover. Ferenc Nagy, leader of the Smallholders' Party and Hungarian premier prior to the Communist seizure of power, was forced into exile and used atrocity stories to emphasize the illegality of the Red Army's (and, by extension, the Communists') presence in Hungary. Indeed, he even employed sexual metaphors to characterize Soviet aggression: 'Communist imperialism is an advancing process of penetration . . . . by its very nature it cannot stop.'[36] In his book *The Struggle Behind the Iron Curtain*, he deliberately picked out examples of rape that would horrify his audience in the west and would illustrate Hungary's status as victim of Soviet aggression:

The barbarism of the Soviet occupying forces can best be judged by the fact that many thousands of Hungarian men were raped or forced to unnatural excesses by Russian women soldiers. The Reds established a recreation camp near Kecskemét for more than thirty thousand sick and convalescent women members of the Soviet army and the police forces. From this camp, for instance, the Russian women banded together at night and swooped down on the surrounding hamlets, kidnapping the men and sometimes holding them captive for days.

Often these abductions led to the peculiar situation of women and girls hiding, not themselves, but their men in the forests and in haystacks to keep them from the disease-ridden Soviet women troops.[37]

In order to emphasize the endemic nature of rape in the Red Army, Nagy stressed the complicity of an unlikely set of perpetrators: incapacitated female soldiers. Drawing on a popular interwar conservative trope of the female Communist sexual predator, he suggested that rapes were not committed solely by rogue individuals, but that organized collectives of women soldiers violated Hungarian men.[38] Moreover, by suggesting that even men were at risk, he implied that all Hungarians, not just vulnerable women, were potential victims. Stories of sexual brutality illustrated the idea of an entire nation victimized and subdued by the representatives of an ideology whose inversion of anticipated gender roles attested to their abnormality and foreignness.

Post-Communist nationalist discourses revived these ways of presenting rape, interweaving stories of sexual violence with the violation of national symbols and the destruction of the Hungarian nation. In the film *A Vád (The Prosecution)* (1998), the director Sándor Sára implied through the linking of two narratives that Hungary herself was 'raped' by the Communists. The central story of the rape of a Hungarian peasant woman (the idealized conservative embodiment of the Hungarian nation), and the trial of her brother for shooting her Red Army rapist, was juxtaposed with scenes showing the events leading to the takeover of the state by the Communist Party. In a similar fashion, the Hungarian Catholic Church used narratives of rape to symbolize the destruction of a Christian nation by a barbarous, heathen force. The Catholic bishop of Győr, Vilmos Apor, was 'martyred' following an unsuccessful attempt to protect Hungarian women at his palace from Soviet troops (he was beatified in 1997). In popular versions of the story of his death, Apor, in full ceremonial dress, was shot three times on Good Friday and died two days later on Easter Sunday. Both the rape of Hungarian women and the murder of a Catholic bishop mirrored and mutually reinforced the narrative of a nation and its traditions destroyed by a marauding enemy army.

The connection between the rape of Hungary's women and the 'rape of the nation' was crucial for nationalists' post-1989 accounts of Communism. For them, Communism was a foreign force, imposed from the outside, under which ordinary Hungarians were simply victims and never complicit in its operation.[39] Any memory of support for Communism or of complex relationships between Communist state and citizen was marginalized. Shocking rape stories reinforced this version of history: Hungarian women were only ever victims of Soviet violence and any memory of fraternization between Soviet troops and Hungarian women was erased.[40] In other nationalist depictions of Hungarian history, the Communist period is left out entirely, as if it were not part of the nation's past at all.[41] In such accounts, the story of rape functioned to mark the point beyond which the Hungarian citizen became a passive victim and the history of the Hungarian nation was put on hold.

Post-Communist nationalist histories sought to draw attention to one specific set of victims – the Hungarian nation under Communism – while deliberately downplaying others – in particular, Hungarian Jewish victims of the Holocaust and political opponents of Fascism. This construction was crucial to the anti-Communist rhetoric of the first conservative government after 1990. Its leaders presented themselves as the inheritors of the anti-Communist, nationalist traditions of the conservative Horthy regime of the interwar years. In doing so, they revived the memory of the wartime efforts of the Hungarian army, who, as heroic Hungarian patriots, had fought the 'evil' Soviet Union and thus had resisted the arrival of Communism in Hungary 'in advance'.[42] The fact that they had been fighting alongside Nazi Germany was of less importance: it was Communism, not Fascism, that had been the greatest threat to the Hungarian nation.[43] The story of victimized Hungarian women again played a significant part in the narrative: the alliance with Nazi Germany was downplayed as Hungarian soldiers were remembered as heroes of a campaign in which they fought to protect their country and its women from the Soviets. Moreover, an emphasis on the sexual brutality of the Soviet army distracted attention from the far greater violence of the Holocaust that had preceded it under the German occupation and the indigenous Hungarian Fascist regime. Nationalist voices often sought to contain the power of the memory of victims of Fascism whose stories had the capacity to drown out appeals to the victims of Communism.[44]

Nationalist histories provided those conservative women who wanted to describe their suffering at the hands of the Red Army with a language of victimhood and trauma. However, this also meant that these women's narratives were shaped by the language of Hungarian nationalism, and that their stories of rape contributed to the marginalization of the memory of Fascism and the Holocaust.[45] Within oral history accounts, conservative women them-selves were prepared to use accounts of rape to illustrate the brutality of the Soviets while simultaneously playing down the violence inflicted on certain sections of the Hungarian population during the German occupation from March 1944.

Many conservative women normalized their experiences of, or down-played, the historic importance of, the German occupation of Hungary and the Fascist regime that followed it. This was despite the fact that after May 1944 the Nazis' political enemies were persecuted and over 600,000 Hungarian Jews perished in the Holocaust:

James: So what was your personal experience of German occupation?
Irén: Nothing special. I have to say nothing special, because we were not, how should I say? – we had nothing to fear. My father was in a good position, he was a director.[46]

Mária too claimed not to have been affected by the German occupation:

We had a very beautiful life . . . that was until [December] 1944 . . . . then the siege came. I still haven't mentioned the war because it did not affect us much . . . where we lived in Buda on Sváb Hill, we say that the war did not touch us there. But then during the siege . . . when the Russians came, then I can say that our lives were turned through 180 degrees.[47]

What matters here is not whether her life was actually beautiful or not (it may well have been), but rather the fact that after revelations about the horrors of the German occupation and of the indigenous Fascist regime, she still did not feel the need to alter her testimony to address her former ignorance of what was happening to others in her society. The absence of right-wing violence and the Holocaust in her testimony suggests that she wanted to present Communism, not Fascism, as the greatest evil of her lifetime.

The sexual brutality of the Red Army was crucial in such narratives. It focused on the evils of the Soviets, and by extension the Communists, while playing down the horrors of the Hungarian experience of Fascism. This point was often made through an explicit contrast between the kindness of German soldiers and the brutality of the Red Army. Moreover, rape was clearly being used to refute the idea that 1945 marked a liberation in any way. Conservatives often refer to Jews who were persecuted at the moment of their 'so-called liberation' by the Red Army: the 'liberated' were mistaken in believing they had been liberated at all:

James: And what was your impression of the German soldiers? Do you remember?

Ildikó: I could go to the country alone and whenever I met a German soldier they were just helpful . . . the German Wehrmacht, the army, were cultured people. And the army, when they came, were just marvellous . . . . My friend, she's very nice, but she's not conservative and she thinks differently about certain things. The Russians, she thinks they saved her life, because she was a Jewish girl, but still these Jewish people were taken by the Communists and sent to prison again. So somebody who came back from Auschwitz was sent to the Gulag. We were very frightened. My father fought against Bolshevism and was in the army. So, of course, until the last drop of our blood, we were against the Russians . . . . I had to leave home because some of them were very interested in me. I was thirteen years old or so and my mother tried to hide me and I went to stay with other families.[48]

Stories of women's suffering should not be seen only as the product of the end of censorship or as part of a society 'coming to terms' with a traumatic past: rather, they were often shaped by nationalist versions of Hungarian history that have deflected attention away from the crimes of Fascism by focusing on those of the Red Army and the Communist regime. It was only women from conservative backgrounds who remembered rape in this way. Nationalism gave them a language with which they could articulate their suffering at the hands of the Red Army and which did not conflict with their own conservative interpretations of history.[49]

Rape Stories: Marginalization and Denial

In oral history testimony, other groups who experienced the Soviet occupation refused to frame the violations they had experienced or witnessed as a significant and traumatic event. Some maintained that rape was of little importance or was not so widespread as to affect their behaviour under Soviet occupation. Some suggested they were not even aware it was happening. Some denied to themselves for many years that rapes had occurred. Others suggested that, where something did happen, it was often as consensual sex between a soldier and a Hungarian woman. Some turned the common understanding of rape as an act of power over women on its head: in their accounts, the Red Army rapist became the true 'victim' of the encounter. For them, the prominence of horrific rape stories in post-Communist culture was not merely the result of a lifting of censorship, but part of a wider, actively produced and highly politicized right-wing account of history.

This perception did not begin in 1989, but had existed before the arrival of the Red Army in Hungary, when stories about the cruelties inflicted on local populations by the Soviets were seen by many as the product of German and Hungarian wartime propaganda. The Nazis had presented Soviet troops as racially inferior, from a lower level of civilization and thus capable of acts of extreme brutality.[50] Recruitment posters for the Hungarian army had suggested that if the Red Army reached Hungary, men would be deported to Siberia and women and children left to suffer under a brutal occupying army (see Figure 16). One well-known poster in Budapest suggestively featured a Red Army soldier ripping a crucifix from a woman's neck.[51] Many oral history respondents remembered radio broadcasts that related the terrible ways in which the Red Army treated women and children.

The Nazis' use of images of Soviet atrocities meant that the issue of rape was politicized even before the arrival of the Red Army. Atrocity stories were immediately distrusted by left-wingers, liberals and Jews, who saw them as an invention of the Fascist propaganda. According to Alexandra Orme, a Polish aristocrat who was in Hungary in 1944–45:

> The papers never used to call the Russians anything but the 'Red Hangmen' or the 'Perverts' and the local wireless station, which was manned by Germans, never tired of broadcasting accounts of the horrible crimes committed by the Russians . . . . We did not believe a word of it. Among ourselves, we would admit the possibility of there being a few isolated cases of Russian soldiers getting drunk and raping a few women who happened to come their way, but on the whole we had the best possible opinion of the Russian army.[52]

In fact, such perceptions meant that many were shocked to discover that some elements of the Red Army did commit rapes:

James: Were there rumours about the Red Army?

Ödön: Yes, but we always thought that whatever bad was said about them was put around deliberately by the authorities so I don't think that my family or the people in the cellar, apart from the Fascist who was hiding with us, believed any of these rumours. I think it came as quite a shock that the first thing they did was rob us . . . . there were two younger women whom they simply selected from the crowd and herded towards the door and everybody knew what this meant, but after a few minutes they reappeared because apparently they were crying and begging them and I suppose even a soldier didn't want that sort of fuss.[53]

By contrast, conservatives who supported the Hungarian-German war effort and saw the Soviet forces as the enemy were easily convinced that accounts of Red Army atrocities were accurate:

James: Do you remember when you heard that the Russians were getting close to Budapest?

Magda: Yes, yes, up till then the radio worked and it was always possible to hear things about it . . . . I felt a great amount of fear, as they depicted them as such wild people . . . they spoke about how cruel they were: they raped the women, they looted, they shot people down. One believed it for a long time and now looking back – it was just propaganda, but there was an awful lot of truth in it as well.

The fact that atrocity stories existed as a form of propaganda prior to the arrival of the Red Army influenced Hungarian attitudes towards the Soviets when they did arrive and subsequent accounts of the Red Army's actions. Conservatives had their prior suspicions about the army's brutality adequately confirmed by the troops' behaviour after their arrival. Moreover, in their explanations of Soviet violence, they drew on Nazi propaganda that had presented World War II as a racial struggle against an inferior 'Asiatic' civilization wanting to impose its barbarous political ideology on Europe.[54] Evidence for this racial interpretation of the war was amply provided by the high number of ill-behaved Central Asian troops among the Soviet occupying force in Budapest. Many conservatives still drew a link between the inferiority of Asiatic-looking troops and their lack of sexual restraint with Hungarian women: 'It [rape] was an everyday thing for the Russians. If they arrived and they could do it, then they did it . . . . the remainder [in the army] were Asiatic; they came from a different level of civilization . . . there was no kind of inhibition in them.'[55]

Yet the experience of occupation did not lead others to present the Red Army as uncivilized barbarian rapists. Some still saw images of sexual violence as the stuff of Nazi propaganda: Alexandra Orme, as late as 1949, found it easy to explain away incidences of brutality and argued for the essential goodness of the Soviet soldier:

I never found one really bad person amongst them. I was to hear much of how they stole, looted and raped. They do that when they are drunk, or when their commander is an evil person himself and exercises a bad influence on them . . . . The Russian soldier ought by right to have been a dreadful and a dangerous person, for he has neither discipline nor even religion to restrain him, and from childhood has been taught that Europe is inhabited by bloodsuckers whom he ought to destroy. But get to know him properly . . . you will see that nowhere are there so many good people as in Russia.[56]

It was striking that former party members, interviewed after 1989, remembered their refusal to admit that rapes had occurred in the immediate postwar period. The Hungarian situation was different from that in Germany, where rape was discussed more publicly and there is substantial evidence that women related openly what had happened to them.[57] In Hungary, the Soviet-dominated Allied Control Commission did not allow stories about rape to be published from winter 1945 onwards; the only hint that rapes occurred existed in the advertisements for abortion procedures that had a regular presence in newspapers in 1945. Research on rape was not allowed at universities.[58] Party members were thus not confronted with the issue, and could construct rumours of rape simply as 'enemy propaganda'. Sándor, for instance, came from a Jewish left-wing family and joined both the Communist Party and an auxiliary unit of the Red Army immediately after the war. Nobody dared to tell him about atrocities. Moreover, his support for the Communists led him to dismiss rumours of rape:

James: I'm also interested in the rumours that were going round about the Soviet army at that time.

Sándor: Well, I mean, I don't know whether I did hear about them raping people and so on. We *now* know they did. This wouldn't have necessarily reached a young man . . . wearing a red armband. And by March or April [1945] when school started we already had guns . . . so nobody would have told me what they thought about it. And for us I think they remained the 'liberators' certainly for some time.

James: Did you hear about rapes at the time, or was it only later?

Sándor: Don't remember. I would have blotted it out, probably . . . . I could very well imagine that, if anything arrived in our family circle, one would have said, 'This is Nazi nonsense' . . . . So we wouldn't have believed it . . . that's the same as the interwar lefties who didn't want to believe the purges of 1937 – that they were just rumours put around by the enemy.

His belief that the new Soviet man was not sexually aggressive was put to the test when, as a young Communist Party member, he supervised a regiment of visiting Soviet trade apprentices in Budapest:

> I think at that time we were still convinced that they [the Soviets] were new men. . . . [They were the] Battalion of Trade Apprentices, who were of course young proletarians from Moscow for whom this was the beautiful west . . . and at night [they] were regularly jumping out of their windows and going to drink somewhere or pick up some whores or whatever else, which we were very embarrassed by. Very embarrassed by them. Didn't denounce them, but we knew about it, because they asked for our help.

Sándor continued to deny that atrocities had occurred as long as he considered the arrival of the Red Army as a liberation, kept his faith in the postwar political transformation that that liberation had allowed and maintained his belief in the potential of the Communist state (even if he had been disillusioned at certain points). He started to believe stories of rape only during his army service in 1954 when faced with the suicides of old men forced to work on collective farms:

> James: So when did you start to believe [in the occurrence of rape]?
> Sándor: . . . As I say, it was during my army service when it became clear what was going on in the country. . . . I think we once or twice tried to keep the old men from hanging themselves. But then I thought that that's not really what we want to do, and kind of decided to 'tend my garden'.[59]

Stories that marginalized the importance of Red Army atrocities, or downplayed the trauma caused by the experience, have not received public attention in post-Communist Hungary. However, they occured frequently in private oral history testimony. These stories have been shaped by the continued political debates over the meaning of World War II and its aftermath in post-Communist culture. As we saw above, nationalist voices in contemporary Hungary moulded women's stories into narratives of brutality and victimization in order to illustrate the righteousness of the Hungarian army's struggle alongside Nazi Germany against the Soviet Union, and the subsequent victimization of the Hungarian nation under the Communist regime. Thus, for many Jewish and left-wing respondents, horror stories of trauma and victimhood were associated with right-wing versions of history that were insufficiently critical of Hungary's experience of Fascism and wartime alliance with Germany.

Some groups in post-Communist Hungarian society still held to the 'anti-Fascist narrative', presenting the arrival of the Red Army as a liberation. For them, the Red Army had defeated Fascism, bringing political persecution and the deportation and extermination of Hungary's Jewish population to an end. Whatever the later consequences of the Soviet presence, for such respondents the Red Army's role as liberator could not be eroded. This position was put most forcefully by Jewish respondents, one of whom recounted an idealized 'saviour' image she still held of the 'liberating army': 'And then on the morning of the liberation [*laughs*], there was, I mean, I think this is not true, but my memory is that this Russian soldier in a white fur coat, with a gleaming sword, I mean, that's how I remember it, came in, and there were people kissing his hand. I don't know how much truth there is in it!'[60] Faced with the contemporary conservative portrayal of the Red Army as brutal occupiers, these respondents, especially Jewish ones, created a counter-narrative: they downplayed rape or provided different accounts of sexual contact between Soviet soldiers and Hungarian women. In doing so, they used rape stories as a different form of 'truth-telling': to highlight their experience of 1945 as a liberation.[61] Miklós directly attacked the dominant conservative representation:

James: And so did you see any of the behaviour of Russian soldiers?

Miklós: Yes. Now, don't expect me to say the usual thing that every Russian was a rapist. No! Many of the girls, even the Jewish girls, were happy to be raped, and they came up [to you] afterwards and said, 'But he was so experienced!' [*laughs*][62]

Both men and women sought to reinstate the Red Army as liberators by challenging rape stories, but did so in different ways. For Jewish or left-wing men, stories of mass rape were often replaced by narratives of consensual sex between Hungarian women and Soviet soldiers. Unlike conservatives, who never mentioned the idea of 'fraternization', these men thought that women might express their gratitude by offering themselves sexually to their liberators: 'When we lived in that air-raid shelter, they wanted to rape my wife's elder sister, but there was another young lady whom they took, and she said, "Please, I owe my life to you, I will volunteer." And instead of Anikó, this woman allowed two or three Russian soldiers to go through her [*sic*].' These men did not present such actions as collaboration: the Red Army was not considered the enemy, and hence women could sleep with them and remain honourable:

James: Did you know anybody who was raped by the Russians?

Mátyás: . . . At our place we were lucky, because in the house where we were there were two women whom they didn't have to rape, because they gave their services to the Russians with a lot of pleasure, and therefore gave us a small kind of defence in this micro-environment, but this was a particularly fortuitous set-up. Two honourable Hungarian women who happily slept with the Russians.[63]

Left-wing and Jewish women did not substitute stories of forced violation with narratives of consensual sex as their male counterparts did. They were much more prepared to admit to the occurrence of rape but nevertheless wanted to show that the experience was very different from the horrific encounters recalled by conservative women. Their accounts still echoed the anti-Fascist accounts of 1945: that excuses should be made for the Red Army's behaviour as a 'liberating army'. Luca was typical in retaining her sympathy for the Red Army despite the near-rape of a family member: 'I don't look at this and say, "Oh terrible Russian troops!" I mean, they were soldiers, they were away from home, they were fighting, I mean, what do you expect? They nearly raped my sister, but again, it was my father who saved her. But again, I look at it, these were people away for years from their girlfriends, what do you expect?'

Others sought to place Soviet violence in context, arguing that it was of far less significance than what the Germans had done. Indeed, some progressives, such as Vera, still reproduced the story that Soviet soldiers commonly told in 1945 about the Germans' violent treatment of babies:[64]

James: So you said you remember people talking about the rapes that took place. What did people say?

Vera: Well, it was common knowledge that they came into a dwelling where there were women, and raped them, several of them in succession. . . . You must understand that the Germans did much worse than that. I saw Germans throwing babies at the wall, you know, their brains popping out, and I didn't see the Russians doing that.[65]

Even the left-wing or Jewish women who were raped did not shape stories of their own violations into ones of trauma and victimization. Katalin was raped by two Red Army soldiers. She came from a wealthy conservative family but had turned to socialism as a young woman and had welcomed the Red Army as liberators. She had hoped that the collapse of Horthy's Hungary would usher in a more equitable, meritocratic society, but was quickly disappointed by her experience of the Communist state, especially as her class background confined her to menial jobs. She was equally disillusioned by post-Communist Hungary, which she saw as an iniquitous society. She therefore sought to provide an image of the Red Army that spoke of her experience of liberation in 1945, and took issue with the stories of mass rapes, which she considered to have been promoted for political reasons in post-Communist Hungary.

She first rejected the idea that women had seen themselves as victims of the Red Army in 1945. She was interviewed with another woman, Éva, who related how her mother had dressed her as a boy in order to prevent her being raped. Katalin immediately challenged the idea that girls needed to disguise themselves: it was mere parroting of German propaganda from 1944:

James: Can you remember what you thought about the Russians coming?

Éva: Yes, I was afraid, because from the radio and from broadcasts you knew that they were bad and they took children and they raped women and girls. . . .

Katalin: Propaganda. . . . German propaganda only. . . .

Éva: But it goes on when a war comes. . . . So my mother made me look like a boy and gave me a boy's name. . . . My hair was cut off to turn me into a boy.

Katalin: What was your age?

Éva: Six or something like this.[66]

Katalin: You weren't in danger whether you were a girl or a boy. . . . Why did she think you were safer as a boy than as a girl of six years? . . . Sixteen years old I would understand, but six years?

James: So did you try to change your appearance when the Russians came?

Katalin: I never . . . I was not afraid . . . I never had the feeling of being in danger. Before the war there was the propaganda that they would rape – but what army doesn't? That was the propaganda and when it happened nobody was astonished. It was just sheer luck whether you were raped or not. Of course, there were women who did it [i.e. slept with Red Army Soldiers] of their own free will, yes, because they got food and clothing and I don't know what. There were two kinds of people: those who spoke about it and those who didn't and denied it all.

She then gave an account of her own rape:

When I had to get up, because nature was calling, they [the Red Army soldiers] noticed that I was not a child, and then the situation began to get tricky because they had already begun to court some of the girls there. When later I had to go out, one or two of them escorted me to the neighbours, and they used the opportunity – when I was already married – but I did not die from it. I was lucky because they were provided with condoms from the Tetenyi rubber factory. So when things happened I was astonished but I said, 'So, alright, we survived, that's no problem' . . . . you must understand that a great many came from a very bad environment in Russia and were very poor.[67]

Katalin's account was moulded by her own politics: her continued sympathy for the Red Army meant that she did not use the story of her own rape to demonize them. First, she presented the soldiers as having 'courted the girls' rather than violated them. Second, she downplayed its importance ('I did not die from it') and chose to stress those elements of the experience that lessened its implications for her: the soldiers brought condoms from the local rubber factory. Third, she did not use the language of victimization or trauma so common in nationalist accounts. She presented her rape in the least psychologically damaging way possible: she did not stress the brutalization or violation that was central to other narratives. Rather, one of the worst aspects was that she was 'already married'. The idea of psychological trauma was also rejected: the rape was neither a defining moment in her life nor did it have a damaging effect on her ('we survived, that's no problem'). Lastly, she sympathized with the culpable soldiers and found reasons for their behaviour. The idea that some were backward and primitive was central to this construction: she turned the Red Army soldiers into objects of sympathy and placed herself above 'poor' and disadvantaged Russians. Her loss of honour was erased by the belief that she was superior to those who raped her.[68] Katalin's testimony vividly illustrates the different narrative frameworks that left-wing women used to couch their accounts of rape at the hands of the Red Army. She avoided presenting her experience as a moment of terrible violation, and herself as a 'rape victim'; this might in part have been because the term 'rape' seemed to her to overdramatize an experience that she had otherwise resisted processing as brutalizing, by a group of people whom she saw as her liberators.[69] Certainly, after 1989, any sense of suffering she might have felt had to be downplayed for fear of legitimizing dominant conservative stories, which might have drawn upon the story of 'her rape' to demonize her 'liberators' and to drown out the memory of greater atrocities.

Conclusion

Within Hungary, telling stories about Red Army rape – either as witness or victim – was a political act in 1944, and continued to be so right into the post-

Communist period. Conservative and nationalist women had multiple public narratives to choose from in trying to make sense of their suffering at the hands of the Red Army. Even before the Soviet troops arrived, Nazi propaganda had supplied a model for their understanding of rape as the brutalization of the Hungarian nation by an Asiatic barbarian horde. Even today, some respondents' testimony suggests that their experiences of fear and brutality at the hands of the Soviets in 1945 were still understood as the confirmation of those images provided under the German occupation. After the war, the demonization of the Red Army as rapists then became a way of describing the roots of the subjugation of the country by the Soviet-backed Hungarian Workers' Party. This interpretation was publicly articulated after 1989: the image of the brutalized rape victim marked the violation of the Hungarian nation and the beginning of its brutal suppression over four decades. Conservative women had thus been able to draw upon a range of scripts that enabled them to understand their individual suffering as part of a systematic, brutal and traumatizing violation of the Hungarian female population.

By contrast, many left-wing, progressive and Jewish women who had been violated by soldiers of the Red Army, or had witnessed others' suffering, did not wish to present themselves as brutalized victims or to testify to others' pain, even after 1989. In 1945, the fact that they associated the idea of rape with Nazi propaganda, held sympathies for those who would then violate them and saw themselves as representatives of a 'guilty nation', meant that they refused to frame their experiences as brutal violations, but rather as understandable, if unfortunate, by-products of war. This 'anti-Fascist' outlook even led some to deny that rapes had occurred at all. Their anti-Fascism, which had drawn them into refusing to condemn the Red Army despite the atrocities they committed, was drowned out after 1948 by an officially imposed state anti-Fascism which repressed the memory of rape altogether and also silenced their sympathetic narratives. Yet their stories enjoyed a revival after 1989: faced with newly dominant discourses that linked the brutality of Soviet soldiers to radical anti-Communist agendas, the imperative to tell their own version of events was given a new impetus. Their stories were a form of 'anti-witnessing', a refusal to testify to the atrocities of a brutal occupier, or to shape their own violations into accounts of a traumatized nation. All these stories demonstrated the degree to which there was still a sense of competitive victimization between those who had suffered variously under Communism and Fascism: left-wing and Jewish women's refusal to witness their own suffering under the Soviets was an attempt to transmit, to a post-Communist world, the importance of both the experience of suffering under Nazism and their liberation from it.

There has been no powerful non-political way for this generation to talk about the atrocities committed by the Red Army in Hungary since the end of the war. As the political theorist and politician István Bibó commented in 1945, the Hungarian population, 'confused by having been exposed to distorted world views for decades . . . envisioned the Russian army exclusively in terms of such stereotypes, and instead of expecting living, flesh-and-blood individuals, they saw the arrival of devils or angels embodying an ideology'.[70] Even after 1989, Red Army soldiers were still imagined as angels or devils, and stories of mass atrocities, rape or its denial, consensual sex or contextualized brutality reflected the political debates and conflicts within Hungarian society. No other meaningful way of understanding rape that could undercut these politicized framings emerged. Women did not come to view themselves simply as victims of war, or of male violence in conflict, for instance: a gendered view of the meaning of sexual brutalization in war did not exist for this generation.[71] Nor could they view their victimization solely in terms of their own personal trauma. Being a victim still signalled, for many, the acceptance of Nazi propaganda and conservative anti-Communist discourses with which they could not identify. Thus, over fifty years after the atrocities themselves, victims' and witnesses' stories were still linked to their mid-twentieth-century political orientations and outlooks. Hungary's wartime past was not 'mastered' after 1989: there was very little sign that consensual accounts of the Red Army's behaviour and of the country's experience of the war, Fascism and Communism could be constructed within post-Communist Hungarian society.

CONCLUSION: DIVIDED SOCIETIES, DEMOCRATIC MEMORY?

The idea that the past was something to be overcome was key for the new cultures that emerged after 1989 in central-eastern Europe. History could not simply be left behind: it demanded to be reworked and mythologized so that the painful legacies it had left for the present could be mastered. Post-Communism was a culture of historical reinvention, in which political parties, state-sponsored historical institutions, cultural sites and individuals packaged the meanings and memories of dictatorship to meet the needs of a new political system. New institutions such as institutes of national memory and history commissions were established to construct and disseminate versions of the past that were deemed appropriate for the post-Communist world. In the cultural sphere, memorial museums at sites of terror and statue parks propagated their own particular understandings of the Communist past. Political parties of both left and right drew upon stories of their resistance to, or suffering under, Communist dictatorship when constructing new political identities. Many of those who had lived through Communism also regarded the process of re-working their life stories for a liberal democratic age as essential: former Communists, the socially mobile and the persecuted all presented post-Communism as an era in which they had had to adapt their understandings of their experiences of dictatorship in response to new political imperatives.

Yet post-Communist cultures in central-eastern Europe were, for the most part, deeply divided over how best to come to terms with their dictatorial history. Various groups, each of which had different relationships to the past, varying understandings of what had occurred in 1989, diverse conceptions of the nature of the democratization that had been achieved and different political visions for the future of post-Communist societies, had, in consequence, divided understandings of the way in which the past should be overcome.

Moreover, in this epoch of rapid reinvention and deep contestations over how to rise above a problematic past, many were forced not simply to articulate their version of history, but to find ways of powerfully demonstrating the validity of their view: these were cultures in which displays of authenticity were vital in order to make these recent reworkings of the past appear meaningful and convincing. Battles thus raged over which voices were the most genuine and where the truth about Communism could best be discovered. Groups were centrally concerned with the promotion of their own credibility, developing a broad range of new rhetorical justifications – 'giving voice to the repressed', 'taming a wild past', 'uncovering hidden horrors' – that attempted to make their reformulations appear obvious and historically persuasive. Likewise, those who criticized these approaches sought to undermine such appeals, framing their opponents in the clash over historical memory as inauthentic charlatans who had distorted their own histories based on the selective use of evidence.

For some elites, whom in broad terms we might describe as radical, or nationalist, anti-Communists, the central issue was the unfinished nature of the political transition. For them, the supposedly victorious events of 1989 had in fact been a defeat as the Communists had not been excluded from participation in the new political system, and the continued presence of former dictators was inimical to the development of both an advanced democracy and a new order based around conservative morality, nationalism and anti-Communism. The invocation of the past was key in their mobilization of nationalist and radical anti-Communist constituencies to complete the 'unfinished revolution'. Some right-wing governments such as Fidesz in Hungary (1998–2002, 2010-) or Law and Justice in Poland (2005–7) framed 1989 as a betrayal, and sought to revive the memory of older anti-Communist struggles in order to inspire an ongoing anti-Communist crusade in the present. In other cases, they presented Communism as a world divided into patriotic victims and traitorous collaborators, and sought to transfer these categories into the post-Communist world. Contemporary political struggles were framed as fights between former victims on the one hand, and the surviving perpetrators, on the other. This work has addressed two powerful *lieux de memoire* where these ideas were articulated after 1989: the site of terror and the post-Communist autobiography. At locations of former violence such as mass graves and political prisons and camps, anti-Communists sought not merely to resurrect the memory of those who had suffered under dictatorship but also to employ the stories of what they had endured as a broader metaphor for the victimization of countries that had stoically withstood violent, anti-national regimes of occupation. In this sense, sites of terror were designed to forge broader anti-Communist constituencies who saw themselves as 'national martyrs' and whose power could be drawn upon to continue the anti-Communist fight in the present. Conservative anti-Communists constructed autobiographies in which they also presented themselves as victims who had suffered and endured a foreign occupation. The oral history conducted for this project demonstrated how even those opponents of the former regime had had very complex experiences of Communism, enjoying periods of professional success, especially in the late Communist period, as well as moments of violence, discrimination and persecution earlier in their lives. Nevertheless, their life stories concentrated upon incidents of victimization, as traumatized sufferers of Red Army atrocities or as the professionally excluded. They were not simply giving voice to experiences which could not be articulated before 1989: their stories of ill-treatment allowed them to claim that they had faithfully served the country during a period of foreign rule, enduring persecution, in order to maintain the nation's traditions and stories within their families and ready to pass them on to a new generation after 1989.

Anti-Communist elites attempted to make their understandings of their countries' pasts powerful in part through the re-creation of a world of Communist crimes and 'totalitarian evil' at sites of memory where these histories of violence and illegality seemed self-evident and unchallengeable. Nationalists gave these locations authenticity by presenting their interventions as simple uncoverings of the truth that Communists had always tried to hide: a powerful rhetorical device that distracted attention from the political agendas that lay behind the very act of uncovering. At sites of terror, they looked to the assistance of professionals such as forensic archaeologists, whose work provided a powerful metaphor for the objective, apolitical, scientific peeling away and revealing of stories that, it seemed, the past had always been waiting to serve up to the present. In a similar fashion, the power of autobiographies of victimization – of which there were many after 1989 – relied on a powerful rhetoric of truth-telling and direct eyewitnessing that underlay the nationalist outlooks that framed the ways in which many victims related stories from their earlier lives. They presented themselves as the powerless downtrodden of history, finally able to reveal the violence that had been inflicted on them. It was for this reason that many who suffered but whose politics did not match that of nationalist anti-Communists refused to draw on the language of trauma to express their suffering or marginalization under Communism. Many victims – of Red Army atrocities, deportation, or of class- or politically-based discrimination – were unwilling to testify to what they had endured precisely because the post-Communist life story was loaded with so much political baggage, and they did not wish to see theirs deployed to confirm a nationalist project of anti-Communist revenge. Thus they constructed autobiographies to undermine a totalitarian reading of their lives, and refused to perform their stories of suffering according to the expectations of a post-Communist world. They sought a language that avoided the reductive categories of victim or perpetrator, and often used their stories of imprisonment or punishment to ridicule the accounts of the Communist past that could not find their way beyond the merely criminal.

Yet, for more moderate, often liberal, anti-Communist elites, the invocation of a criminal Communist world from which the post-Communist present had not escaped, and the insistence that the anti-Communist struggle needed to be recreated in the present, were in themselves inimical to democratic development. The notion of the unfinished revolution, although it might properly describe some unfortunate legacies of Communism, had both deeply divided the post-Communist polity and prompted a crisis in popular identification with it. For the moderate anti-Communists, the events of 1989 could not only be understood as an incomplete process: the Round Table negotiations of that year also represented a civilized agreement that embodied the democratic values of negotiation and compromise in action, and hence symbolized a defeat for authoritarian practices. These were the early stages of a longer-term process of post-Communist democratization. Moderates did not identify the physical survival of Communists as a barrier to democratic development as radical anti-Communists did, but rather pinpointed the post-Communist nation's incapacity to identify with the new political system and reluctance to celebrate the democratic achievements already realized as the central problems to be tackled. They wanted to convince post-Communist societies that an imperfect, but stable and evolving form of democracy had been achieved, and to encourage citizens to identify with it.

They therefore engaged in work that sought to build a new unifying 'national memory' that they believed could heal past divides and underpin a proper liberal, democratic identity. While some championed the commemoration of the negotiations of 1989 as a victory over dictatorship, the unheroic, exclusive and elitist nature of these settlements made their mythologization difficult; thus, other approaches – embodied in the work of history commissions and institutes of national memory – sought new ways to narrate the break with dictatorship that would make the reality of a political caesura clear and meaningful to post-Communist societies. Like radical nationalist anti-Communists, they were keen to construct an image of Communism as a criminal world inhabited by perpetrators and victims. Yet, unlike them, they were not interested in mobilizing victims against perpetrators in the present, but rather wanted to show that these divisions had been overcome. They promoted the idea of a criminal Communist world in order to demonstrate what had in fact been achieved in 1989: an escape from a system based on force and illegality in which individuals were reduced to the status of victims or perpetrators to one based on human rights and protections for the individual from a once overbearing, violent state. A world of illegality was constructed as a mirror to the present, in which post-Communist populations might better view what they had left behind and hence commit to the superior form of democratic development that had started in 1989.

As we saw above, radical anti-Communist elites argued that the truth about Communism was to be found at physical locations of former terror – mass graves, former political prisons and camps. More moderate voices, by contrast, focused on the archives of the former secret police which provided them with powerful authentic written sources that documented the criminality of Communism. While nationalists relied on archaeologists to uncover the physical remains of Communist terror, more moderate anti-Communists looked to archivists and historians to reveal the crimes of collaboration and victimization through their work for history commissions and institutes of national memory. Their claims to authenticity lay in a number of propositions. They often evoked the idea of 'facing up to the past', a strategy that was presented as an advanced, civilized approach to dealing with the legacies of history drawn from western Europeans' reckoning with Nazism. Hence these moderate anti-Communists suggested that the adoption of such practices was a prerequisite for their societies becoming truly western and modern. They framed the choice not to reckon with dictatorship – by which they meant rejecting the idea of a criminal past of victims and perpetrators – as a mark of cultural backwardness, which would consign their societies to the margins of Europe where Communism had once placed them. At other points, they presented themselves as 'healers of a wounded past': while radical Communists sought to divide the post-Communist polity with appeals to continue past battles, moderates at the institutes and commissions envisaged their work as neutral arbiters of a divided past, who, through their judicious, balanced and supposedly apolitical use of the archives they controlled, could resolve present conflicts. They regarded themselves as the ones who would build a new unifying 'national memory' through the forging of a broad-based social and political consensus around the need to reject a criminal past.

It was not only anti-Communists who tried to reshape the way in which the national past was understood: former Communists who remained in the political system after 1989 as democratic socialists also needed to work through their relationship with dictatorship in order to compete in a new political age. Some rejected their pasts: apologies, and signs of atonement were often necessary to reposition parties of the ex-Communist left. Yet in many cases their appeals were more subtle. They did not unequivocally attack the leftist project of the second half of the twentieth century or criminalize it all; rather, they sought to sift through the wreckage of the postwar left's accommodations with dictatorship, and select out those parts of their movement's history that still had the potential to be revived and could be claimed as democratic. Moreover, they rejected the idea that they could simply be considered anti-national, traitorous, collaborating quislings, and looked to their pasts to make it appear so. Moments of resistance both to Fascism, and to Stalinist dictatorship by reform Communists were reworked into a democratic heritage for ex-Communists after 1989. Their claims to authenticity in post-Communism lay in the assertion that they had mounted the most sustained attack on dictatorship in the twentieth century, or, in other cases, that they had sought to protect the nation under constrained circumstances. Thus, while anti-Communists established the authenticity of their approaches to the past at sites of victimhood, former Communists preferred sites of resistance both to Fascism and Communism. Just as much as rightist parties, former Communists supported attempts to commemorate the heroic moments of Communist-era resistance such as the Hungarian Uprising of 1956 and the Polish Solidarity movement. In doing so, they were able either to demonstrate that they had once fought both dictatorship and excessive foreign domination, or at the very least were able to emphasize that the movement that they had once worked for had been truly defeated and that ex-Communists were thus no threat to liberal democracy. These reformulations were found in their post-Communist life stories too; for the reform-minded Communists of the postwar generation, the fight against Fascism in the 1940s and then against the excesses of Stalinism in the 1950s and 1960s confirmed their contribution to the struggle for a more progressive and democratic political culture. For a younger generation, the party's role in initiating the Round Table discussions of 1989 allowed them to create the myth of a democratic heritage in which even former party members had fought to erode the system from within. Although many found these claims unconvincing and historically inaccurate, they were a crucial feature of post-Communism: they demonstrated that even ex-Communists were keen to create a democratic heritage for themselves out of the memories of dictatorship.

Those who advocated these new procedures invariably presented themselves as trying to help their country properly overcome its difficult history. For some, this meant the re-animation of the struggles of the dictatorial past in the continued fight against the Communists who had remained within the post-1989 political system. For others, dealing with the past was about the creation of a unified new national memory that addressed the fractured understandings of dictatorship that lay behind the deep political divides of post-Communism. In other contexts, remembering the past correctly became a way of showing that one had become western and modern, and had truly left the backwardness of the Communist past behind. Recognizing the criminality of Communism and commemorating the Holocaust were promoted both to western political bodies and to domestic audiences as ways in which post-Communist societies were modernizing themselves in ways that would ensure their 'return to Europe'. Yet some were sceptical that these processes in fact represented any sort of overcoming past habits at all. Critics of the criminalization of the past often remarked on the similarities to the pre-1989 period: anti-Communist attempts to 'take revenge on the past', to criminalize its histories and build monolithic institutions devoted to imposing a new national memory 'from above', were legacies of politicized and authoritarian impulses drawn from the Communist era, and deleterious to a deeper form of liberal democratic development. Indeed, other critical voices suggested that such top-down politically-driven processes were incapable of engendering a widely accepted and honestly felt reckoning with the dictatorial past. Moreover, as oral histories collected here demonstrated, those who lived through the postwar period brought their distinctively Communist understandings of autobiography, loaded with political meaning and intent, into the present; where once they had constructed stories of anti-Fascist and class-based struggle in public to demonstrate loyalty to the Communist regime, or maintained anti-Communist family stories at home, they now carried these same politicized and divisive autobiographical habits with them into the post-1989 era. Nationalists deployed their stories of suffering to bolster the idea of a reconstituted nation that was still battling Communists; former Communists presented autobiographies of resistance to dictatorships in order to declare their allegiance to the new system. Thus, the very idea that post-Communist societies had to remake their pasts for a new political age was as much a legacy of four decades of a dictatorial system that had stressed both public and private reinvention, as it was a response to the encounter after 1989 with a western set of norms that demanded commemoration and the working through of difficult pasts as the key to overcoming dictatorship.

NOTES

Introduction

1. Lee Edwards, 'Is Communism Dead?' at <http://www.tfas.org/Document.Doc?id=30> (accessed 27 July 2009).

2. This figure for the number of victims of Communism was popularized by *the Black Book of Communism* a multi-authored work which documented the number of people killed under Communist regimes during the twentieth century. See Stéphane Courtois et al., *The Black Book of Communism: Crimes, Terror, Repression*, trans. Jonathan Murphy (Cambridge, MA: Harvard University Press, 1999). Opponents of the *Black Book's* approach criticized it for including a large number of deaths under Communist regimes that were either only indirectly caused by, or unrelated to, the practice of Communist ideology itself, and for including a wide range of dictatorships with different practices under the rubric of 'Communist'. More fundamentally, opponents objected to its 'numbers game', which obscured a more complex understanding of the causes of suffering, appeared to set up a competition between the victims of Communism and Fascism, and dangerously conflated historical research with a moralizing discourse in its attempt to deny the uniqueness of the Holocaust: Carolyn J. Dean, 'Recent French Discourses on Stalinism, Nazism and "Exorbitant" Jewish Memory', *History & Memory* 18/1 (2006): 49–52; Richard Golsan, 'The Politics of History and Memory in France in the 1990s', in *Stalinism and Nazism: History and Memory Compared*, ed. Henry Rousso (Lincoln, NB: University of Nebraska Press, 2004), xvii–xxi.

3. Tsao Tsing-Yuan, 'The Birth of the Goddess of Democracy', in *Popular Protest and Political Culture in Modern China*, ed. Jeffrey N. Wasserstrom and Elizabeth J. Perry (Boulder, CO: Westview Press, 1994), 140–47. Members of the committee had initially wanted to build a museum for the victims of Communism that would provide a counterpart to the Holocaust Museum in Washington. However, they were unable to raise enough money. They also considered a memorial based on other designs such as a replica of the Berlin Wall, a Gulag prison, or a boat used by Cuban or Vietnamese refugees; see John J. Miller, 'A Goddess for Victims', *National Review Online*, 28 May 2007 at <http://nrd.nationalreview.com/article/?q=YWNiODY4Y2FmNTM3YTI0YjhlYTc4ZGY0ZjE4ZDIyNDQ=> (accessed 27 July 2009).

4. Edwards, 'Is Communism Dead?', 4–5.

5. This habit of using the victims of totalitarianism to evidence America's global mission was not confined to monuments to Communism. Nathan Rappaport's monument 'Liberation' in Battery Park, outside New York's Holocaust Museum, was built across from the Statue of Liberty and Ellis Island, and represented an American GI rescuing an almost lifeless survivor of the Nazi camps. Both the form chosen for the memorial and its location wrote the Holocaust into the American national self-image: the Holocaust was used to represent its mission to spread freedom and crush tyranny, and to present America itself as a place of refuge and liberty. James E. Young, 'The Art of Memory: Holocaust Memorials in History', in *The Art of Memory: Holocaust Memorials in History*, ed. James E. Young (Munich: Prestel, 1994), 33.

6. George W. Bush's speech on 12 June 2007. In this context, the collapse of Communism was used to inspire a new generation in the 'War on Terror'. According to President Bush, former Communist adversaries were replaced by jihadists who held similar totalitarian ideologies.
7. For the most famous expression of this idea, see Francis Fukuyama, *The End of History and the Last Man* (London: Hamish Hamilton, 1992).
8. On the necessity of the victory over 'eastern' Communist ideologies for western identity, see Nataša Kovačević, *Narrating Post/Communism: Colonial Discourse and Europe's Borderline Civilization* (London: Routledge, 2008), 1–2.
9. Thus, the expression 'post-Communist' rather than 'liberal democratic' is used to describe the period after 1989. It implies an era that is a departure from the past, but for which the exact ideological direction of travel is unclear.
10. There is no neutral term to describe the region from which the selection of states between Russia and Germany under study are chosen. The descriptors 'eastern Europe' and 'central Europe' have been variously thought to include all the countries included here. 'Eastern Europe' was popular in the west during the Cold War, when these countries were within the Communist bloc and the term could be used to denote the economic and political underdevelopment of the region. Its connotation of backwardness means that its use is sometimes considered derogatory; nevertheless, it is still commonly employed both within, and outside, the region. 'Central Europe', by contrast, was more often used in the context of the region's aspiration to 'return to Europe' after 1989, and was drawn upon by domestic advocates of European Union accession to denote that the countries in question had natural 'western' inclinations and traditions and hence should be early candidates for membership. Thus, representatives of the second tier of European Union applicants in south-eastern European countries sometimes argued that the term 'central' was being used to draw new lines between the naturally 'western' (Poland, Czech Republic and so on) and the supposedly intrinsically eastern and backward (The Balkans). The terms 'east central' or 'central-eastern' have fewer problematic connotations. This is not only because they avoid the obvious value judgements immediately implied by choosing 'eastern' or 'central', and evade the unresolved problem of defining which countries belong to either geographical category, but also because they capture the ambiguity in definitions of the region. (Are we eastern? Are we really western?). These terms do, of course, have their own histories and political meanings, but these being for the most part historically submerged, they are less politically suggestive to the modern reader. The term 'east central Europe' is more commonly used by historians; the term 'central-eastern' by political and social scientists and economists. For the history of these concepts, see, for example, Robin Okey, 'Central Europe/Eastern Europe: Behind the Definitions', *Past and Present* 137/1 (1992): 102–33; Maria Todorova, *Imagining the Balkans* (New York and Oxford: Oxford University Press, 1997); Larry Wolff, *Inventing Eastern Europe: The Map of Civilization on the Mind of the Enlightenment* (Stanford, CA: Stanford University Press, 1994).
11. See Luisa Passerini, 'Memories between Silence and Oblivion', in *Contested Pasts: The Politics of Memory*, ed. Katharine Hodgkin and Susannah Radstone (London: Routledge, 2003), 238–54. See also, on the silencing of the Korean War in American memory, Marilyn Young, 'An Incident at No Gun Ri', in *Crimes of War: Guilt and Denial in the Twentieth Century*, ed. Omer Bartov, Atina Grossmann and Mary Nolan (New York: New Press, 2002), 242–58.
12. There were some exceptions to this, such as the Memorial of Rebirth in Bucharest, Romania, dedicated to the struggles of the Romanian Revolution and inaugurated in 2005, The first day of the Velvet Revolution in Czechoslovakia, 17 November 1989, became a 'Day of Freedom' in the Czech Republic, but even here, it was not considered a particularly important celebration, at least until the twentieth anniversary. Thanks to Michal Kopeček for this information.
13. This is close to Jeffrey Olick's concept of the 'politics of regret'. Memory is now much less invoked to stress historical continuity and legacy and much more to talk about 'learning the lessons of history'; see Jeffrey K. Olick, *The Politics of Regret: On Collective Memory and Historical Responsibility* (New York: Routledge, 2007), 16.
14. The idea that the past could be erased was less important in those countries that had been ruled by hardline Communist regimes in the late Communist period, such as the German Democratic Republic, Czechoslovakia and Romania.
15. Adam Michnik, 'The Velvet Restoration', in *The Revolutions of 1989*, ed. Vladimir Tismăneanu (London: Routledge, 1999), 239–45.

16. On the relationship between conservatism and the re-establishment of 'national continuity' as a means to 'come to terms' with a difficult past, see Max Paul Friedman and Padraic Kenney, 'History in Politics', in *Partisan Histories: The Past in Contemporary Global Politics*, ed. Max Paul Friedman and Padraic Kenney (New York: Palgrave Macmillan, 2005), 4–5.

17. Many examples of this are beautifully described and analysed in Katherine Verdery, *The Political Lives of Dead Bodies: Reburial and Post-Socialist Change* (New York: Columbia University Press, 1999); see also István Rév, 'Parallel Autopsies', *Representations* 49 (1995): 32–33; Richard S. Esbenshade, 'Remembering to Forget: Memory, History, National Identity in Postwar East-Central Europe', *Representations* 49 (1995): 73.

18. Tatiana Zhurzhenko, 'The Geopolitics of Memory', *Eurozine* 5 October 2007, at <http://www.eurozine.com/articles/2007-05-10-zhurzhenko-en.html> (accessed 27 July 2009). In Romania, former Communists won the first post-Communist elections; in Hungary and Poland, they won the second elections.

19. On competing ideas about the nature of 'incompleteness', see Magdalena Zolkos, 'The Conceptual Nexus of Human Rights and Democracy in the Polish Lustration Debates 1989–97', *Journal of Communist Studies and Transition Politics* 22/2 (2006): 228–48.

20. On the necessity of new myths for democratization in post-Communist eastern Europe, see Harald Wydra, 'Introduction', in *Democracy and Myth in Russia and Eastern Europe*, ed. Alexander Wöll and Harald Wydra (London: Routledge, 2008), 15–20.

21. The 'memory boom' was not confined to democracies and post-dictatorial societies: even in 1990s China, an explosion in the political, commercial and personal remembering of the early revolutionary era was apparent; see Ching Kwan Lee and Guobin Yang, 'Introduction: Memory, Power and Culture', in *Re-envisioning the Chinese Revolution*, ed. Ching Kwan Lee and Guobin Yang (Stanford, 2007), 1–2.

22. Konrad Jarausch, for example, asserts that although the 1968 generation constructed itself as the first to achieve a proper reckoning with the Nazi past, in fact it was merely the one that 'dramatized and popularized' a process that had begun much earlier. The idea of a postwar European failure to 'come to terms' with its Fascist past was, however, important in sustaining the 68ers' generational identity; see Konrad Jarausch, 'Critical Memory and Civil Society: The Impact of the 1960s on German Debates about the Past', in *Coping with the Nazi Past: West German Debates on Nazism and Generational Conflict, 1955–1975*, ed. Philipp Gassert and Alan E. Steinweis (Oxford: Berghahn Books, 2006), 20–23. See also A. Dirk Moses, *German Intellectuals and the Nazi Past* (Cambridge: Cambridge University Press, 2007), 186–218.

23. For an excellent survey of the political agendas of the 68ers and their uses of memory, see Hans Kundnani, *Utopia or Auschwitz: Germany's 1968 Generation and the Holocaust* (London: Hurst, 2009).

24. Jarausch, 'Critical Memory', 24.

25. Konrad H. Jarasuch, Hinrich C. Seeba and David P. Conradt, 'The Presence of the Past: Culture, Opinion and Identity in Germany', in *After Unity: Reconfiguring German Identities*, ed. Konrad H. Jarausch (Oxford: Berghahn, 1997), 53–55.

26. Jennifer A. Yoder, 'Truth without Reconciliation: An Appraisal of the Enquete Commission on the SED Dictatorship in Germany', *German Politics* 8/3 (1999): 59–80.

27. Andrew Beattie, *Playing Politics with History: The Bundestag Inquiries into East Germany* (New York and Oxford: Berghahn, 2008), 2–3.

28. For this argument, see Dan Diner, 'Restitution and Memory: The Holocaust in European Political Cultures', *New German Critique* 90 (2003): 36–44.

29. Maria Mälksoo, 'The Discourse of Communist Crimes in the European Memory Politics of World War II', paper presented at the 'Ideology and Discourse Analysis' conference, Roskilde University, Denmark, 22 October 2008.

30. Lavinia Stan, 'Truth Commissions in Post-Communism: The Overlooked Solution?', *The Open Political Science Journal* 2 (2009): 1. Some liberals in Poland suggested the post-Franco 'Spanish model' of overcoming the past through silencing former conflicts, but Germany remained the primary model. On the closing down of the possibility, in the early 1990s, of an imitation of Argentinean, Chilean or South African models of public tribunals involving public testimony in Germany, see A. James McAdams, *Judging the Past in Unified Germany* (Cambridge and New York: Cambridge University Press, 2001), 122. It was only ex-Communists who looked beyond Europe, particularly to the model of South Africa and 'reconciliation'; see Adrian Cioflâncă, 'Politics of Oblivion in Postcommunist Romania', *The Romanian Journal of Political Sciences* 2 (2002): 93.

31. Adrian Cioflâncă, 'Istorie şi justiţie: Un model german pentru procesul comunismului', *Echinox Notebooks* 13 (2007): 121–32.
32. For a comparison of Russian and western memory cultures, see Alexander Etkind, 'Post-Soviet Hauntology: Cultural Memory of the Soviet Terror', *Constellations: An International Journal of Critical and Democratic Theory* 16/1 (2009): 182–200. Given the much greater volume of literature on the subject, and the fact that the reckoning with Communism occurred in a different political context (as part of unification), the German case is excluded from this study.
33. On these groups, see Kathleen E. Smith, *Remembering Stalin's Victims: Popular Memory and the End of the USSR* (Ithaca: Cornell University Press, 1996); and Catherine Merridale, 'Redesigning History in Contemporary Russia', *Journal of Contemporary History* 38/1 (2003): 18–20.
34. See Richard Sakwa, 'Myth and Democratic Identity in Russia', in *Democracy and Myth*, 202–18.
35. See, for example, the work of Boris Mironov, discussed in Dina Khapaeva, 'Historical Memory in Post-Soviet Gothic Society', *Social Research: An International Quarterly of Social Sciences* 76/1 (2009): 359–94.
36. Etkind, 'Hauntology', 193. Indeed, President Yeltsin suggested the creation of a memorial for the victims of the Russian Civil War (as a gesture of reconciliation to former opponents), but did not consider a memorial for the victims of Stalinism.
37. In July 2007, opinion polls carried out in St Petersburg, Kazan and Ulyanovsk found that nearly half of respondents saw the Soviet past in a positive light, and only 23 per cent saw Stalin's impact on Russian history as negative; quoted in Dina Khapaeva, 'History without Memory: Gothic Morality in Post-Soviet Society', *Eurozine*, 20 February 2002 at <http://www.eurozine.com/articles/2009-02-02-khapaeva-en.html> (accessed 23 July 2009). On the revival of the Soviet past, see also Kathleen Smith, *Myth-Making in the New Russia: Politics and Memory during the Yeltsin Era* (Ithaca, NY: Cornell University Press, 2002), especially chapters 4 and 9; Adam Hochschild, *The Unquiet Ghost: Russians Remember Stalin* (London: Serpent's Tail, 1995); Nanci Adler, 'The Future of the Soviet Past Remains Unpredictable: The Resurrection of Stalinist Symbols amidst the Exhumation of Mass Graves', *Europe-Asia Studies* 57/8 (2005): 1093–1119.
38. Interviews were conducted with historians, archivists, prosecutors, activists, archaeologists and curators: they explored individuals' journeys into issues of memory, their intellectual or ideological approaches, their everyday activities at sites of memory, and their broader reflections on the way in which their country was dealing with its past. Relevant details about specific interviews are given where referenced.
39. This, of course, echoed reform socialist calls in 1968 for 'socialism with a human face'.
40. See, for example, the silences in leftist memory that were maintained even after the collapse of the Franco regime, Ángela Cenarro, 'Memory beyond the Public Sphere: The Francoist Repression Remembered in Aragon', *History & Memory* 14/1 (2002): 174–76. On the way in which people talking about their experiences in apartheid South Africa and Nazi Germany edit their stories in the face of an interviewer who represents a culture that condemns those systems, see Michelle Mouton and Helena Pohlandt-McCormick, 'Boundary Crossings: Oral History of Nazi Germany and Apartheid South Africa – a Comparative Perspective', *History Workshop Journal* 48 (1999): 46–48.
41. On the explosion of witnessing the past in Europe in the 1980s and 1990s, see Annette Wieviorka, *The Era of the Witness* (Ithaca, NY: Cornell University Press, 2006). For a counter-view that oral history was hampered by multiple silences about the Communist past, at least in the context of the former Soviet Union, see Daniel Bertaux, Anna Rotkirch and Paul Thompson, 'Introduction', in Daniel Bertaux, Paul Thompson and Anna Rotkirch, eds, *On Living Through Soviet Russia* (London and New York: Routledge, 2004), 7–9.
42. Irina Paperno, 'Personal Accounts of Soviet Experience', *Kritika* 3/4 (2002): 577–610.
43. These fears were on display in 1989 (see below, pages 5–6), but were not apparent later. Although some – especially ex-Communists – suggested that too much remembering of the Communist period was divisive and deleterious to democratic development, very few seriously asserted that it would provoke a return to serious civil conflict. This work does not include the break-up of Yugoslavia where revivals of the memory of World War II and the Communist period were of course dangerous.

44. Only one interviewee ever refused an interview on this basis.
45. Even in a united Germany there were exceptions, as the case of Brandenburg demonstrates.
46. See, for example, polls that addressed whether Hungarians believed that the arrival of the Red Army in 1945 still constituted a liberation, or whether Poles still believed the Communists' claim that Martial Law was a necessity to prevent Soviet intervention in 1981.
47. For an example of how successful Czechoslovak professionals attempted to create acceptable life stories after 1989, see Vladimir Andrle, 'Neither a Dinosaur Nor a Weathercock: The Construction of a Reputably Continuous Self in Czech Post-Communist Life Stories', *Qualitative Sociology* 23/2 (2000): 215–30.
48. For some of the best: István Rév, *Retroactive Justice: Prehistory of Post-Communism* (Stanford: Stanford, CA: University Press, 2005); Françoise Mayer, *Les Tchèques et leur communisme: mémoire et identités politiques* (Paris: Editions de l'ecole des Hautes Études en Sciences Sociales, 2004); Stefan Troebst and Ulf Brunnbauer, eds, *Zwischen Nostalgie und Amnesie: Die Erinnerung an den Kommunismus in Südosteuropa* (Cologne: Böhlau, 2007); Oksana Sarkisova and Péter Apor, eds, *Past for the Eyes: East European Representations of Communism in Cinema and Museums after 1989* (Budapest: CEU Press, 2008); Michal Kopeček, ed., *Past in the Making: Historical Revisionism in Central Europe after 1989* (Budapest: CEU Press, 2008); Sorin Antohi, Balázs Trencsényi and Péter Apor, eds, *Narratives Unbound: Historical Studies in Post-Communist Eastern Europe* (Budapest: CEU Press, 2007); Ene Kõresaar, Epp Lauk and Kristin Kuutma, eds, *The Burden of Remembering: Recollections and Representations of the Twentieth Century* (Helsinki: SKS Kirjat, 2009); Maria Todorova, ed., *Remembering Communism: Genres of Representation* (New York: Social Science Research Council, Columbia University Press, 2010); Maria Todorova and Zsuzsa Gillie, eds, *Post-Communist Nostalgia* (New York and Oxford: Berghahn Books, 2010); Volkhard Knigge and Ulrich Mählert, eds, *Der Kommunismus im Museum: Formen der Auseinandersetzung in Deutschland und Ostmitteleuropa* (Cologne: Böhlau, 2005); Vladimir Tismăneanu, *Fantasies of Salvation: Post-Communist Political Mythologies* (Princeton, NJ: Princeton University Press, 1998); Kristina Kaiserová and Gert Röhrborn, eds, *Present Tensions: European Writers on Overcoming Dictatorships* (Budapest: CEU Press, 2009).
49. See, for example, Caroline Humphrey, *The Unmaking of Soviet Life: Everyday Economies after Socialism* (Ithaca, NY: Cornell University Press, 2002); Ruth Mandel and Caroline Humphrey, eds, *Markets and Moralities: Ethnographies of Postsocialism* (Oxford: Berg, 2002); Daphne Berdahl, Matti Bunzl and Martha Lampland, eds, *Altering States: Ethnographies of Transition in Eastern Europe and the Former Soviet Union* (Ann Arbor, MI: University of Michigan Press, 2000); Daphne Berdahl, *Where the World Ended: Re-unification and Identity in the German Borderland* (Berkeley, CA: University of California Press, 1999); Katherine Verdery, *What Was Socialism and What Comes Next?* (Princeton, NJ: Princeton University Press, 1996); and Rogers Brubaker et al., *Nationalist Politics and Everyday Ethnicity in a Transylvanian Town* (Princeton, NJ: Princeton University Press, 2006).
50. For a sophisticated and convincing use of oral history to this end, see Kate Fisher, *Birth Control, Sex and Marriage in Britain, 1918–1960* (Oxford: Oxford University Press, 2006).
51. Paula Hamilton and Linda Shopes, 'Introduction: Building Partnerships between Oral History and Memory Studies', in *Oral History and Public Memories*, ed. Paula Hamilton and Linda Shopes (Philadelphia, PA: Temple University Press, 2008), viii–xii; Susannah Radstone and Katharine Hodgkin, 'Regimes of Memory: An Introduction', in *Memory Cultures: Memory, Subjectivity, and Recognition*, ed. Susannah Radstone and Katharine Hodgkin (New Brunswick, NJ: Transaction Publishers, 2006), 2–3.
52. The Soviet and post-Soviet liberal human rights organisation Memorial started collecting testimonies, mainly from the victims of Stalinism, in 1989. The individual researcher Irina Sherbakova started collecting testimonies of Gulag survivors in the 1970s.
53. In the early 1980s, Karta established the so-called 'Eastern Archive' where approximately 1,200 interviews with Poles repressed by the Soviet Army were stored. In post-Communist central-eastern Europe, the other main oral history groupings are located within the Institute of Contemporary History in Prague, the Czech Republic; Babeş-Bolyai University, Cluj, Romania; the Intercultural Institute in Timişoara, Romania; and the University of Sofia, Bulgaria.
54. For an example of the focus on the repressed and those who opposed the Communist state, see, for example, the *Anuarul de Istorie Orală* of Babeş-Bolyai University, Cluj in Romania.

55. For critiques of which groups' biographies were valorized after 1989, see Neringa Klumbyte, 'Ethnographic Note on Nation: Narratives and Symbols of Early Post-Socialist Nationalism in Lithuania', *Dialectical Anthropology* 27/3–4 (2003): 281; Marianne Liljestrom, 'Success Stories from the Margins: Soviet Women's Autobiographical Sketches from the Late Soviet Period', in *On Living Through Soviet Russia*, 235–36.

56. Daniela Koleva, 'The Colour of Memory: Doing Oral History in Post-Socialist Settings', in *Remembering after the Fall of Communism: Oral History and (Post-)Socialist Societies*, ed. Julia Obertreis and Anke Stephan (Essen: Klartext Verlag 2009), 207. See, for example, the work of Smaranda Vultur, who has recovered the suffering of German minorities during the Communist period: Smaranda Vultur, *Istorie trăită – istorie povestită. Deportarea în Bărăgan, 1951–1956* (Timişoara: Amarcord, 1997).

57. The Institute of Oral History in Cluj, Romania, declares that it is using oral history to promote multiculturalism and the diversity of social identities and religious confessions in Transylvania and Romania, and to construct a civic identity in tune with European values.

58. See the discussion in Julia Obertreis, 'Memory, Identity and Facts: The Methodology of Oral History and Researching (Post-)Socialist Societies', in *Remembering after the Fall of Communism: Oral History and (Post-)Socialist Societies* (Essen: Klartext Verlag 2009), 45–46; for a major exception to this rule, see the pioneering work in working-class industrial communities collected in Lutz Niethammer, ed., *Fragen an das Deutsche Gedächtnis: Aufsätze zur Oral History* (Essen: Klartext, 2007); Lutz Niethammer, Alexander von Plato and Dorothee Wierling, *Die Volkseigene Erfahrung: Eine Archäologie des Lebens in der Industrieprovinz der DDR: 30 Biografische Eröffnungen* (Berlin: Rowohlt, 1991). Younger scholars started to examine working-class culture with oral history; see, for example, Eszter Bartha, ' "Te és az üzemed": Szocialista kollektívák és munkáspolitika az 1970-es és 1980-as években az NDK-ban és Magyarországon', in *Mindennapi Rákosi és Kádár Korában*, ed. Sándor Horváth (Budapest: Nyitott Könyvműhely, 2008), 231–63. For a rich work that uses oral history to access pre-Communist and Communist values, see Catherine Merridale, *Night of Stone: Death and Memory in Russia* (London: Granta, 2000).

59. The work of Warsaw's Karta Centre came closest to this. It conducted interviews in the Ukraine (mostly with ethnic Poles) and in Germany (mostly with Germans 'expelled' from today's Polish territories). These projects were in part conceived of as ways of counteracting international misunderstandings over history, and thus could be seen as reconciliation activities, although Karta does not present them in this way.

60. There were some attempts to use oral history to enable dialogue between former enemies; see, for example, the dissident Adam Michnik's conversations with the architect of Martial Law in Poland, Wojciech Jaruzelski, reproduced in Adam Michnik, *Letters from Freedom: Post-Cold War Realities and Perspectives* (Berkeley, CA: University of California Press, 1998); see also Vladimir Tismăneanu's historical dialogue with former apparatchik and post-Communist president Ion Iliescu in Ion Iliescu and Vladimir Tismăneanu, *Communism, Post-Communism and Democracy: The Great Shock at the End of a Short Century* (Boulder, CO: East European Monographs, 2006); different elite and dissident perspectives on normalization in Czechoslovakia are presented in Miroslav Vaněk, ed., *Mocní? A Bezmocní?: Politické elity a disent v období tzv. normalizace: Interpretační studie životopisných interview* (Prague: Prostor, 2006). By contrast, one of the most revealing oral projects of the period immediately prior to the collapse – Teresa Torańska's 'Them' – used dialogues between the older generation of male party leaders and a young female activist interviewer to reveal the huge gulf between 'us' and 'them' in the final years of the Polish People's Republic. Teresa Torańska, *Them: Stalin's Polish Puppets* (New York: Harper & Row, 1987).

61. See, for example, Portelli's exploration of how postwar Italian liberal democracy shaped the way in which people remembered their stories of wartime Nazi massacres: Alessandro Portelli, 'The Massacre at the Fosse Ardeatine', in *Memory, History, Nation*, 29–41; idem, *The Order Has Been Carried Out* (Basingstoke: Palgrave Macmillan, 2007); Luisa Passerini, 'Oral Memory of Fascism', in *Rethinking Italian Fascism: Capitalism, Populism and Culture*, ed. David Forgacs (London: Lawrence and Wishart, 1986), 185–96; idem, *Fascism in Popular Memory: The Cultural Experience of the Turin Working Class* (Cambridge: Cambridge University Press, 1987). For an advocate of this approach, see Michael Frisch, *A Shared Authority: Essays on the Craft and Meaning of Oral and Public History* (Albany, NY: State University of New York Press, 1990), especially chapter 8; for a discussion of the

relationship between personal and public discourses on memory, see Susannah Radstone, 'Re-conceiving Binaries: The Limits of Memory', *History Workshop Journal* 59 (2005): 134–50; for a good discussion of examples, see Penny Summerfield, 'Culture and Composure: Creating Narratives of the Gendered Self in Oral History Interviews', in *Cultural and Social History* 1/1 (2004): 67–70.

62. Silences were often viewed as the result of traumas of the Communist period and thus as a methodological problem to be overcome. Some focused on whether the peculiarities of the Communist experience made oral history respondents unreliable narrators. The traumas of the Soviet period, the frequent necessity of hiding the past from the public gaze, the fact that people learnt to keep two biographies and only present an official version to strangers such as the oral historian, all meant that testimony was considered 'impeded'; Bertaux, Rotkirch and Thompson, 'Introduction', in *On Living Through Soviet Russia*, 8–9.

63. On using oral history to explore overcoming the silence surrounding the Gulag, see Irina Sherbakova, 'The Gulag in Memory', in Luisa Passerini, ed., *Memory and Totalitarianism: International Yearbook of Oral History and Life Stories, Vol. 1*, (Oxford: Oxford University Press, 1992), 103–15.

64. On the use of oral history to examine, for example, the ways in which Communist ideology shaped East Germans' understanding of their own experiences under Nazism, on how concentration camp survivors 'learnt' to narrate their experiences in Slovenia, on how Bulgarians remember the war and on Uzbek peasant attitudes towards collectivization, see Dorothee Wierling, 'A German Generation of Reconstruction: The Children of the Weimar Republic in the GDR', in *Memory and Totalitarianism*, 71–88; Silvija Kavčič, 'Etablierung eines Erzählmusters', in *Remembering after the Fall*, 221–32; Daniela Koleva, 'What Do You Remember of 9th September 1944? Remembering Communism: Official and Unofficial Discourses', *Echinox Notebooks* 1 (2001): 140–46; Marianne Kamp, 'Soviet and Uzbek on the Collective Farm', in *Remembering after the Fall*, 233–42.

65. See Liljestrom, 'Success Stories', 235–36, for a critique of how oral historians dealing with Communism and gender after 1989 valorized women's stories of victimization and ignored biographies of successful women as unrepresentative.

66. The Bulgarian oral historian Daniela Koleva has taken up the constructivist memory-centred approach to post-Communist testimony; see, for example, her 'Memories of the War and the War of Memories in Post-Communist Bulgaria', *Oral History* 34/2 (2006): 44–55; *idem*, 'Histoire orale et mémoire du communisme', *Divinatio* 27 (2008): 211–25; *idem*, 'Histoire orale et micro-histoire: Un cas de Béléné, Bulgarie', *Divinatio* 29 (2009): 59–74. On how children of persecuted participants in the Hungarian 1956 Uprising made sense of the revolution both under Communism and post-Communism: Zsuzsanna Kőrösi and Adrienne Molnár, *Carrying a Secret in my Heart: Children of the Victims of the Reprisals after the Hungarian Revolution in 1956: An Oral History* (Budapest: CEU Press, 2003). There have been small-scale projects which have touched on this issue; see, for example, Sidonia Nedeianu Grama, 'Memory Features of the 1989 Revolution: Competing Narratives on the Revolution', in *Remembering after the Fall*, 91–108; Vladimir Andrle, 'Neither a Dinosaur Nor a Weathercock'. Many works touch on these issues but do not make them their central focus.

67. The details of these separate projects are as follows: interviews with seventy-eight respondents from interwar Hungarian middle-class and intellectual families about their experience of the Communist state; interviews with twenty respondents conducted for a comparative project on Hungarian, Czechoslovak and Polish party members and their autobiographies in the 1940s and 1950s; and interviews with a further twenty Czechoslovak and Polish respondents on varieties of anti-Communist opposition. The vast majority of interviews were conducted with those born in the interwar period (1918–40) who thus experienced the establishment of Communism during their young lives. The sample contained individuals with a wide variety of relationships with the Communist state: party members and oppositionists, the socially mobile and the persecuted, as well as the apolitical and politically demobilized.

68. On the development of late Communist culture and the 'hegemony of form' over genuine ideological content and meaning, see Alexei Yurchak, 'Soviet Hegemony of Form: Everything Was Forever, Until It Was No More', *Comparative Studies in Society and History* 45/3 (2003); *idem, Everything Was Forever, Until It Was No More: The Last Soviet Generation* (Princeton, NJ: Princeton University Press, 2006). Rotkirch has charted the journey from the

collective nature of the memory of the postwar generation to the more individualistic memory of the 1960s and 1970s generations as a development that undermined the Communist state's ability to construct collective solidarities: Anna Rotkirch, *The Man Question: Loves and Lives in Late 20th Century Russia* (Helsinki: University of Helsinki Department of Social Policy Research Reports, 2000). On the autobiographical urge in the late Soviet Union, see Irina Paperno, 'Personal Accounts', 577–610. For late Soviet oral auto-biographies, see Donald Raleigh, *Russia's Sputnik Generation: Baby Boomers Talk About their Lives* (Bloomington, IN: Indiana University Press, 2006).

69. Even if one came from the wrong background, writing the correct biography – in which the individual might attack his or her own family as 'bourgeois oppressors' – could at certain moments be enough to ensure mobility within the system: Daniela Koleva, 'Between Testimony and Power: Autobiographies in Socialist Bulgaria', paper presented at the 'Texts of Testimony: Autobiography, Life-Story Narratives and the Public Sphere' conference in Liverpool, 23–25 August 2001, 4; James Mark, 'Discrimination, Opportunity and Middle-Class Success in Early Communist Hungary', *The Historical Journal* 48/2 (2005): 510; Lutz Niethammer, 'Biographie und Biokratie: Rückblick auf eine Sondierung in der DDR fünf Jahre nach ihrem Ende', in Niethammer, *Fragen an das deutsche Gedächtnis*.

70. Whereas many scholars have worked on Stalinist-era autobiographies and explored how Communist subjects wrote themselves 'biographically' into the regime's ideological project, little attention has been paid to the legacies of these Stalinist forms in post-Communism. On the idea that Communist forms of biography lived on after 1989, see Jochen Hellbeck, 'Galaxy of Black Stars: The Power of Soviet Biography', *American Historical Review* 115 (2009): 622–23.

71. Many oral history respondents did indeed draw upon these identities when describing their lives: this was not particularly surprising given that these terms were widely used in the Communist period too, although the conception of how these groups were constituted was of course radically different.

72. Many works have explored the idea of family stories as transmission vehicles for alternative memories: see Daniel Bertaux, 'Transmission in Extreme Situations: Russian Families Expropriated by the October Revolution', in *Pathways to Social Class: A Qualitative Approach to Social Mobility*, ed. Daniel Bertaux and Paul Thompson (Oxford: Oxford University Press, 1997), 230–58, and Cenarro, 'Memory beyond the Public Sphere'.

73. For a call to analyse the impact of the collapse on the form of oral narratives, and not to regard oral testimony simply as evidence of an alternative world that embodied values sepa-rate to those of the Communist state, see Péter Apor, 'The Joy of Everyday Life: Microhistory and the History of Everyday Life in the Socialist Dictatorships', *East-Central Europe* 35/1–2 (2007–08): 200–01.

74. On the complex ways in which victim stories are told in different post-Communist environ-ments, see Anselma Gallinat, 'Life-Stories in Interviews and in Social Interaction', in *Remembering after the Fall*, 275–86; see also J. K. Coetzee and H. Otakar, 'Oppression, Resistance and Imprisonment', in *Trauma and Life Stories: International Perspectives*, ed. Kim Lacey Rogers, Selma Leydesdorff and Graham Dawson (London: Routledge, 1999), 80–94.

Chapter 1: The Unfinished Revolution

1. In Hungary, images of the Round Table are part of the commonplace visual narratives of 1989; see Renáta Uitz, 'Communist Secret Services on the Screen', in *Past for the Eyes: East European Representations of Communism in Cinema and Museums after 1989*, ed. Oksana Sarkisova and Péter Apor (Budapest: CEU Press, 2008), 57.

2. Peter Siani-Davies, *The Romanian Revolution of December 1989* (Ithaca, NY: Cornell University Press, 2005), chapter 7.

3. It is worth noting that it was political figures from outside central-eastern Europe repre-senting the broader global story who dominated proceedings (George H. Bush, Margaret Thatcher and Mikhail Gorbachev in Berlin in 1999, for instance). There was some indication that the levels of popular involvement in Prague and Berlin were beginning to change in 2009. The first day of the Velvet Revolution in Czechoslovakia, 17 November 1989, became a 'Day of Freedom' in the Czech Republic; despite being an official anniversary, it was

not considered to be particularly important for a long time. Only on the occasion of the twentieth anniversary did popular events and political demonstrations begin to suggest changes in attitudes towards 1989. Thanks to Michal Kopeček for this information. On 9 November 2009, a thousand foam domino tiles, some of them decorated by Berlin residents and others by artists from places that had experienced their own divides (e.g. South Korea, Palestine, Cyprus) were placed along the line of the former Wall and then torn down. Here, the framing of the Wall's fall linked the domestic experience with a broader narrative of an ongoing global mission to overcome political divisions.

4. For an excellent discussion, see Aleksander Smolar and Magdalena Potocka, 'History and Memory: The Revolutions of 1989–91', *Journal of Democracy* 12/3 (2001), 15. Representatives from the former GDR were not included until pressure was placed on the organizers of the Berlin commemoration.

5. There were some exceptions to this, such as the Memorial of Rebirth in Bucharest, Romania, dedicated to the struggles of the Romanian Revolution and inaugurated in 2005.

6. Adam Michnik, 'The Velvet Restoration', in Vladimir Tismăneanu, ed., *The Revolutions of 1989*, ed. Vladimir Tismăneanu (London: Routledge, 1999), 239–45.

7. Jan Kubik and Amy Lynch, 'The Original Sin of Poland's Third Republic: Discounting "Solidarity" and its Consequences for Political Reconciliation', *Polish Sociological Review* 153 (2006): 9–38. In Hungary, there is even disagreement over when Communism ended: for Fidesz, the anti-Communist party, it was 1990 (with the first democratic elections), not 1989 (the date of the Round Table). In Romania, one of the anti-Communists' major demands was for an 'honest' enquiry into the role of the army and security forces in the revolution; they regarded the parliamentary enquiries in the 1990s as cover-ups: Lavinia Stan, 'Truth Commissions in Post-Communism: The Overlooked Solution?', *The Open Political Science Journal* 2 (2009): 3.

8. Kubik and Lynch, 'Original Sin', 16. They state: 'these two central cleavages in Polish politics have been more "cultural" than in other post-communist Central European states. They have their origin in the *unrealized ritual closure* of both the Round Table negotiations and the entire Polish People's Republic period.'

9. For a range of voices and interpretations of the Hungarian 1989, including those lamenting the 'unfinished revolution', see István Elek, *Rendszerváltoztatók húsz év után* (Budapest: Heti Válasz Lap- és Könyvkiadó, 2009), especially 9–14 ('Nincs meg a cezúra').

10. See Andrew Wolpert, *Remembering Defeat: Civil War and Civic Memory in Ancient Athens* (Baltimore, MD and London: Johns Hopkins University Press, 2001) for a contrasting way to forget defeat and gloss over it in civic memory.

11. This chapter will focus on the cases of Poland and Hungary as two countries that experienced significant episodes of resistance to Communism and negotiated elite settlements that brought an end to dictatorship, and in which the memory of anti-Communist resistance has played a significant role in political and cultural life since the collapse of the system. However, this model could be applied to many other countries, albeit in different ways.

12. Kubik and Lynch, 'Original Sin', 14.

13. András Bozóki, 'Introduction: The Significance of the Roundtable Talks', in *The Roundtable Talks of 1989: The Genesis of Hungarian Democracy: Analysis and Documents*, ed. András Bozóki (Budapest: CEU Press, 2001), xxiii. In 1988, the Hungarian Socialist Party still hoped for a form of limited pluralism in which it would play a leading role; by February 1989, it had accepted the inevitability of a multiparty system.

14. Kenneth Benoit and John W. Shiemann, 'Institutional Choice in New Democracies: Bargaining over Hungary's 1989 Electoral Law', *Journal of Theoretical Politics* 13/2 (2001): 153–82.

15. For a discussion of this, see Leszek Koczanowicz, 'Memory of Politics and the Politics of Memory: Reflections on the Construction of the Past in Post-Totalitarian Poland', *Studies in East European Thought* 49 (1997): 263.

16. See István Rév, *Retroactive Justice: Prehistory of Post-Communism* (Stanford, CA: Stanford University Press, 2005), 42–43.

17. János M. Rainer, *Ötvenhat Után* (Budapest: 1956-os Intézet, 2003), 233–47. Here, Rainer explores how 1956 was used as both a warning and a threat in 1989.

18. Even the radicals within the SZDSZ and Fidesz were only prepared to incorporate 56ers if they renounced earlier calls to violence. Likewise, during the Polish Round Tables, both sides attempted to avoid reviving the memory of past conflicts; according to one participant from Solidarity, 'Another [condition of successful negotiations] that was very important was the principle of not discussing symbolic problems. We were to solve the future, and avoid arguing about the past. We believed, and I think most of us agreed here, that if we started getting into discussions about the past wrongs, we wouldn't accomplish anything. We had to accept the fact that we looked at different things from the past in different ways, and that we had different visions of various symbolic problems. There were situations when someone couldn't help raising such a problem, and the emotions flared, but I think we were in "Solidarity" trying to weaken these emotions during the negotiations'. See Donna Parmelee, ed., *Communism's Negotiated Collapse: The Polish Round Table, Ten Years Later. A Conference at the University of Michigan. April 7–10, 1999. English Transcript of the Conference Proceedings*, trans. Kasia Kietlinska (Ann Arbor, MI: The University of Michigan Center for Russian and East European Studies, 1999) at <www.umich.edu/~iinet/PolishRoundTable/frame.html> (accessed 3 July 2009).

19. Indeed, in 1990, even right-wing papers such as *Magyar Fórum* presented 1989 as the heroic culmination of the hopes of 1956; see, for example, Konrád Salamon, 'A magyar dicsőséges forradalom 1989–1990', *Magyar Fórum*, 24 March 1990: 2.

20. Quoted in György Litván, ed., *The Hungarian Revolution of 1956: Reform, Revolution, Repression, 1953–1963* (Harlow, Essex: Longman, 1996), x.

21. On the reinterpretation of the liberal settlements of 1848 as 'bloodless transitions' that prefigured 1989, see András Bozóki, 'The Roundtable Talks of 1989: Participants, Political Visions and Historical References', *Hungarian Studies* 14/2 (2000): 250; Gábor Ittzés, 'Ritual and National Self-Interpretation: The Nagy Imre Funeral', *Religion and Society in Central and Eastern Europe* 1 (2005): 11.

22. On the importance of cultural identities – partly based on interpretations of history – in the definition of post-Communist Hungarian political cleavages, see Emilia Palonen, 'Political Polarisation and Populism in Contemporary Hungary', *Parliamentary Affairs* 62/2 (2009): 318–34.

23. György Litván places the shift at the 1992 anniversary of 1956; György Litván, 'Politikai Beszéd 1956-ról 1989 után', in *Évkönyv 2002. Magyarország a Jelenkorban*, ed., Rainer M. Janos and Éva Standeisky (Budapest: 1956-os Intézet, 2002), 258–63 at 261.

24. András Bozóki saw this as a shift from a symbolic politics that bolstered a new political system and its institutions as a whole, to a symbolic politics that was used to bolster particular interest groups and divided Hungary into two; see András Bozóki, 'Consolidation or Second Revolution? The Politics of the New Right in Hungary', *Slovak Foreign Policy Affairs* 1 (2005): 17–28.

25. He had also been very critical at the time of Imre Nagy's reburial of reform Communists' sudden celebration of Nagy and the other martyrs of the revolution: 'We cannot understand that those who were eager to slander the revolution and its prime minister have suddenly changed into great supporters of Imre Nagy. Nor can we understand that the party leaders, who made us study from books that falsified the Revolution, now rush to touch the coffins as if they were charms of good luck'. Quoted in Karl P. Benziger, 'The Funeral of Imre Nagy: Contested History and the Power of Memory Culture', *History and Memory* 12/2 (2000): 153. Fidesz had not signed the pact (but had not attempted to veto it either).

26. Quoted by Csilla Kiss, 'From Liberalism to Conservatism: The Federation of Young Democrats in Post-Communist Hungary', *East European Politics and Societies* 16/3 (2002): 741–42.

27. Heino Nyyssönen, 'History in the First Parliament; The Politics of Memory in Hungary 1990–1994', *Hungarologische Beiträge* 14 (2002): 175. Kiss, 'From Liberalism to Conservatism', 744.

28. Brigid Fowler, 'Concentrated Orange: Fidesz and the Remaking of the Hungarian Centre-Right, 1994–2002', *Journal of Communist Studies and Transition Politics* 20/3 (2004): 80–114. The Hungarian middle class was hit by the so-called 'Bokros Package'.

29. In fact, both left and right appealed to the 'losers' of the transition: the ex-Communists to the working class and Fidesz to the middle class.

30. Zoltán Ripp, *Eltékozolt Esélyck: A rendszerváltás értelme és értelmezései* (Napvilág Kiadó: Budapest, 2009), 159–61.
31. This was in part to provide an integrative idea that avoided the splintering of the right as in other places such as Poland. See, for example, Bozóki, 'Consolidation or Second Revolution?', 22.
32. He was never tried as the principle of retroactivity never became law. See Csilla Kiss, 'The Misuses of Manipulation: The Failure of Transitional Justice in Post-Communist Hungary', *Europe-Asia Studies* 58/6 (2006): 932–33.
33. Heino Nyyssönen, *The Presence of the Past in Politics: '1956' after 1956 in Hungary* (Jyväskylä: SoPhi, 1999), 280.
34. Litván, 'Politikai Beszéd 1956-ról 1989 után', 261.
35. From Fidesz's party literature from 1996: *A Polgári Magyarországért. 'Két pogány közt egy hazáert'. A Fidesz Magyar Polgári Párt vitairata* (Budapest: Fidesz Országos Elnöksége-Fidesz Központi Hivatal, 1996).
36. Gábor Egry, '1956 Emlékezete Itthon és külföldön', *Regio: kisebbség, politika, társadalom* 18/3 (2007): 19.
37. This is a reference to the westward migration of ethnic Magyars to the Carpathian Basin in the ninth century.
38. <http://www.orbanviktor.hu/in_english_article/commemoration_of_the_1956_revolution> (accessed 20 May 2010).
39. Mónika Mátay and Ildikó Kaposi, 'Radicals Online: The Hungarian Street Protests of 2006 and the Internet', in *Finding the Right Place on the Map: Central and Eastern European Media Change in a Global Perspective*, ed. Karol Jakubowicz and Miklós Sükösd (Bristol: Intellect, 2008), 289–90.
40. István Rév argued that it was not incidental that resistance took the form of occupying, and remaking the historical meaning of, public space in the capital. He suggested that the rightist demonstrators attempted to create a 'counter-topography' to undermine the socialist government's attempts at controlling the commemorations of 1956 in 2006. His work pointed to the importance of 'performative memory' – demonstrations, occupations, and so on – as a means of invoking the past for the right. See István Rév, untitled paper presented at the School of Slavonic and East European Studies, 8 June 2007.
41. Attila Gyulai, 'Egy Diszkurzív Stratégia Értelmében Felfogott Igazságról és Hazugságról', *Politikatudományi Szemle* 2 (2007): 115; Anna Seleny, 'Communism's Many Legacies in East-Central Europe', *Journal of Democracy* 18/3 (2007): 160.
42. This was not possible, as state television had already gone off the air for the night.
43. Gyurcsány, in turn, tried to break the link that protesters made between 1956 and 2006: Egry, '1956 Emlékezete', 15.
44. See 'A Felvonulási téri 1956-os emlékmű: éket ver, vagy egyesít? – Képriport', *Gondola.hu*, 30 October 2006 at <http://gondola.hu/cikkek/51004> (accessed 3 July 2009).
45. The Workers' Militia (Munkásőrség) was a special police force used by the re-established regime to help regain order. Membership was voluntary, but it grew quickly.
46. See, for example, Paweł Machcewicz, 'Polityka historyczna to nic nowego', *Gazeta Wyborcza*, 20 April 2006: 20; Barbara Szacka, ' "Solidarity" and Martial Law in the Collective Memory of Polish History', *Polish Sociological Review* 153/1 (2006). Plans to commemorate Solidarity often revealed deep fissures in the way in which it was remembered. The commemorative events planned for 2000 became caught up with the presidential candidacy of Marian Krzaklewski, who, as a former activist, claimed the right to speak for the legacy of Solidarity. President Kwaśniewski (a former Communist) was not invited to the commemoration, and so no heads of state took part. At first, Lech Wałęsa was also kept at arm's length. In 2006, Lech Wałęsa refused to attend, as it was hosted by the radically anti-Communist Lech Kaczyński of the Law and Justice party.
47. It was at the local rather than national level that Solidarity was more commonly remembered. The European Solidarity Centre was funded by the city of Gdańsk in conjunction with the European Union, but without the participation of the Polish state. The construction of the centre was estimated at €100 million, 25–30 per cent of which came from the city of Gdańsk. Over thirty world leaders and ex-leaders signed the document to confirm the founding of the centre. The poles bearing the flags of the ten new eastern members of the European Union were made by Gdańsk shipyard workers and installed outside the European

Parliament in Strasbourg on 3 May 2004. By contrast, it was striking that the many sites commemorating the victims of Communism did not receive support from the European Union. For a call for greater emphasis to be placed on the study of memory politics at a local level, see Ewa Ochman, 'Municipalities and the Search for the Local Past: Fragmented Memory of the Red Army in Upper Silesia', *East European Politics and Societies* 23/3 (2009): 392–420.

48. During the period when the largest opposition movement to Communism anywhere in central-eastern Europe – Solidarity – was legal, the Communist regime allowed it to build its own monuments. One of the most famous of these was the '1956 memorial' in Poznan, which consists of two crosses tied together. On one is a reference to the June Revolt in 1956 – a workers' uprising whose demands focused on better working conditions and political relaxation, and is seen as the starting point for the softening of the regime in the late 1950s. On the other cross is a list of dates – 1968, 1970, 1976, 1980 and 1981 – marking a series of workers' revolts against the regime that had been put down. Here was Solidarity invoking itself as part of a glorious, but tragic, tradition of resistance to the Communist regime. Monuments to workers' resistance were built in other places too: the 'Monument to the Worker' commemorating the strikes of June 1980 in Lublin was set up outside the car factory where they occurred. See Izabella Main, 'Memory and History in the Cityscapes in Poland: The Search for Meaning', in *Inquiries into Past and Present*, ed. Deanna Gard et al (Vienna: IWM Junior Visiting Fellows' Conferences, Vol. 17, 2005) at <http://www.iwm.at/index.php?option=com_content&task=view&id=301&Itemid=276> (accessed 3 July 2009).

49. Jan Kubik, *The Power of Symbols against the Symbols of Power: The Rise of Solidarity and the Fall of State Socialism in Poland* (University Park, PA: Pennsylvania State University Press, 1994).

50. Robin Okey, *The Demise of Communist East Europe: 1989 in Context* (London: Arnold, 2004), 68.

51. See Michnik, 'The Velvet Restoration'. See also Jacek Kuron, 'Overcoming Totalitarianism', in *The Revolutions of 1989*, ed. Vladimir Tismăneanu (London: Routledge, 1999), 198–201; Kuron defends the Round Table negotiations as truly revolutionary events, since they were by their very nature a 'denial of totalitarianism': 'we don't want to destroy the system by force . . . . If we are to have a truly democratic revolution, it must be achieved through a gradual process' (200–01); see also Michael D. Kennedy, *Cultural Formations of Post-Communism: Emancipation, Transition, Nation and War* (Minneapolis, MN: University of Minnesota Press, 2002), Chapter 1.

52. Adam Michnik also refers to populist right-wingers as 'anti-Communists with a Bolshevik face'. See Michnik, 'The Velvet Restoration', 250.

53. There are other interpretations of the 'defeat of Solidarity', most notably the leftist critique that the democratic practices of the movement and the link between liberals and workers were lost in the late 1980s as Solidarity's leaders came to embrace the free market, shock therapy and individualism. For such a critique, see David Ost, 'Solidarity: 25 Years Later', *Skalny Center for Polish and Central European Studies Newsletter*, spring (2006): 1–2.

54. Susan C. Pearce, 'The Polish Solidarity Movement in Retrospect: In Search of a Mnemonic Mirror', *International Journal of Politics, Culture, and Society* 22 (2009): 177.

55. Kubik and Lynch, 'Original Sin', 28.

56. On the conspiracy theories that surround the deal between pinks and reds, see Jacek Kurczewski, 'The Spoiled Drama of Emancipation: Conflicting Narratives', *Polish Sociological Review* 4/168 (2009): 547–54. The idea that post-Communist liberals had come from Communist families, had had 'leftist periods' in the 1960s and early 1970s before their conversion to liberalism, and hence were not true anti-Communists, was argued by the right in Hungary too. It emerged soon after the transition; for an example, see the unsigned 'Apák és Fiúk [Fathers and Sons]', *Magyar Fórum*, 31 March 1990: 2.

57. Gavin Rae, 'Back to the Future: The Resurgence of Poland's Conservative Right', *Debatte: Journal of Contemporary Central and Eastern Europe* 15/2 (2007): 221–32.

58. Michal Wenzel, 'Solidarity and Akcja Wyborcza "Solidarność". An Attempt at Reviving the Legend', *Communist and Post-Communist Studies* 31/2 (1998): 139–56.

59. The resignation of prime minister Józef Oleksy following accusations of collaboration with Soviet security forces allowed anti-Communists to characterize the post-Communist left as direct descendants of the Communist elite.

60. '[P]olitical groups, social groups, and people, for whom truth, justice and interpersonal solidarity are the indispensable elements in building an independent, just, and democratic
Poland', taken from the *Solidarity Electoral Action Declaration*, 8 June 1996.

61. 'Cultural War and Polish Politics', *Rzeczpospolita*, 7–8 July 2007: A9.

62. Zdzisław Krasnodębski, *Demokracja peryferii* (Gdańsk: Slowo/Obraz Terytoria), 226,
quoted in Rae, 'Back to the Future', 227.

63. Bronisław Wildstein, *A Long Shadow of the Polish People's Republic or the Decommunization
That Never Happened* (Krakow: Arcana, 2005).

64. Indeed, the museum begins not with the rising itself but with the persecution of the insurgents by the Communist regime in the late 1940s. Janusz Kurtyka, the second head of
Poland's Institute for National Remembrance (see below, Chapter 2), argued that the
Uprising against the Nazi occupiers was mainly aimed at keeping the Soviets out of the
capital, and was a declaration of freedom in anticipation of the Red Army's arrival from
the east; Janusz Kurtyka, interview with Polish Radio 1 on 1 August 2007. The institute also
organized events with the theme 'Warsaw 1944 – the Battle of Poland', which presented the
Uprising in these terms.

65. Towards the end of the exhibition, the importance of the revival of the memory of
the Warsaw Uprising in inspiring Solidarity dissidents was shown. However, here it was
the national Catholic aspect of Solidarity in 1980–81 that was emphasized. Its role in the
collapse of Communism in 1989 was never mentioned.

66. See, for example, Anna M. Grzymała-Busse, *Redeeming the Communist Past: The Regeneration of Communist Successor Parties in East Central Europe after 1989* (Cambridge:
Cambridge University Press, 2002), 77–80: 'Centralization was the structural side of party
metamorphosis, but this rebirth also consisted of a symbolic aspect. Breaking with the past
consisted of denouncing the symbolic dimension of the party identity: its name, symbols
and historical justifications. . . . most of the party's past forms and actions had outlived
whatever usefulness and legitimacy they once had. Denouncing former misdoings and
crimes signalled to both current and potential supporters that the party recognized why it
was so discredited.'

67. This was also true in Romania, where Ion Iliescu – the former party apparatchik who
became the first post-Communist president – identified with the (very minor) outbursts of
resistance to the Ceaușescu regime, and portrayed himself as the hero of the 1989 revolution. For a detailed examination of this, see Dragoș Petrescu, 'Dilemmas of Transitional
Justice in Post-1989 Romania', in *Lustration and Consolidation of Democracy and the Rule of
Law in Central and Eastern Europe*, ed. Vladimíra Dvořáková and Anđelko Milardović
(Zagreb: Political Science Research Centre, 2007), 128–30. See also Ion Iliescu and Vladimir
Tismăneanu, *Communism, Post-Communism and Democracy: The Great Shock at the End of
a Short Century* (Boulder, CO: East European Monographs, 2008).

68. The continuity in membership was striking: over 90 per cent of its members in 1991 had
been in the party prior to 1989. See Grzymała-Busse, *Redeeming the Communist Past*, 112.

69. Ibid., 113–14.

70. On the incapacity of the Communist elite to utter Nagy's name before the summer of 1989,
see István Rév, 'The Necronym', *Representations* 64 (1998): 76–108.

71. Zoltán Ripp, '1956 emlékezete és az MSZMP', *Évkönyv 2002*: 248–49.

72. For a good discussion of this, see András Mink, 'The Revisions of the 1956 Hungarian
Revolution', in *Past in the Making: Historical Revisionism in Central Europe after 1989*, ed.
Michal Kopeček (Budapest: CEU Press, 2008), 172–73.

73. The ex-Communists, who embraced globalization and neo-liberal reforms to a greater
extent than the right, did not of course draw on certain socialist aspects of the Uprising, such
as the Workers' Councils that had advocated greater worker democracy.

74. During these parliamentary debates, the socialists' right to commemorate the revolution was
frequently questioned by conservatives who viewed them as suppressors of the revolution and
demanded that they first make amends for their role in the post-revolutionary terror. Karl P.
Benziger, 'Imre Nagy and the Unsettled Past: The Politics of Memory in Contemporary
Hungary', paper presented at 'The 7th Annual New School for Social Research, Sociology and
Historical Studies Joint Conference: History Matters: Spaces of Violence, Spaces
of Memory', 23–24 April 2004 at <www.newschool.edu/nssr/historymatters/papers/
KarlBenziger.pdf>: 12 (accessed 3 July 2009). Moreover, they claimed Nagy as a left-wing

martyr of national independence and democracy. The socialists (along with the liberal party, the Free Democrats) therefore opposed the removal of his name from the First Act of the post-Communist period (which declared him a martyr of the revolution) in 1990, and then had him officially recognized as a 'martyr of the nation' in 1996. See Benziger, 'The Funeral of Imre Nagy'.

75. Roger Gough, *A Good Comrade: János Kádár, Communism and Hungary* (London: I. B. Tauris, 2006), 257.

76. Ex-Communists still thought it legitimate to hark back to the stability that characterized the late Communist period. In 1994, Gyula Horn claimed, 'when I was in the government [i.e. in 1988–89] wasn't it true that it was better then?'

77. András Mink, 'The Kádár of History', *Budapest Review of Books* (2001): 44–46.

78. According to Ferenc Laczó, '[They] rely on a revised version of the convergence thesis popular in the 1960s, which presupposed the reconcilability of reform Communism and social democracy'. See Ferenc Laczó, 'The Many Moralists and the Few Communists: Approaching Morality and Politics in Post-Communist Hungary', in Michal Kopeček, ed. *Past in the Making*, 159.

79. For this argument from the first democratically elected former Communist prime minister of post-Communist Hungary, see 'Miért lett pártvezér? Mezei András beszélgetése dr. Horn Gyulával I', *Élet és Irodalom*, 17 May 1991: 7.

80. Laczó, 'The Many Moralists and the Few Communists', 160.

81. See, for example, the socialists' claim that members of the Hungarian right wanted to commemorate those who idealized the interwar political system, and even Fascists, during the debate on enshrining Imre Nagy's martyrdom in law. Benziger, 'Imre Nagy and the Unsettled Past', 13; István Rév, 'Counterrevolution', in *Between Past and Future: The Revolutions of 1989 and their Aftermath*, ed. Sorin Antohi and Vladimir Tismăneanu (Budapest: CEU Press, 2000), 247–71.

82. Ferenc Gyurcsány, the socialist prime minister from 2002 to 2008, often spoke of the role that the Soviets had played in liberating Hungary and made it clear he wished to align Hungary with modern 'western' approaches to history in which it was acceptable, following the end of the Cold War, to commemorate the major role that the Soviets had played in freeing Europe from Fascism.

83. According to the Socialist Party chairman István Hiller, speaking in 2005: 'This is a spiritual heritage that the progressive Hungarian left has an obligation to respect. Nagy wanted to give communism a "human face", to mould it to Hungarian traditions and society, and to prevent any more of the bloody purges that blighted Hungary after the Second World War, under Stalinist dictator Mátyás Rákosi.'

84. Paloma Aguilar and Carsten Humlebaek, 'Collective Memory and National Identity in the Spanish Democracy: The Legacies of Francoism and the Civil War', *History and Memory* 14 (2002): 121–64.

85. Although, as Paczkowski quipped in 1999, 'Another rather universally held conviction claims that from 1956 on no other factor, apart from the communist party, was the true generator of transformations aiming at democracy and independence. Quite possibly, we might soon come across an opinion demonstrating that the Polish United Workers' Party strove consistently at the restitution of private ownership and market economy, a belief based on the fact that the free market reforms were initiated several months prior to the Round Table.' See Andrzej Paczkowski, 'Communist Poland 1944–1989: Some Controversies and a Single Conclusion', *Polish Review* 44/2 (1999): 222–23.

86. For a discussion of this, see Koczanowicz, 'Memory of Politics and Politics of Memory', 261.

87. The ex-Communist Mieczysław Rakowski argued this in Michael D. Kennedy, 'Power, Privilege and Ideology in Communism's Negotiated Collapse', in *Communism's Negotiated Collapse: The Polish Round Table, Ten Years Later*, ed. Donna, Parmelee, 77.

88. See below, Chapter 5, for interviews with former Communists.

89. This picked up on earlier myths of the Communists' role in preventing the incorporation of Poland as the 'seventeenth republic' into the Soviet Union, or in blocking Soviet attempts to rule directly within Poland itself. See the discussion of this in Paczkowski, 'Communist Poland 1944–1989', 219.

90. Aleksander Kwaśniewski, quoted in 'Documents on Democracy', *Journal of Democracy* 16/4 (2005): 182–85.

91. This was why it was so important for anti-Communist historians to disprove this 'necessity of Martial Law' argument.
92. Aleksander Kwaśniewski, Polish Radio 1, 13 December 2001. This is an excerpt from a speech the president gave at a conference commemorating the twentieth anniversary of the imposition of Martial Law.
93. Since 2005, a younger generation of Social Democrats has deliberately referred back to Solidarity's twenty-one demands; they view Solidarity as defeated, but in the sense that workers' aspirations were crushed in the wake of Communism's collapse. For the revival of this class-based interpretation, see David Ost, 'Solidarity: 25 Years Later', 2.
94. Quoted in Małgorzata Subotic, 'How Kwaśniewski Won', Polish News Bulletin, 27 November 1995.
95. On the importance of anti-Nazi resistance memory in the west, see, for example, Bill Niven, Facing the Nazi Past: United Germany and the Legacy of the Third Reich (London: Routledge, 2001), chapter 3; Douglas Peifer, 'Commemoration of Mutiny, Rebellion and Resistance in Post-war Germany: Public Memory, History and the Formation of "Memory Beacons" ', Journal of Military History 65/1 (2001): 1013–52.
96. The desire to take revenge on the past can be translated into a national memorial day; see the example of Cambodia's 'Day to Remain Tied to Anger' on 20 May every year, when the genocide of Pol Pot's regime is remembered.
97. For an exploration of the way in which the victories of 1989 were connected to the colour revolutions in the Ukraine and Georgia more than a decade later, see Andrés Schipani-Adúriz, 'Through an Orange-Colored Lens: Western Media, Constructed Imagery, and Color Revolutions', Demokratizatsiya: The Journal of Post-Soviet Democratization 15/4 (2007): 459–64.
98. See below, Chapter 4, for an exploration of the competition between western European discourses on the Holocaust and central-eastern European commemorations for the victims of Communism.
99. José Manuel Barroso's speech commemorating the fiftieth anniversary of 1956: 'Acting Together: The Legacy of 1956', Budapest, 23 October 2006 at <http://www.europa-eu-un.org/articles/en/article_6387_en.htm> (accessed 3 July 2009).
100. Laczó, 'The Many Moralists and the Few Communists', 164. Here, he concludes that this representation was 'largely external to the Hungarian story – the story of those who lived through it'.

Chapter 2: Completing the Revolution: History Commissions and Institutes of National Memory

1. On the limited nature of Vergangenheitsbewältigung (the struggle to come to terms with the past) in post-Nazi Germany, there is a large amount of literature; see, for example, Norbert Frei, Adenauer's Germany and the Nazi Past: The Politics of Amnesty and Integration (New York: Columbia University Press, 2002); Robert G. Moeller, War Stories: The Search for a Usable Past in the Federal Republic of Germany (Berkeley, CA and London: University of California Press, 2003); Bill Niven, ed., Germans as Victims: Remembering the Past in Contemporary Germany (Basingstoke, Hampshire: Palgrave Macmillan, 2006); Alf Lüdtke, 'Coming to Terms with the Past: Illusions of Remembering, Ways of Forgetting Nazism in West Germany', Journal of Modern History 65 (1993): 542–72. Many scholars have argued that there is a close link between processes of justice and collective memory: courtroom proceedings are in themselves fundamentally concerned with establishing convincing stories about the past. Prominent trials (which are often well covered by the media and widely discussed) can have a far greater impact on public debates about the past than can historians, as the principles on which cases are chosen and prosecuted educate populations into concepts that will be the foundation for a new political order. See, for example, Mark Osiel, Mass Atrocity, Collective Memory, and the Law (New Brunswick, NJ and London: Transaction, 1997).
2. See, in particular, Paloma Aguilar, Memory and Amnesia: The Role of the Spanish Civil War in the Transition to Democracy (New York and Oxford: Berghahn Books, 2002).
3. For a critical take that assesses why democracies see remembering as so important and suggests that memory is not always an effective support for democratization, see Barbara

A. Misztal, *Theories of Social Remembering* (Maidenhead, Berkshire: Open University Press, 2003), chapter 6.

4. Lavinia Stan, 'Truth Commissions in Post-Communism: The Overlooked Solution?', *The Open Political Science Journal* 2 (2009): 1. Some liberals in Poland suggested the post-Franco 'Spanish model' of overcoming the past through silencing former conflicts, but Germany remained the primary model. On the closing down of the possibility, in the early 1990s, of an imitation of Argentinean, Chilean or South African models of public tribunals involving public testimony in Germany, see A. James McAdams, *Judging the Past in Unified Germany* (Cambridge and New York: Cambridge University Press, 2001), 122. It was only ex-Communists who looked beyond Europe, particularly to the model of South Africa and 'reconciliation'; see Adrian Cioflâncă, 'Politics of Oblivion in Postcommunist Romania', *The Romanian Journal of Political Sciences* 2 (2002): 93.

5. There are many examples of this. See, for instance, the importance of the participation of the working class in the Bolsheviks' myth of the Russian Revolution; Frederick C. Corney, *Telling October: Memory and the Making of the Bolshevik Revolution* (Ithaca, NY: Cornell University Press, 2004).

6. Alex Boraine, 'Truth and Reconciliation Commission in South Africa Amnesty: The Price of Peace', in *Retribution and Reparation in the Transition to Democracy*, ed. Jon Elster (Cambridge: Cambridge University Press, 2006), 311. On the relationship between narrative and legitimization, see Claire Moon, *Narrating Political Reconciliation: South Africa's Truth and Reconciliation Commission* (Lanham, MD: Lexington Books, 2008); Richard Wilson, *The Politics of Truth and Reconciliation in South Africa: Legitimizing the Post-Apartheid State* (Cambridge and New York: Cambridge University Press, 2001).

7. Of course, this model was heavily criticized by those who believed that justice was sacrificed on the altar of a fake new social solidarity. However, this chapter mostly concerns the political intentions of those who set up 'truth-telling' procedures.

8. See Jacek Kuron, 'Overcoming Totalitarianism', in *The Revolutions of 1989*, ed. Vladimir Tismăneanu (London: Routledge, 1999), 198–201.

9. Michnik referred to this as the 'amnesty, not amnesia' programme. For an excellent discussion, see Magdalena Zolkos, 'The Conceptual Nexus of Human Rights and Democracy in the Polish Lustration Debates 1989–97', *Journal of Communist Studies and Transition Politics* 22/2 (2006): 233–37.

10. Jan Kubik and Amy Lynch, 'The Original Sin of Poland's Third Republic: Discounting "Solidarity" and its Consequences for Political Reconciliation', *Polish Sociological Review* 153 (2006): 9–38. The authors quote Ireneusz Krzemiński as saying: 'a symbolic picture of the end of the old order and the beginning of the new order has not emerged. Such a symbol, that would dwell in the everyday consciousness and that would constitute a focal point for public rituals, practically does not exist; and yet it is sorely needed' (18).

11. Ibid., 17.

12. For a discussion of this in the Hungarian context, see István Rév, *Retroactive Justice: Prehistory of Post-Communism* (Stanford, CA: Stanford University Press, 2005), 30. In his formulation, '[Communism's] strange death fooled the people one more time by denying them the experience of their sovereignty. Communism killed itself instead of letting the people do it themselves.'

13. Only Germany and Czechoslovakia experimented with de-Communization, and even in these countries the number of those purged was much lower than originally anticipated. In Czechoslovakia, for instance, following the Lustration Law of October 1991, 310,000 people were vetted, 15,000 were deemed to have been 'collaborators', but very few were excluded from public office because the law only related to those in high-ranking positions. See Wojciech Sadurski, *Rights before Courts: A Study of Constitutional Courts in Post-Communist States of Central and Eastern Europe* (Dordrecht: Springer, 2005), 236; John Borneman, *Settling Accounts: Violence, Justice and Accountability in Postsocialist Europe* (Princeton, NJ: Princeton University Press, 1997), 152. On the options for justice, see Noel Calhoun, *Dilemmas of Justice in Eastern Europe's Democratic Transitions* (New York: Palgrave Macmillan, 2004), 8–14.

14. See the Romanian case below, page 33.

15. Although, as some scholars note, the law is often an effective arena in which to shape new collective memories. On the role of the law in suppressing unwanted memories from

the German Democratic Republic, see Inga Markovits, 'Selective Memory: How the Law Affects What We Remember and Forget about the Past – the Case of East Germany', *Law and Society Review* 35/3 (2001): 513–63. See also Csilla Kiss, 'The (Re)Construction of Post-Communist Memory', in *The Burden of Remembering: Recollections and Representations of the Twentieth Century*, ed. Ene Kõresaar, Epp Lauk and Kristin Kuutma (Helsinki: SKS Kirjat, 2009): 119–38.

16. This did not mean that the producers of this new liberal democratic memory denied that continuities existed in political practice across the threshold of 1989, or that the system change had been limited; rather, they believed that the narrative of the clean break was necessary to mobilize populations in support of, and to strengthen, the post-Communist system.

17. Jarosław Kaczyński, 'Democrats Cannot Be Tolerant to Communism', speech at the Institute of National Remembrance, 21 February 2007.

18. The German case was the exception here: the establishment of a History Commission occurred much earlier in the context of unification. Given that the east was integrated immediately into West German political structures (which also provided the cultural-historical norms) here too a History Commission might also be read as a necessary prerequisite for integration into the West.

19. This coalition between the National Liberal Party and the Democratic Party was formed in order to create a united anti-Communist bloc to defeat the ex-Communist Social Democrats.

20. Organisations such as the Group for Social Dialogue (Grupul pentru Dialog Social) who seek to promote civil liberties and a democratic culture.

21. For an account that stresses the politics behind the commission, see Ruxandra Cesereanu, 'The Final Report on the Holocaust and the Final Report on the Communist Dictatorship in Romania', *East European Politics and Societies* 22 (2008): 274.

22. The Council for the Study of Securitate Archives (CNSAS) had been founded in 1999 by Romania's first anti-Communist government under Emil Constantinescu, but was repeatedly blocked by both the government itself and the SRI (the successor to the domestic branch of the Securitate) in its attempts to transfer security-service files: Lavinia Stan, 'Moral Cleansing, Romanian Style', *Problems of Post-Communism* 49/4 (2002): 52. It should be noted that the CNSAS's mandate was strictly related to Securitate files, which were inherited after 1989 by the SRI. The only other files housed by the CNSAS were those created by the Securitate in prisons, mainly consisting of interrogation reports on dissidents. It should be emphasized that the CNSAS was not mandated to make all Communist-era files accessible: no military intelligence and no files from other ministries could be transferred. My thanks to Lavinia Stan for this information.

23. For Iliescu's comments in Israel, see Ruxandra Cesereanu, 'The Final Report', 270–81.

24. The commission was under pressure to produce the report before the accession date of 1 January 2007.

25. On the emergence of the idea of new official 'national memories', see Michal Kopeček, 'In Search of "National Memory": The Politics of History, Nostalgia and the Historiography of Communism in the Czech Republic and East Central Europe', in *Past in the Making: Historical Revisionism in Central Europe after 1989*, ed. Michal Kopeček (Budapest: CEU Press, 2008), 75–95.

26. Băsescu's speech before parliament, 18 December 2006, published on the website of the Presidency of Romania at <http://cpcader.presidency.ro/upload/8288-en.pdf> (accessed 20 May 2010).

27. Dragoș Petrescu, 'Dilemmas of Transitional Justice in Post-1989 Romania', in *Lustration and Consolidation of Democracy and the Rule of Law in Central and Eastern Europe*, ed. Vladimíra Dvořáková and Anđelko Milardović (Zagreb: Political Science Research Centre, 2007), 128.

28. Vladimir Tismăneanu, Dorin Dobrincu and Cristian Vasile, *Comisia Prezidențială pentru Analiza Dictaturii Comuniste din România, Raport Final* (Bucharest: Humanitas, 2006), 624.

29. Unlike Poland, there was no equivalent of the Round Table, no negotiation and political reconciliation between former enemies, and no declaration from Communists that they had rejected the former system. This partly explains why an anti-anti-Communist force that advocated celebrating the values of 1989 did not emerge in Romania.

30. Figure from 2002, taken from Adrian Cioflâncă, 'Politics of Oblivion in Post-Communist Romania', *The Romanian Journal of Political Sciences* 2 (2002): 90.
31. Tismăneanu et al, *Comisia Prezidenţială*, 27.
32. Ion Iliescu and Vladimir Tismăneanu, *Communism, Post-Communism and Democracy: The Great Shock at the End of a Short Century* (Ann Arbor, MI: University of Michigan Press, 2008), 121, 151.
33. Petrescu, 'Dilemmas of Transitional Justice', 132–33.
34. For an examination of Iliescu's promotion of the idea of 'authentic revolution', see Cristian Tileaga, 'What Is a "Revolution"?: National Commemoration, Collective Memory and Managing Authenticity in the Representation of a Political Event', *Discourse and Society* 19/3 (2008): 359–82.
35. Neagu Cosma, *Securitatea, Poliţia Politică, Dosare, Informatori* (Bucharest: Globus, 1998). This author was picked out as inimical to a new democratic mentality by Dorin Dobrincu: interview with the author, Bucharest, May 2008. On the maintenance of national Communist outlooks in historiography, see Cristina Petrescu and Dragoş Petrescu, 'Mastering vs. Coming to Terms with the Past: A Critical Analysis of Post-Communist Romanian Historiography', in *Narratives Unbound: Historical Studies in Post-Communist Eastern Europe*, ed. Sorin Antohi, Balázs Trencsényi and Péter Apor (Budapest: CEU Press, 2007), 319.
36. It was based on the assumption that the story had to be told in one way; even when commission members admitted that it was not perfect, they suggested their official story was still 'perfectible'.
37. Interviews with commission members Cristian Vasile and Dorin Dobrincu with the author, Bucharest, May 2007. Dobrincu in particular stressed the strength of the nationalist Communist account of the past in the 1990s and the need to provide a liberal democratic alternative.
38. At both the 1996 and 2000 elections, the ex-Communist Social Democrats raised the possibility that de-Communization might bring about 'civil war' and called for reconciliation. See Alexandru Gussi, Usages de passé et démocratization (Unpublished doctoral thesis, Institut d'Etudes Politiques de Paris, 2007), 178.
39. Vladimir Tismăneanu, 'Democracy and Memory: Romania Confronts its Communist Past', *The Annals of the American Academy of Political and Social Science* 617 (2008): 171; Armand Goşu, one of the commission members, suggested that with ex-Communist involvement it would have been a historical whitewash; interview with the author, Bucharest, May 2008.
40. There were other 'victims of Communism' on the commission – such as Monica Lovinescu and Virgil Ierunca – but they did not represent broader constituencies.
41. Tismăneanu, 'Democracy and Memory', 169. On make-up and tensions, see Cristian Vasile, 'Cine a scris Raportul Tismăneanu', *Revista 22* (2007) at <http://www.revista22.ro/cine-a-scris-raportul-Tismăneanu-3336.html> (accessed 6 July 2009). There were also twenty political, historical and sociological experts who assisted the commission.
42. This was also a problem for the Enquete Commission in unified Germany, where the trials received much more attention, were publicly contested and thus provoked greater debate over the past. See Jennifer A. Yoder, 'Truth without Reconciliation: An Appraisal of the Enquete Commission on the SED Dictatorship in Germany', *German Politics* 8/3 (1999): 72.
43. Some claimed that as the commission developed and it became clearer that President Băsescu and his Democratic Liberals did not support lustration, its focus began to be limited. The short time allocated to the production of the report also meant that there was little room to ensure that a consistent academic tone was given to the variety of its contributions.
44. The commission initially included twenty members, but two of them (Sorin Antohi and Nicolae Corneanu) had to step down because of accusations that they had collaborated with the Securitate. Only Cristian Vasile, Vladimir Tismăneanu, Gail Kligman, Stelian Tănase, Andrei Pippidi, Alexandru Zub and Marius Oprea had written on Communism before being appointed as commission members. Some issues connected with membership were contested at the time. For some Romanians, the fact that former dissident Paul Goma refused the invitation to join meant that it had no legitimacy to deal with the Communist past. Some contested the right of Vladimir Tismăneanu to be commission chairman because he had started his career as a Marxist.

45. Tismăneanu et al., *Comisia Prezidenţială*, 19–20.
46. Greg Grandin, 'The Instruction of Great Catastrophe: Truth Commissions, National History, and State Formation in Argentina, Chile, and Guatemala', *The American Historical Review*, 110/1 (2005): 46. Here, the first commissions in Bolivia and Argentina are quoted as having been 'state-sanctioned investigations into past episodes of political terror [and] one part of this transition's agenda to cultivate a notion of liberal citizenship that viewed the state not as a potential executor of social justice but as an arbiter of legal disputes and protector of individual rights'.
47. See, for example, Greg Grandin, *The Last Colonial Massacre: Latin America in the Cold War* (Chicago: University of Chicago Press, 2004), vii.
48. Tismăneanu, 'Democracy and Memory', 173.
49. Some argued that because the ideology of Communism was still accepted by groups in the west, they could only reject it in terms of its criminal practice: to condemn it ideologically would be taken as an intolerant, illiberal rejection of political pluralism.
50. Tismăneanu, 'Democracy and Memory', 171.
51. Tismăneanu et al., *Comisia Prezidenţială*, 626.
52. Ibid., 626.
53. Michael Humphrey, 'From Victim to Victimhood: Truth Commissions and Trials as Rituals of Political Transition and Individual Healing', *The Australian Journal of Anthropology* 14/2 (2003): 172.
54. Tismăneanu, 'Democracy and Memory', 171–72.
55. Tismăneanu et al., *Comisia Prezidenţială*, 161. Two sections on the late Communist period deal with 'fear' and 'misery' as sources of social control, but do not address the widespread co-optation of society.
56. Monica Ciobanu, 'Criminalising the Past and Reconstructing Collective Memory: The Romanian Truth Commission', *Europe-Asia Studies* 61/2 (2009): 328.
57. Where co-optation was addressed, it was very brief and used to frame a section on the rejection of the system by a small number of dissidents; see *ibid.*, 363–64. This was a frustrating omission for some members of the commission: see the interview by the author with Dragoş Petrescu, Bucharest, May 2008.
58. See also its use of terms such as 'Fascist-Communist Baroque': Tismăneanu et al., *Comisia Prezidenţială*, 150–51. Communism was no longer the antithesis of Nazism but rather its brother: similarities between the discourse of Nicolae Ceauşescu and the political actions of Corneliu Zelea Codreanu, Romanian Fascist leader in the 1930s, were drawn out and categorised together as part of a continuous style of leadership termed 'Fascist-Communist Baroque': Caius Dobrescu, 'Barocul Fascisto-Comunist ca Fenomen Global', paper presented at 'Gulag şi Holocaust în Conştiinţă Romanească' conference Babeş-Bolyai University 25–26 May 2007 at <http://www.memoria.ro/?location=view_article&id=1744> (accessed 7 July 2009).
59. This term was used immediately after the collapse of Communism in Romania; see, for example, Vladimir Trebici, *Genocid şi Demografie* (Bucharest: Humanitas, 1991).
60. Stéphane Courtois et al., eds, *The Black Book of Communism: Crimes, Terror, Repression*, trans. Jonathan Murphy (Cambridge, MA and London: Harvard University Press, 1999).
61. Gheorghe Boldur-Lăţescu, *Genocidul comunist în România* (Bucharest: Albatros, 1992).
62. It should be noted that the Soviets exerted significant influence over the framing of the Genocide Convention in 1948 and successfully petitioned for the exclusion of the extermination of 'political groupings' from the definition of genocide. See Amir Weiner, 'In the Long Shadow of War: The Second World War and the Soviet and Post-Soviet World', *Diplomatic History* 25/3 (2001): 446; Tismăneanu et al., *Comisia Prezidenţială*, 158.
63. For Romanian criticisms of the use of this term to describe Communist crimes, see the interview with Michael Shafir in Dan Tapalagă, 'Raportul Tismăneanu, notat cu şapte', *Ziua de Cluj*, 12 January 2007.
64. Ciobanu, 'Criminalising the Past', 334.
65. Humphrey, 'From Victim to Victimhood', 171; see also Bain Attwood, 'In the Age of Testimony: The Stolen Generations Narrative, "Distance," and Public History', *Public Culture* 20/1 (2008): 75–96.
66. Grandin, 'The Instruction of Great Catastrophe', part 13.
67. Ibid., part 12; Julie Taylor, 'Body Memories: Aide-Memoires and Collective Amnesia in the Wake of Argentine Terror', in *Body Politics: Disease, Desire, and the Family*, ed. Michael Ryan (Boulder, CO: Westview Press, 1994), 192–203.

68. Like many other truth commissions, the Romanian one purged the ideological context in which the dictatorship operated from its historical account in favour of focusing on the violence and criminality inherent in the relationship between perpetrators and victims. Just as the South African Truth and Reconciliation Commission received criticism for seeming to equate the violence perpetrated by the apartheid state and African National Congress resistance and ignoring the power inequalities and different ideological outlooks of these forces, so the Romanian Presidential Commission was criticized for equalizing the victims of Communism, irrespective of their (sometimes anti-democratic) ideological attachments.

69. Tismăneanu, 'Democracy and Memory', 173.

70. Interview with Dobrincu.

71. Some suggest that resistance mythologies were especially important for post-Communist intellectuals who had not resisted under Communism and for whom '1989' had not provided a powerful anti-Communist moment through which they could construct an anti-Communist tradition.

72. Interview with Petrescu.

73. Tismăneanu et al., *Comisia Prezidenţială*, 625.

74. Ibid., 332–33.

75. Interview with Petrescu.

76. On the divided interpretations of 1989 among ex-Communists and anti-Communists, see Alexandru Gussi, 'Décembre 1989: prémisses du débat sur le passé récent en Roumanie', *Romanian Political Science Review* 1 (2006): 115–34; Tileaga, 'What Is A "Revolution"?', 359; Peter Siani-Davies, *The Romanian Revolution of December 1989* (Ithaca, NY: Cornell University Press, 2005), especially chapter 7; Sanda Cordoş, 'Revoluţia, un prag între două vieţi', *Echinox* 6 (2004): 124–28.

77. Lavinia Stan, 'Truth Commissions in Post-Communism', 3. Indeed, the narrative of heroic deaths was utilized at sites such as the Military Museum in Bucharest, where the memory of the fallen was used to promote the idea of authentic system change.

78. Interview with Goşu.

79. See Tismăneanu et al., *Comisia Prezidenţială*, 626–27. On the importance of the participation in, and the myth of, the University Square protests in the formation of a Romanian anti-Communist identity after 1989, see Julia Brotea and Daniel Béland, ' "Better Dead than Communist!" Contentious Politics, Identity Formation, and the University Square Phenomenon in Romania', *Spaces of Identity* 7/2 (2007) at <https://pi.library.yorku.ca/ojs/index.php/soi/article/vi/ew/7971/7103> (accessed 7 July 2009); Ruxandra Cesereanu, 'Fenomenul Piaţa Universităţii', *Revista 22* (2003) at <http://www.revista22.ro/fenomenul-piata-universitatii-1990-445.html> (accessed 7 July 2009).

80. President Traian Băsescu's speech before parliament, 18 December 2006.

81. Ciobanu, 'Criminalising the Past', 332.

82. In 2008, the report was attacked in the volume *Iluzia Anticomunismului* ('The Illusion of Anti-Communism') by a group of both leftist and non-leftist scholars who objected to the use of the term 'genocide' and the failure to attribute any form of social development to the Communist period: Vasile Ernu, Costi Rogozanu and Ciprian Şiulea, eds, *Iluzia Anticomunismului: Lecturi Critice ale Raportului Tismăneanu* (Chisinau: Cartier, 2008).

83. Material from the report was included in the language and literature baccalaureate: see 'Examenul de Bacalaureat Limba şi Litertura Română, 2008', *Ministerul Educaţiei, Cercetării şi Tineretului Centrul Naţional pentru Curriculum şi Evaluare în Învăţământul Preuniversitar.*

84. Interviews by the author with Andrei Pippidi and Armand Goşu, Bucharest, May 2008.

85. Kopeček, 'In Search of "National Memory"', 88.

86. There was little interest in the files in Poland in the immediate aftermath of the collapse, unlike in Germany; see Noel Calhoun, *Dilemmas of Justice in Eastern Europe's Democratic Transitions* (New York: Palgrave Macmillan, 2004), 102–03. For the documents transferred, see <http//www.ipn.gov.pl/wai/en/22/55/Groups_of_Archival_Documents.html> (accessed 7 July 2009).

87. Polymeris Voglis, 'The Greek Civil War and the Politics of Memory', Colloque international: les sociétés européennes du XXI siècle face à leur passé, Reims, France, 5–7 May 2008. See, for instance, Greece, where, in 1989, parliament voted to destroy the country's records relating to the civil war between Communists and nationalists. The end of the Cold War elicited a collective desire to forget these memories, which were not deemed useful in a new political context.

88. For details of how it was established in the Czech Republic, see Vladimíra Dvořáková, 'The Institute of National Memory: Historical Memory as a Political Project', in *Lustration and Consolidation*, 153–68.

89. In Romania, these processes were divided between three institutions: a Presidential Commission to give an official account of the past, an Institute for the Investigation of Communist Crimes to compile evidence for the prosecution of past criminal behaviour, and the National Council for the Study of the Securitate Archives to control access to documentation, carry out official screening of suspected Communist-era officials and to conduct research.

90. See Adam Czarnota, 'The Politics of the Lustration Law in Poland, 1989–2006', in *Justice as Prevention: Vetting Public Employees in Transitional Societies*, ed. Alexander Mayer-Rieckh and Pablo de Greiff (New York: Social Science Research Council, 2007), 232.

91. This was a particular concern under the Law and Justice government (2005–07), but was less so under its predecessor (Democratic Left Alliance) and its successor (Civic Platform).

92. The Lustration Bureau replaced the body formerly responsible for verifying vetting declarations, the Office of the Spokesman of Public Interest, which had operated independently of the Institute of National Remembrance, but had used its archive. Thus, although the archive had been previously used for vetting, the Lustration Bureau brought it 'in house', and moreover was mandated to increase very significantly the scale of this process.

93. Interview with Leon Kieres, first director of the Institute of National Remembrance, in *The Warsaw Voice*, 4 August 2002.

94. Interview with Paweł Machcewicz, first head of the Public Education Bureau, Warsaw, April 2008: 'for me this is about truth and justice and not about revenge and political manipulation.'

95. *Institute of National Remembrance Annual Report*, 2003.

96. Paweł Machcewicz, 'The Institute of National Remembrance and Coming to Terms with a Difficult Past: World War II and the Communist Dictatorship', *InterMarium* 8/3 (2006): 1–10.

97. It had to revive knowledge that had been repressed during the Communist period, such as information about the Soviet deportations of Poles to Siberia.

98. This debate was sparked off by Jan Gross's book *Neighbors*, which dealt with a massacre of Jews by their 'Polish neighbours' on 10 July 1941; see Jan Gross, *Neighbors: The Destruction of the Jewish Community in Jedwabne* (Princeton, NJ: Princeton University Press, 2001).

99. Interview by the author with an anonymous member of the Public Education Bureau, Warsaw, April 2008.

100. Interview with Machcewicz.

101. These institutions placed a large emphasis on public education, producing monographs and exhibitions, training history teachers, and preparing lists of Communist symbols and memorials to be removed.

102. Interview with Machcewicz.

103. Csilla Kiss, 'The (Re)Construction of Post-Communist Memory'.

104. Act of Parliament, 18 December 1998, on the Institute of National Remembrance – Commission for the Prosecution of Crimes against the Polish Nation (*Journal of Laws*, 19 December 1998).

105. Interview by the author with an anonymous member of the Public Education Bureau, Warsaw, April 2008.

106. This is from the institute's Founding Act (1998).

107. Interview with Machcewicz.

108. It was the one part of the institute that was not independent of government, as it was responsible to both the institute's board and the Ministry of Justice. (The head of the Main Commission was also the deputy national prosecutor and was answerable to hearings of both the lower chamber and Senate in parliament.)

109. Of the 1,271 investigations carried out by the Main Commission before 2007, 937 related to Communist crimes, 245 to Nazi crimes and 89 to other crimes.

110. Interview by the author with Dariusz Gabrel, head of the Main Commission, Warsaw, April 2008.

111. *Institute of National Remembrance Annual Report,* 2003.
112. Once sufficient material had been gathered from the archives of the secret police and elsewhere, it was sent to public prosecutors who decided if the case should be heard in court. During the institute's first two years, its prosecutors made 24 indictments, 6 sentences were handed down and 4 people were found guilty. There were 200 indictments out of 5,000 cases over the period between 2000 and 2007. This low success rate was in part due to the fact that many victims were already dead or elderly, and testimony was often difficult to obtain because of trauma or memory loss. Yet the institute's head suggested that these cases were crucial information-gathering exercises, even where insufficient evidence led to the discontinuance of the case: 'Our success is the indictments sent to the courts and also the decisions of discontinuance after having established all the circumstances and the victims.' Interview with Gabrel.
113. This work remained unfinished after protests from a Jewish organization concerning the exhumation of Jewish bodies.
114. The conservative Law and Justice party was critical of the institute's framing of Poles as perpetrators in the Jedwabne case; according to Paweł Machcewicz, 'Law and Justice was from the very beginning really interested in history . . . they wanted to use the institution to [carry this out]. . . . To put it in a nutshell they said that the Polish democratic state after '89 failed in its obligations to promote the plight of Poles regarding their history. . . . When the institute concentrated Polish public opinion on Jedwabne – which they considered shaming for the Poles – it meant there was not enough concentration on more glorious aspects of Polish history.' Interview with Machcewicz. The institute's second president, Janusz Kurtyka (2005–10), rejected the earlier emphasis on dark episodes from the Polish past and encouraged his historians to concentrate on unifying histories. Interview by the author with Łukasz Kamiński, deputy head of the Public Education Bureau, Warsaw, April 2008.
115. A first parliamentary motion on lustration was passed in Poland in 1992, but it was not until 1997 that the first Lustration Law was passed. However, it was not effective, in part because of the failure to establish a 'Lustration Court' to verify investigations; see Adam Czarnota, 'The Politics of the Lustration Law'.
116. Quoted in Cynthia M. Horne, 'Late Lustration Programmes in Romania and Poland: Supporting or Undermining Democratic Transitions?', *Democratization* 16/2 (2009): 352.
117. Ibid. The new Lustration Law was expanded to include not only public officials but also teachers, journalists and 'those in positions of public trust', a category which could include those in the private sector such as business leaders and lawyers (353).
118. My thanks to Krzysztof Persak of the Institute of National Remembrance for this information.
119. This was controversial, because the idea had been overturned by the Supreme Court in 2000. See Horne, 'Late Lustration Programmes', 353.
120. It should be noted that the institute contained many (relatively) autonomous units and individuals, and that, in interviews conducted in 2008, some did not agree with the new elite consensus and continued aspects of their work according to other models.
121. Interview by the author with Jacek Wygoda, head of the Lustration Bureau, Warsaw, April 2008: 'it is very delayed compensation because this [institute] wasn't established until 1998 . . . the truth is that apart from Romania there were no revolutions in any of our countries.'
122. *Faces of Security* exhibition (in Polish, *Bezpieka*, a derogatory term for state-security officers).
123. Horne, 'Late Lustration Programmes', 354.
124. After 1997, when the first major vetting law was introduced, lustration in a Polish context usually meant the revelation of a person's collaboration (as an informer or state-security-service employee) and the judgement of that person at the ballot box or by an employer, rather than automatic purging from public service. The situation was different in Czechoslovakia and Germany, where lustration meant that collaboration could lead directly to exclusion from office. For a discussion of the history of this approach, see Czarnota, 'The Politics of the Lustration Law', 232.
125. The archive could also be used as a source of fear; some of it was destroyed at the end of the Communist period, although the precise extent of the losses was only partly known, and even less publicized. Between 1998 and 2007, those accused of collaboration could not access the archive: only former victims of the regime could consult their files. Thus, individuals with

problematic pasts often had to guess at the likelihood of incriminating evidence surviving in the secret police archive when making their declarations. This restriction was deemed unconstitutional in 2007 and nearly all citizens – including so-called 'collaborators' – were given access to their personal material. This change allowed many accused to check their files before deciding how to answer on their vetting forms. However, former state security employees or secret informers were still denied access to documents that they had helped to 'produce'. Interview by the author with Wojciech Sawicki, Archive, Institute of National Remembrance, Warsaw, April 2008.

126. Under the 1997 law, punishment was legally mandated as ten years and could not be adjusted. From 2007 onwards, however, both the size of the lie and the seriousness of the collaboration with the security services could be taken into consideration in determining the level of punishment. The Lustration Bureau presented the slow pace of vetting as proof that the institution was democratic: '[This] may come to a dead end in democratic societies . . . only in autocratic societies can lustration really work . . . most important are citizens' rights, not spectacular successes.' Interview by the author with Prosecutor Stawowy, Lustration Bureau, Warsaw, April 2008.

127. A Constitutional Court ruling in 2007 prohibited the Lustration Bureau from assessing positive statements, except in the case of MPs and local government office holders.

128. Those in the vetting office pointed out that shame was often an insufficient punishment, citing the use by former 'collaborators' of the Polish website 'Schoolfriends Reunited', which provided a forum for them to discuss their activities publicly.

129. In Romania, during similar processes organized by the CNSAS, some defendants, including many members of the Securitate, contested this process not by denying their former involvement, but rather by denying on the vetting form that they had been 'agents' (which had a negative connotation). Instead, they stated that they had been 'officers' who had worked with the state-security services but who should not be criminalized as they had not broken the laws of that era. Interview with Claudiu Secașiu, CNSAS, Bucharest, April 2008.

Chapter 3: Criminalizing Communism?: History at Terror Sites and in Statue Parks and National Museums

1. On the social silence about Nazism after 1945, see, for example, Alf Lüdtke, ' "Coming to Terms with the Past": Illusions of Remembering, Ways of Forgetting Nazism in West Germany', *Journal of Modern History* 65/3 (1993): 542–72. On collective forgetting in Spain as an important part of the negotiated transition to democracy, see, for example, Joan Ramon Resina, ed., *Disremembering the Dictatorship: The Politics of Memory in the Spanish Transition to Democracy* (Amsterdam: Rodopi, 2000). This silence about the past meant that Francoist interpretations were not challenged in public spaces; many Catholic churches retained memorials to priests murdered by Communists, and major Francoist monuments – such as the Valley of the Fallen – were left untouched. The last statue of Franco was removed only in 2009, thirty-four years after the dictator's death.

2. See, for example, the collection of memorials to Ceaușescu at the Craiova Leisure Park, Romania; the reopened Zhivkov Museum in Pravets, Bulgaria; and the plans for a museum dedicated to Stalin near Krasnoyarsk.

3. See, for example, the display of everyday Communist-era objects at the 'Open Depot' in Eisenhüttenstadt as an example of 'leftist melancholia' in Charity Scribner, *Requiem for Communism* (Cambridge, MA: MIT, 2003).

4. On the choice of prisons for museums, see Péter Apor, 'Eurocommunism. Commemorating Communism in Contemporary Eastern Europe', in Małgorzata Pakier and Bo Stråth, eds, *A European Memory? Contested Histories and Politics of Remembrance* (Oxford: Berghahn Books, 2010).

5. 'Premier Neglects Hungary's National Interests – Controversial Museum Head', *Népszabadság*, 4 August 2005.

6. Mária Schmidt, 'Ne Hass, ne Alkoss, ne Gyarapíts! A Terror Háza Múzeum első éve', in *Magyarország Politikai Évkönyve 2003 I–II* (Budapest: Demokrácia Kutatások Magyar Központja Közhasznú Alapítvány, 2003).

7. Hungarian TV2, 24 February 2003.

8. Quoted on the Sighet Memorial website at <http://www.memorialsighet.ro/index.php? lang=en> (accessed 9 July 2009). See above, Chapter 2, for an in-depth exploration of the idea of the 'unfinished revolution' for Romanian anti-Communists after 1989.
9. Quoted in Alexandra Laignel-Lavastine, 'Fascism and Communism in Romania: The Comparative Stakes and Uses', in *Stalinism and Nazism: History and Memory Compared*, ed. Henry Rousso (Lincoln, NE: University of Nebraska Press, 1999), 175.
10. See Sighet Memorial website at <http://www.memorialsighet.ro/> (accessed 9 July 2009).
11. Ana Blandiana, 'Memoria ca Formă de Justiţie', *Dilema* 518 (2003): 10. Indeed, the first official state-endorsed report to condemn Romanian Communism as a criminal system, published seventeen years after the end of the Communist regime, recommended the opening of more prison museums where Communism could be 'culturally tried' and condemned. After the report was published, preparations were made to open new prison museums at sites such as Făgăraş castle.
12. The House of Terror's director, Mária Schmidt, also presented her institution as a way of containing the past in the absence of revenge or justice. See Schmidt, 'Ne Hass, ne Alkoss, ne Gyarapíts!', 176–77.
13. Ana Blandiana, 'Die Gedenkstätte Memorial Sighet – Ein Lebendiges Museum', in *Der Kommunismus im Museum: Formen der Auseinandersetzung in Deutschland und Ostmitteleuropa*, ed. Volkhard Knigge and Ulrich Mählert (Cologne: Böhlau, 2005), 173.
14. This simplifying of victims' life stories was a complaint made by László Rajk Jnr, son of the executed former Hungarian Communist minister of the interior: 'The lack of complexity is a problem not only of the House of Terror but of the whole approach to Communism in Eastern Europe. . . . Because of a lack of analysis, people fall into the same trap as the Communists did 50 years ago. . . . What bothers me is not that my father is on the wall of the guilty or of the victims or both. The problem is the oversimplification of his career'; quoted in Kim Lucian, 'Budapest Revisits its Recent Horrors', *Boston Globe*, 6 April 2003: A16.
15. See Robert Fürtös, 'Sighet, preambul al Holocaustului, punct central al Gulagului', *Caietele Echinox*, 13 (2007): 226–41. Around twelve thousand Jews were deported from Sighet to Nazi extermination camps.
16. For a detailed discussion of this, see Chapter 4.
17. There is an attempt at the Sighet Memorial prison museum to reflect the ethnic diversity of the area where it was situated. There are, for example, rooms on the suffering of ethnic Hungarians and Germans under Communism. However, the main focus is on the heroic Romanian martyrs and the loss of 'ethnic Romanian lands' to the Soviet Union after World War II.
18. Laignel-Lavastine, 'Fascism and Communism', 174. The founders of the House of Terror had also visited Holocaust sites such as the Washington Holocaust Museum when considering their design.
19. For an examination of how the House of Terror uses stylistic devices from Fascist-era museums, see István Rév, *Retroactive Justice: Pre-History of Post-Communism* (Stanford, CA: Stanford University Press, 2005), 294–98.
20. On the use of banks of photographs of victims taken by a genocidal regime, see Rachel Hughes, 'The Abject Artefacts of Memory: Photographs from Cambodia's Genocide', *Media, Culture & Society* 25/3 (2003): 23, 25.
21. Visitors to the Tuol Seng Genocide Museum in Phnom Penh tried to subvert the museum's intention by scrawling names or personal information on top of photographs left unidentified. By contrast, the museum attempted to deny the photographic subjects' individuality in order to emphasize their objectification and the mass terror. However, the relatives of those who perished wished to reclaim their individual memory and present it to other visitors. See ibid.
22. Interviews with the architect of the rebuilt camp and a former political prisoner, Vojna Camp, June 2004. The architect also reported that he had visited Auschwitz to 'get ideas' for the reconstruction of the camp. Despite having no Fascist heritage, the tour of the site presents it as the continuation of Nazi methods into the Communist era; according to one guide interviewed for Czech radio: 'While the former Nazi concentration camps were preserved in the West as memorials to honour its victims, on the other side of the Berlin Wall, little changed but the uniforms worn by the guards and the inmates.' Interviewee quoted in *Radio Praha* at <http://www.radio.cz/en/article/73278> (accessed 9 July 2009).

23. Nevertheless, the Northern Transylvania Holocaust Memorial Museum was opened in Şimleu Silvaniei in 2005 in an area which had been under the control of the Hungarian state during World War II after the Second Vienna Award.

24. Gheorghe Petrov and Cosmin Budeancă, '*Raport Privind Cercetările Arheologice Desfăşurate în Cimitirul Săracilor din Sighetu Marmaţiei*' (Bucharest: Institute for the Investigation of Communist Crimes in Romania, 2006)

25. Interview with Marius Oprea, director of the Institute for the Investigation of Communist Crimes in Romania, May 2008.

26. For accounts that historicize the discipline and explore its linkages with the ideologies of late twentieth-century democratization: Laurent Olivier, 'The Archaeology of the Contemporary Past', in ed. *Archaeologies of the Contemporary Past* Victor Buchli and Gavin Lucas, ed (London and New York: Routledge, 2001); Zoe Crossland, 'Buried Lives: Forensic Archaeology and the Disappeared in Argentina', *Archaeological Dialogues* 7 (2000): 146–59; Roxana Ferllini, 'The Development of Human Rights Investigations since 1945', *Science and Justice* 43/4 (2003): 219–24; Pedro Funari, Andres Zarankin and Melisa Salerno, eds, *Memories from Darkness: Archaeology of Repression and Resistance in Latin America* (New York: Springer, 2009). In Argentina, relatives of victims criticized forensic archaeologists for focusing too heavily on bones as objects of evidence, rather than seeing their recovery as important for humanitarian purposes and in providing comfort for the families of the dead. They also believed that excavations removed the symbolic power of the mass grave site, which was 'no longer haunted by the uneasy ghosts of the disappeared'; see Zoe Crossland, 'Violent Spaces: Conflict over the Reappearance of Argentina's Disappeared', in *Matériel Culture: The Archaeology of Twentieth Century Conflict*, ed. John Schofield, William Gray Johnson and Colleen M. Beck (London: Routledge, 2002), 130.

27. Interview with Oprea.

28. Its aims were 'to investigate and to identify the crimes, the abuses and human rights violations during the Communist regime in Romania, as well as to notify the state's criminal investigation departments when such cases are discovered'. See 'Activity Report May–December 2006', *The Institute for the Investigation of Communist Crimes in Romania, Investigations Department*, 3 at <http://www.crimelecomunismului.ro/pdf/en/activity_report_06/activity_report_2006.pdf> (accessed 9 July 2009). It mainly carried out excavations at the request of relatives of those killed for political reasons. It also produced films such as *Testimonies of Suffering* and *The Dead* which dealt with the excavation of the executed.

29. Petrov and Budeancă, *Raport privind cercetările arheologice desfăşurate în Cimitirul Săracilor din Sighetu Marmatiei.*

30. Interview with Cosmin Budeancă, archaeologist on the Sighet excavation, May 2008.

31. Figure from 2002, taken from Adrian Cioflâncă, 'Politics of Oblivion in Postcommunist Romania', *The Romanian Journal of Political Sciences* 2 (2002): 90.

32. In June 2001, for example, President Ion Iliescu, a member of the former *nomenklatura*, called for 'national reconciliation' based on 'erasing the problems of the past' and providing amnesty for those who had committed violent acts during the Romanian revolution.

33. Sidonia Grama, 'In Between Places of Remembrance and Realms of Memory: The 15-Year Commemoration of the Romanian Revolution in Timişoara', *Philobiblon* 10–11 (2005–06): 310–41.

34. *Sighet Memorial Guide.*

35. *Ibid.*

36. Gail Kligman, *The Wedding of the Dead: Ritual, Poetics and Popular Culture in Transylvania* (Berkeley, CA: University of California Press, 1998), 177.

37. Ibid., 156.

38. These were not placed at the actual locations of graves, as they are unknown.

39. Inscription on the Ciugureanu Cross, Cemetery of the Poor.

40. Zsolt K. Horváth, 'The Redistribution of the Memory of Socialism: Identity Formations of the "Survivors" in Hungary after 1989', in *Past for the Eyes: East European Representations of Communism in Cinema and Museums after 1989*, ed. Oksana Sarkisova and Péter Apor (Budapest: CEU Press, 2008), 270.

41. Grūtas Park also wanted to recreate the feeling of being deported by using cattle wagons to take visitors to its displays; it was banned from doing so.

42. For a discussion of narrative museums, see Elaine Heumann Gurian, *Civilizing the Museum: The Collected Writings of Elaine Heumann Gurian* (London: Routledge, 2006),

50–51. Examples include the Washington Holocaust Museum and the Jewish Museum in Berlin.

43. It was striking that this was the one site of terror that chose to incorporate the building's Fascist history; at other sites, which placed much more emphasis on accurate reconstruction, it was feared that the power of a recovered Holocaust victim's cell could have drowned out the story of Communist victimization they wished to tell.

44. Schmidt suggested that the Hungarian Jewish experience of terror was more appropriately dealt with at international sites such as Auschwitz or at the Budapest Holocaust Museum. See Schmidt, 'Ne Hass, ne Alkoss, ne Gyarapíts!', 191–93.

45. See Gyula Pauer's sculpture *Shoes on the Danube Promenade*, a memorial to those Jews shot on the Pest embankment by the Arrow Cross.

46. In the weeks from 15 May to 8 July 1944, long before the Arrow Cross came to power, 400,000 out of the approximately 600,000 Hungarian Jews killed in the Holocaust were deported for extermination.

47. However, it is noteworthy that, although the building ceased to be used by the Communist secret police in 1956, the exhibition extends to the post-1956 reprisals and the trial of Imre Nagy in 1958, and then deals with the collapse of Communism in 1989.

48. In the first years of the museum, there were serious disputes over the fact that Nazism and the Holocaust did not receive the same treatment as Communism. The museum's supporters considered these accusations misguided, viewing the Budapest Holocaust Memorial Centre, founded at almost the same time as the House of Terror Museum by the same government, as the more appropriate location at which to deal with these subjects. Moreover, the House of Terror's historical exhibition was closely linked to its building, which was used by the Hungarian Arrow Cross and then the Communists. The majority of Hungarian Jews were killed under the German occupation of the country, before the Arrow Cross took power on 15 October 1944, so they considered it inappropriate to examine the Shoah in depth at this site. It is, however, referenced in the exhibition. They suggest that the House of Terror was instituted to address periods of totalitarianism under Hungarian rule and was designed to focus on a wide range of forms of political terror (including persecution on account of social status, religion, and political conviction): for this reason, the period of so-called 'goulash socialism' (which did not see the levels of violence of the earlier period) is omitted, and the exhibition on Arrow Cross rule considers the terror meted out on the political opposition alongside Jewish persecution.

49. The absence of a liberation narrative angered some Russian nationalist correspondents who visited the museum: 'The House of Terror museum, created this past spring by the rightist government, seeks to equalize the Szálasists, responsible for the death of hundreds of thousands of Hungarian Jews, and Soviet liberators who saved the country from Nazism.' See 'Imre Kertész: "I've Been Through Worse" ', *Moscow News* 23 October 2002.

50. House of Terror guide.

51. For an exploration of how ideas about 'Judeo-Bolshevism', first constructed in the 1930s, inhabit post-Communist debates about perpetrators, see Laignel-Lavastine, 'Fascism and Communism'.

52. In addition, by emphasizing that Communism was an extension of Fascism, they closed down the possibility that Communism could be seen as a reaction to it. They also rejected the story of those radicalized by their experience of Fascism into supporting Communism, as this has the potential to evoke sympathy for the Communist experience and to place the suffering under Fascism above that under the later Soviet occupation.

53. Speech given by Viktor Orbán outside the House of Terror, 24 February 2002.

54. BBC Monitoring Europe, 8 May 2002.

55. See Rév, *Retroactive Justice*, 290–91.

56. A statue park was also established in Moscow, but this is outside the geographical frame of reference of this work.

57. One of the first plans for such a park came in fact from Lenin in the 1920s, who wanted to exhibit monuments from the tsarist regime. This was, however, never realized.

58. Beverly A. James, *Imagining Postcommunism: Visual Narratives of Hungary's 1956 Revolution* (College Station, TX: Texas A&M University Press, 2005), 29. The responsibility for dealing with Communist memorialization was given to local government in many countries, such as Poland, Estonia and Hungary. This policy has repeatedly been reconsidered in the light of

'inappropriate local forms of memorialization'; see, for example, the conflicts over the Forbidden Structures Act (2007) in Estonia (discussed below in Chapter 4).

59. Maya Nadkarni, 'The Death of Socialism and the Afterlife of its Monuments: Making and Marketing the Past in Budapest's Statue Park Museum', in *Contested Pasts: The Politics of Memory*, ed. Katharine Hodgkin and Susannah Radstone (London: Routledge, 2003), 199–200.

60. Renatas Berniunas, 'Agency, Cognitive Anchors and Memory: Why Soviet Icons Matter', in *The Burden of Remembering: Recollections and Representations of the Twentieth Century*, ed. Ene Kõresaar, Epp Lauk and Kristin Kuutma (Helsinki: SKS Kirjat, 2009): 174.

61. Gediminas Lankauskas, 'Sensuous (Re)Collections: The Sight and Taste of Socialism at Grūtas Statue Park, Lithuania', *Senses and Society* 1/1 (2006): 47. Lankauskas also notes a generational divide in attitudes towards Grūtas: the older generation, especially those born before World War II, tended to see it as a 'criminal place'; for the younger generation, it had no power to inspire fear.

62. Letter to the secretary general of the UN, 'For the eradication of the exposition of the leaders of Communism and their henchmen in Grūtas forest in the district of Varėna', 2 September 1999.

63. Berniunas, 'Cognitive Anchors':174.

64. Critics of these sites frequently made reference to the 'unimaginability' of exhibiting Nazi statuary after 1945. 'Imagine that in your country, one day armed KGB men come to your door. They beat your neighbour, rape your sister, your mother, kill your brothers . . . and exile your family', Kerosierius was quoted as saying by the *National Post* newspaper. 'And now someone is building monuments to these killers, these rapists? No country has ever built monuments for tyrants. Are there any monuments for Hitler or Goebbels?' Quoted in Lee Greenwald, *The Ottowa Citizen*, 7 April 2001.

65. 'Lithuania's Parliamentary Chair Sees Ban on Soviet Symbols as Secondary Matter', *Baltic News Service*, 28 September 2005: B1.

66. Interview with Viliumas Malinauskas, August 2005.

67. Lankauskas, 'Sensuous (Re)Collections', 38.

68. These were added to the site in 2008.

69. These biographies were written by professional historians and curators connected to the Genocide and Resistance Research Centre of Lithuania in Vilnius. They were also responsible for the Museum of Genocide Victims located at the former KGB headquarters in Vilnius (see Chapter 4 for a detailed discussion of this site). Given this, it is not surprising that the iconography of the site of terror is reproduced at Grūtas.

70. Quoted in Nadkarni, 'Statue Park', 205.

71. Lankauskas, 'Sensuous (Re)Collections', 37–38.

72. Paul Williams, 'The Afterlife of Communist Statuary: Hungary's Szoborpark and Lithuania's Grūtas Park', *Forum for Modern Language Studies* 44/2 (2008): 196.

73. See ibid., 194.

74. Szoborpark guide, statement from Ákos Eleőd from 1994, 3.

75. Nadkarni, 'Statue Park', 197.

76. The sense that the site is a monument to the victory of capitalism and liberal democracy is echoed in some of the guest book comments: 'Thank God, this is now a museum!!!'

77. István Kiss, the sculptor of the monument to the 1919 Béla Kun Communist Republic of Councils, argued that statues should stay in their public locations despite the change of regime as they are 'as much a part of Hungarian history as [those of] any other period'. See 'Budapest Watches Statues Trundle In and Out of Exile', *The New York Times*, 4 October 1992: 14.

78. István Rév, head of the Open Society Archives in Budapest, argued that the statues should have remained in place and been labelled with information about the previous era; see Kristen Schweizer and Tünde Kaposi, 'Monuments a Bust: Campaign in Hungary to Remove Old Soviet Statues Angers Russia', *National Post*, 24 February 2007: A19.

79. Laurier Turgeon and Élise Dubuc argued that its popularity lay in its erasure of the Communist period from Romanian history. Its displays harked back to the traditional rural culture of a pre-industrial, pre-Communist Romania. Laurier Turgeon and Élise Dubuc, 'Ethnology Museums. New Challenges and New Directions', *Ethnologies* 24/2 (2002): 19–32.

80. Andrei Pleşu, minister of culture (1990–91), quoted in Gabriela Cristea and Simina Radu-Bucurenci, 'Raising the Cross: Exorcising Romania's Communist Past in Museums, Memorials, and Monuments', in Sarkisova and Apor, eds, *Past for the Eyes*, ed. Oksana Sarkisova and Péter Apar, 287.

81. Ioana Popescu, 'Peasant Museum', interview with Simina Radu-Bucurenci, in ibid., 289.

82. Duncan Light, 'An Unwanted Past: Contemporary Tourism and the Heritage of Communism in Romania', *International Journal of Heritage Studies* 6/2 (2000): 156.

83. Thus, the museum reflected many of the historical narratives of ex-Communists after 1989, including a new exhibition on the events of 1989 which presented the military as heroic (for abandoning Ceauşescu and supporting the revolutionaries) and the revolution as an final severance with the Communist past.

84. Horea Bernea, quoted in Cristea and Radu-Bucurenci, 'Raising the Cross', 296.

85. Compensating for the excessive politicization of Communist-era displays was a common theme in interviews with museum curators. Interviews with Sarmīte Baltiņa, curator, Museum of War, Riga, August 2005, and István Ihász, curator, National Museum, Budapest, May 2009.

86. A large amount of new material was also collected for the *Red Cage* exhibition.

87. The whole museum was renovated and reopened in 1996 for the 1,100th anniversary of the foundation of the Hungarian state.

88. Interview with Ihász.

89. Interview with Baltiņa.

90. Interview with Ihász.

91. For this idea, see Cristea and Radu-Bucurenci, 'Raising the Cross', 292–93.

92. However, it does not intend to deal with the American Army's use of the facility.

93. Paula M. Krebs, ' "The Last of the Gentlemen's Wars": Women in the Boer War Concentration Camp Controversy', *History Workshop Journal* 33/1 (1992): 41.

94. Ahmed Kathrada, 'Opening Address: The Robben Island Exhibition', quoted in Carolyn Strange and Michael Kempa, 'Shades of Dark Tourism: Alcatraz and Robben Island', *Annals of Tourism Research* 30/2 (2003): 394–95.

95. See Bill Nasson, 'Commemorating the Anglo-Boer War in Post-Apartheid South Africa', in *Memory and the Impact of Political Transformation in Public Space*, ed. Daniel J. Walkowitz and Lisa Maya Knauer (Durham, NC: Duke University Press, 2004), 277–94.

96. These memorials ignored the mixed-race graves in the camps and excluded from the list of the dead all those blacks with Afrikaner names and Afrikaaners with English names. The designers of these sites wanted it to be clear that Afrikaaners were the victims par excellence. On this, see Liz Stanley and Helen Dampier, 'Aftermaths: Post/Memory, Commemoration and the Concentration Camps of the South African War 1899–1902', *European Review of History* 12/1 (2005): 91–119.

97. J. H. Jacobs, 'Narrating the Island: Robben Island in South African Literature', *Current Writing* 4 (1992): 74.

Chapter 4: Containing Fascism: Anti-Communism in the Age of Holocaust Memory

1. Some of the material in this chapter appeared as part of my 'Containing Fascism: History in Post-Communist Baltic Occupation and Genocide Museums', in Oksana Sarkisova and Péter Apor, eds, *Past for the Eyes: East European Representations of Communism in Cinema and Museums after 1989* (Budapest and New York: CEU Press, 2008), 333–67.

2. See, for example, Zvi Gitelman, 'Politics and the Historiography of the Holocaust in the Soviet Union', in *Bitter Legacy: Confronting the Holocaust in the USSR*, ed. Zvi Gitelman (Bloomington, IN: Indiana University Press, 1997), 14–42; Thomas C. Fox, 'The Holocaust under Communism', in *Historiography of the Holocaust*, ed. Dan Stone (Basingstoke, Hampshire: Palgrave Macmillan, 2005), 420–39; Jeffrey Herf, *Divided Memory: The Nazi Past in the Two Germanys* (Cambridge, MA: Harvard University Press, 1997), 16–25; Michael Steinlauf, *Bondage to the Dead: Poland and the Memory of the Holocaust* (Syracuse, NY: Syracuse University Press, 1997); Thomas Fox, *Stated Memory: East Germany and the Holocaust* (Woodbridge, Suffolk: Camden House, 1999).

3. Mark Temple, 'The Politicization of History: Marshal Antonescu and Romania', *East European Politics and Societies* 10/3 (1996): 457–503. On the celebration of Hungarian soldiers fighting alongside Nazi Germany, see István Deák, 'A Fatal Compromise? The

Debate over Collaboration and Resistance in Hungary', *East European Politics and Societies* 9/2 (1995): 209–33. On the commemoration of right-wing anti-Semitic anti-Communism in Poland, see Adam Michnik, 'Mantra: Rather Than Discourse', *Common Knowledge* 8/3 (2002): 516–25.

4. On the necessity of creating a 'post-Communist anti-Fascism' that was not associated with Communist dictatorship, see Ana Bazac, 'Can Antifascism Still Play a Role? A Case Study of Romania', *Critique* 34/1 (2006): 61–80. Gáspár Miklós Tamás argued for the necessity of a 'post-antifascism'. See below, Chapter 5, for a more in-depth discussion.

5. The European Union played a large role in establishing the Task Force for International Co-operation on Holocaust Education, which from 2003 promoted the teaching of Holocaust history in all school systems within the European Union, and encouraged all member states to adopt 27 January, the date of the liberation of Auschwitz, as a memorial day. The specificity of German guilt became less emphasized; rather, the Holocaust became more commonly presented as a part of the collective heritage of all European nations, from which common lessons could be drawn to ensure a free, tolerant continent. See Henry Rousso, 'History of Memory, Policies of the Past: What For?', in *Conflicted Memories: Europeanizing Contemporary Histories*, ed. Konrad H. Jarausch and Thomas Lindenberger (New York and Oxford: Berghahn Books, 2007), 32–34; Andrew H. Beattie, 'Learning from the Germans? History and Memory in German and European Projects of Integration', *PORTAL Journal of Multidisciplinary International Studies* 4/2 (2007): 1022; Gerard Delanty, 'The Quest for European Identity', in *Making the European Polity: Reflexive Integration in the European Union*, ed. Erik Oddvar Eriksen (Abingdon, Oxfordshire: Routledge, 2005), 127–42; Georges Mink and Laure Neumayer, eds, *L'Europe et ses passés douloureux* (La Découverte: Paris, 2007); Christian Joerges, Matthias Mahlmann and Ulrich K. Preuß, eds, *'Schmerzliche Erfahrungen der Vergangenheit' und der Prozess der Konstitutionalisierung Europas* (VS-Verlag: Wiesbaden, 2008); Claus Leggewie, 'A Tour of the Battleground: The Seven Circles of Pan-European Memory', *Social Research: An International Quarterly of Social Sciences* 75/1 (2008): 217–34; Lothar Proebst, 'Founding Myths of Europe and the Role of the Holocaust', *New German Critique*, 90 (2003), 45–58; Benoît Challand, '1989, Contested Memories and the Shifting Cognitive Maps of Europe', *European Journal of Social Theory* 12/3 (2009): 398.

6. For this argument, see Dan Diner, 'Restitution and Memory: The Holocaust in European Political Cultures', *New German Critique* 90 (2003): 36–44. On the idea of the Holocaust as a new 'global' memory, see Daniel Levy and Natan Sznaider, *The Holocaust and Memory in the Global Age* (Philadelphia, PA: Temple University Press, 2006).

7. Maria Mälksoo, 'The Discourse of Communist Crimes in the European Memory Politics of World War II', paper presented at the 'Ideology and Discourse Analysis' conference, Roskilde University, Denmark, 22 October, 2008. See also the Körber Foundation/EU-supported project Eustory, which attempts to 'disarm' history's capacity to divide Europe at <http://www.eustory.eu/> (accessed 14 July 2009).

8. On Putin's role, see Eva-Clarita Onken, 'The Baltic States and Moscow's 9 May Commemoration: Analysing Memory Politics in Europe', *Europe-Asia Studies* 59/1 (2007): 32.

9. Robin Ostow, '(Re)Visualizing Jewish History in Warsaw: The Privatization and Externalization of Nation Building', in *(Re)Visualizing National History: Museums and National Identities in Europe in the New Millennium*, ed. Robin Ostow (Toronto and London: University of Toronto Press, 2008), 157.

10. Eva-Clarita Onken, 'The Politics of Finding Historical Truth: Reviewing Baltic History Commissions and their Work', *Europe-Asia Studies* 38/1 (2007): 109–16.

11. Ibid., 110.

12. Ostow, '(Re)Vizualizing Jewish History', 169. Some cities have sought to present themselves as 'European' by celebrating their multicultural pasts, often concentrating on their (now absent) German communities: for example, Gdańsk in Poland and Sibiu in Romania. See the discussion in James Koranyi, *Between East and West: Romanian German Identities since 1945* (PhD diss., University of Exeter, 2008), chapter 5. It was often the case that international funds – usually from Israel or the United States – paid for projects to reconstruct Jewish monuments and buildings, such as the Great Synagogue in Budapest or most of Jewish Kazaimierz in Krakow.

13. Stuart Burch and David J. Smith, 'Empty Spaces and the Value of Symbols: Estonia's "War of Monuments" from Another Angle', *Europe-Asia Studies* 59/6 (2007): 920–25. The Act also

allowed the Estonian government to clamp down on Russian minority projects which appeared to celebrate symbols of Russian and Soviet imperialism.

14. Martin Malia, 'Foreword: The Uses of Atrocity', in *The Black Book of Communism: Crimes, Terror, Repression*, ed. Stéphane Courtois et al (Cambridge, MA: Harvard University Press, 1999), xii.

15. Jan-Werner Müller, *Constitutional Patriotism* (Princeton, NJ: Princeton University Press, 2007), chapter 3.

16. See, for example, Judith E. Berman, 'Holocaust Commemoration in London and Anglo-Jewish (Dis)-Unity', *Journal of Modern Jewish Studies* 3/1 (2004): 51–71; Helga Embacher, 'Britishness and Ethnic Counter-Memories – Jewishness versus Muslim Memories in Great Britain', paper presented at the 'Memory from Transdisciplinary Perspectives' conference, University of Tartu, Estonia, 11–14 January 2007. Indeed, the German nationalist right sometimes argues that Holocaust remembrance in Germany is shaped in large part for purposes of 'external validation': A. Dirk Moses, 'Stigma and Sacrifice in the Federal Republic of Germany', *History and Memory* 19/2 (2007): 163–64.

17. Mälksoo, 'The Discourse of Communist Crimes'. On the inability of Romanian German communities to identify with EU 'master narratives' that centre on the Holocaust, see Koranyi, *Between East and West*, chapter 5.

18. Maria Mälksoo, 'The Memory Politics of Becoming European: The East European Subalterns and the Collective Memory of Europe', *European Journal of International Relations* 15/4 (2009): 656–57; Maria Mälksoo, *The Politics of becoming European: a study of Polish and Baltic post-Cold War security imaginaries* (London and New York: Routledge, 2010), chapter 5. On the advantages of respecting historical difference over attempting to construct a 'fake' common European memory, see Siobhan Kattago, 'Agreeing to Disagree on the Legacies of Recent History. Memory, Pluralism and Europe after 1989', *European Journal of Social Theory* 12/3 (2009): 375–95.

19. Stefan Rohdewald, 'Post-Soviet Remembrance of the Holocaust and National Memories of the Second World War in Russia, Ukraine and Lithuania', *Forum for Modern Language Studies* 44/2 (2008): 173–74; Klas-Göran Karlsson, 'The Holocaust and Russian Historical Culture', in *Echoes of the Holocaust: Historical Cultures in Contemporary Europe*, ed. Klas-Göran Karlsson and Ulf Zander (Lund: Nordic Academic Press, 2003): 201–22. In a speech given on Victory Day in 2005, Putin quoted at great length from Stalin's speech that had greeted Soviet victory in 1945.

20. Anatoly M. Khazanov, 'Whom to Mourn and Whom to Forget? (Re)constructing Collective Memory in Contemporary Russia', *Totalitarian Movements and Political Religions* 9/2–3 (2008): 305.

21. Ibid., 303.

22. The Holocaust Educational Centre in Moscow, established in 1992, organized a travelling exhibition in order to foster awareness of the Jewish experience in Russia. In its displays and educational material it dwelt much more on the role of Jews fighting Nazi Germany than it did on the victims of the Holocaust. See ibid., 174–75.

23. Anna M. Cienciala, Natalia S. Lebedeva and Wojciech Materski, eds, *Katyn: A Crime Without Punishment* (New Haven, CT: Yale University Press, 2007), 259. The investigation that followed was eventually closed down in 2004, having produced no report or official Russian apology.

24. Rohdewald, 'Post-Soviet Remembrance', 174.

25. Speaking before the sixtieth anniversary of the end of World War II, István Hiller, the chair of the Socialist Party, argued that Hungary needed to celebrate the Soviet liberation and the victory over Fascism by the 'democratic forces of the world', despite objections from conservative Fidesz politicians that they were celebrating an occupation. According to a poll published in *Népszabadság*, one-third of Hungarians saw the arrival of the Soviets as a liberation, one-third as an occupation, and one-third said these descriptions did not adequately describe these events. 'Hungarians Divided over World War II Endgame', *Hungarian News Agency (MTI)*, 2 April 2005.

26. Michael D. Kennedy, 'The Cultural Politics of Military Alliances and Energy Security', paper presented at the University of Michigan, 23 September 2005: 13 at <http://www.maxwell.syr.edu/moynihan/programs/ces/pcconfpdfs/Kennedy.pdf> (accessed 14 July 2009). Kennedy notes that when Vladimir Putin visited Auschwitz in 2005, he failed to mention the Soviet alliance with Hitler at the beginning of the war. Moreover, even in the 1990s there was no

mention of the Polish Home Army's contribution in the displays on the heroes of the anti-Fascist struggle at Moscow's main commemorative area dedicated to the memory of World War II, Victory Park.

27. On the relationship between the notion of being modern and civilized, and the acceptance of the post-Soviet Russian 'liberation' narrative, see the excellent discussion of the various decisions Baltic leaders made with regard to attending the Victory Day celebrations in Moscow in 2005: Onken, 'Moscow's May Commemoration', 23–46.

28. For a detailed discussion of this in a Lithuanian setting, see Alfred Erich Senn, 'Perestroika in Lithuanian Historiography: The Molotov-Ribbentrop Pact', *Russian Review* 49/1 (1990): 43–53.

29. Dovile Budryte, *Taming Nationalism? Political Community Building in the Post-Soviet Baltic States* (Aldershot, Hampshire: Ashgate, 2005), 181. On the use of a restricted set of life stories of the deported to establish a new historical truth in Lithuania, see Neringa Klumbyte, 'Ethnographic Note on Nation: Narratives and Symbols of Early Post-Socialist Nationalism in Lithuania', *Dialectical Anthropology* 27/3–4 (2003): 281.

30. Budryte, *Taming Nationalism*, 183. She describes how 14 June ceremonies, which commemorated the beginnings of the mass deportations in 1941, were much better attended in the late 1980s and early 1990s. She also cites a survey of Lithuanian teenagers, conducted in 2004, which suggested that many considered it important to remember the periods of repression, while most were not attracted by official state remembrance.

31. Bella Zisere, 'The Memory of the Shoah in Post-Soviet Latvia', *East European Jewish Affairs* 35/2 (2005): 160.

32. Ieva Gundare, 'Overcoming the Legacy of History for Ethnic Integration in Latvia', *Intermarium* 5/3 (2003): 17 at <http://www.columbia.edu/cu/sipa/REGIONAL/ECE/vol5no3/latvia.pdf> (accessed 14 July 2009).

33. Dov Levin, 'Lithuania', in *The World Reacts to the Holocaust*, ed. David S. Wyman and Charles H. Rosenzveig (Baltimore, MD: Johns Hopkins University Press, 1996), 345.

34. This remains the only Holocaust museum in the Baltics; it is small, difficult to find, and poorly funded.

35. Zisere, 'The Memory of the Shoah', 156.

36. Others in the Baltics were the KGB Cells Museum in Tartu, Estonia and the Ninth Fort outside Kaunas, Lithuania, which was not only the site of the murder of 45,000 Jews and Russian prisoners of war (mainly by local Lithuanian forces) under the German occupation, but was also a holding centre from which Lithuanian nationals were deported to Siberia during the first Soviet occupation in 1940–41. It then functioned as a Soviet prison between 1945 and 1948.

37. In post-Communist Lithuania in the 1990s, the term 'genocide' was much more likely to refer to Soviet-era deportation and killing of Lithuanians than it was to the extermination of Lithuanian Jews (despite the fact that 94 per cent of them were killed in the Holocaust): Zisere, 'The Memory of the Shoah', 247. Criticism of the use of the term to describe Stalinist policies came from the Lithuanian Jewish community, who suggested the word should not be used to describe a policy aimed at untrustworthy social classes, and from prominent exiles such as Tomas Venclova. See Budryte, *Taming Nationalism*, 183–84. It also ignored the ways in which the Soviet experience in fact facilitated the growth of a Lithuanian space, particularly in Vilnius, where Soviets ethnically cleansed the city of Poles after World War II. See Theodore R. Weeks, 'Remembering and Forgetting: Creating a Soviet Lithuanian Capital. Vilnius 1944–1949', *Journal of Baltic Studies* 39/4 (2008): 517–33.

38. The rest of the building was gradually transformed into a research centre and archive which included former KGB collections.

39. Interview by the author with Virginija Rudienė, Museum of Genocide Victims, Vilnius, August 2005.

40. In fact, this building also has an interesting pre-Soviet history: it was a political prison under the Russian Empire, the square it faces was a site for public executions before 1917, and the road on which it is situated was called Victim Street before World War II.

41. An exhibition on the period 1939–41 which mainly dealt with Soviet oppression and KGB activity was opened in 2002; displays on anti-Soviet resistance including the postwar partisan struggle, and on deportation and labour camps, were opened in 2004; in 2005, plans were made for an exhibition on dissidents and resistance from the 1960s to the 1980s.

42. For a fascinating exploration of a site where, in the early 1990s, two different walks – one that showed the visitor the victims of Fascism and another the victims of the Soviets – gave

the memorial site's two constituencies very different experiences of a camp formerly used by both the Nazis and Soviets; see Sarah Farmer, 'Symbols That Face Both Ways: Commemorating the Victims of Stalinism and Nazism at Buchenwald and Sachsenhausen', *Representations* 49 (1995): 97–119.

43. The director placed a great deal of emphasis on the authenticity of the building: '[E]ven now you see the prison building, aside from a few exceptions, as the KGB left it in August 1991.' Quoted in Eugenijus Peikštenis, 'Das Museum für die Opfer des Genozids, Vilnius', in *Der Kommunismus im Museum: Formen der Auseinandersetzung in Deutschland und Ostmitteleuropa*, ed. Volkhard Knigge and Ulrich Mählert (Cologne: Böhlau, 2005), 132. Former prisoners from the Communist era were used as guides to provide visitors with powerful recollections of the Soviet jail and to make their visit more authentic.

44. Interview by the author with Vilma Juozevičiūtė, Press Officer, Museum of Genocide Victims, Vilnius, August 2005.

45. In the late Communist period, some cells were still used to hold political dissidents, but most had been converted to house the archives of the KGB.

46. Uncovering hidden atrocities is, of course, a compelling story in many post-dictatorial societies; however, this narrative had a particularly strong appeal in Lithuania. During the glasnost period, the KGB revealed its willingness to disclose the locations of many mass graves in the Soviet bloc, including that at Katyn. Lithuania was excluded from this policy as the Soviet elite feared that such revelations would encourage the nationalist independence movement. The KGB then destroyed documentary evidence of these sites in 1990–91; see Rokas M. Tracevskis, 'A Grave Fit for Whom?', *Transitions Online* 3 October 2003 at <http://www.tol.cz/look/TOLnew/tolprint.tpl?IdLanguage=1&IdPublication=4&NrIssue=4 4&NrSection=2&NrArticle=9017&ST1=body&ST_T1=tol&ST_AS1=1&ST_max=1> (accessed 14 July 2009).

47. The director stated that over a thousand prisoners were killed here under the Soviet occupation. See Peikštenis, 'Das Museum für die Opfer des Genozids', 138.

48. Interview with Juozevičiūtė.

49. Audio guide, Museum of Genocide Victims.

50. Forensic archaeology emerged as a discipline in Lithuania in the 1960s.

51. See the 'Law on the responsibility for the genocide of the population of Lithuania', passed 9 April 1992.

52. Although uncommon, DNA testing was used in some eastern European mass grave excavations to identify individuals. See Sarah E. Wagner, *To Know Where He Lies: DNA Technology and the Search for Srebrenica's Missing* (Berkeley, CA and London: University of California Press, 2008), chapter 3.

53. Kirsten Juhl, *The Contribution by (Forensic) Archaeologists to Human Rights Investigations of Mass Graves* (Stavanger: Arkeologisk museum i Stavanger, 2005), 23.

54. Rimantas Jankauskas et al., 'Forensic Archaeology in Lithuania: The Tuskulėnai Mass Grave', *Acta Medica Lituanica* 12/1 (2005): 71.

55. Ibid., 72.

56. The Genocide and Resistance Research Centre of Lithuania was not heavily involved in the initial excavations, as it had only recently been founded. However, it was subsequently the major player in the memorialization at the site, and became responsible for administering families' requests for searches for relatives' remains among the exhumed material.

57. 'Tuskulėnai: Victims of Execution and their Henchmen (1944–1947)', summary produced by the Genocide and Resistance Research Centre. The KGB archives lacked documentation on 157 people shot in the prison.

58. Emmanuel Zingeris, quoted in Tracevskis, 'A Grave Fit for Whom?', 3.

59. This is usually a very expensive procedure and is only carried out after 'politicized mass fatalities in wealthy countries' (such as 9/11 and the London Bombings of July 2005); see Margaret Cox, Ambika Flavel and Ian Hanson, 'Introduction and Context', in *The Scientific Investigation of Mass Graves: Towards Protocols and Standard Operating Procedures*, ed. Margaret Cox et al (Cambridge: Cambridge University Press, 2008), 306.

60. Personal correspondence of the author with the museum, February 2007.

61. Weeks, 'Remembering and Forgetting', 519–20.

62. For a discussion of this, see John Czaplicka, 'The Palace Ruins and Putting the Lithuanian Nation into Place: Historical Settings in Vilnius', in *Memory and the Impact of Political*

Transformation in Public Space, ed. Daniel J. Walkowitz and Lisa Maya Knauer (Durham, NC: Duke University Press, 2004), 179.

63. Ibid., 180–81.
64. Weeks, 'Remembering and Forgetting', 520–25.
65. See, for example, the rebuilding of the Great Synagogue in Vilnius.
66. Vilna Goan Jewish State Museum.
67. Interview by the author with Professor Dr Rimantas Jankauskas, forensic archaeologist at the Tuskulėnai excavation, September 2008. For background information, see Didier Raoult et al., 'Evidence for Louse-Transmitted Diseases in Soldiers of Napoleon's Grand Army in Vilnius', *The Journal of Infectious Diseases* 193/1 (2006), 112–20.
68. Dovile Budryte, *Taming Nationalism?* 184; see also James Mark, 'Containing Fascism', 333.
69. In 1991, a poll found that 69 per cent of Lithuanians identified themselves as Catholics. The Catholic Church played a large role in developing and preserving national culture, especially during those periods when Lithuanians had no state.
70. Athena S. Leoussi, 'National Symbols: Ethnicity and Historical Continuity in Post-Communist "New Europe"', in Grosby *Nationalism and Ethnosymbolism: History, Culture and Ethnicity in the Formation of Nations*, ed. Steven Elliot Grosby and Athena S. Leoussi (Edinburgh: Edinburgh University Press, 2007), 179.
71. On 14 June 1941, the NKVD started the mass arrests and deportations of Lithuanians during the first Soviet occupation.
72. In addition, the buildings of the Tuskulėnai Manor, which were used both by the KGB and the Association of Water Sports as a sanatorium under Soviet rule, will be converted by the museum to house an exhibition on the 'spiritual genocide' of the Communist period, focusing on the attempts to turn the Lithuanian national into the *homo sovieticus*.
73. Interview with Jankauskas.
74. Ellen Cassedy, 'A Controversy Exhumes Long-Buried Memories', *Forward*, 12 November 2004.
75. Meike Wulf, 'The Struggle for Official Recognition of "Displaced" Group Memories in Post-Soviet Estonia', in *Past in the Making: Historical Revisionism in Central Europe after 1989*, ed. Michal Kopeček (Budapest: CEU Press, 2008), 221–45.
76. Onken, 'Moscow's 9 May Commemoration', 34.
77. Baltic News Service, 8 June 2006. In June 2006, the Defence Ministry provided the museum with its first state funding, in order to upgrade the building's security following threats connected with the installation of the Lagedi statue.
78. See 'Statement by Foreign Minister Ojuland Concerning the Lihula Monument', 3 September 2004 at <http://www.vm.ee/eng/kat_138/4791.html> (accessed 21 February 2007).
79. Baltic News Service, 1 February 2007. The introduction of this parliamentary Act was also triggered by controversies over the 'Bronze Soldier' in Tallinn, and plans by the municipal council of Narva (where the population is over 90 per cent Russian-speaking) to erect a monument to Peter the Great.
80. Quoted in E. Doyle Stevick, 'The Politics of the Holocaust in Estonia; Historical Memory and Social Divisions in Estonian Education', in *Reimagining Civic Education: How Diverse Societies Form Democratic Citizens*, ed. E. Doyle Stevick and Bradley A. Levinson (Lanham, MD: Rowman & Littlefield, 2007), 217–18.
81. Zisere, 'The Memory of the Shoah', 162–63. Some small-scale local initiatives such as the Holocaust Museum in Vilnius came from below, however.
82. Budryte, *Taming Nationalism?*, 186.
83. The Latvian commission included members of the Jewish community, émigré Latvian historians, and international experts and diplomats. The Estonian International Commission for the Investigation of Crimes Against Humanity was entirely non-Estonian, and mainly consisted of well-known diplomatic and political figures.
84. 'This Commission has a strong external function – to satisfy Western demands by acknowledging the Holocaust in Latvia, and to counterbalance this demand by confronting the West with the crimes of the Soviet regime.' Gundare, 'Overcoming the Legacy', 23.
85. See <http://www.okupatsioon.ee/english/activities/index.html> (accessed 15 July 2009). Olga Kistler-Ritso donated 35 million Kroons towards its establishment.
86. For a more in-depth exploration of this shift, see Budryte, *Taming Nationalism?*, 183–86.

87. Interview by the author with Paulis Lazda, the founder of the Riga Museum of the Occupation of Latvia, February 2007. After 2000, however, the Ministry of Culture began to make contributions to the museum. Helena Demakova, Latvian culture minister (2004–9) was particularly supportive. There were very few private donations from within Latvia itself; Lazda ascribed this to an absence of a post-Communist culture of charitable giving and a reluctance to donate on the part of some Latvian companies who feared that it might affect their economic relationship with Russia.
88. This was Lazda's description of his role.
89. Interview with Lazda.
90. Stefan Wagstyl, 'Peacetime Collaboration', *Financial Times*, 7 May 2005.
91. Interview by the author with Richard Petersons, Historian and Curator, Museum of the Occupation of Latvia, Riga, August 2005.
92. For example, Queen Elizabeth II stopped at the museum on a state visit in October 2006. In 2000, Paulis Lazda himself was awarded Latvia's top civilian honour, Commander of the Order of Three Stars, for his work with the museum. The available annual visitor figures for the museum are as follows: 2001–2002: 40,000 visitors; 2004: 65,000; see Gundega Michel and Valters Nollendorfs, 'Das Lettische Okkupationsmuseum, Riga', in *Der Kommunismus im Museum*, ed. Knigge and Mählert, 122.
93. Romuald J. Misiunas, 'Soviet Historiography on World War II and the Baltic States, 1944–1974', in *The Baltic States in Peace and War 1917–1945*, ed. V. Stanley Vardys and Romuald J. Misiunas (University Park, PA: Pennsylvania State University Press, 1978), 189–90.
94. Senn, 'Perestroika in Lithuanian Historiography', 43–56.
95. This is also true of post-Communist Russian history textbooks. While now acknowledging the existence of the Molotov-Ribbentrop Pact and the secret protocols, they still present World War II primarily as the story of the Soviet Union's heroic role in liberating Europe from Fascism: James V. Wertsch, 'Patching Up Blank Spots in History: Revising the Official Narrative of the Molotov-Ribbentrop Pact', in *The Burden of Remembering. Recollections and Representations of the Twentieth Century*, ed. Ene Kõresaar, Epp Lauk and Kristin Kuutma (Helsinki: SKS Kirjat, 2009): 37–56.
96. A museum of occupation opened in Georgia in 2006 on 26 May, the anniversary of Georgia's declaration of independence from the Russian Empire in 1918. Russian president Vladimir Putin criticized the establishment of the museum; see BBC Monitoring, Former Soviet Union, 10 July 2006.
97. Indeed, one of the reasons for the lack of preparedness to accept the idea that Soviets were also occupiers arose from the fear that this admission would strengthen the hand of nationalist forces and threaten Russian-speaking communities in the Baltics: Thomas Sherlock, 'History and Myth in the Soviet Empire and the Russian Republic', in *Teaching the Violent Past: History Education and Reconciliation*, ed. Elizabeth A. Cole (Lanham, MD: Rowman & Littlefield, 2007), 236; Mälksoo, 'Discourse of Communist Crimes', 10.
98. Unlike in Lithuania (6 per cent), Russian-language communities make up significant minorities in both Latvia (30 per cent) and Estonia (28 per cent). Curators usually distinguished between those 'historical' pre-Soviet Russian minorities who were less likely to hold to these views, and Soviet-era 'colonizers' who were more likely to. It is interesting to note that occupation museums – the primary aim of which was to refute the narrative of liberation – were only established in those two Baltic states where large Soviet settler populations remained.
99. Interview with Petersons. Divides in social memory between Soviet immigrant populations and local Baltic populations were frequently noted both by academics and journalists. In a survey of Russian- and Latvian-language school examinations, the political scientist Juris Dubrovskij noted: 'the fact that problems still exist in Latvia can be attested to by final examinations in high schools. We can underline general tendencies in the answers of students studying in Russian or in Latvian. Whilst the former idealize the USSR and present contemporary Latvia as a country of apartheid, the works of Latvian-speaking schoolchildren present an "eternal Latvia" that is constantly being occupied . . . and Latvians were and still are victims of history'. Juris Dubrovskij, *Kholokost v latviiskikh velebnikakh istorii*, quoted in Zisere, 'The Memory of the Shoah', 158.
100. According to a late Soviet-era publication on Tallinn's monuments, 'The Bronze figure of a soldier mourning his comrades is free of unnecessary pathos, full of courage and

confidence': Mart Eller, *Monuments and Decorative Sculpture of Tallinn*, trans. Kristi Tarand (Tallinn: Perioodika, 1978), 25.

101. Some of these bodies were claimed by their families. For a discussion of this incident, see Marko Lehti, Matti Jutila and Markku Jokisipilä, 'Never-Ending Second World War: Public Performances of National Dignity and the Drama of the Bronze Soldier', *Journal of Baltic Studies* 39/4 (2008): 393–418.

102. Steven Lee Myers, 'Estonia Sparks Outrage in Russia', *International Herald Tribune*, 24 January 2007.

103. James V. Wertsch, 'Collective Memory and Narrative Templates', *Social Research* 75/1 (2008): 136.

104. Olivier Truc, 'Une statue soviétique sème la discorde entre nationalistes estoniens et russophones', *Le Monde*, 16 January 2007. For a website that defends the 'Bronze Soldier' and suggests that its demolition would be a victory for Fascism, see <http://bronze-soldier .com/> (accessed 15 July 2009).

105. Wulf, 'Struggle for Official Recognition', 236–37. She notes that this is a similar solution to that found in the *Neue Wache* in Berlin, where a monument to the victims of all tyrannies and wars in modern German history was constructed in the wake of German reunification.

106. Ibid.

107. 'Estonians Protest Controversial Memorial', *Baltic Times*, 22 May 2006. This suggestion was made in speeches at the protest against the Bronze Soldier on 20 May 2006.

108. The curators of the Riga Museum of Occupation needed to deal with the pro-Soviet and anti-Fascist history of their building. In 1970, a Memorial Museum to the Latvian Red Riflemen, situated in a purpose-built structure in the form of an elongated cube raised off the ground on stilts on Latvian Red Riflemen Square, was opened as part of the centenary celebration of Lenin's birth. This institution told the story of the Latvian Riflemen, a group who had served the Bolshevik cause during the Russian Revolution and the ensuing Civil War. It was a propaganda museum that represented the Soviets as liberators of Latvia and was used to emphasize the role that Latvians themselves had played in the establishment of the Soviet Union. In 1991, it was closed and the building leased to the Museum of Occupation by the state. After the collapse of Communism, for those still ideologically attached to the former system, it retained its symbolic significance as a site that formerly represented Soviet power and liberation: it was used as a starting point for marches on anniversaries of Soviet days of remembrance. Given the structure's continuing power to invoke politically undesirable responses, the new museum attempted to make a clear break with its building's past: none of the old exhibits were retained. There was no reference to the Latvian riflemen – a group whose story had the potential to demonstrate the role that political ideology had on Latvians – in the new museum.

109. 'Estonia: Prime Minister Issues Statement on International Holocaust Remembrance Day', *US Federal News*, 27 January 2007.

110. Gundare, 'Overcoming the Legacy', 24.

111. These were the numbers provided in the museum display. For a discussion of these figures, see Aivars Stranga, 'The Holocaust in Occupied Latvia: 1941–1945', in *The Hidden and Forbidden History of Latvia under Soviet and Nazi Occupations 1940–1991*, ed. Valters Nollendorfs and Erwin Oberländer (Riga: Institute of the History of Latvia, 2005), 161.

112. It is estimated that the Arājs Commando 'directly killed' at least 26,000 civilians, and were 'indirectly involved' in the murder of around 60,000. The membership of the organization probably constituted a few thousand. Ibid., 167.

113. Andrew Ezergailis, *The Holocaust in Latvia 1941–1944: The Missing Centre* (Washington, D.C.: United States Holocaust Memorial Museum, 1996), 70.

114. For a discussion of the myth of Latvian Jews as '[Soviet] tank kissers', see Zisere, 'The Memory of the Shoah', 158. The deportation of Baltic Jews by the Soviets in 1940 can be instrumentalized in other ways, too; Estonian historian Meelis Maripuu deliberately equates Communism with Nazism by describing the Soviet deportation of five hundred Estonian Jews as the 'first act of the Holocaust'. In this instance, the Soviets are demonized by association with the Holocaust. For a discussion of this, see Wulf, 'Struggle for Official Recognition'.

115. Anton Weiss-Wendt, 'Why the Holocaust Does Not Matter to Estonians', *Journal of Baltic Studies* 39/4 (2008): 477.

116. Interview by the author with Heiki Ahonen, Museum Director, Museum of Occupations, Tallinn, August 2005.
117. Many objects were therefore deliberately presented with minimal or no explanatory text.
118. Interview with Ahonen.
119. Seventy thousand native Latvian Jews, 20,000 from the Reich and 1,000 from Lithuania were killed in Latvia; see Stranga, 'The Holocaust in Occupied Latvia', 161.
120. This figure is quoted in Budryte, *Taming Nationalism?*, 180. For a detailed description of the different ways in which Estonians suffered, and the numbers involved, see Heiki Ahonen, 'Wie Gründet Man ein Museum? Zur Entstehungsgeschichte des Museums der Okkupationen in Riga', in *Der Kommunismus im Museum*, ed. Knigge and Mählert, 116. See also Jaak Kangilaski et al., *The White Book: Losses Inflicted on the Estonian Nation by Occupation Regimes 1940–1991*, ed. Vello Salo et al, trans. Mari Ets et al (Tallinn: Estonian Encyclopaedia Publishers, 2005) for a detailed analysis of Estonia's population losses.
121. Weiss-Wendt, 'Why the Holocaust', 476.
122. The description of the Battle of Kurzeme in the Riga museum had 'Latvian pitted against Latvian'.
123. The reason for her presence at Klooga was not made clear. It was a site where mainly foreign Jews were taken.
124. Interview with Petersons.
125. 'The Nazi occupation and the war hinder the development of Latvian culture, albeit with fewer restrictions than during the year of Soviet occupation where the expression of inappropriate ideas most often ended in imprisonment or threat of death. Although subject to censorship, private publishing houses . . . are allowed to resume work': Museum of the Occupation of Latvia, Riga.
126. This is not true everywhere in western Europe. In democratic Spain, where the 'pact of silence' after Franco's death meant that earlier Francoist historical narratives were not immediately challenged, it was possible to represent links between Nazi Germany and Spain in World War II in an uncritical manner. Until very recently, the Military Museum in Madrid, for example, had a relatively positive display on the Blue Division (those troops sent by Franco to fight alongside Nazi Germany to 'save Europe from Communism'); my thanks to Tim Rees for this point.
127. Gundare, 'Overcoming the Legacy', 24. Gundare quoted one comment in Russian from the guest book: 'The exhibit concentrates on victims, not on perpetrators. We can only guess whom you are blaming for all the sufferings.' This was despite the fact that the Riga museum translated its texts into Russian and deliberately attempted to avoid demonization on the basis of ethnicity. According to the director of Tallinn's Museum of Occupations, 'Few Russians come in. Actually you can say that very few older people come but the youngsters are fascinated. When we opened our [internet] home page, it was in Estonian, someone obviously Russian and not too elderly . . . wrote to us telling us we should also do it in Russian, because Estonians tend to accuse Russians and local Russians do not understand what for. Some would like to know.'

Chapter 5: Remaking the Autobiography: Communists and their Pasts

1. A far greater number of oral history projects have been carried out with victims and resisters than with former party members and representatives of the regime. For some exceptions, see Barbara Miller, *Narratives of Guilt and Compliance in Unified Germany: Stasi Informers and their Impact on Society* (London: Routledge, 2002); Aili Aarelaid-Tart, 'Estonian-Inclined Communists as Marginals', in *Biographical Research in Eastern Europe: Altered Lives and Broken Biographies*, ed. Robin Humphrey, Robert Miller and Elena (Aldershot, Hampshire: Ashgate, 2003), 71–100. Most of the work on the 'subjectivity' of those who supported the regime has come from the study of party documents and diaries; see, for example, Jochen Hellbeck, 'Fashioning the Stalinist Soul: The Diary of Stepan Podlubnyi', in *Stalinism: New Directions*, ed. Sheila Fitzpatrick (London: Routledge, 2000), 77–116; Jochen Hellbeck, *Revolution on my Mind: Writing a Diary under Stalin* (Cambridge, MA: Harvard University Press, 2006); Igal Halfin, *Terror in my Soul: Communist Autobiographies on Trial* (Cambridge, MA: Harvard University Press, 2003); Sheila Fitzpatrick, *Tear Off the Masks!: Identity and Imposture in Twentieth-Century Russia* (Princeton, NJ: Princeton University Press, 2005).

2. For the ways in which even those from bourgeois backgrounds could learn to represent their pasts in politically appropriate ways in order to ensure their social mobility, see James Mark, 'Discrimination, Opportunity and Middle-Class Success in Early Communist Hungary', *Historical Journal* 48/2 (2005): 499–521; Daniela Koleva, ' "Socialist Individualism": Modernization and the Biographical Self', in *Talking History: Proceedings of the International Oral History Conference, 23–27 September 1999*, ed. Daniela Koleva (Kiten: LIK, 2000), 107–8.

3. On ways of demonizing one's own past, see Daniela Koleva, 'Between Testimony and Power: Autobiographies in Socialist Bulgaria', paper presented at the 'Texts of Testimony: Autobiography, Life-Story Narratives and the Public Sphere' conference, John Moores University, Liverpool, 23–25 August 2001.

4. On the role of the anti-Fascist autobiography in various central-eastern European Communist systems, see Catherine Epstein, 'The Politics of Biography: The Case of East German Old Communists', *Daedalus* 128/2 (1999): 1–30; Lutz Niethammer, 'Biographie und Biokratie: Nachdenken zu einem Westdeutschen Oral History-Projekt in der DDR Fünf Jahre nach der Deutschen Vereinigung', paper presented at the 'International Oral History' conference, São Paulo, 1995; Daniela Koleva, 'Between Testimony'; Galia Valtchinova, 'Ismail Kadare's The H-File and the Politics of Memory', in *Talking History*, ed. Daniela Koleva (Sofia: LIK, 2000), 172–83; Mark, 'Discrimination', 511–12.

5. On the development of late Communist culture and the 'hegemony of form', see Alexei Yurchak, 'Soviet Hegemony of Form: Everything Was Forever, Until It Was No More', *Comparative Studies in Society and History* 45/3 (2003). On the increasingly individualistic autobiography of the late Communist period, see Anna Rotkirch, *The Man Question: Loves and Lives in late 20th Century Russia*, (Helsinki: University of Helsinki Department of Social Policy Research Reports, 2000).

6. On the afterlife of anti-Fascism in East Germany, see Ingo Loose, 'The anti-Fascist Myth of the German Democratic Republic and its Decline after 1989', in *Past in the Making: Historical Revisionism in Central Europe after 1989*, ed. Michal Kopeček (Budapest: CEU Press, 2008), 63–68; Mary Nolan, 'Antifascism under Fascism: German Visions and Voices', *New German Critique* 67 (1996): 33–55.

7. Michael W. Jackson quotes different scholars' estimates for central and eastern European participants in the International Brigades. They average out at 3,900 Germans, 3,501 Poles, and 979 Hungarians. Although small in number, they were celebrated as the first great anti-Fascist fighters, particularly because some of the most prominent Communists in the GDR and Hungary had been in Spain during the Civil War. See Michael W. Jackson, *Fallen Sparrows: The International Brigades in the Spanish Civil War* (Philadelphia: American Philosophical Society, 1994), 46, 75.

8. On the memory and treatment of Spanish Civil War veterans in the GDR, see Josie McLellan, *Antifascism and Memory in East Germany: Remembering the International Brigades, 1945–1989* (Oxford: Clarendon Press, 2004); Arnold Krammer, 'The Cult of the Spanish Civil War in East Germany', *Journal of Contemporary History* 39/4 (2004): 531–60; Michael Uhl, *Mythos Spanien: Das Erbe der Internationalen Brigaden in der DDR* (Bonn: Dietz, 2004).

9. Marek Jan Chodakiewicz, 'Affinity and Revulsion: Poland Reacts to the Spanish Right 1936–1939 (and Beyond)', in *Spanish Carlism and Polish Nationalism: The Borderlands of Europe in the 19th and 20th Centuries*, ed. Marek Jan Chodakiewicz and John Radziłowski, (Charlottesville, VA: Leopolis Press, 2003), 94–95.

10. See, for example, the statue to the International Brigadiers in the Spanish Civil War that was removed to Szoborpark in Budapest.

11. A Polish anti-Fascist youth culture magazine, *Never Anymore*, called for the renewed remembrance of the International Brigades. See Chodakiewicz, 'Affinity and Revulsion', 95.

12. Spanish conservatives did not oppose the granting of Spanish citizenship to International Brigadiers but wanted to do it in silence, without openly celebrating their heroism and reviving memories of the Spanish Civil War; see Carsten Jacob Humlebaek, 'Political Uses of the Recent Past in Spanish Post-Authoritarian Democracy', in *Partisan Histories: The Past in Contemporary Global Politics*, ed. Max Paul Friedman and Padraic Kenney (New York: Palgrave Macmillan, 2005), 80.

13. Epstein, 'The Politics of Biography', 1–30.

14. On the revival of anti-Fascism among the Serbian left as a way of celebrating Yugoslav multiculturalism and aligning itself with western European norms, see Todor Kuljić,

'The New (Changed) Past as Value Factor of Development', *Sociologija* 48/3 (2006): 219–30.

15. For the way in which the myth of the anti-Fascist struggle of the Great Patriotic War overlaid earlier emphases on the class struggle in the Soviet Union, see, for example, Geoffrey Hosking, 'The Second World War and Russian National Consciousness', *Past and Present* 175/1 (2002): 162–87; Amir Weiner, *Making Sense of War: The Second World War and the Fate of the Bolshevik Revolution* (Princeton, NJ: Princeton University Press, 2002); and Amir Weiner, 'In the Long Shadow of War: The Second World War and the Soviet and Post-Soviet World', *Diplomatic History* 25/3 (2001): 443–56.

16. Péter Apor, 'The Creative Fear: Fascism, Anti-Semitism, Democracy and the Foundation of the People's Democracy in Hungary', in *Myth and Memory in the Construction of Community: Historical Patterns in Europe and Beyond*, ed. Bo Stråth (Brussels: Peter Lang, 2000), 263–80; Geoff Eley, *Forging Democracy: The Left in Europe, 1850–2000* (Oxford: Oxford University Press, 2002), 261–98; Anson Rabinbach, 'Introduction: Legacies of anti-Fascism', *New German Critique* 67 (1996): 3–4.

17. This was true of all Hungarian and Czechoslovak testimony; Polish testimony was often more ambiguous. For many Poles, even on the left, the Soviets could not be unambiguous liberators, given their alliance with Nazi Germany in 1939 and their joint occupation of Poland in that year.

18. On the widespread belief in anti-Fascist politics in 1945 itself, see István Bibó, 'The Crisis of Hungarian Democracy', in *Democracy, Revolution, Self-Determination*, ed. István Bibó (Boulder, CO: Social Science Monographs, 1991), 91.

19. Csaba, b. 1931, Pécs, Catholic, professional family (interview December 2000). All respondents were promised anonymity, hence all names are pseudonyms.

20. Sheila Fitzpatrick, 'Ascribing Class: The Construction of Social Identity in Soviet Russia', *The Journal of Modern History* 65/4 (1993), 745–70.

21. A derogatory term for a rich peasant, introduced by the Bolsheviks when they began to impose Marxist class structures to describe the Soviet village in the 1920s. It was used to mark out richer landowning villagers (although it might also be applied to political enemies or be used by villagers to demonize their enemies) and could lead to dispossession, discrimination and/or deportation. The term was introduced into central-eastern Europe with the Communist takeovers of the late 1940s.

22. Jerzy, b. 1927, village in south-eastern Poland, non-religious peasant family, joined party 1951 (interview October 2004).

23. On conversion narratives in Soviet-era autobiographies, see Halfin, *Terror in my Soul*, 64–78.

24. This occurred on 21 January 1945. Later in February, the Communist Party suggested that Mussolini Square (Oktogon) should be renamed 'Red Army Square'. This plan was never realized. See Martin Mevius, *Agents of Moscow: The Hungarian Communist Party and the Origins of Socialist Patriotism, 1941–1953* (Oxford: Clarendon Press, 2005), 200.

25. Mátyás, b. 1929, Budapest, Jewish, father a factory administrator, joined party 1948 (interview May 2000).

26. They came from a region of southern Slovakia that had been part of Hungary immediately after World War I.

27. Tomáš, b. 1927, south-eastern Slovakia, parents small shopkeepers, joined party 1945 (interview December 2004).

28. With the exception of Czechoslovakia, the rhetoric of the class struggle became less important to many central-eastern European Communist regimes from the 1960s onwards. In Hungary, for instance, it was possible from the early 1960s to ridicule earlier obsessions with class: Szonja Szelényi, *Equality by Design: The Grand Experiment in Destratification in Socialist Hungary* (Stanford, CA: Stanford University Press, 1998), 15.

29. For an examination of whether anti-Fascism still had democratic content after the GDR, see Konrad Jarausch, 'The Failure of East German Antifascism: Some Ironies of History as Politics', *German Studies Review* 14/1 (1991): 94–95; James J. Ward, 'Was Bleibt? (What's Left?): Antifascism as Historical Experience and Contemporary Politics in Post-Marxist (East) Germany', *New Political Science* 12/1 (1993): 39–57.

30. Alajos, b. 1934, Budapest, Jewish petty-bourgeois/intellectual family, never joined party (interviews November 1998, February 1999).

31. An 'eternal flame' was constructed by Hungarian nationalists in 1926 to the memory of Lajós Batthyány, who, as prime minister of Hungary, was executed during the war for independence against Austria in 1848–49.

32. A major poet and journalist who joined the Communist Party in 1930. He was soon expelled and then committed suicide in 1937, but his work was later appropriated by the Communist state.

33. Benedek, b. 1930, Szeghalom, assimilated Jewish, merchant family, joined party late 1940s (interview September 1998).

34. Indeed, in the following years, commemorations of the date of the suppression of the Uprising – 4 November – took place by the monument to the Soviet liberators of Hungary from Fascism in 1945. The two events were thus closely connected in late Communist-era public memory.

35. András Mink, 'The Revisions of the 1956 Hungarian Revolution', in *Past in the Making*, ed. Michal Kopeček, 171.

36. Membership of the party had stood at 859,037 in January 1956 before the revolution; see Sándor Rákosi, 'Magyar Dolgozók Pártja', in *Legyőzhetetlen erő. A magyar kommunista mozgalom szervezeti fejlődésének 50 éve*, ed. Tibor Erényi and Sándor Rákosi (Budapest: Kossuth Könyvkiadó, 1968), 224–25. Membership fell to 151,000 in its immediate aftermath and had only risen to 416,646 by 1959; see Iván Szenes, *A Kommunista Párt újjászervezése Magyarországon 1956–1957* (Budapest: Kossuth Könyvkiadó, 1976), 249–50. It was only in the 1980s that party membership began to approach pre-1956 levels again.

37. 'Counter-revolution' was used as a term in meetings between Dubček and the Soviet leadership in 1968, and it became increasingly instrumentalized by the anti-reformist clique who requested Soviet intervention to ward off 'right-wing forces [who] have created conditions suitable for a counterrevolutionary coup'. On the 'Letter of Invitation' sent to Brezhnev to help ward off an 'imminent counter-revolution', see Alan Levy, *So Many Heroes* (Sagaponack: Second Chance Press, 1980), 166.

38. This did not really occur after the Poznan Rising in 1956 in Poland, where the Communist elite refrained from using the language of 'counter-revolution', but rather listened in limited ways to workers' demands.

39. Kieran Williams, *The Prague Spring and its Aftermath: Czechoslovak Politics, 1968–1970* (Cambridge: Cambridge University Press, 1997), 231.

40. *Ibid.*, 240–41. Those who did recant could also be demoted: for example, Oldřich Černík was prime minister between 1968 and 1970 but lost his position on account of his continued support for reform Communism. He was prepared to denounce those who condemned the Soviet invasion but was nevertheless relegated to a research institute and later commented, 'I have shat away my position and my honour' (241).

41. *Ibid.*, 236. For an interesting discussion between 68ers over whether to accept the state's terminology of counter-revolution, see Milan Šimečka's correspondence with Ludvík Vaculík, where he refers to the purge as 'civilized violence'. See also Pavel Kohout, *From the Diary of a Counterrevolutionary* (New York: McGraw-Hill, 1972).

42. Olga, b. 1939, near Ostrava, non-believer although Catholic church-going parents, mining family, joined party 1959 (interview, December 2004).

43. For an introduction, see Jerzy Eisler, 'March 1968 in Poland', in *1968: The World Transformed*, ed. Carole Fink, Philipp Gassert and Detlef Junker (Cambridge: Cambridge University Press, 1998), 237–51.

44. Joanna Wawrzyniak, 'Negotiating the Nation's Official Past: The Politics of Commemoration of World War II in Communist Poland', 16–17 at <http://98.129.116.150/tcds/Wawrzyniak.pdf> (accessed 18 July 2009). See also *idem*, 'Union of Fighters for Freedom and Democracy as an Example of the Role of People Living Off Stories of Nazi Occupation', *Kwartalnik Historii Żydów (Jewish History Quarterly)* 4 (2008): 427–46.

45. Bishop Bronisław Dembowski described how '[I was a] (m)ember of the "Grey Ranks" (Szare Szeregi), a private in the seventy-second regiment of the Home Army Radom Region, [swore the] oath of allegiance in 1943, at the age of sixteen, and [was] a participant of Action Storm from August to November 1944. In April of 1945, in Radom, I saw posters, "Away with the Home Army bandits", and "the drooling reactionary dwarf". And that was the reward. . . . I have tears in my eyes now . . . this was the reward for the boy who was ready to die for Poland . . . "The drooling reactionary dwarf"? I apologize, well, can you see how it's still alive, it's all coming back?' Quoted in Donna Parmelee, ed., *Communism's Negotiated*

Collapse: The Polish Round Table Ten Years Later: Transcription of a Conference at the University of Michigan, April 7–10, 1999, trans. Kasia Kietlinska (Ann Arbor: The University of Michigan Center for Russian and East European Studies, 1999), 74, available at <http://www.ii.umich.edu/PolishRoundTable/engtranstoc.html> (accessed 3 July 2009).

46. Andrzej, b. 1930, Warsaw, Jewish, professional family, joined party around 1949 (interview October 2004).

47. Communist 1960s propaganda aimed at equating an 'aggressive Israel' with Nazi Germany; see Joanna Wawrzyniak, 'Kriegsgeschichten: Juden als Deutsche in Polen, 1967–1968', in *Die Destruktion des Dialogs: Zur Innenpolitischen Instrumentalisierung Negativer Fremd- und Feindbilder. Polen, Tschechien, Deutschland und die Niederlande im Vergleich, 1900 bis Heute*, ed. Dieter Bingen, Peter Oliver Loew and Kazimierz Wóycicki (Wiesbaden: Harrassowitz, 2007), 162–75.

48. Wawryzniak, 'Negotiating the Nation's Official Past', 20. She also notes that, despite the anti-Semitism of the campaign, it was nevertheless the first prominent example of the regime acknowledging the separate plight of the Jews, since in order to refute this position the regime had to claim that Poles did indeed save Jews from 'their persecution' during the war.

49. Indeed, unlike in Hungary and Czechoslovakia, the Polish Communist Party substantially increased its membership in these years, from just over one million in 1956–57 to just over three million by the end of the 1970s: Eric Hanley, 'A Party of Workers or a Party of Intellectuals? Recruitment into Eastern European Communist Parties 1945–1988', *Social Forces* 81 (2003): Appendix Table 2.

50. Krzysztof, b. 1942, Warsaw, Catholic family but non-believer, father 'managerial elite', joined party 1974 (interview October 2004). For the members of the '1968 generation' who joined the party in Poland, the justifications they present are different from those of the postwar generation. Whereas for party members who joined in the 1940s and 1950s coming to terms with anti-Fascist commitments was the centre of their story, those who joined from the 1960s onwards often presented themselves in much more nationalistic terms: they remained party members only as long as they could tell themselves they were defending the national interest. It was very common that those who joined as 'endo-Communists' (nationalist Communists) in Poland in the 1960s then presented their departure, or attempts at departure, from the party at the moment of Solidarity's birth in 1980–81. In the late 1960s, the party had made them feel they could reconcile their patriotism with party membership; Solidarity in the early 1980s was instrumental in showing them that they could not.

51. On calls to reform the public memory of the Slovak Uprising by emphasising the role of national forces and not simply viewing it as directed from Moscow, see Shari J. Cohen, *Politics without a Past: The Absence of History in Post-Communist Nationalism* (Durham, NC: Duke University Press, 1999), 100–01.

52. Ágota, b. 1930, village in western Hungary, Catholic family but non-believer, professional family, joined party 1951 (interview May 2000).

53. Zdeněk, b. 1927, northern Bohemia, father a self-employed tailor, joined party 1946 (interview December 2004).

54. For a much fuller examination of this phenomenon, see James Mark, 'Antifascism, the 1956 Revolution and the Politics of Communist Autobiographies in Hungary 1944–2000', *Europe-Asia Studies* 58/8 (2006): 1228–39.

55. See above, Chapter 1, for the political equivalent of this autobiographical narrative.

56. For explorations of collective silencing, see Zsuzsanna Kőrösi and Adrienne Molnár, *Carrying a Secret in my Heart: Children of the Victims of the Reprisals after the Hungarian Revolution in 1956: An Oral History* (Budapest: CEU Press, 2003), 2; Gábor Gyáni, '1956 elfelejtésének régi-új Mítosza', *Élet és Irodalom*, 9 February 2001; and Péter György, *Néma hagyomány. Kollektív felejtés és a kései múltértelmezés 1956 1989-ben* (Budapest: Magvető, 2000).

57. Silencing of the past was not a feature of all respondents' testimony; however, nearly all respondents took care to protect their social position from the intrusion of past political actions.

58. Károly, b. 1930, Vienna, Catholic family but non-believer, father mechanical engineer, joined party 1948–49 (interview May 2000).

59. On the necessity of creating a 'post-Communist anti-Fascism' that was not associated with Communist dictatorship, see Ana Bazac, 'Can Anti-Fascism Still Play a Role? A Case Study of Romania', *Critique* 34/1 (2006): 61–80.

60. See Chapter 1 above, for a more detailed analysis of this.
61. Jenő, b. 1929, Budapest, Jewish, father a factory manager, joined party 1947 (interview May 2000).
62. In his radio address of 3 November 1956, Cardinal Mindszenty, following his release from prison, refuted the idea that 1956 was a revolution, preferring to characterize it as a 'fight for freedom' to re-establish the historical traditions that had been broken by the arrival of the Red Army in 1945. This conservative platform rejected not just Communism, but also aspects of the progressive, democratic system that had emerged between 1945 and 1948.
63. It is striking that respondents from a variety of political traditions reproduced, in the post-Communist period, aspects of the Kádár-era conception of 1956 as a counter-revolution intent on restoring a bourgeois, 'reactionary' state to Hungary. Anti-Communist respondents used it positively to suggest that the revolution was intent on re-establishing a bourgeois order, and that reform socialists played only a minor role. Reform socialists (such as Károly, above) used the threat of a right-wing restoration to suggest that reactionaries had sabotaged the reform process by inviting the Stalinists to suppress the revolution. Supporters of the Kádár system still produce counter-revolutionary rhetoric in their post-Communist testimony.
64. After the collapse of Communism, the female figure representing liberation was allowed to remain, but the Soviet soldiers at the base of the monument were removed and placed in Budapest's Szoborpark.
65. Judit, b. 1932, Budapest, Jewish, father factory owner, joined party 1945 (interview December 2000).
66. Stanislav Rostotsky, dir., *At Dawn, It's Quiet Here* (1972).
67. Quoted in Paulina Bren, '1968 East and West: Visions of Political Change and Student Protest', in *Transnational Moments of Change: Europe 1945, 1968, 1989* Horn and Padraic Kenney (Lanham, MD: Rowman & Littlefield, 2004), 120.
68. Catherine Epstein, *The Last Revolutionaries: German Communists and their Century* (Cambridge, MA: Harvard University Press, 2003), 194. These published autobiographies had previously been seen as 'something out of the ordinary and regarded as unseemly immodesty to write down one's own life and thoughts'.
69. For an oral history investigation into generational experience under Communism, see Dorothee Wierling, *Geboren im Jahr Eins: Der Jahrgang 1949 in der DDR: Versuch einer Kollektivbiographie* (Berlin: Ch. Links, 2002). Other scholars have noted the collective nature of the memory of the postwar generation and the more individualistic tone of the 1960s and 1970s generations, a development which undermined the Communist states' ability to construct collective solidarities. See, for example, Anna Rotkirch, *The Man Question: Loves and Lives* in *Late 20th Century Russia* (Helsinki: University of Helsinki Department of Social Policy Research Reports, 2000).
70. Jarosław, b. 1940, eastern Poland, Catholic, family of rural gentry, originally nobility, joined party late 1960s (interview 2004).

Chapter 6: Victims' Stories

1. Neringa Klumbyte, 'Ethnographic Note on Nation: Narratives and Symbols of Early Post-Socialist Nationalism in Lithuania', *Dialectical Anthropology* 27/3–4 (2003): 281: 'while many people were deported to Siberia after World War II, the experience of life there is communicated though books by selected authors . . . who become part of the school curriculum. They are personal and literal; the legitimacy and representativeness of personal memoirs are not questioned.' In some countries, such as the Soviet Union, the revelation of stories of Stalinist-era suffering occurred during the perestroika period.
2. There are large numbers of interviews collected from Gulag survivors by the Memorial Society and oral historians such as Irina Sherbakova and Nanci Adler. On the shift from the Communist-era biographies of female heroines to the post-Communist obsession with collecting women's stories of victimization, see Marianne Liljeström, 'Success Stories from the Margins: Soviet Women's Autobiographical Sketches from the Late Soviet Period', in *On Living Through Soviet Russia*, ed. Daniel Bertaux, Paul Thompson and Anna Rotkirch (London and New York: Routledge, 2004), 235–36; for a collection of stories of women's suffering, see, for example, Tiina Kirss, Ene Kõresaar and Marju Lauristin, eds, *She Who Remembers Survives: Interpreting Estonian Women's Post-Soviet Life Stories* (Tartu: Tartu

University Press, 2004). By contrast, on the absence of narrative forms that Gulag survivors can draw on to relate their own experiences (compared with Holocaust survivors) in the post-Soviet context, see Jehanne M. Gheith, ' "I Never Talked": Enforced Silence, Non-Narrative Memory, and the Gulag', *Mortality* 12/2 (2007): 159–75.

3. Csilla Kiss, 'The (Re)Construction of Post-Communist Memory', in *The Burden of Remembering: Recollections and Representations of the Twentieth Century*, ed. Ene Kõresaar, Epp Lauk and Kristin Kuutma (Helsinki: SKS Kirjat, 2009): 119–38.

4. See above, Chapter 2.

5. On the problems of narrating accounts of professional success in post-Communist life stories, see, for example, James Mark, 'Discrimination, Opportunity and Middle-Class Success in Early Communist Hungary', *The Historical Journal* 48/2 (2005): 514–20; Vladimir Andrle, 'The Buoyant Class: Bourgeois Family Lineage in the Life Stories of Czech Business Elite Persons', *Sociology* 35/4 (2001): 815–33.

6. On the complex interaction between public expectations of victim stories and more complex private memories, see Anselma Gallinat, 'Life-Stories in Interviews and in Social Interaction: Victims of the GDR Talk and Argue About the Past', in *Remembering after the Fall of Communism: Oral History and (Post-)Socialist Societies*, ed. Julia Obertreis and Anke Stephan (Essen: Klartext, 2009), 275–86; *idem*, 'Difficult Stories: Public Discourse and Narrative Identity in Eastern Germany', *Ethnos: Journal of Anthropology* 71/3 (2006): 343–66.

7. This was both the security-service headquarters and a prison in central Budapest. It was often used as a shorthand for the violence and oppressive nature of the Communist state.

8. István, b. 1933, Budapest, Catholic, family originally aristocrats, grew up with mother who ran a dress shop (interview April 2000).

9. István's coda to his family's story illustrates this point. Despite the level of his exclusion and punishment, he was not prepared to collaborate with the state by becoming an informant in order to ease his suffering.

10. This is a central difference between Communist and anti-Communist life stories. As we saw in Chapter 5, supporters of the former regime often saw their autobiographies as shaped, or even 'contaminated', by their engagement with the autobiographical processes insisted upon before 1989; hence some argued that they needed to 'come to terms' not only with what they had done but also with the complicity embedded in the very structure of their life stories. Anti-Communists, by contrast, were convinced that their autobiographies remained unpolluted by Communist-era public narratives and were the only place where the true stories of the nation had been kept safe. Many scholars of the Communist period now explore the ways in which the Communist Party did in fact attempt to appropriate the discourse of the nation; see, for example, Martin Mevius, *Agents of Moscow: The Hungarian Communist Party and the Origins of Socialist Patriotism, 1941–1953* (Oxford: Clarendon Press, 2005); Marcin Zaremba, *Komunizm, legitymizacja, nacjonalizm: nacjonalistyczna legitymizacja władzy komunistycznej w Polsce* (Warsaw: Trio: Instytut Studiów Politycznych Polskiej Akademii Nauk, 2005); David Brandenberger, *National Bolshevism: Stalinist Mass Culture and the Formation of Modern Russian National Identity, 1931–1956* (Cambridge, MA: Harvard University Press, 2002).

11. Other works have explored the idea of family stories as transmission vehicles for alternative memories; see Daniel Bertaux, 'Transmission in Extreme Situations: Russian Families Expropriated by the October Revolution', in *Pathways to Social Class: A Qualitative Approach to Social Mobility*, ed. Daniel Bertaux and Paul Thompson (Oxford: Clarendon Press, 1997), 230–58; Irina Krovushkina Paert, 'Memory and Survival in Stalin's Russia: Old Believers in the Urals during the 1930s–50s', in *On Living Through Soviet Russia*, 195–213.

12. József, b. 1949, Warsaw, Catholic, professional and business family (interview October 2004).

13. Bálint, b. 1922, Budapest, Catholic, high-ranking professional family (interview December 2000).

14. The term 'Poland A' refers to the more industrialized west of the country, and 'Poland B' to the less developed east.

15. Bronisław, b. 1937, Vilnius, Catholic, educated theatrical family (interview October 2004).

16. On the integration of the old middle class in Hungary, see James Mark, 'Discrimination' and János M. Rainer, 'Submerging or Clinging On Again: József Antall, Father and Son, in Hungary after 1956', *Contemporary European History* 14/1 (2005): 66–67. On middle-class integration into the Czechoslovak Communist Party, see Muriel Blaive, 'The Czechs and their Communism, Past and Present', in *Inquiries into Past and Present*, ed. Deanna Gard et al.

(Vienna: IWM Junior Visiting Fellows' Conferences, 2005) at <http://www.iwm.at/index2.php?option=com_content&do_pdf=1&id=293> (accessed 3 July 2009); on measures designed to increase working-class participation in Polish universities from the early 1950s, see John Connelly, *Captive University: The Sovietization of East German, Czech, and Polish Higher Education, 1945–1956* (Chapel Hill, NC: The University of North Carolina Press, 2000), 239.

17. In Hungary, the percentage of students from non-manual backgrounds attending university hardly dropped from its immediate postwar level even in the period of greatest anti-middle-class discrimination: Albert Simkus and Rudolf Andorka, 'Inequalities in Educational Attainment in Hungary, 1923–1973', *American Sociological Review* 47 (1982): 745; Szonja Szelényi, *Equality by Design: The Grand Experiment in Destratification in Socialist Hungary* (Stanford, CA: Stanford University Press, 1998), 125–26. The former middle class maintained a large presence in higher education: in Czechoslovakia, for example, students from worker-peasant backgrounds never filled more than 43 per cent of university places. In both Hungarian and Czechoslovak cases, this reflected the failure to recruit sufficient numbers of working-class students into a rapidly expanding university sector. It should be noted that these experiences of rewriting autobiographies were almost entirely absent from testimony in Czechoslovakia concerning the early Communist period, where the regime did not seriously attempt to challenge the dominance of its middle-class elite. Prospective students thus did not face the class-based counter-selective quotas and the anti-bourgeois rhetoric that greeted Hungarian university applicants. See Connelly, *Captive University*, 266–72. Only in East Germany did the state's long-term commitment to worker education, an aspirational proletariat and the flight of middle-class students to West Germany ensure a worker-peasant-dominated student body and a professional-intellectual elite. See ibid., 273–79.

18. On the aristocracy and the remaking of autobiography and identity in the Soviet Union, see Matthew Rendle, 'The Problems of "Becoming Soviet": Former Nobles in Soviet Society, 1917–41', *European History Quarterly* 38/7 (2008): 7–33.

19. Jan, b. 1929, Falenty, Catholic, Polish aristocratic family (interview October 2004).

20. A study on social mobility in Bulgaria noted that members of the pre-Communist elite learnt how to demonize members of their families in their public autobiographies by using class-conscious terms such as 'oppressor' and 'petty-bourgeois philistine'; see Daniela Koleva, ' "Socialist Individualism": Modernization and the Biographical Self', in *Talking History: Proceedings of the International Oral History Conference, Kiten, 24–27 September 1999*, ed. Daniela Koleva (Kiten: LIK, 1999), 108.

21. See Lutz Niethammer, 'Biographie und Biokratie', *Mitteilungen aus der Kulturwissenschaftlichen Forschung* 37 (1997): 370–87; Daniela Koleva, 'Between Testimony and Power: Autobiographies in Socialist Bulgaria', paper presented at the 'Texts of Testimony: Autobiography, Life-Story Narratives and the Public Sphere' conference, John Moores University, Liverpool, 23–25 August 2001; Galia Valtchinova, 'Ismail Kadare's *The H-File* and the Politics of Memory', in *Talking History*, ed. Daniela Koleva, 172–83; Jack R. Friedman, 'Furtive Selves: Proletarian Contradictions, Self-Presentation, and the Party in 1950s Romania', *International Labor and Working-Class History* 68 (2005): 9–23.

22. Flóra, b. 1935, Kalocsa, Catholic, father a shopkeeper with employees (interview October 1998).

23. Mária. M. Kovács and Antal Örkény, 'Promoted Cadres and Professionals in Post-War Hungary', in *Economy and Society in Hungary*, ed. Rudolf Andorka and László Bertalan (Budapest: Karl Marx University of Economic Sciences, 1986), 151.

24. Correspondence with Hanna Świda-Ziemba, sociologist, 2005.

25. Erzsébet, b. 1936, Székesfehérvár, Catholic, professional family (interview March 2000).

26. J. K. Coetzee and H. Otakar, 'Oppression, Resistance and Imprisonment: A Montage of Different But Similar Stories in Two Separate Countries', in *Trauma and Life Stories: International Perspectives*, ed. Kim Lacey Rogers, Selma Leydesdorff and Graham Dawson (London: Routledge, 1999), 80–94. They compare examples of South African and Czechoslovak persecution under apartheid and Communism respectively, analysing why South Africans saw the suffering in their lives as a basis for political action, whereas Czechs did not.

27. See James Mark, 'Society, Resistance and Revolution: The Budapest Middle Class and the Hungarian Communist State 1948–56', *The English Historical Review* 120/488 (2005): 963–86.

28. Nationalist accounts often included stories of relatives' resistance to Communism or other 'occupying regimes' prior to the Communist takeover itself, as these illustrated the family's longer-term commitment to anti-leftism and the nation. However, they downplayed, or

refused to testify to, their resistance during the Communist period, as these stories marked them out as someone who had politically engaged with the regime (however combatively), had thus entered into a dialogue, and hence had the potential to be ideologically changed by the experience. True anti-Communists, from this perspective, withdrew from all forms of political activity after 1948 as they tried to stay true to national ideals.

29. Dezső, b. 1929, Rákosliget, Catholic, professional family (interview December 1998).
30. Irén, b. 1929, Budapest, Catholic, father a neurologist and sanatorium director (interview May 2000).
31. Ryszard, b. 1932, village near Kraków, Catholic, soldiering and shopkeeping family (interview September 2004).
32. Reproduced in Adam Michnik, *Letters from Freedom: Post-Cold War Realities and Perspectives* (Berkeley, CA: University of California Press, 1998), 231.
33. Anna, b. 1930, Vác, Catholic, father a train driver, married into a professional family (interview May 2000).
34. Csaba, b. 1931, Pécs, Catholic professional family (interview December 2000); on the idea of the tacit agreement between the bourgeoisie and the Communist state after 1956 in Hungary, see Rainer, 'Submerging or Clinging On Again', 66.
35. Edit, b. 1907, Jánosháza, Jewish upper-middle-class family, father a company director (interview January 2000).
36. Urszula, b. 1930, Warsaw, Catholic, professional family, mother a doctor, father a lawyer (interview September 2004).
37. This was a common rebuttal that former dissidents used when they were criticized for not supporting lustration policies: Vladimir Andrle, 'Czech Dissidents: A Classically Modern Community', in *Biographical Research in Eastern Europe: Altered Lives and Broken Biographies*, ed. Robin Humphrey, Robert Miller and Elena Zdravomyslova (Aldershot, Hampshire: Ashgate, 2003), 126.
38. Jiří, b. 1945, Tábor, professional family (interview November 2004). On the rejection of the idea of victimization and moralistic discourses concerning the Communist past, see Kiss, 'The (Re)Construction of Post-Communist Memory' and Alexander von Plato, ' "Entstasifizierung" im Öffentlichen Dienst der Neuen Bundesländer nach 1989: Umorientierung und Kontinuität in der Lehrerschaft', *Jahrbuch für Historische Bildungsforschung* 5 (1999): 313–42.
39. Jiří Gruša, *The Questionnaire: Or Prayer for a Town and a Friend* (London: Blond & Briggs, 1982); Milan Kundera, *Slowness* (New York: HarperCollins Publishers, 1997).
40. In the late Communist period in Hungary and Poland, the insistence on politically appropriate autobiographies was much lower. The hardline Czechoslovak regime that emerged to 'normalize' the country in the wake of the defeat of the reform Communist movement in 1968 reawakened the biocratic culture of the early Communist period described above, in Chapter 5.
41. For this argument, see Nataša Kovačević, 'History on Speed: Media and the Politics of Forgetting in Milan Kundera's *Slowness*', *Modern Fiction Studies* 52/3 (2006): 634–55.

Chapter 7: The Afterlife of Atrocity: Remembering Red Army Rape after 1989

1. This chapter is based partly on my article 'Remembering Rape: Divided Social Memory and the Red Army in Hungary 1944–1945', *Past and Present* 188 (2005): 133–61.
2. Atina Grossmann notes the fascination with calculating numbers to capture events whose scale can never be truly known, and explains it as part of some historians' desire to assert the rightful place of women's suffering in an account of World War II: Atina Grossmann, 'A Question of Silence: The Rape of German Women by Occupation Soldiers', *October* 72 (1995): 46.
3. The figures quoted are conservative estimates. Andrea Pető, 'Memory and the Narrative of Rape in Budapest and Vienna in 1945', in *Life after Death: Approaches to a Cultural and Social History of Europe during the 1940s and the 1950s*, ed. Richard Bessel and Dirk Schumann (Cambridge: Cambridge University Press, 2003), 132; Grossmann, 'A Question of Silence', 46.
4. Eastern Prussia was a scene of particular brutality, where an estimated 1.4 million Polish and German women were raped: Catherine Merridale, *Ivan's War: The Red Army 1939–45* (London: Faber and Faber, 2005), 269–70. On Slovakia, see Karel Kaplan, *Československo v poválečné Evropě* (Prague: Univerzita Karlova v Praze, Nakladatelství Karolinum, 2004),

341–42; on Hungary, see Andrea Pető, 'Átvonuló hadsereg, maradandó trauma: Az 1945 ös budapesti nemi erőszak esetek emlékezete', *Történelmi Szemle* 41/1–2 (1999): 85–107.

5. Norman M. Naimark, *The Russians in Germany: A History of the Soviet Zone of Occupation, 1945–1949* (Cambridge, MA and London: Belknap Press of Harvard University Press, 1995), 129–40

6. Pető, 'Memory and the Narrative of Rape', 130.

7. See, for example, Anke Pinkert, *Film and Memory in East Germany* (Bloomington, IN: Indiana University Press, 2008), 165. She discusses Konrad Wolf's film *I Was Nineteen* (1968), in which rape is alluded to, but placed in the broader context of the responsibility of ordinary Germans for the war and the far greater suffering of Russian women under German occupation. Rape victims in north-eastern Yugoslavia had their cases officially investigated; see Naimark, *Russians in Germany*, 71. A new interest in local history in Hungary in the early 1970s spawned studies of the liberation period that included mentions of sexual contact between Hungarians and Russians: Pető, 'Memory and the Narrative of Rape', 146.

8. For this point, see Atina Grossmann, 'Trauma, Memory and Motherhood: German and Jewish Displaced Persons in Post-Nazi Germany, 1945–1949', *Archiv für Sozialgeschichte* 38 (1998): 225. For details of American fraternization, see John Willoughby, 'The Sexual Behaviour of American GIs during the Early Years of the Occupation of Germany', *Journal of Military History* 62/1 (1998): 155–74.

9. Elizabeth Heineman, 'Gender, Sexuality, and Coming to Terms with the Nazi Past', *Central European History* 38/1 (2005): 55. On Austrian women, see Andrea Pető, 'Memory and the Narrative of Rape', 132.

10. This is the argument of Elizabeth Heineman, 'The Hour of the Woman: Memories of Germany's "Crisis Years" and West German National Identity', *The American Historical Review*, 101/2 (1996): 354–95.

11. Catherine Merridale, 'Culture, Ideology and Combat in the Red Army', *Journal of Contemporary History* 41/2 (2006): 311.

12. Merridale, *Ivan's War*, 269.

13. Boris Slutsky, *Things That Happened*, ed. and trans. G. S. Smith (Moscow: Glas, 1999), 148. Rape was also addressed in Lev Kopelev, *No Jail for Thought* (London: Secker and Warburg, 1977). For a post-Communist Russian discussion of the issue, see Leonid Rabichev, 'Voina vse spishet', *Znamya* 2 (2005): 163 (quoted in Merridale, *Ivan's War*).

14. See above, Chapter 4, for a more detailed examination of this.

15. Feminist documentary-maker Helke Sander's *The Liberators Take Liberties* was the most well-known manifestation of this phenomenon: Helke Sander, dir., *Befreier und Befreite: Krieg, Vergewaltigungen, Kinder* (Germany: Bremer Institut Film, 1992). Andrea Pető, a feminist historian from Budapest, played a large role in the recovery of women's stories. Unlike Sander, however, she noted the problems of applying ideas about rape that developed in the 1970s to those who experienced it in World War II: Pető, 'Memory and the Narrative of Rape', 145.

16. Laurel Cohen-Pfister, 'Rape, War and Outrage: Changing Perceptions on German Victimhood in the Period of Post-Unification', in *Victims and Perpetrators: 1933–1945. (Re)Presenting the Past in Post-Unification Culture*, ed. Laurel Cohen-Pfister and Dagmar Wienroeder-Skinner (Berlin: de Gruyter, 2006), 316.

17. Alaine Polcz, *Asszony a fronton: egy fejezet életemből* (Budapest: Pont Kiadó, 2002).

18. See the project of Dr Philipp Kuwert at the University of Greifswald in eastern Germany: Philipp Kuwert and Harald Jürgen Freyberger, 'The Unspoken Secret: Sexual Violence in World War II', *International Psychogeriatrics* 19/4 (2007): 782–84. Their aim was not to provide women with counselling but rather to chart the long-term effects of wartime rape.

19. Antony Beevor, *Berlin: The Downfall, 1945* (London: Viking, 2002); Anonymous, *A Woman in Berlin: Diary 20 April 1945 to 22 June 1945* (London: Virago, 2005); Max Färberböck, dir., *A Woman in Berlin [Eine Frau in Berlin]* (Germany: Constantin Film Produktion, 2008). The diary was republished in Germany in 2003; the film was released in 2008.

20. For this critique, see Grossmann, 'A Question of Silence', 48–49.

21. Testimony from raped women was often used uncritically to illustrate the horrors of occupation, with little analysis of the complex reasons behind the decisions some women take in relating their suffering publicly. For an exploration of the ways in which the 'emotional

power of individual victims' voices' taken from the period of Soviet occupation were manipulated by historians in the German Federal Republic, see Robert G. Moeller, *War Stories: The Search for a Usable Past in the Federal Republic of Germany* (Berkeley, CA and London: University of California Press, 2003), 54–55.

22. Cohen-Pfister, 'Rape, War and Outrage', 321.

23. The interviews for this chapter were conducted between 1998 and 2000. The analysis was based on interviews with thirty-one female and forty-five male respondents. As a man interviewing about rape, I found that by showing appropriate sensitivity it was possible to obtain detailed testimony. During some interviews, women stressed that it was important that as a man I should understand 'women's experiences'. Moreover, my main focus was on collective understandings about rape rather than on gathering detailed information about what happened to individual women. Any reluctance on the part of raped women to talk about their experiences to a man was therefore not crucial to this particular project. In addition, I was equally interested in how men see the issue of rape; in an interview situation, men may have found it much more difficult to talk to a woman interviewer about this sensitive subject.

24. Due to the social silence that surrounded the issue in 1945, and the destruction of written materials under the Communist regime, an exact figure for the number of women raped in Budapest is unlikely to emerge. Ungváry suggests a figure of 10 per cent of the female population: Krisztián Ungváry, *Battle for Budapest: 100 Days in World War II* (London: I. B. Tauris, 2002), 289. This chapter will focus almost exclusively on male-on-female rape. Some conservative writers have used stories of female Red Army soldiers raping Hungarian men for propagandistic purposes, although I have found no evidence of such rapes having actually occurred. I have also not discovered any evidence of homosexual rape, and for this reason the chapter will not address the issue.

25. After the war, the Soviet regime awarded two sets of medals: those for cities 'liberated' and others for cities 'conquered'. Soldiers who fought during the siege of Budapest were categorized as 'conquerors': Martin Mevius, *Agents of Moscow: The Hungarian Communist Party and the Origins of Socialist Patriotism, 1941–1953* (Oxford: Clarendon Press, 2005), 63.

26. For other attempts to use oral history to investigate communities that were divided in their understandings of atrocities, see Pamela Ballinger, 'Who Defines and Remembers Genocide after the Cold War? Contested Memories of Partisan Massacre in Venezia Giulia in 1943–1945', *Journal of Genocide Research*, 2/1 (2000), 11–30; Francesca Cappelletto, 'Public Memories and Personal Stories: Recalling the Antifascist Massacres', in *Memory and World War II: An Ethnographic Approach*, ed. Francesca Cappelletto (Oxford: Berg, 2005), 101–30.

27. A medium-sized town north-west of Budapest on the present-day Slovak–Hungarian border.

28. Erzsébet, b. 1936, Székesfehérvár, Catholic, professional family (interview March 2000).

29. Post-Communist histories emphasized the role of Hungarians as victims of the Red Army. See, for example, Ungváry, *Battle for Budapest*, 285–95. Although he admits that the civilian experience of the Red Army was varied, he focuses on atrocities committed on the local population.

30. Márta, b. 1929, Budapest, father a dentist (interview 2000).

31. Magda, b. 1932, Budapest, Reformed (Calvinist), father a judge (interview 2000).

32. See Albert Tezla, 'Introduction', in Alaine Polcz, *A Wartime Memoir: Hungary 1944–1945* (Budapest: Corvina Books, 1998), 20.

33. See, for example, Ruth Harris, 'The "Child of the Barbarian": Rape, Race and Nationalism during the First World War', *Past and Present* 141 (1993): 206. In France, following World War I, women were seen as embodiments of a 'violated, innocent female nation'. Their stories were therefore taken seriously and collected. After World War II, women were presented not as victims but as 'horizontal collaborators' and were stigmatized.

34. On the social silence that surrounded rape in Budapest immediately after the war, see Pető, 'Memory and the Narrative of Rape', 132. On the contrasting preparedness of women in Berlin to retell rape stories both privately and publicly with a 'certain bravado and "Berliner Schnauze" (sarcastic humour)', see Grossmann, 'A Question of Silence', 55.

35. See, for example, Tezla, 'Introduction', 9.

36. Ferenc Nagy, *Struggle behind the Iron Curtain*, trans. Stephen K. Swift (New York: MacMillan, 1948), xi.

37. Ibid., 63.

38. Klaus Theweleit, *Male Fantasies: Women, Floods, Bodies, History* (Cambridge: Polity, 1987), 70–79. Here, he discusses the interwar German fear of the threat of castration by the proletarian 'rifle-woman'.

39. In this interpretation, Hungarians under the Nazi and Soviet occupations were seen as helpless victims, stripped of any responsibility for what was done in their country during these years.

40. There is little historical record of the extent of fraternization, or the 'taking of a male protector' among Hungarian women. One historian suggests that the number of prostitutes in Budapest went up twenty-fold after the arrival of the Red Army: Ungváry, *Battle for Budapest*, 289.

41. See István Rév, 'Parallel Autopsies', *Representations* 49 (1995): 32–33. Here, he explores how similarities in the symbolism and ritual between the burial of the first leader of post-Communist Hungary and the almost contemporaneous reburial of the interwar and wartime leader Admiral Horthy established the sense of a natural continuity between 1944 and 1989 and erased the intervening years of Communism in the national imagination.

42. For an exploration of this historical mindset: ibid., 31–34. See above, Chapter 4, for a discussion of this theme in a Baltic setting.

43. Some nationalist histories saw the beginning of the German occupation in March 1944 as the point at which national history was put 'on hold': the Holocaust was simply the responsibility of the German occupiers.

44. See, for example, the discussion of the House of Terror above, in Chapter 3.

45. This does not mean that all these respondents had Fascist sympathies, but rather that for many interviewees, particularly conservative respondents, Fascism was not perceived to be as great an evil as Communism and was not presented as a defining moment in their life story or their nation's history. The absence of an emphasis on a rejection of Fascism within post-Communist Hungary is explored in István Rév, 'Counterrevolution', in *Between Past and Future: the Revolutions of 1989 and their Aftermath*, ed. Sorin Antohi and Vladimir Tismăneanu (Budapest: CEU Press, 2000), 247–71.

46. Irén, b. 1929, Budapest, Catholic, father a neurologist and sanatorium director (interview 2000).

47. Mária, b. 1928, Budapest, Catholic, father a minister in the Horthy government (interview 2000).

48. Ildikó, b. 1930, Budapest, Catholic, father a soldier and taxi driver (interview 2000).

49. For another exploration of the way in which nationalists have used stories of women's suffering, see Pető, 'Memory and the Narrative of Rape', 147–48.

50. Similar images of the Red Army as animalistic and subhuman were produced in Nazi Germany; see Grossmann, 'A Question of Silence', 50.

51. Polcz, *A Wartime Memoir*, 93.

52. Alexandra Orme, *From Christmas to Easter: A Guide to the Russian Occupation*, trans. M. A. Meyer and L. Meyer (London: William Hodge and Company Limited, 1949), 4. This was a memoir, published four years after the war, based on a diary kept in 1944–45.

53. Ödön, b. 1933, Budapest, non-practising Reformed (Calvinist), father an orchestral musician and mother a piano teacher (interview 1999).

54. See, for example, Wolfram Wette, 'Német propaganda és a csatlósországok: Magyarország, Románia és Bulgária (1941–43)', *Történelmi Szemle* 22 (1979): 478–79. See also Balázs Sipos, 'Szovjetbarát és Szovjetellenes Nyilas Propaganda 1939–1941', *Múltunk* 41 (1996): 107–32. On Austrian women who still reproduce aspects of Nazi propaganda in their stories of the Soviet occupation, see Irene Bandhauer-Schöffmann, 'Women's Fight for Food in Post-War Vienna', in *When the War Was Over* (London: Leicester University Press, 2000), 81.

55. Győző, b. 1933, Biharnagybajom, Reformed (Calvinist), father a 'middling peasant' (interview 2000).

56. Orme, *From Christmas to Easter*, 85.

57. Grossmann, 'A Question of Silence', 50.

58. It was reported that after 1945 at the Faculty of Law in Budapest a notice stated, 'No dissertation will be considered on the law of rape and on the doctrine of the Holy Crown': László Péter, 'The Holy Crown of Hungary, Visible and Invisible', *Slavonic and East European Review*, 81/3 (2003): 422.

59. Sándor, b. 1930, Budapest, assimilated Jewish, father a research economist (interview 2000).

60. Luca, b. 1933, Budapest, assimilated Jewish, father a chemical engineer (interview September 1998).

61. See how the images of the French 'Tondues' – women who were humiliated in public at the point of liberation in 1945 for their 'horizontal collaboration' – have been used by the right in France both to show collaboration as passive and feminine (rather than active and masculine), and to complicate the idea of the 'heroic liberation': Alison M. Moore, 'Photography of the Tondues: Visuality of the Vichy Past through the Silent Image of Women', *Gender and History* 17/3 (2005): 659.

62. Miklós, b. 1926, Putnok, Jewish, father an ironmonger (interview 2000).

63. Mátyás, b. 1929, Budapest, Jewish, father a factory administrator (interview May 2000).

64. This story seems to have been communicated by the Red Army across central-eastern Europe: see Grossmann, 'A Question of Silence', 51.

65. Vera, b. 1936, Budapest, assimilated Jewish, father an industrial chemist (interview 2000).

66. Éva, b. 1936, Budapest, Evangelical, father a chemical engineer (interview 2000).

67. Katalin, b. 1923, Budapest, Catholic, father a factory director (interview 2000).

68. This point was also made about German women's representations of rape in Grossmann, 'A Question of Silence', 59–60.

69. There are other ways in which this could be interpreted. Some scholars of psychology argue that the notion of 'rape' is a dramatizing construct that does not always help women assimilate their experiences of non-consensual sex, and as such is not always used to make sense of the experience: Darcy McMullin and Jacquelyn W. White, 'Long-Term Effects of Labelling a Rape Experience', *Psychology of Women Quarterly* 30/1 (2006): 96–105; Zoe D. Peterson and Charlene L. Muehlenhard, 'Was It Rape? The Function of Women's Rape: Myth, Acceptance and Definitions of Sex in Labeling their Own Experiences', *Sex Roles* 51/3-4 (2004): 129–44. My thanks to Alison Moore for these references. On the problems of 'coming to terms' with being raped by 'your liberator', see Cohen-Pfister, 'Rape, War and Outrage', 316–17. For an account of how a woman who was sexually violated in the 1970s did not consider herself a victim at the time but later came to revise the meaning of her experience, see Mary Beard, 'Diary', *London Review of Books* 24 August 2000.

70. István Bibó, 'The Crisis of Hungarian Democracy', in *Democracy, Revolution, Self-Determination*, István Bibó (Boulder, CO: Social Science Monographs, 1991), 91.

71. For a critique of the weakness of feminism in post-Communist Hungary, see Joanna Goven, 'Gender Politics in Hungary: Autonomy and Antifeminism', in *Gender Politics and Post Communism: Reflections from Eastern Europe and the Former Soviet Union*, ed. Nanette Funk and Magda Mueller (New York: Routledge, 1993), 224–40.

BIBLIOGRAPHY

Aarelaid-Tart, Aili. 'Estonian-Inclined Communists as Marginals.' In Robin Humphrey, Robert Miller and Elena Zdravomyslova, eds. *Biographical Research in Eastern Europe: Altered Lives and Broken Biographies.* Aldershot: Ashgate, 2003.

'Activity Report May–December 2006.' *The Institute for the Investigation of Communist Crimes in Romania, Investigations Department.* Available from http://www.crimelecomunismului.ro/pdf/en/activity_report_06/activity_report_2006.pdf. Accessed 9 July 2009.

Adler, Nanci. 'The Future of the Soviet Past Remains Unpredictable: The Resurrection of Stalinist Symbols amidst the Exhumation of Mass Graves.' *Europe-Asia Studies.* 57/8 (2005): 1093–1119.

Aguilar, Paloma and Carsten Humlebaek. 'Collective Memory and National Identity in the Spanish Democracy: The Legacies of Francoism and the Civil War.' *History and Memory.* 14 (2002): 121–64.

Aguilar, Paloma. *Memory and Amnesia: The Role of the Spanish Civil War in the Transition to Democracy.* New York and Oxford: Berghahn Books, 2002.

Ahonen, Heiki. 'Wie Gründet Man ein Museum? Zur Entstehungsgeschichte des Museums der Okkupationen in Riga.' In Volkhard Knigge and Ulrich Mählert, eds. *Der Kommunismus im Museum: Formen der Auseinandersetzung in Deutschland und Ostmitteleuropa.* Cologne: Böhlau, 2005.

Andorka, Rudolf, and László Bertalan, eds. *Economy and Society in Hungary.* Budapest: Karl Marx University of Economic Sciences, 1986.

Andrle, Vladimir. 'Neither a Dinosaur Nor a Weathercock: The Construction of a Reputably Continuous Self in Czech Post-Communist Life Stories.' *Qualitative Sociology.* 23/2 (2000): 215–30.

Andrle, Vladimir. 'The Buoyant Class: Bourgeois Family Lineage in the Life Stories of Czech Business Elite Persons.' *Sociology.* 35/4 (2001): 815–34.

Andrle, Vladimir. 'Czech Dissidents: A Classically Modern Community.' In Robin Humphrey, Robert Miller and Elena Zdravomyslova, eds. *Biographical Research in Eastern Europe: Altered Lives and Broken Biographies.* Aldershot: Ashgate, 2003.

Anon, 'Apák és Fiúk [Fathers and Sons].' *Magyar Fórum.* 31 March 1990: 2.

Anon, 'Budapest Watches Statues Trundle In and Out of Exile.' *The New York Times.* 4 October 1992.

Anon, 'Imre Kertész: "I've Been Through Worse".' *Moscow News.* 23 October 2002.

Anon, 'Hungarians Divided over World War II Endgame.' *Hungarian News Agency (MTI).* 2 April 2005.

Anon, 'Lithuania's Parliamentary Chair Sees Ban on Soviet Symbols as Secondary Matter.' *Baltic News Service.* 28 September 2005.

Anon, 'Premier Neglects Hungary's National Interests – Controversial Museum Head.' *Népszabadság.* 4 August 2005.

Anon. *A Woman in Berlin: Diary 20 April 1945 to 22 June 1945.* London: Virago, 2005.

Anon, 'A Felvonulási téri 1956-os emlékmű: éket ver, vagy egyesít? – Képriport.' *gondola.hu*. 30 October 2006. Available from http://gondola.hu/cikkek/51004. Accessed 3 July 2009.

Anon, 'Estonians Protest Controversial Memorial.' *Baltic Times*. 22 May 2006.

Anon, 'Cultural War and Polish Politics.' *Rzeczpospolita*. 7–8 July 2007: A9.

Anon, 'Estonia: Prime Minister Issues Statement on International Holocaust Remembrance Day.' *US Federal News*. 27 January 2007.

Antohi, Sorin, and Vladimir Tismăneanu, eds. *Between Past and Future: The Revolutions of 1989 and their Aftermath*. Budapest: CEU Press, 2000.

Antohi, Sorin, Balázs Trencsényi and Péter Apor, eds. *Narratives Unbound: Historical Studies in Post-Communist Eastern Europe*. Budapest: CEU Press, 2007.

Apor, Péter. 'The Creative Fear: Fascism, Anti-Semitism, Democracy and the Foundation of the People's Democracy in Hungary.' In Bo Stråth, ed. *Myth and Memory in the Construction of Community: Historical Patterns in Europe and Beyond*. Brussels: Peter Lang, 2000.

Apor, Péter. 'The Joy of Everyday Life: Microhistory and the History of Everyday Life in the Socialist Dictatorships.' *East-Central Europe*. 35/1–2 (2007–08): 185–218.

Apor, Péter. 'Eurocommunism: Commemorating Communism in Contemporary Eastern Europe.' In Małgorzata Pakier and Bo Stråth, eds. *A European Memory? Contested Histories and Politics of Remembrance*. Oxford: Berghahn Books, 2010.

Attwood, Bain. 'In the Age of Testimony: The Stolen Generations Narrative, "Distance", and Public History.' *Public Culture*. 20/1 (2008): 75–96.

Ballinger, Pamela. 'Who Defines and Remembers Genocide after the Cold War? Contested Memories of Partisan Massacre in Venezia Giulia in 1943–1945.' *Journal of Genocide Research*. 2/1 (2000): 11–30.

Bandhauer-Schöffmann, Irene. 'Women's Fight for Food in Post-War Vienna.' In Claire Duchen and Irene Bandhauer-Schöffmann, eds. *When the War Was Over*. London: Leicester University Press, 2000.

Bandhauer-Schöffmann, Irene, and Claire Duchen, eds. *When the War Was Over*. London: Leicester University Press, 2000.

Barroso, José Manuel. 'Acting Together: The Legacy of 1956.' Budapest: 23 October 2006. Available from http://www.europa-eu-un.org/articles/en/article_6387_en.htm. Accessed 3 July 2009.

Bartha, Eszter. ' "Te és az üzemed": Szocialista kollektívák és munkáspolitika az 1970-es és 1980-as években az NDK-ban és Magyarországon.' In Sándor Horváth, ed. *Mindennapok Rákosi és Kádár Korában*. Budapest: Nyitott Könyvműhely, 2008.

Bartov, Omer, Atina Grossmann and Mary Nolan, eds. *Crimes of War: Guilt and Denial in the Twentieth Century*. New York: New Press, 2002.

Băsescu, Traian, Speech before Parliament, 18 December 2006.

Bazac, Ana. 'Can Anti-Fascism Still Play a Role? A Case Study of Romania.' *Critique*. 34/1 (2006): 61–80.

Beard, Mary. 'Diary.' *London Review of Books*. 24 August 2000.

Beattie, Andrew H. 'Learning from the Germans? History and Memory in German and European Projects of Integration.' *PORTAL Journal of Multidisciplinary International Studies*. 4/2 (2007): 1–22.

Beattie, Andrew H. *Playing Politics with History: The Bundestag Inquiries into East Germany*. New York and Oxford: Berghahn, 2008.

Beevor, Antony. *Berlin: The Downfall, 1945*. London: Viking, 2002.

Benoit, Kenneth, and John W. Schiemann. 'Institutional Choice in New Democracies: Bargaining over Hungary's 1989 Electoral Law.' *Journal of Theoretical Politics*. 13/2 (2001): 153–82.

Benziger, Karl P. 'The Funeral of Imre Nagy: Contested History and the Power of Memory Culture.' *History and Memory*. 12/2 (2000): 142–64.

Benziger, Karl P. 'Imre Nagy and the Unsettled Past: The Politics of Memory in Contemporary Hungary.' Paper presented at the 7th Annual New School for Social Research Sociology and Historical Studies Joint Conference: History Matters: Spaces of Violence, Spaces of Memory. 23–24 April 2004. Available from www.newschool.edu/nssr/historymatters/papers/KarlBenziger.pdf. Accessed 3 July 2009.

Berdahl, Daphne. *Where the World Ended: Re-unification and Identity in the German Borderland*. Berkeley: University of California Press, 1999.

Berdahl, Daphne, Matti Bunzl and Martha Lampland, eds. *Altering States: Ethnographies of Transition in Eastern Europe and the Former Soviet Union*. Ann Arbor: University of Michigan Press, 2000.

Berman, Judith E. 'Holocaust Commemoration in London and Anglo-Jewish (Dis)-Unity.' *Journal of Modern Jewish Studies*. 3/1 (2004): 51–71.

Berniunas, Renatas. 'Agency, Cognitive Anchors and Memory: Why Soviet Icons Matter.' In Ene Kõresaar, Epp Lauk and Kristin Kuutma, eds. *The Burden of Remembering: Recollections and Representations of the Twentieth Century*. Helsinki: SKS Kirjat, 2009.

Bertaux, Daniel. 'Transmission in Extreme Situations: Russian Families Expropriated by the October Revolution.' In Daniel Bertaux and Paul Thompson, eds. *Pathways to Social Class: A Qualitative Approach to Social Mobility*. Oxford: Clarendon Press, 1997.

Bertaux, Daniel, and Paul Thompson, eds. *Pathways to Social Class: A Qualitative Approach to Social Mobility*. Oxford: Clarendon Press, 1997.

Bertaux, Daniel, Paul Thompson and Anna Rotkirch, eds. *On Living Through Soviet Russia*. London and New York: Routledge, 2004.

Bertaux, Daniel, Anna Rotkirch and Paul Thompson. 'Introduction.' In Daniel Bertaux, Paul Thompson and Anna Rotkirch, eds. *On Living Through Soviet Russia*, London and New York: Routledge, 2004.

Bessel, Richard and Dirk Schumann, eds. *Life after Death: Approaches to a Cultural and Social History of Europe during the 1940s and the 1950s*. Cambridge: Cambridge University Press, 2003.

Bibó, István, *Democracy, Revolution, Self-Determination*. Boulder: Social Science Monographs, 1991.

Bibó, István. 'The Crisis of Hungarian Democracy.' In István Bibó, ed., *Democracy, Revolution, Self-Determination*. Boulder, CO: Social Science Monographs, 1991.

Bingen, Dieter, Peter Oliver Loew and Kazimierz Wóycicki, eds. *Die Destruktion des Dialogs: Zur Innenpolitischen Instrumentalisierung Negativer Fremd- und Feindbilder. Polen, Tschechien, Deutschland und die Niederlande im Vergleich, 1900 bis Heute*. Wiesbaden: Harrassowitz, 2007.

Blaive, Muriel. 'The Czechs and their Communism, Past and Present.' In Deanna Gard et al., eds. *Inquiries into Past and Present*. Vienna: IWM Junior Visiting Fellows' Conferences. 17 (2005). Available from http://www.iwm.at/index.php?option=com_content&task=view&id= 301&Itemid=276. Accessed 3 July 2009.

Blandiana, Ana. 'Memoria ca Formă de Justiție.' *Dilema*. 518 (2003): 10.

Blandiana, Ana. 'Die Gedenkstätte Memorial Sighet – Ein Lebendiges Museum.' In Volkhard Knigge and Ulrich Mählert, eds. *Der Kommunismus im Museum: Formen der Auseinandersetzung in Deutschland und Ostmitteleuropa*. Cologne: Böhlau, 2005.

Boldur-Lățescu, Gheorghe. *Genocidul comunist în România*. Bucharest: Albatros, 1992.

Boraine, Alex. 'Truth and Reconciliation Commission in South Africa. Amnesty: The Price of Peace.' In Jon Elster, ed. *Retribution and Reparation in the Transition to Democracy*. Cambridge: Cambridge University Press, 2006.

Borneman, John. *Settling Accounts: Violence, Justice and Accountability in Postsocialist Europe*. Princeton, NJ: Princeton University Press, 1997.

Bozóki, András. 'The Roundtable Talks of 1989: Participants, Political Visions and Historical References.' *Hungarian Studies*. 14/2 (2000): 241–57.

Bozóki, András, ed. *The Roundtable Talks of 1989: The Genesis of Hungarian Democracy: Analysis and Documents*. Budapest: CEU Press, 2001.

Bozóki, András. 'Introduction: The Significance of the Roundtable Talks.' In András Bozóki, ed. *The Roundtable Talks of 1989: The Genesis of Hungarian Democracy: Analysis and Documents*. Budapest: CEU Press, 2001.

Bozóki, András. 'Consolidation or Second Revolution? The Politics of the New Right in Hungary.' *Slovak Foreign Policy Affairs*. 1 (2005): 17–28.

Brandenberger, David. *National Bolshevism: Stalinist Mass Culture and the Formation of Modern Russian National Identity, 1931–1956*. Cambridge, MA: Harvard University Press, 2002.

Bren, Paulina. '1968 East and West: Visions of Political Change and Student Protest.' In Gerd-Rainer Horn and Padraic Kenney, eds. *Transnational Moments of Change: Europe 1945, 1968, 1989*. Lanham, MD: Rowman & Littlefield, 2004.

Brotea, Julia, and Daniel Béland. ' "Better Dead than Communist!" Contentious Politics, Identity Formation, and the University Square Phenomenon in Romania.' *Spaces of Identity*. 7/2 (2007). Available from https://pi.library.yorku.ca/ojs/index.php/soi/article/view/7971/7103. Accessed 7 July 2009.

Brubaker, Rogers et al. *Nationalist Politics and Everyday Ethnicity in a Transylvanian Town.* Princeton, NJ: Princeton University Press, 2006.

Buchli, Victor, and Gavin Lucas, eds. *Archaeologies of the Contemporary Past.* London and New York: Routledge, 2001.

Budryte, Dovile. *Taming Nationalism? Political Community Building in the Post-Soviet Baltic States.* Aldershot: Ashgate, 2005.

Burch, Stuart, and David J. Smith. 'Empty Spaces and the Value of Symbols: Estonia's "War of Monuments" from another Angle.' *Europe-Asia Studies.* 59/6 (2007): 913–36.

Calhoun, Noel. *Dilemmas of Justice in Eastern Europe's Democratic Transitions.* New York: Palgrave Macmillan, 2004.

Cappelletto, Francesca, ed. *Memory and World War II: An Ethnographic Approach.* Oxford: Berg, 2005.

Cappelletto, Francesca. 'Public Memories and Personal Stories: Recalling the Antifascist Massacres.' In Francesca Cappelletto, ed. *Memory and World War II: An Ethnographic Approach.* Oxford: Berg, 2005.

Cassedy, Ellen. 'A Controversy Exhumes Long-Buried Memories.' *Forward.* 12 November 2004.

Cenarro, Ángela. 'Memory Beyond the Public Sphere: The Francoist Repression Remembered in Aragon.' *History and Memory.* 14/1 (2002): 165–88.

Cesereanu, Ruxandra. 'The Final Report on the Holocaust and the Final Report on the Communist Dictatorship in Romania.' *East European Politics and Societies.* 22 (2008): 270–81.

Cesereanu, Ruxandra. 'Fenomenul Piața Universității.' *Revisita.* 22 (2003). Available from http://www.revista22.ro/fenomenul-piata-universitatii-1990–445.html. Accessed 7 July 2009.

Challand, Benoît. '1989, Contested Memories and the Shifting Cognitive Maps of Europe.' *European Journal of Social Theory.* 12/3 (2009): 397–408.

Chodakiewicz, Marek Jan, and John Radziłowski, eds. *Spanish Carlism and Polish Nationalism: The Borderlands of Europe in the 19th and 20th Centuries.* Charlottesville: Leopolis Press, 2003.

Chodakiewicz, Marek Jan. 'Affinity and Revulsion: Poland Reacts to the Spanish Right 1936–1939 (and Beyond).' In Marek Jan Chodakiewicz and John Radziłowski, eds. *Spanish Carlism and Polish Nationalism: The Borderlands of Europe in the 19th and 20th Centuries.* Charlottesville: Leopolis Press, 2003.

Cienciala, Anna M., Natalia S. Lebedeva and Wojciech Materski, eds. *Katyn: A Crime without Punishment.* New Haven, CT: Yale University Press, 2007.

Ciobanu, Monica. 'Criminalising the Past and Reconstructing Collective Memory: The Romanian Truth Commission.' *Europe-Asia Studies.* 61/2 (2009): 313–36.

Cioflâncă, Adrian. 'Politics of Oblivion in Postcommunist Romania.' *The Romanian Journal of Political Sciences.* 2 (2002): 85–93.

Cioflâncă, Adrian. 'Istorie și justiție: Un model german pentru procesul comunismului.' *Echinox Notebooks.* 13 (2007): 121–32.

Coetzee, J. K., and H. Otakar. 'Oppression, Resistance and Imprisonment: A Montage of Different But Similar Stories in Two Separate Countries.' In Kim Lacey Rogers, Selma Leydesdorff and Graham Dawson, eds. *Trauma and Life Stories: International Perspectives.* London: Routledge, 1999.

Cohen, Shari J. *Politics without a Past: The Absence of History in Post-Communist Nationalism.* Durham, NC: Duke University Press, 1999.

Cohen-Pfister, Laurel. 'Rape, War and Outrage: Changing Perceptions on German Victimhood in the Period of Post-Unification.' In Laurel Cohen-Pfister and Dagmar Wienroeder-Skinner, eds. *Victims and Perpetrators: 1933–1945: (Re)Presenting the Past in Post-Unification Culture.* Berlin: de Gruyter, 2006.

Cohen-Pfister, Laurel, and Dagmar Wienroeder-Skinner, eds. *Victims and Perpetrators: 1933–1945: (Re)Presenting the Past in Post-Unification Culture.* Berlin: de Gruyter, 2006.

Cole, Elizabeth A., ed. *Teaching the Violent Past: History Education and Reconciliation.* Lanham, MD: Rowman & Littlefield, 2007.

Connelly, John. *Captive University: The Sovietization of East German, Czech, and Polish Higher Education, 1945–1956.* Chapel Hill: The University of North Carolina Press, 2000.

Cordoş, Sanda. 'Revoluția, un prag între două vieți.' *Echinox.* 6 (2004): 124–28.

Corney, Frederick C. *Telling October: Memory and the Making of the Bolshevik Revolution.* Ithaca: Cornell University Press, 2004.

Cosma, Neagu. *Securitatea, Poliția Politică, Dosare, Informatori.* Bucharest: Globus, 1998.

Courtois, Stéphane et al., eds. *The Black Book of Communism: Crimes, Terror, Repression.* Trans. Jonathan Murphy. Cambridge, MA: Harvard University Press, 1999.

Cox, Margaret, Ambika Flavel and Ian Hanson. 'Introduction and Context.' In Margaret Cox et al., eds. *The Scientific Investigation of Mass Graves: Towards Protocols and Standard Operating Procedures.* Cambridge: Cambridge University Press, 2008.

Cox, Margaret et al., eds. *The Scientific Investigation of Mass Graves: Towards Protocols and Standard Operating Procedures.* Cambridge: Cambridge University Press, 2008.

Cristea, Gabriela, and Simina Radu-Bucurenci. 'Raising the Cross: Exorcising Romania's Communist Past in Museums, Memorials, and Monuments.' In Oksana Sarkisova and Péter Apor, eds. *Past for the Eyes: East European Representations of Communism in Cinema and Museums after 1989.* Budapest: CEU Press, 2008.

Crossland, Zoe. 'Buried Lives: Forensic Archaeology and the Disappeared in Argentina.' *Archaeological Dialogues.* 7 (2000): 146–59.

Crossland, Zoe. 'Violent Spaces: Conflict over the Reappearance of Argentina's Disappeared.' In John Schofield, William Gray Johnson and Colleen M. Beck, eds. *Matériel Culture: The Archaeology of Twentieth Century Conflict.* London: Routledge, 2002.

Czaplicka, John. 'The Palace Ruins and Putting the Lithuanian Nation into Place: Historical Settings in Vilnius.' In Daniel J. Walkowitz and Lisa Maya Knauer, eds. *Memory and the Impact of Political Transformation in Public Space.* Durham, NC: Duke University Press, 2004.

Czarnota, Adam. 'The Politics of the Lustration Law in Poland, 1989–2006.' In Alexander Mayer-Rieckh and Pablo de Greiff, eds. *Justice as Prevention: Vetting Public Employees in Transitional Societies.* New York: Social Science Research Council, 2007.

Dampier, Helen, and Liz Stanley. 'Aftermaths: Post/Memory, Commemoration and the Concentration Camps of the South African War 1899–1902.' *European Review of History.* 12/1 (2005): 91–119.

Deák, István. 'A Fatal Compromise? The Debate Over Collaboration and Resistance in Hungary.' *East European Politics and Societies.* 9/2 (1995): 209–33.

Dean, Carolyn J. 'Recent French Discourses on Stalinism, Nazism and "Exorbitant" Jewish Memory.' *History & Memory.* 18/1 (2006): 43–85.

Delanty, Gerard. 'The Quest for European Identity.' In Erik Oddvar Eriksen, ed. *Making the European Polity: Reflexive Integration in the European Union.* Abingdon: Routledge, 2005.

Diner, Dan. 'Restitution and Memory: The Holocaust in European Political Cultures.' *New German Critique.* 90 (2003): 36–44.

Dobrescu, Caius. 'Barocul Fascisto-Comunist ca Fenomen Global.' Paper presented at the 'Gulag şi Holocaust în Conştiinţă Romaneasca' conference. Babeş-Bolyai University, 25–26 May 2007. Available from http://www.memoria.ro/?location=view_article&id=1744. Accessed 7 July 2009.

Duchen, Claire and Irene Bandhauer-Schöffmann, eds. *When the War Was Over.* London: Leicester University Press, 2000.

Dvořáková, Vladimíra. 'The Institute of National Memory: Historical Memory as a Political Project.' In Vladimíra Dvořáková and Anđelko Milardović, eds. *Lustration and Consolidation of Democracy and the Rule of Law in Central and Eastern Europe.* Zagreb: Political Science Research Centre, 2007.

Dvořáková, Vladimíra, and Anđelko Milardović, eds. *Lustration and Consolidation of Democracy and the Rule of Law in Central and Eastern Europe.* Zagreb: Political Science Research Centre, 2007.

Edwards, Lee. *Is Communism Dead?* Available from http://www.tfas.org/Document.Doc?id=30. Accessed 27 July 2009.

Egry, Gábor. '1956 Emlékezete Itthon és külföldön.' *Regio: kisebbség, politika, társadalom.* 18/3 (2007): 3–21.

Eisler, Jerzy. 'March 1968 in Poland.' In Carole Fink, Philipp Gassert and Detlef Junker, eds. *1968: The World Transformed.* Cambridge: Cambridge University Press, 1998.

Elek, István. *Rendszerváltoztatók húsz év után.* Budapest: Heti Válasz Lap- és Könyvkiadó, 2009.

Eley, Geoff. *Forging Democracy: The Left in Europe, 1850–2000.* Oxford: Oxford University Press, 2002.

Eller, Mart-Ivo, ed. *Monuments and Decorative Sculpture of Tallinn.* Trans. Kristi Tarand. Tallinn: Perioodika, 1978.

Elster, Jon, ed. *Retribution and Reparation in the Transition to Democracy.* Cambridge: Cambridge University Press, 2006.

Embacher, Helga. 'Britishness and Ethnic Counter-Memories – Jewishness versus Muslim Memories in Great Britain.' Paper presented at the 'Memory from Transdisciplinary Perspectives' conference. University of Tartu, 11–14 January 2007.

Epstein, Catherine. 'The Politics of Biography: The Case of East German Old Communists.' *Daedalus.* 128/2 (1999): 1–30.

Epstein, Catherine. *The Last Revolutionaries: German Communists and their Century.* Cambridge, MA: Harvard University Press, 2003.

Erényi, Tibor, and Sándor Rákosi, eds. *Legyőzhetetlen erő. A magyar kommunista mozgalom szervezeti fejlődésének 50 éve.* Budapest: Kossuth Könyvkiadó, 1968.

Eriksen, Erik Oddvar, ed. *Making the European Polity: Reflexive Integration in the European Union.* Abingdon: Routledge, 2005.

Ernu, Vasile, Costi Rogozanu and Ciprian Şiulea, eds. *Iluzia Anticomunismului: Lecturi Critice ale Raportului Tismăneanu.* Chisinau: Cartier, 2008.

Esbenshade, Richard S. 'Remembering to Forget: Memory, History, National Identity in Postwar East-Central Europe.' *Representations.* 49 (1995): 72–96.

Etkind, Alexander. 'Post-Soviet Hauntology: Cultural Memory of the Soviet Terror.' *Constellations: An International Journal of Critical and Democratic Theory.* 16/1 (2009): 182–200.

'Examenul de Bacalaureat Limba şi Literturа Română, 2008.' *Ministerul Educaţiei, Cercetării şi Tineretului Centrul Naţional pentru Curriculum şi Evaluare în Învăţământul Preuniversitar.*

Ezergailis, Andrew. *The Holocaust in Latvia 1941-1944: The Missing Centre.* Washington, D.C.: United States Holocaust Memorial Museum, 1996.

Färberböck, Max. dir. *A Woman in Berlin [Eine Frau in Berlin].* Germany: Constantin Film Produktion, 2008.

Farmer, Sarah. 'Symbols That Face Both Ways: Commemorating the Victims of Stalinism and Nazism at Buchenwald and Sachsenhausen.' *Representations.* 49 (1995): 97–119.

Ferllini, Roxana. 'The Development of Human Rights Investigations since 1945.' *Science and Justice.* 43/4 (2003): 219–24.

Fink, Carole, Philipp Gassert and Detlef Junker, eds. *1968: The World Transformed.* Cambridge: Cambridge University Press, 1998.

Fisher, Kate. *Birth Control, Sex and Marriage in Britain, 1918–1960.* Oxford: Oxford University Press, 2006.

Fitzpatrick, Sheila. 'Ascribing Class: The Construction of Social Identity in Soviet Russia.' *The Journal of Modern History.* 65/4 (1993): 745–70.

Fitzpatrick, Sheila, ed. *Stalinism: New Directions.* London: Routledge, 2000.

Fitzpatrick, Sheila. *Tear Off the Masks!: Identity and Imposture in Twentieth-Century Russia.* Princeton, NJ: Princeton University Press, 2005.

Forgacs, David, ed. *Rethinking Italian Fascism: Capitalism, Populism and Culture.* London: Lawrence and Wishart, 1986.

Fowler, Brigid. 'Concentrated Orange: Fidesz and the Remaking of the Hungarian Centre-Right, 1994–2002.' *Journal of Communist Studies and Transition Politics.* 20/3 (2004): 80–114.

Fox, Thomas C. *Stated Memory: East Germany and the Holocaust.* Woodbridge: Camden House, 1999.

Fox, Thomas C. 'The Holocaust under Communism.' In Dan Stone, ed. *Historiography of the Holocaust.* Basingstoke: Palgrave Macmillan, 2005.

Frei, Norbert. *Adenauer's Germany and the Nazi Past: The Politics of Amnesty and Integration.* New York: Columbia University Press, 2002.

Friedman, Jack R. 'Furtive Selves: Proletarian Contradictions, Self-Presentation, and the Party in 1950s Romania.' *International Labor and Working-Class History.* 68 (2005): 9–23.

Friedman, Max Paul, and Padraic Kenney. 'History in Politics.' In Max Paul Friedman and Padraic Kenney, eds. *Partisan Histories: The Past in Contemporary Global Politics.* New York: Palgrave Macmillan, 2005.

Friedman, Max Paul, and Padraic Kenney, eds. *Partisan Histories: The Past in Contemporary Global Politics.* New York: Palgrave Macmillan, 2005.

Frisch, Michael. *A Shared Authority: Essays on the Craft and Meaning of Oral and Public History.* Albany: State University of New York Press, 1990.

Fürtös, Robert. 'Sighet, Preambul al Holocaustului, Punct Central al Gulagului.' *Echinox.* 13 (2007): 226–41.

Fukuyama, Francis. *The End of History and the Last Man.* London: Hamish Hamilton, 1992.

Funari, Pedro, Melisa Salerno and Andres Zarankin, eds. *Memories from Darkness: Archaeology of Repression and Resistance in Latin America*. New York: Springer, 2009.

Funk, Nanette, and Magda Mueller, eds. *Gender Politics and Post Communism: Reflections from Eastern Europe and the Former Soviet Union*. New York: Routledge, 1993.

Gallinat, Anselma. 'Difficult Stories: Public Discourse and Narrative Identity in Eastern Germany.' *Ethnos: Journal of Anthropology*. 71/3 (2006): 343–66.

Gallinat, Anselma. 'Life-Stories in Interviews and in Social Interaction: Victims of the GDR Talk and Argue About the Past.' In Julia Obertreis and Anke Stephan, eds. *Remembering after the Fall of Communism: Oral History and (Post-)Socialist Societies*. Essen: Klartext, 2009.

Gard, Deanna, et al., eds. *Inquiries into Past and Present*. Vienna: IWM Junior Visiting Fellows' Conferences. 17 (2005). Available from http://www.iwm.at/index.php?option=com_content &task=view&id=301&Itemid=276. Accessed 3 July 2009.

Gassert, Philipp, and Alan E. Steinweis, eds. *Coping with the Nazi Past: West German Debates on Nazism and Generational Conflict, 1955–1975*. Oxford: Berghahn Books, 2006.

Gheith, Jehanne M. ' "I Never Talked": Enforced Silence, Non-Narrative Memory, and the Gulag.' *Mortality*. 12/2 (2007): 159–75.

Gitelman, Zvi. 'Politics and the Historiography of the Holocaust in the Soviet Union.' In Zvi Gitelman, ed. *Bitter Legacy: Confronting the Holocaust in the USSR*. Bloomington: Indiana University Press, 1997.

Gitelman, Zvi, ed. *Bitter Legacy: Confronting the Holocaust in the USSR*. Bloomington: Indiana University Press, 1997.

Golsan, Richard. 'The Politics of History and Memory in France in the 1990s.' In Henry Roussou, ed. *Stalinism and Nazism: History and Memory Compared*. Lincoln, NB: University of Nebraska Press, 2004.

Gough, Roger. *A Good Comrade: János Kádár, Communism and Hungary*. London: I. B. Tauris, 2006.

Goven, Joanna. 'Gender Politics in Hungary: Autonomy and Antifeminism.' In Nanette Funk and Magda Mueller, eds. *Gender Politics and Post Communism: Reflections from Eastern Europe and the Former Soviet Union*. New York: Routledge, 1993.

Grama, Sidonia. 'In Between Places of Remembrance and Realms of Memory: The 15 Year Commemoration of the Romanian Revolution in Timişoara.' *Philobiblon*. 10, 11 (2005–6): 310–41.

Grama, Sidonia. 'Memory Features of the 1989 Revolution: Competing Narratives on the Revolution.' In Julia Obertreis and Anke Stephan, eds. *Remembering after the Fall of Communism: Oral History and (Post-)Socialist Societies*. Essen: Klartext, 2009.

Grandin, Greg. *The Last Colonial Massacre: Latin America in the Cold War*. Chicago: University of Chicago Press, 2004.

Grandin, Greg. 'The Instruction of Great Catastrophe: Truth Commissions, National History, and State Formation in Argentina, Chile, and Guatemala.' *The American Historical Review*. 110/1 (2005): 46–67.

Grosby, Steven Elliot, and Athena S. Leoussi, eds. *Nationalism and Ethnosymbolism: History, Culture and Ethnicity in the Formation of Nations*. Edinburgh: Edinburgh University Press, 2007.

Gross, Jan. *Neighbors: The Destruction of the Jewish Community in Jedwabne*. Princeton, NJ: Princeton University Press, 2001.

Grossmann, Atina. 'A Question of Silence: The Rape of German Women by Occupation Soldiers.' *October*. 72 (1995): 42–63.

Grossmann, Atina. 'Trauma, Memory and Motherhood: German and Jewish Displaced Persons in Post-Nazi Germany, 1945–1949.' *Archiv für Sozialgeschichte*. 38 (1998): 215–39.

Gruša, Jiří. *The Questionnaire: Or Prayer for a Town and a Friend*. London: Blond & Briggs, 1982.

Grzymała-Busse, Anna M. *Redeeming the Communist Past: The Regeneration of Communist Successor Parties in East Central Europe after 1989*. Cambridge: Cambridge University Press, 2002.

Gundare, Ieva. 'Overcoming the Legacy of History for Ethnic Integration in Latvia.' *Intermarium*. 5/3 (2003). Available from http://www.columbia.edu/cu/sipa/REGIONAL/ECE/vol5no3/latvia.pdf. Accessed 14 July 2009.

Gurian, Elaine Heumann. *Civilizing the Museum: The Collected Writings of Elaine Heumann Gurian*. London: Routledge, 2006.

Gussi, Alexandru. 'Décembre 1989: prémisses du débat sur le passé récent en Roumanie.' *Romanian Political Science Review*. 1 (2006): 115–34.
Gussi, Alexandru. Usages de passé et démocratization. Unpublished doctoral thesis. Institut d'Études Politiques de Paris, 2007.
Gyáni, Gábor. '1956 elfelejtésének régi-új mítosza.' *Élet és Irodalom*. 9 February 2001.
György, Péter. *Néma hagyomány. Kollektív felejtés és a kései múltértelmezés 1956 1989-ben*. Budapest: Magvető, 2000.
Gyulai, Attila. 'Egy Diszkurzív Stratégia Értelmében Felfogott Igazságról és Hazugságról.' *Politikatudományi Szemle*. 2 (2007): 105–24.
Halfin, Igal. *Terror in my Soul: Communist Autobiographies on Trial*. Cambridge, MA: Harvard University Press, 2003.
Hamilton, Paula, and Linda Shopes. 'Introduction: Building Partnerships between Oral History and Memory Studies.' In Paula Hamilton and Linda Shopes, eds. *Oral History and Public Memories*. Philadelphia: Temple University Press, 2008.
Hamilton, Paula, and Linda Shopes, eds. *Oral History and Public Memories*. Philadelphia: Temple University Press, 2008.
Hanley, Eric. 'A Party of Workers or a Party of Intellectuals? Recruitment into Eastern European Communist Parties 1945–1988.' *Social Forces*. 81/4 (2003): 1073–106.
Harris, Ruth. 'The "Child of the Barbarian": Rape, Race and Nationalism during the First World War.' *Past and Present* 141 (1993): 170–206.
Heineman, Elizabeth. 'The Hour of the Woman: Memories of Germany's "Crisis Years" and West German National Identity.' *American Historical Review*, 101/2 (1996), 354–95.
Heineman, Elizabeth. 'Gender, Sexuality, and Coming to Terms with the Nazi Past.' *Central European History*. 38/1 (2005): 41–74.
Hellbeck, Jochen. 'Fashioning the Stalinist Soul: The Diary of Stepan Podlubnyi.' In Sheila Fitzpatrick, ed. *Stalinism: New Directions*. London: Routledge, 2000.
Hellbeck, Jochen. *Revolution on my Mind: Writing a Diary under Stalin*. Cambridge, MA: Harvard University Press, 2006.
Hellbeck, Jochen. 'Galaxy of Black Stars: The Power of Soviet Biography.' *American Historical Review*. 115 (2009): 615–24.
Herf, Jeffrey. *Divided Memory: The Nazi Past in the Two Germanys*. Cambridge, MA: Harvard University Press, 1997.
Hochschild, Adam. *The Unquiet Ghost: Russians Remember Stalin*. London: Serpent's Tail, 1995.
Hodgkin, Katharine, and Susannah Radstone, eds. *Contested Pasts: The Politics of Memory*. London: Routledge, 2003.
Horn, Gerd-Rainer, and Padraic Kenney, eds. *Transnational Moments of Change: Europe 1945, 1968, 1989*. Lanham, MD: Rowman & Littlefield, 2004.
Horn, Gyula. 'Miért lett pártvezér? Mezei András beszélgetése dr. Horn Gyulával I.' *Élet és Irodalom*. 17 May 1991: 7.
Horne, Cynthia M. 'Late Lustration Programmes in Romania and Poland: Supporting or Undermining Democratic Transitions?' *Democratization*. 16/2 (2009): 344–76.
Horváth, Sándor, ed. *Mindennapok Rákosi és Kádár Korában*. Budapest: Nyitott Könyvműhely, 2008.
Horváth, Zsolt K. 'The Redistribution of the Memory of Socialism: Identity Formations of the "Survivors" in Hungary after 1989.' In Oksana Sarkisova and Péter Apor, ed. *Past for the Eyes: East European Representations of Communism in Cinema and Museums after 1989*. Budapest: CEU Press, 2008.
Hosking, Geoffrey. 'The Second World War and Russian National Consciousness.' *Past and Present*. 175/1 (2002): 162–87.
Hughes, Rachel. 'The Abject Artefacts of Memory: Photographs from Cambodia's Genocide.' *Media, Culture and Society*. 25/3 (2003): 23–44.
Humlebaek, Carsten Jacob. 'Political Uses of the Recent Past in Spanish Post-Authoritarian Democracy.' In Max Paul Friedman and Padraic Kenney, eds. *Partisan Histories: The Past in Contemporary Global Politics*. New York: Palgrave Macmillan, 2005.
Humphrey, Caroline. *The Unmaking of Soviet Life: Everyday Economies after Socialism*. Ithaca: Cornell University Press, 2002.

Humphrey, Michael. 'From Victim to Victimhood: Truth Commissions and Trials as Rituals of Political Transition and Individual Healing.' *The Australian Journal of Anthropology.* 14/2 (2003): 171–87.

Humphrey, Robin, Robert Miller and Elena Zdravomyslova, eds. *Biographical Research in Eastern Europe: Altered Lives and Broken Biographies.* Aldershot: Ashgate, 2003.

Iliescu, Ion, and Vladimir Tismăneanu. *Communism, Post-Communism and Democracy: The Great Shock at the End of a Short Century.* Boulder: East European Monographs, 2006.

Institute of National Remembrance Annual Report 2003. Available from http://www.ipn.gov.pl/wai/en/22/55/Groups_of_Archival_Documents.html. Accessed 7 July 2009.

Ittzés, Gábor. 'Ritual and National Self-Interpretation: The Nagy Imre Funeral.' *Religion and Society in Central and Eastern Europe.* 1 (2005): 1–19.

Jackson, Michael W. *Fallen Sparrows: The International Brigades in the Spanish Civil War.* Philadelphia: American Philosophical Society, 1994.

Jacobs, J. H. 'Narrating the Island: Robben Island in South African Literature.' *Current Writing.* 4 (1992): 73–84.

Jakubowicz, Karol, and Miklós Sükösd, eds. *Finding the Right Place on the Map: Central and Eastern European Media Change in a Global Perspective.* Bristol: Intellect, 2008.

James, Beverly A. *Imagining Postcommunism: Visual Narratives of Hungary's 1956 Revolution.* College Station: Texas A&M University Press, 2005.

Jankauskas, Rimantas, et al. 'Forensic Archaeology in Lithuania: The Tuskulénai Mass Grave.' *Acta Medica Lituanica.* 12/1 (2005): 70–74. Available from http://images.katalogas.lt/maleidykla/Act51/ActM_070_074.pdf. Accessed 15 July 2009.

Jarausch, Konrad H. 'The Failure of East German Antifascism: Some Ironies of History as Politics.' *German Studies Review.* 14/1 (1991): 85–102.

Jarausch, Konrad H., ed. *After Unity: Reconfiguring German Identities.* Oxford: Berghahn, 1997.

Jaraush, Konrad H. 'Critical Memory and Civil Society: The Impact of the 1960s on German Debates about the Past.' In Philipp Gassert and Alan E. Steinweis, eds. *Coping with the Nazi Past: West German Debates on Nazism and Generational Conflict, 1955–1975.* Oxford: Berghahn Books, 2006.

Jarausch, Konrad H., and Thomas Lindenberger, eds. *Conflicted Memories: Europeanizing Contemporary Histories.* New York and Oxford: Berghahn Books, 2007.

Jarausch, Konrad H., Hinrich C. Seeba and David P. Conradt. 'The Presence of the Past: Culture, Opinion and Identity in Germany.' In Konrad H. Jarausch, ed. *After Unity: Reconfiguring German Identities.* Oxford: Berghahn, 1997.

Joerges, Christian, Matthias Mahlmann and Ulrich K. Preuß, eds. *'Schmerzliche Erfahrungen der Vergangenheit' und der Prozess der Konstitutionalisierung Europas.* Wiesbaden: VS-Verlag, 2008.

Juhl, Kirsten. *The Contribution by ('Forensic') Archaeologists to Human Rights Investigations of Mass Graves.* Stavanger: Arkeologisk museum i Stavanger, 2005.

Kaczyński, Jarosław. 'Democrats Cannot Be Tolerant to Communism.' Speech at the Institute of National Remembrance. 21 February 2007.

Kaiserová, Kristina, and Gert Röhrborn, eds. *Present Tensions: European Writers on Overcoming Dictatorships.* Budapest: CEU Press, 2009.

Kamp, Marianne. 'Soviet and Uzbek on the Collective Farm.' In Julia Obertreis and Anke Stephan, eds. *Remembering After the Fall of Communism: Oral History and (Post-)Socialist Societies.* Essen: Klartext, 2009.

Kangilaski, Jaak, et al. *The White Book. Losses Inflicted on the Estonian Nation by Occupation Regimes 1940–1991.* Ed. Vello Salo et al. Trans. Mari Ets et al. Tallinn: Estonian Encyclopaedia Publishers, 2005.

Kaplan, Karel. *Československo v poválečné Evropě.* Prague: Univerzita Karlova v Praze, Nakladatelství Karolinum, 2004.

Karlsson, Klas-Göran. 'The Holocaust and Russian Historical Culture.' In Klas-Göran Karlsson and Ulf Zander, eds. *Echoes of the Holocaust: Historical Cultures in Contemporary Europe.* Lund: Nordic Academic Press, 2003.

Karlsson, Klas-Göran, and Ulf Zander, eds. *Echoes of the Holocaust: Historical Cultures in Contemporary Europe.* Lund: Nordic Academic Press, 2003.

Kattago, Siobhan. 'Agreeing to Disagree on the Legacies of Recent History. Memory, Pluralism and Europe after 1989.' *European Journal of Social Theory.* 12/3 (2009): 375–95.

Kavčič, Silvija. 'Etablierung eines Erzählmusters.' In Julia Obertreis and Anke Stephan, eds. *Remembering after the Fall of Communism: Oral History and (Post-)Socialist Societies*. Essen: Klartext, 2009.

Kennedy, Michael D. 'Power, Privilege and Ideology in Communism's Negotiated Collapse.' In Donna Parmelee, ed. *Communism's Negotiated Collapse: The Polish Round Table, Ten Years Later. A Conference at the University of Michigan. April 7–10, 1999*. Trans. Kasia Kietlinska. Ann Arbor: The University of Michigan Center for Russian and East European Studies, 1999. Available from http://www.umich.edu/~iinet/PolishRoundTable/pdf/kennedy. pdf. Accessed 3 July 2009.

Kennedy, Michael D. *Cultural Formations of Post-Communism: Emancipation, Transition, Nation and War*. Minneapolis: University of Minnesota Press, 2002.

Kennedy, Michael D. 'The Cultural Politics of Military Alliances and Energy Security.' Paper presented at the University of Michigan, Ann Arbor, 23 September 2005. Available from http://www.maxwell.syr.edu/moynihan/programs/ces/pcconfpdfs/Kennedy.pdf. Accessed 14 July 2009.

Khapaeva, Dina. 'History without Memory: Gothic Morality in Post-Soviet Society.' *Eurozine*. 20 February 2002. Available from http://www.eurozine.com/articles/2009-02-02-khapaeva-en.html. Accessed 23 July 2009.

Khapaeva, Dina. 'Historical Memory in Post-Soviet Gothic Society.' *Social Research: An International Quarterly of Social Sciences*. 76/1 (2009): 359–94.

Khazanov, Anatoly M. 'Whom to Mourn and Whom to Forget? (Re)constructing Collective Memory in Contemporary Russia.' *Totalitarian Movements and Political Religions*. 9/2–3 (2008): 293–310.

Kirss, Tiina, Ene Kõresaar and Marju Lauristin, eds. *She Who Remembers Survives: Interpreting Estonian Women's Post-Soviet Life Stories*. Tartu: Tartu University Press, 2004.

Kiss, Csilla. 'From Liberalism to Conservatism: The Federation of Young Democrats in Post-Communist Hungary.' *East European Politics and Societies*. 16/3 (2002): 739–63.

Kiss, Csilla. 'The Misuses of Manipulation: The Failure of Transitional Justice in Post-Communist Hungary.' *Europe-Asia Studies*. 58/6 (2006): 925–40.

Kiss, Csilla. 'The (Re)Construction of Post-Communist Memory.' In Ene Kõresaar, Epp Lauk and Kristin Kuutma, eds. *The Burden of Remembering: Recollections and Representations of the Twentieth Century*. Helsinki: SKS Kirjat, 2009.

Klumbyte, Neringa. 'Ethnographic Note on Nation: Narratives and Symbols of the Early Post-Socialist Nationalism in Lithuania.' *Dialectical Anthropology*. 27/3–4 (2003): 279–95.

Knigge, Volkhard, and Ulrich Mählert, eds. *Der Kommunismus im Museum: Formen der Auseinandersetzung in Deutschland und Ostmitteleuropa*. Cologne: Böhlau, 2005.

Koczanowicz, Leszek. 'Memory of Politics and Politics of Memory: Reflections on the Construction of the Past in Post-Totalitarian Poland.' *Studies in East European Thought*. 49/4 (1997): 259–70.

Kohout, Pavel. *From the Diary of a Counterrevolutionary*. New York: McGraw-Hill, 1972.

Koleva, Daniela. ' "Socialist Individualism": Modernization and the Biographical Self.' In Daniela Koleva, ed. *Talking History: Proceedings of the International Oral History Conference, 23–27 September 1999*. Kiten: LIK, 2000.

Koleva, Daniela, ed. *Talking History: Proceedings of the International Oral History Conference, 23–27 September 1999*. Kiten: LIK, 2000.

Koleva, Daniela. 'Between Testimony and Power: Autobiographies in Socialist Bulgaria.' Paper presented at the 'Texts of Testimony: Autobiography, Life-Story Narratives and the Public Sphere' conference. John Moores University, Liverpool, 23–25 August 2001.

Koleva, Daniela. 'What Do You Remember of 9th September 1944? Remembering Communism: Official and Unofficial Discourses.' *Echinox Notebooks*. 1 (2001): 140–46.

Koleva, Daniela. 'Memories of the War and the War of Memories in Post-Communist Bulgaria.' *Oral History*. 34/2 (2006): 44–55.

Koleva, Daniela. 'Histoire orale et Mémoire du communisme.' *Divinatio*. 27 (2008): 211–25.

Koleva, Daniela. 'Histoire orale et micro-histoire: Un cas de Béléné, Bulgarie.' *Divinatio*. 29 (2009): 59–74.

Koleva, Daniela. 'The Colour of Memory: Doing Oral History in Post-Socialist Settings.' In Julia Obertreis and Anke Stephan, eds. *Remembering after the Fall of Communism: Oral History and (Post-)Socialist Societies*. Essen: Klartext Verlag, 2009.

Kopeček, Michal. 'In Search of "National Memory": The Politics of History, Nostalgia and the Historiography of Communism in the Czech Republic and East Central Europe.' In Michal Kopeček, ed. *Past in the Making. Historical Revisionism in Central Europe after 1989*. Budapest: CEU Press, 2008.

Kopeček, Michal, ed. *Past in the Making: Historical Revisionism in Central Europe after 1989*. Budapest: CEU Press, 2008.

Kopelev, Lev. *No Jail for Thought*. London: Secker and Warburg, 1977.

Koranyi, James. Between East and West: Romanian German Identities since 1945. Unpublished Doctoral Thesis. University of Exeter, 2008.

Kõresaar, Ene, Epp Lauk and Kristin Kuutma, eds. *The Burden of Remembering: Recollections and Representations of the Twentieth Century*. Helsinki: SKS Kirjat, 2009.

Kőrösi, Zsuzsanna, and Adrienne Molnár. *Carrying a Secret in my Heart: Children of the Victims of the Reprisals after the Hungarian Revolution in 1956: An Oral History*. Budapest: CEU Press, 2003.

Kovačević, Nataša. 'History on Speed: Media and the Politics of Forgetting in Milan Kundera's *Slowness*.' *Modern Fiction Studies*. 52/3 (2006): 634–55.

Kovačević, Nataša. *Narrating Post/Communism: Colonial Discourse and Europe's Borderline Civilization*. London: Routledge, 2008.

Kovács, Mária. M., and Antal Örkény. 'Promoted Cadres and Professionals in Post-War Hungary.' In Rudolf Andorka and László Bertalan, eds. *Economy and Society in Hungary*. Budapest: Karl Marx University of Economic Sciences, 1986.

Krammer, Arnold. 'The Cult of the Spanish Civil War in East Germany.' *Journal of Contemporary History*. 39/4 (2004): 531–60.

Krebs, Paula M. 'The Last of the "Gentlemen's Wars": Women in the Boer War Concentration Camp Controversy.' *History Workshop Journal*. 33/1 (1992): 38–56.

Kubik, Jan. *The Power of Symbols against the Symbols of Power: The Rise of Solidarity and the Fall of State Socialism in Poland*. University Park: Pennsylvania State University Press, 1994.

Kubik, Jan, and Amy Lynch. 'The Original Sin of Poland's Third Republic: Discounting "Solidarity" and its Consequences for Political Reconciliation.' *Polish Sociological Review*. 153 (2006): 9–38.

Kuljić, Todor. 'The New (Changed) Past as Value Factor of Development.' *Sociologija*. 48/3 (2006): 219–30.

Kundani, Hans. *Utopia or Auschwitz: Germany's 1968 Generation and the Holocaust*. London: Hurst, 2009.

Kundera, Milan. *Slowness*. New York: HarperCollins Publishers, 1997.

Kurczewski, Jacek. 'The Spoiled Drama of Emancipation: Conflicting Narratives.' *Polish Sociological Review* 4/168 (2009): 547–54.

Kuron, Jacek. 'Overcoming Totalitarianism.' In Vladimir Tismăneanu, ed. *The Revolutions of 1989*. London: Routledge, 1999.

Kuwert, Philipp, and Harald Jürgen Freyberger. 'The Unspoken Secret: Sexual Violence in World War II.' *International Psychogeriatrics*. 19/4 (2007): 782–84.

Kwaśniewski, Aleksander. 'Documents on Democracy.' *Journal of Democracy*. 16/4 (2005): 182–85.

Lacey, Kim Rogers, Selma Leydesdorff and Graham Dawson, eds. *Trauma and Life Stories: International Perspectives*. London: Routledge, 1999.

Laczó, Ferenc. 'The Many Moralists and the Few Communists: Approaching Morality and Politics in Post-Communist Hungary.' In Michal Kopeček, ed. *Past in the Making: Historical Revisionism in Central Europe after 1989*. Budapest: CEU Press, 2008.

Laignel-Lavastine, Alexandra. 'Fascism and Communism in Romania: The Comparative Stakes and Uses.' In Henry Rousso, ed. *Stalinism and Nazism: History and Memory Compared*. Lincoln: University of Nebraska Press, 1999.

Lankauskas, Gediminas. 'Sensuous (Re)Collections: The Sight and Taste of Socialism at Grūtas Statue Park, Lithuania.' *Senses and Society*. 1/1 (2006): 27–52.

Lee, Ching Kwan, and Guobin Yang. 'Introduction: Memory, Power and Culture.' In Ching Kwan Lee and Guobin Yang, eds. *Re-envisioning the Chinese Revolution: The Politics and Poetics of Collective Memories in Reform China*. Stanford: Stanford University Press, 2007.

Lee, Ching Kwan, and Guobin Yang, eds. *Re-envisioning the Chinese Revolution: The Politics and Poetics of Collective Memories in Reform China*. Stanford: Stanford University Press, 2007.

Leggewie, Claus. 'A Tour of the Battleground: The Seven Circles of Pan-European Memory.' *Social Research: An International Quarterly of Social Sciences*. 75/1 (2008): 217–34.

Lehti, Marko, Matti Jutila and Markku Jokisipilä. 'Never-Ending Second World War: Public Performances of National Dignity and the Drama of the Bronze Soldier.' *Journal of Baltic Studies*. 39/4 (2008): 393–418.

Leoussi, Athena S. 'National Symbols: Ethnicity and Historical Continuity in Post-Communist "New Europe".' In Steven Elliot Grosby and Athena S. Leoussi, eds. *Nationalism and Ethnosymbolism: History, Culture and Ethnicity in the Formation of Nations*. Edinburgh: Edinburgh University Press, 2007.

Levin, Dov. 'Lithuania.' In David S. Wyman and Charles H. Rosenzveig, eds. *The World Reacts to the Holocaust*. Baltimore: Johns Hopkins University Press, 1996.

Levy, Alan. *So Many Heroes*. Sagaponack: Second Chance Press, 1980.

Levy, Daniel, and Natan Sznaider. *The Holocaust and Memory in the Global Age*. Philadelphia: Temple University Press, 2006.

Light, Duncan. 'An Unwanted Past: Contemporary Tourism and the Heritage of Communism in Romania.' *International Journal of Heritage Studies*. 6/2 (2000): 145–60.

Liljeström, Marianne. 'Success Stories from the Margins: Soviet Women's Autobiographical Sketches from the Late Soviet Period.' In Daniel Bertaux, Paul Thompson and Anna Rotkirch, eds. *On Living Through Soviet Russia*, London and New York: Routledge, 2004.

Litván, György, ed. *The Hungarian Revolution of 1956: Reform, Revolution, Repression, 1953–1963*. Harlow: Longman, 1996.

Litván, György. 'Politikai Beszéd 1956-rólx 1989 után.' In Rainer M. János and Éva Standeisky, eds. *Évkönyv 2002: Magyarország a Jelenkorban*. Budapest: 1956-os Intézet, 2002.

Loose, Ingo. 'The Antifascist Myth of the German Democratic Republic and its Decline after 1989.' In Michal Kopeček, ed. *Past in the Making: Historical Revisionism in Central Europe after 1989*. Budapest: CEU Press, 2008.

Lucian, Kim. 'Budapest Revisits its Recent Horrors.' *Boston Globe*. 6 April 2003.

Lüdtke, Alf. ' "Coming to Terms with the Past". Illusions of Remembering, Ways of Forgetting Nazism in West Germany.' *Journal of Modern History*. 65/3 (1993): 542–72.

Machcewicz, Paweł. 'The Institute of National Remembrance and Coming to Terms with a Difficult Past: World War II and the Communist Dictatorship.' *InterMarium*. 8/3 (2006): 1–10.

Machcewicz, Paweł. 'Polityka historyczna to nic nowego.' *Gazeta Wyborcza*. 20 April 2006.

Main, Izabella. 'Memory and History in the Cityscapes in Poland: The Search for Meaning.' In Deanna Gard et al., eds. *Inquiries into Past and Present*. Vienna: IWM Junior Visiting Fellows' Conferences. 17 (2005). Available from http://www.iwm.at/index.php?option=com _content&task=view&id=301&Itemid=276. Accessed 3 July 2009.

Malia, Martin. 'Foreword: The Uses of Atrocity.' In Courtois, Stéphane et al., eds. *The Black Book of Communism: Crimes, Terror, Repression*. Trans. Jonathan Murphy. Cambridge, MA: Harvard University Press, 1999.

Mälksoo, Maria. 'The Discourse of Communist Crimes in the European Memory Politics of World War II.' Paper presented at the 'Ideology and Discourse Analysis' conference. Roskilde University, Denmark, 22 October 2008.

Mälksoo, Maria. 'The Memory Politics of Becoming European: The East European Subalterns and the Collective Memory of Europe.' *European Journal of International Relations*. 15/4 (2009): 653–80.

Mälksoo, Maria, *The Politics of becoming European: a study of Polish and Baltic post-Cold War security imaginaries*. London and New York: Routledge, 2010.

Mandell, Ruth, and Caroline Humphrey, eds. *Markets and Moralities: Ethnographies of Postsocialism*. Oxford: Berg, 2002.

Mark, James. 'Remembering Rape: Divided Social Memory and the Red Army in Hungary 1944–1945.' *Past and Present*. 188 (2005): 133–61.

Mark, James. 'Society, Resistance and Revolution: The Budapest Middle Class and the Hungarian Communist State 1948–56.' *The English Historical Review*. 120/488 (2005): 963–86.

Mark, James. 'Discrimination, Opportunity and Middle-Class Success in Early Communist Hungary.' *Historical Journal*. 48/2 (2005): 499–521.

Mark, James. 'Antifascism, the 1956 Revolution and the Politics of Communist Autobiographies in Hungary 1944–2000.' *Europe-Asia Studies*. 58/8 (2006): 1209–40.

Mark, James. 'Containing Fascism: History in Post-Communist Baltic Occupation and Genocide Museums.' In Oksana Sarkisova and Péter Apor, eds. *Past for the Eyes: East European representations of Communism in cinema and museums after 1989*. Budapest: CEU Press, 2008.

Markovits, Inga. 'Selective Memory: How the Law Affects What We Remember and Forget about the Past – the Case of East Germany.' *Law and Society Review*. 35/3 (2001): 513–63.

Mátay, Mónika, and Ildikó Kaposi. 'Radicals Online: The Hungarian Street Protests of 2006 and the Internet.' In Karol Jakubowicz and Miklós Sükösd, eds. *Finding the Right Place on the Map: Central and Eastern European Media Change in a Global Perspective*. Bristol: Intellect, 2008.

Mayer, Françoise. *Les Tchèques et leur communisme: mémoire et identités politiques*. Paris: Éditions de l'École des Hautes Études en Sciences Sociales, 2004.

Mayer-Rieckh, Alexander, and Pablo de Greiff, eds. *Justice as Prevention: Vetting Public Employees in Transitional Societies*. New York: Social Science Research Council, 2007.

McAdams, A. James. *Judging the Past in Unified Germany*. Cambridge and New York: Cambridge University Press, 2001.

McLellan, Josie. *Antifascism and Memory in East Germany: Remembering the International Brigades, 1945–1989*. Oxford: Clarendon Press, 2004.

McMullin, Darcy, and Jacquelyn W. White. 'Long-Term Effects of Labelling a Rape Experience.' *Psychology of Women Quarterly*. 30/1 (2006): 96–105.

Melegh, Atilla. *On the East-West Slope: Globalization, Nationalism, Racism and Discourses on Central and Eastern Europe*. Budapest: CEU Press, 2006.

Merridale, Catherine. 'Culture, Ideology and Combat in the Red Army.' *Journal of Contemporary History*. 41/2 (2006): 305–24.

Merridale, Catherine. 'Redesigning History in Contemporary Russia.' *Journal of Contemporary History*. 38/1 (2003): 13–28.

Merridale, Catherine. *Night of Stone: Death and Memory in Russia*. London: Granta, 2000.

Merridale, Catherine. *Ivan's War: The Red Army 1939–45*. London: Faber and Faber, 2005.

Mevius, Martin. *Agents of Moscow: The Hungarian Communist Party and the Origins of Socialist Patriotism, 1941–1953*. Oxford: Clarendon Press, 2005.

Michel, Gundega, and Valters Nollendorfs. 'Das Lettische Okkupationsmuseum, Riga.' In Volkhard Knigge and Ulrich Mählert, eds. *Der Kommunismus im Museum: Formen der Auseinandersetzung in Deutschland und Ostmitteleuropa*. Cologne: Böhlau, 2005.

Michnik, Adam. *Letters from Freedom: Post-Cold War Realities and Perspectives*. Berkeley: University of California Press, 1998.

Michnik, Adam. 'The Velvet Restoration.' In Vladimir Tismăneanu, ed. *The Revolutions of 1989*. London: Routledge, 1999.

Michnik, Adam. 'Mantra: Rather than Discourse.' *Common Knowledge*. 8/3 (2002): 516–25.

Miller, Barbara. *Narratives of Guilt and Compliance in Unified Germany: Stasi Informers and their Impact on Society*. London: Routledge, 2002.

Miller, John J. 'A Goddess for Victims.' *National Review Online*. 28 May 2007. Available from http://nrd.nationalreview.com/article/?q=YWNiODY4Y2FmNTM3YTI0YjhlYTc4ZGY0ZjE4 ZDIyNDQ=. Accessed 27 July 2009.

Mink, András. 'The Kádár of History.' *Budapest Review of Books*. 2001: 37–47.

Mink, András. 'The Revisions of the 1956 Hungarian Revolution.' In Michal Kopeček, ed. *Past in the Making: Historical Revisionism in Central Europe after 1989*. Budapest: CEU Press, 2008.

Mink, Georges, and Laure Neumayer, eds. *L'Europe et ses passés douloureux*. Paris: La Découverte, 2007.

Mironov, Boris, and Dina Khapaeva. 'Historical Memory in Post-Soviet Gothic Society.' *Social Research: An International Quarterly of Social Sciences*. 76/1 (2009): 359–94.

Misiunas, Romuald J. 'Soviet Historiography on World War II and the Baltic States, 1944–1974.' In V. Stanley Vardys and Romuald J. Misiunas, eds. *The Baltic States in Peace and War 1917–1945*. University Park: Pennsylvania State University Press, 1978.

Misztal, Barbara A. *Theories of Social Remembering*. Maidenhead: Open University Press, 2003.

Moeller, Robert G. *War Stories: The Search for a Usable Past in the Federal Republic of Germany*. Berkeley, CA and London: University of California Press, 2003.

Moon, Claire. *Narrating Political Reconciliation: South Africa's Truth and Reconciliation Commission*. Lanham, MD: Lexington Books, 2008.

Moore, Alison M. 'Photography of the Tondues: Visuality of the Vichy Past through the Silent Image of Women.' *Gender and History*. 17/3 (2005): 657–81.

Moses, A. Dirk. 'Stigma and Sacrifice in the Federal Republic of Germany.' *History and Memory*. 19/2 (2007): 139–80.

Moses, A. Dirk. *German Intellectuals and the Nazi Past*. Cambridge: Cambridge University Press, 2007.

Mouton, Michelle, and Helena Pohlandt-McCormick. 'Boundary Crossings: Oral History of Nazi Germany and Apartheid South Africa – a Comparative Perspective.' *History Workshop Journal*. 48 (1999): 41–63.

Müller, Jan-Werner. *Constitutional Patriotism*. Princeton, NJ: Princeton University Press, 2007.

Myers, Steven Lee. 'Estonia Sparks Outrage in Russia.' *International Herald Tribune*. 24 January 2007.

Nadkarni, Maya. 'The Death of Socialism and the Afterlife of its Monuments: Making and Marketing the Past in Budapest's Statue Park Museum.' In Katharine Hodgkin and Susannah Radstone, eds. *Contested Pasts: The Politics of Memory*. London: Routledge, 2003.

Nagy, Ferenc. *Struggle behind the Iron Curtain*. Trans. Stephen K. Swift. New York: Macmillan Company, 1948.

Naimark, Norman M. *The Russians in Germany: A History of the Soviet Zone of Occupation, 1945–1949*. Cambridge, MA and London: Belknap Press of Harvard University Press, 1995.

Nasson, Bill. 'Commemorating the Anglo-Boer War in Post-Apartheid South Africa.' In Daniel J. Walkowitz and Lisa Maya Knauer, eds. *Memory and the Impact of Political Transformation in Public Space*. Durham, NC: Duke University Press, 2004.

Niethammer, Lutz. 'Biographie und Biokratie: Nachdenken zu einem Westdeutschen Oral History-Projekt in der DDR Fünf Jahre nach der Deutschen Vereinigung.' Paper presented at the 'International Oral History' conference. São Paulo, 1995.

Niethammer, Lutz. 'Biographie und Biokratie.' *Mitteilungen aus der Kulturwissenschaftlichen Forschung*. 37 (1997): 370–87.

Niethammer, Lutz. 'Biographie und Biokratie: Rückblick auf eine Sondierung in der DDR fünf Jahre nach ihrem Ende.' In Lutz Niethammer, ed. *Fragen an das deutsche Gedächtnis: Aufsätze zur Oral History*. Essen: Klartext, 2007.

Niethammer, Lutz, ed. *Fragen an das Deutsche Gedächtnis: Aufsätze zur Oral History*. Essen: Klartext, 2007.

Niethammer, Lutz, Alexander von Plato and Dorothee Wierling. *Die Volkseigene Erfahrung: Eine Archäologie des Lebens in der Industrieprovinz der DDR: 30 Biographische Eröffnungen*. Berlin: Rowohlt, 1991.

Niven, Bill. *Facing the Nazi Past: United Germany and the Legacy of the Third Reich*. London: Routledge, 2001.

Niven, Bill, ed. *Germans as Victims: Remembering the Past in Contemporary Germany*. Basingstoke: Palgrave Macmillan, 2006.

Nolan, Mary. 'Antifascism under Fascism: German Visions and Voices.' *New German Critique*. 67 (1996): 33–55.

Nyyssönen, Heino. *The Presence of the Past in Politics: '1956' after 1956 in Hungary*. Jyväskylä: SoPhi, 1999.

Nyyssönen, Heino. 'History in the First Parliament; The Politics of Memory in Hungary 1990–1994.' *Hungarologische Beiträge*. 14 (2002): 163–89.

Oberländer, Erwin, and Valters Nollendorfs, eds. *The Hidden and Forbidden History of Latvia under Soviet and Nazi Occupations 1940–1991*. Riga: Institute of the History of Latvia, 2005.

Obertreis, Julia. 'Memory, Identity and Facts: The Methodology of Oral History and Researching (Post-)Socialist Societies.' In Julia Obertreis and Anke Stephan, eds. *Remembering after the Fall of Communism: Oral History and (Post-)Socialist Societies*. Essen: Klartext Verlag, 2009.

Obertreis, Julia, and Anke Stephan, eds. *Remembering after the Fall of Communism: Oral History and (Post-)Socialist Societies*. Essen: Klartext Verlag, 2009.

Ochman, Ewa. 'Municipalities and the Search for the Local Past: Fragmented Memory of the Red Army in Upper Silesia.' *East European Politics and Societies*. 23/3 (2009): 392–420.

Okey, Robin. 'Central Europe/Eastern Europe: Behind the Definitions.' *Past and Present*. 137/1 (1992): 102–33.

Okey, Robin. *The Demise of Communist East Europe: 1989 in Context*. London: Arnold, 2004.

Olick, Jeffrey K. *The Politics of Regret: On Collective Memory and Historical Responsibility*. London and New York: Routledge, 2007.

Olivier, Laurent. 'The Archaeology of the Contemporary Past.' In Victor Buchli and Gavin Lucas, eds. *Archaeologies of the Contemporary Past*. London and New York: Routledge, 2001.

Onken, Eva-Clarita. 'The Baltic States and Moscow's 9 May Commemoration: Analysing Memory Politics in Europe.' *Europe-Asia Studies*. 59/1 (2007): 23–46.

Onken, Eva-Clarita. 'The Politics of Finding Historical Truth: Reviewing Baltic History Commissions and their Work.' *Europe-Asia Studies*. 38/1 (2007): 109–16.

Orbán, Viktor, Speech at the House of Terror. 31 October 2007. Available from http://www.orbanviktor.hu/in_english_article/commemoration_of_the_1956_revolution. Accessed 20 May 2010.

Orme, Alexandra. *From Christmas to Easter: A Guide to the Russian Occupation*. Trans. M. A. Michael and L. Meyer. London: William Hodge and Company, 1949.

Osiel, Mark. *Mass Atrocity, Collective Memory, and the Law*. New Brunswick and London: Transaction, 1997.

Ost, David. 'Solidarity: 25 Years Later.' *Skalny Center for Polish and Central European Studies Newsletter*. Spring (2006): 1–2.

Ostow, Robin. '(Re)Visualizing Jewish History in Warsaw: The Privatization and Externalization of Nation Building.' In Robin Ostow, ed. *(Re)Visualizing National History: Museums and National Identities in Europe in the New Millennium*. Toronto and London: University of Toronto Press, 2008.

Ostow, Robin, ed. *(Re)Visualizing National History: Museums and National Identities in Europe in the New Millennium*. Toronto and London: University of Toronto Press, 2008.

Paczkowski, Andrzej. 'Communist Poland 1944–1989: Some Controversies and a Single Conclusion.' *Polish Review*. 44/2 (1999): 217–25.

Paert, Irina Krovushkina. 'Memory and Survival in Stalin's Russia: Old Believers in the Urals during the 1930s–50s.' In Daniel Bertaux, Paul Thompson and Anna Rotkirch, eds. *On Living Through Soviet Russia*, London and New York: Routledge, 2004.

Pakier, Małgorzata, and Bo Stråth, eds. *A European Memory? Contested Histories and Politics of Remembrance*. Oxford: Berghahn Books, 2010.

A Polgári Magyarországért. 'Két pogány közt egy hazáert.' A Fidesz Magyar Polgári Párt vitairata. Budapest: Fidesz Országos Elnöksége-Fidesz Központi Hivatal, 1996.

Palonen, Emilia. 'Political Polarisation and Populism in Contemporary Hungary.' *Parliamentary Affairs*. 62/2 (2009): 318–34.

Paperno, Irina. 'Personal Accounts of Soviet Experience.' *Kritika*. 3/4 (2002): 577–610.

Parmelee, Donna, ed. *Communism's Negotiated Collapse: The Polish Round Table, Ten Years Later. A Conference at the University of Michigan. April 7–10, 1999*. Trans. Kasia Kietlinska. Ann Arbor: The University of Michigan Center for Russian and East European Studies, 1999. Available from www.umich.edu/~iinet/PolishRoundTable/frame.html. Accessed 3 July 2009.

Passerini, Luisa. 'Oral Memory of Fascism.' In David Forgacs, ed. *Rethinking Italian Fascism: Capitalism, Populism and Culture*. London: Lawrence and Wishart, 1986.

Passerini, Luisa. *Fascism in Popular Memory: The Cultural Experience of the Turin Working Class*. Cambridge: Cambridge University Press, 1987.

Passerini, Luisa, ed. *Memory and Totalitarianism: International Yearbook of Oral History and Life Stories, Vol. 1*. Oxford: Oxford University Press, 1992.

Passerini, Luisa. 'Memories between Silence and Oblivion.' In Katherine Hodgkin and Susannah Radstone, eds. *Contested Pasts: The Politics of Memory*. London: Routledge, 2003.

Pearce, Susan C. 'The Polish Solidarity Movement in Retrospect: In Search of a Mnemonic Mirror.' *International Journal of Politics, Culture, and Society*. 22 (2009): 159–82.

Peifer, Douglas. 'Commemoration of Mutiny, Rebellion and Resistance in Post-War Germany: Public Memory, History and the Formation of "Memory Beacons".' *Journal of Military History*. 65/1 (2001): 1013–52.

Peikštenis, Eugenijus. 'Das Museum für die Opfer des Genozids, Vilnius.' In Volkhard Knigge and Ulrich Mählert, eds *Der Kommunismus im Museum: Formen der Auseinandersetzung in Deutschland und Ostmitteleuropa*. Cologne: Böhlau, 2005.

Péter, László. 'The Holy Crown of Hungary, Visible and Invisible.' *Slavonic and East European Review*. 81/3 (2003): 421–510.

Peterson, Zoe D., and Charlene L. Muehlenhard. 'Was It Rape? The Function of Women's Rape: Myth, Acceptance and Definitions of Sex in Labeling their Own Experiences.' *Sex Roles*. 51/3–4 (2004): 129–44.

Pető, Andrea. 'Átvonuló hadsereg, maradandó trauma: Az 1945-ös budapesti nemi erőszak esetek emlékezete.' *Történelmi Szemle*. 41/1–2 (1999): 85–107.

Pető, Andrea. 'Memory and the Narrative of Rape in Budapest and Vienna in 1945.' In Richard Bessel and Dirk Schumann, eds. *Life after Death: Approaches to a Cultural and Social History of Europe during the 1940s and the 1950s*. Cambridge: Cambridge University Press, 2003.

Petrescu, Cristina, and Dragoş Petrescu. 'Mastering vs. Coming to Terms with the Past: A Critical Analysis of Post-Communist Romanian Historiography.' In Sorin Antohi, Balázs Trencsényi and Péter Apor, eds. *Narratives Unbound: Historical Studies in Post-Communist Eastern Europe*. Budapest: CEU Press, 2007.

Petrescu, Dragoş. 'Dilemmas of Transitional Justice in Post-1989 Romania.' In Vladimíra Dvořáková and Anđelko Milardović, eds. *Lustration and Consolidation of Democracy and the Rule of Law in Central and Eastern Europe*. Zagreb: Political Science Research Centre, 2007.

Petrov, Gheorge, and Cosmin Budeancă. *Raport Privind Cercetările Arheologice Desfăşurate în Cimitirul Săracilor din Sighetu Marmaţiei*. Bucharest: Institute for the Investigation of Communist Crimes in Romania, 2006.

Pinkert, Anke. *Film and Memory in East Germany*. Bloomington, IN: Indiana University Press, 2008.

Polcz, Alaine. *A Wartime Memoir: Hungary 1944–1945*. Ed. and trans. Albert Tezla. Budapest: Corvina Books, 1998; *Asszony a fronton: egy fejezet életemből*. Budapest: Pont Kiadó, 2002.

Portelli, Alessandro. 'The Massacre at the Fosse Ardeatine.' In Katharine Hodgkin and Susannah Radstone, eds. *Contested Pasts: The Politics of Memory*, London: Routledge, 2003.

Portelli, Alessandro. *The Order Has Been Carried Out*. Basingstoke: Palgrave Macmillan, 2007.

Proebst, Lothar. 'Founding Myths of Europe and the Role of the Holocaust.' *New German Critique*. 90 (2003): 45–58.

Rabinbach, Anson. 'Introduction: Legacies of Antifascism.' *New German Critique*. 67 (1996): 3–18.

Radstone, Susannah. 'Re-conceiving Binaries: The Limits of Memory.' *History Workshop Journal*. 59 (2005): 134–50.

Radstone, Susannah, and Katharine Hodgkin. 'Regimes of Memory: An Introduction.' In Susannah Radstone and Katharine Hodgkin, eds. *Memory Cultures: Memory, Subjectivity, and Recognition*. New Brunswick: Transaction Publishers, 2006.

Radstone, Susannah, and Katharine Hodgkin, eds. *Memory Cultures: Memory, Subjectivity, and Recognition*. New Brunswick: Transaction Publishers, 2006.

Rae, Gavin. 'Back to the Future: The Resurgence of Poland's Conservative Right.' *Debatte: Journal of Contemporary Central and Eastern Europe*. 15/2 (2007): 221–32.

Rainer, János M. *Ötvenhat Után*. Budapest: 1956-os Intézet, 2003.

Rainer, János M. 'Submerging or Clinging On Again: József Antall, Father and Son, in Hungary after 1956.' *Contemporary European History*. 14/1 (2005): 65–106.

Rainer, János M., and Éva Standeisky, eds. *Évkönyv 2002. Magyarország a Jelenkorban*. Budapest: 1956-os Intézet, 2002.

Rákosi, Sándor. 'Magyar Dolgozók Pártja.' In Tibor Erényi and Sándor Rákosi, eds. *Legyőzhetetlen erő. A magyar kommunista mozgalom szervezeti fejlődésének 50 éve*. Budapest: Kossuth Könyvkiadó, 1968.

Raleigh, Donald. *Russia's Sputnik Generation: Baby Boomers Talk about their Lives*. Bloomington: Indiana University Press, 2006.

Raoult, Didier, et al. 'Evidence for Louse-Transmitted Diseases in Soldiers of Napoleon's Grand Army in Vilnius.' *The Journal of Infectious Diseases*. 193/1 (2006): 112–20.

Rendle, Matthew. 'The Problems of "Becoming Soviet": Former Nobles in Soviet Society, 1917–41.' *European History Quarterly*. 38/7 (2008): 7–33.

Resina, Joan Ramon, ed. *Disremembering the Dictatorship: The Politics of Memory in the Spanish Transition to Democracy*. Amsterdam: Rodopi, 2000.

Rév, István. 'Parallel Autopsies.' *Representations*. 49 (1995): 15–39.

Rév, István. 'The Necronym.' *Representations*. 64 (1998): 76–108.

Rév, István. 'Counterrevolution.' In Sorin Antohi and Vladimir Tismăneanu, eds. *Between Past and Future: The Revolutions of 1989 and their Aftermath*. Budapest: CEU Press, 2000.

Rév, István. *Retroactive Justice: Prehistory of Post-Communism*. Stanford: Stanford University Press, 2005.

Rév, István. Untitled paper presented at the School of Slavonic and East European Studies, London, 8 June 2007.

Ripp, Zoltán. '1956 emlékezete és az MSZMP.' In János M. Rainer and Éva Standeisky, eds. *Évkönyv 2002. Magyarország A Jelenkorban*. Budapest: 1956-os Intézet, 2002.

Ripp, Zoltán. *Eltékozolt Esélyek: A rendszerváltás értelme és értelmezései.* Napvilág Kiadó: Budapest, 2009.

Rohdewald, Stefan. 'Post-Soviet Remembrance of the Holocaust and National Memories of the Second World War in Russia, Ukraine and Lithuania.' *Forum for Modern Language Studies.* 44/2 (2008): 173–84.

Rostotsky, Stanislav, dir. *At Dawn, It's Quiet Here.* 1972.

Rotkirch, Anna. *The Man Question: Loves and Lives in Late 20th Century Russia.* Helsinki: University of Helsinki Department of Social Policy Research Reports, 2000.

Rousso, Henry, ed. *Stalinism and Nazism: History and Memory Compared.* Lincoln: University of Nebraska Press, 1999.

Rousso, Henry. 'History of Memory, Policies of the Past.' In Konrad H. Jarausch and Thomas Lindenberger, eds. *Conflicted Memories: Europeanizing Contemporary Histories.* New York and Oxford: Berghahn Books, 2007.

Ryan, Michael, ed. *Body Politics: Disease, Desire, and the Family.* Boulder: Westview Press, 1994.

Sadurski, Wojciech. *Rights before Courts: A Study of Constitutional Courts in Post-Communist States of Central and Eastern Europe.* Dordrecht: Springer, 2005.

Sakwa, Richard. 'Myth and Democratic Identity in Russia.' In Alexander Wöll and Harald Wydra, eds. *Democracy and Myth in Russia and Eastern Europe.* London: Routledge, 2008.

Salamon, Konrád. 'A magyar dicsőséges forradalom 1989–1990.' *Magyar Fórum.* 24 March 1990.

Sander, Helke. dir. *Befreier und Befreite: Krieg, Vergewaltigungen, Kinder.* Germany: Bremer Institut Film, 1992.

Sarkisova, Oksana and Péter Apor, eds. *Past for the Eyes: East European Representations of Communism in Cinema and Museums after 1989.* Budapest: CEU Press, 2000.

Schipani-Adúriz, Andrés. 'Through an Orange-Colored Lens: Western Media, Constructed Imagery, and Color Revolutions.' *Demokratizatsiya: The Journal of Post-Soviet Democratization.* 15/4 (2007): 459–64.

Schmidt, Mária. 'Ne Hass, ne Alkoss, ne Gyarapíts! A Terror Háza Múzeum első éve.' In *Magyarország Politikai Évkönyve 2003 I–II.* Budapest: Demokrácia Kutatások Magyar Központja Közhasznú Alapítvány, 2003.

Schofield, John, William Gray Johnson and Colleen M. Beck, eds. *Matériel Culture: The Archaeology of Twentieth Century Conflict.* London: Routledge, 2002.

Schweizer, Kristen, and Tünde Kaposi. 'Monuments a Bust: Campaign in Hungary to Remove Old Soviet Statues Angers Russia.' *National Post.* 24 February 2007.

Scribner, Charity. *Requiem for Communism.* Cambridge, MA: MIT, 2003.

Seleny, Anna. 'Communism's Many Legacies in East-Central Europe.' *Journal of Democracy.* 18/3 (2007): 156–70.

Senn, Alfred Erich. 'Perestroika in Lithuanian Historiography: The Molotov-Ribbentrop Pact.' *Russian Review.* 49/1 (1990): 43–53.

Sherbakova, Irina. 'The Gulag in Memory.' In Luisa Passerini, ed. *Memory and Totalitarianism: International Yearbook of Oral History and Life Stories, Vol. 1.* Oxford: Oxford University Press, 1992.

Sherlock, Thomas. 'History and Myth in the Soviet Empire and the Russian Republic.' In Elizabeth A. Cole, ed. *Teaching the Violent Past: History Education and Reconciliation.* Lanham, MD: Rowman & Littlefield, 2007.

Siani-Davies, Peter. *The Romanian Revolution of December 1989.* Ithaca: Cornell University Press, 2005.

Simkus, Albert, and Rudolf Andorka. 'Inequalities in Educational Attainment in Hungary, 1923–1973.' *American Sociological Review.* 47 (1982): 740–51.

Sipos, Balázs. 'Szovjetbarát és Szovjetellenes Nyilas Propaganda 1939–1941.' *Múltunk.* 41 (1996): 107–32.

Slutsky, Boris. *Things That Happened.* Ed. and trans. G. S. Smith. Moscow: Glas, 1999.

Smith, Kathleen E. *Remembering Stalin's Victims: Popular Memory and the End of the USSR.* Ithaca: Cornell University Press, 1996.

Smith, Kathleen. *Myth-Making in the New Russia: Politics and Memory during the Yeltsin Era.* Ithaca: Cornell University Press, 2002.

Smolar, Aleksander, and Magdalena Potocka. 'History and Memory: The Revolutions of 1989–91.' *Journal of Democracy.* 12/3 (2001): 5–19.

Solidarity Electoral Action Declaration, June 8 1996.

Stan, Lavinia. 'Moral Cleansing, Romanian Style.' *Problems of Post-Communism*. 49/4 (2002): 52–62.
Stan, Lavinia. 'Truth Commissions in Post-Communism: The Overlooked Solution?' *The Open Political Science Journal*. 2 (2009): 1–13.
'Statement by Foreign Minister Ojuland Concerning the Lihula Monument.' 3 September 2004. Available from http://www.vm.ee/eng/kat_138/4791.html. Accessed 21 February 2007.
Steinlauf, Michael. *Bondage to the Dead: Poland and the Memory of the Holocaust*. Syracuse, NY: Syracuse University Press, 1997.
Stevick, E. Doyle. 'The Politics of the Holocaust in Estonia; Historical Memory and Social Divisions in Estonian Education.' In E. Doyle Stevick and Bradley A.U. Levinson, eds. *Reimagining Civic Education: How Diverse Societies Form Democratic Citizens*. Lanham, MD: Rowman & Littlefield, 2007.
Stevick, E. Doyle, and Bradley A.U. Levinson, eds. *Reimagining Civic Education: How Diverse Societies Form Democratic Citizens*. Lanham, MD: Rowman & Littlefield, 2007.
Stranga, Aivars. 'The Holocaust in Occupied Latvia: 1941–1945.' In Erwin Oberländer and Valters Nollendorfs, eds. *The Hidden and Forbidden History of Latvia under Soviet and Nazi Occupations 1940–1991*. Riga: Institute of the History of Latvia, 2005.
Strange, Carolyn, and Michael Kempa, eds. 'Shades of Dark Tourism: Alcatraz and Robben Island.' *Annals of Tourism Research* 30/2 (2003): 386–405.
Stråth, Bo, ed. *Myth and Memory in the Construction of Community: Historical Patterns in Europe and Beyond*. Brussels: Peter Lang, 2000.
Subotic, Małgorzata. 'How Kwaśniewski Won.' *Polish News Bulletin*. 27 November 1995.
Summerfield, Penny. 'Culture and Composure: Creating Narratives of the Gendered Self in Oral History Interviews.' *Cultural and Social History*. 1/1 (2004): 65–93.
Szacka, Barbara. ' "Solidarity" and the Martial Law in the Collective Memory of Polish History.' *Polish Sociological Review*. 153/1 (2006): 75–89.
Szelényi, Szonja. *Equality by Design: The Grand Experiment in Destratification in Socialist Hungary*. Stanford: Stanford University Press, 1998.
Szenes, Iván. *A Kommunista Párt újjászervezése Magyarországon 1956–1957*. Budapest: Kossuth Könyvkiadó, 1976.
Tănăsoiu, Cosmina. 'Intellectuals and Post-Communist Politics in Romania: An Analysis of Public Discourse, 1990–2000.' *East European Politics and Societies*. 22/1 (2008): 80–113.
Tapalagă, Dan. 'Raportul Tismăneanu, notat cu şapte.' *Ziua de Cluj*. 12 January 2007.
Taylor, Julie. 'Body Memories: Aide-Memoires and Collective Amnesia in the Wake of Argentine Terror.' In Michael Ryan, ed. *Body Politics: Disease, Desire, and the Family*. Boulder: Westview Press, 1994.
Temple, Mark. 'The Politicization of History: Marshal Antonescu and Romania.' *East European Politics and Societies*. 10/3 (1996): 457–503.
Tezla, Albert. 'Introduction.' In Alaine Polcz. *A Wartime Memoir: Hungary 1944–1945*. Ed. and trans. Albert Tezla. Budapest: Corvina Books, 1998.
Theweleit, Klaus. *Male Fantasies: Women, Floods, Bodies, History*. Cambridge: Polity, 1987.
Tileaga, Cristian. 'What Is a "Revolution"?: National Commemoration, Collective Memory and Managing Authenticity in the Representation of a Political Event.' *Discourse and Society*. 19/3 (2008): 359–82.
Tismăneanu, Vladimir. *Fantasies of Salvation: Post-Communist Political Mythologies*. Princeton, NJ: Princeton University Press, 1998.
Tismăneanu, Vladimir, ed. *The Revolutions of 1989*. London: Routledge, 1999.
Tismăneanu, Vladimir. 'Democracy and Memory: Romania Confronts its Communist Past.' *The Annals of the American Academy of Political and Social Science*. 617 (2008): 166–80.
Tismăneanu, Vladimir, Dorin Dobrincu and Cristian Vasile. *Comisia Prezidenţială pentru Analiza Dictaturii Comuniste din România, Raport Final*. Bucharest: Humanitas, 2006.
Todorova, Maria. *Imagining the Balkans*. Oxford and New York: Oxford University Press, 1997.
Todorova, Maria, ed. *Remembering Communism: Genres of Representation*. New York: Social Science Research Council, Columbia University Press, 2010.
Todorova, Maria and Zsuzsa Gille, eds. *Post-Communist Nostalgia*. New York and Oxford: Berghahn Books, 2010.
Torańska, Teresa. *Them: Stalin's Polish Puppets*. New York: Harper & Row, 1987.
Tracevskis, Rokas M. 'A Grave Fit for Whom?' *Transitions Online*. 3 October 2003. Available from http://www.tol.cz/look/TOLnew/tolprint.tpl?IdLanguage=1&IdPublication=4&NrIssue

=44&NrSection=2&NrArticle=9017&ST1=body&ST_T1=tol&ST_AS1=1&ST_max=1. Accessed 14 July 2009.

Trebici, Vladimir. *Genocid şi Demografie*. Bucharest: Humanitas, 1991.

Troebst, Stefan, and Ulf Brunnbauer. *Zwischen Nostalgie und Amnesie: Die Erinnerung an den Kommunismus in Südosteuropa*. Cologne: Böhlau, 2007.

Truc, Olivier. 'Une statue soviétique sème la discorde entre nationalistes estoniens et russophones.' *Le Monde*. 16 January 2007.

Tsing-Yuan, Tsao. 'The Birth of the Goddess of Democracy.' In Jeffrey N. Wasserstrom and Elizabeth J. Perry, eds. *Popular Protest and Political Culture in Modern China*. Boulder: Westview Press, 1994.

Turgeon, Laurier, and Élise Dubuc. 'Ethnology Museums: New Challenges and New Directions.' *Ethnologies*. 24/2 (2002): 19–32.

Uhl, Michael. *Mythos Spanien: Das Erbe der Internationalen Brigaden in der DDR*. Bonn: Dietz, 2004.

Uitz, Renáta. 'Communist Secret Services on the Screen.' In Oksana Sarkisova and Péter Apor, eds. *Past for the Eyes: East European Representations of Communism in Cinema and Museums after 1989*. Budapest: CEU Press, 2008.

Ungváry, Krisztián. *Battle for Budapest: 100 Days in World War II*. London: I. B. Tauris, 2002.

Valtchinova, Galia. 'Ismail Kadare's *The H-File* and the Politics of Memory.' In Daniela Koleva, ed. *Talking History: Proceedings of the International Oral History Conference, 23–27 September 1999*. Kiten: LIK, 2000.

Vaněk, Miroslav, ed. *Mocní? A Bezmocní?: Politické elity a disent v období tzv. normalizace: Interpretační studie životopisných*. Interview. Prague: Prostor, 2006.

Vardys, V. Stanley, and Romuald J. Misiunas, eds. *The Baltic States in Peace and War 1917–1945*. University Park: Pennsylvania State University Press, 1978.

Vasile, Cristian. 'Cine a scris Raportul Tismăneanu.' *Revista*. 22 (2007). Available from http://www.revista22.ro/cine-a-scris-raportul-Tismăneanu-3336.html. Accessed 6 July 2009.

Verdery, Katherine. *What Was Socialism and What Comes Next?* Princeton, NJ: Princeton University Press, 1996.

Verdery, Katherine. *The Political Lives of Dead Bodies: Reburial and Post-Socialist Change*. New York: Columbia University Press, 1999.

Voglis, Polymeris. 'The Greek Civil War and the Politics of Memory.' *Colloque international: les sociétés européennes du XXI siècle face à leur passé*. Reims, 5–7 May 2008.

von Plato, Alexander. ' "Entstasifizierung" im Öffentlichen Dienst der Neuen Bundesländer nach 1989: Umorientierung und Kontinuität in der Lehrerschaft.' *Jahrbuch für Historische Bildungsforschung*. 5 (1999): 313–42.

Vultur, Smaranda. *Istorie trăită – istorie povestită. Deportarea în Bărăgan, 1951–1956*. Timişoara: Amarcord, 1997.

Wagner, Sarah E. *To Know Where he Lies: DNA technology and the Search for Srebrenica's Missing*. Berkeley, CA and London: University of California Press, 2008.

Wagstyl, Stefan. 'Peacetime Collaboration.' *Financial Times*. 7 May 2005.

Walkowitz, Daniel J., and Lisa Maya Knauer, eds. *Memory and the Impact of Political Transformation in Public Space*. Durham, NC: Duke University Press, 2004.

Ward, James J. 'Was Bleibt? (What's Left?): Antifascism as Historical Experience and Contemporary Politics in Post-Marxist (East) Germany.' *New Political Science*. 12/1 (1993): 39–57.

Wasserstrom, Jeffrey N., and Elizabeth J. Perry, eds. *Popular Protest and Political Culture in Modern China*. Boulder: Westview Press, 1994.

Wawrzyniak, Joanna. 'Kriegsgeschichten: Juden als Deutsche in Polen, 1967–1968.' In Dieter Bingen, Peter Oliver Loew and Kazimierz Wóycicki, eds. *Die Destruktion des Dialogs: Zur Innenpolitischen Instrumentalisierung Negativer Fremd- und Feindbilder. Polen, Tschechien, Deutschland und die Niederlande im Vergleich, 1900 bis Heute*. Wiesbaden: Harrassowitz, 2007.

Wawrzyniak, Joanna. 'Negotiating the Nation's Official Past: The Politics of Commemoration of World War II in Communist Poland.' Available from http://98.129.116.150/tcds/Wawrzyniak.pdf. Accessed 18 July 2009.

Wawrzyniak, Joanna. 'Union of Fighters for Freedom and Democracy as an Example of the Role of People Living Off Stories of Nazi Occupation.' *Kwartalnik Historii Żydów*. 4 (2008): 427–46.

Weeks, Theodore R. 'Remembering and Forgetting: Creating a Soviet Lithuanian Capital. Vilnius 1944–1949.' *Journal of Baltic Studies*. 39/4 (2008): 517–33.

Weiner, Amir. 'In the Long Shadow of War: The Second World War and the Soviet and Post-Soviet World.' *Diplomatic History*. 25/3 (2001): 443–56.

Weiner, Amir. *Making Sense of War: The Second World War and the Fate of the Bolshevik Revolution*. Princeton, NJ: Princeton University Press, 2002.

Weiss-Wendt, Anton. 'Why the Holocaust Does Not Matter to Estonians.' *Journal of Baltic Studies*. 39/4 (2008): 475–97.

Wenzel, Michal. 'Solidarity and Akcja Wyborcza "Solidarność". An Attempt at Reviving the Legend.' *Communist and Post-Communist Studies*. 31/2 (1998): 139–56.

Wertsch, James V. 'Collective Memory and Narrative Templates.' *Social Research*. 75/1 (2008): 133–55.

Wertsch, James V. 'Patching Up Blank Spots in History: Revising the Official Narrative of the Molotov-Ribbentrop Pact.' In Ene Kõresaar, Epp Lauk and Kristin Kuutma, eds. *The Burden of Remembering. Recollections and Representations of the Twentieth Century*. Helsinki: SKS Kirjat, 2009.

Wette, Wolfram. 'Német propaganda és a csatlósországok: Magyarország, Románia és Bulgária (1941–43).' *Történelmi Szemle*. 22 (1979): 478–79.

Wierling, Dorothee. 'A German Generation of Reconstruction: The Children of the Weimar Republic in the GDR.' In Luisa Passerini, ed. *Memory and Totalitarianism: International Yearbook of Oral History and Life Stories, Vol. 1*. Oxford: Oxford University Press, 1992.

Wierling, Dorothee. *Geboren im Jahr Eins: Der Jahrgang 1949 in der DDR: Versuch einer Kollektivbiographie*. Berlin: Ch. Links Verlag, 2002.

Wieviorka, Annette. *The Era of the Witness*. Ithaca: Cornell University Press, 2006.

Wildstein, Bronisław. *A Long Shadow of the Polish People's Republic or the Decommunization That Never Happened*. Krakow: Arcana, 2005.

Williams, Kieran. *The Prague Spring and its Aftermath: Czechoslovak Politics, 1968–1970*. Cambridge: Cambridge University Press, 1997.

Williams, Paul. 'The Afterlife of Communist Statuary: Hungary's Szoborpark and Lithuania's Grūtas Park.' *Forum for Modern Language Studies*. 44/2 (2008): 185–98.

Willoughby, John. 'The Sexual Behaviour of American GIs during the Early Years of the Occupation of Germany.' *Journal of Military History*. 62/1 (1998): 155–74.

Wilson, Richard. *The Politics of Truth and Reconciliation in South Africa: Legitimizing the Post-Apartheid State*. Cambridge and New York: Cambridge University Press, 2001.

Wolff, Larry. *Inventing Eastern Europe: The Map of Civilization on the Mind of the Enlightenment*. Stanford, CA: Stanford University Press, 1994.

Wöll, Alexander, and Harald Wydra, eds. *Democracy and Myth in Russia and Eastern Europe*. London: Routledge, 2008.

Wolpert, Andrew. *Remembering Defeat: Civil War and Civic Memory in Ancient Athens*. Baltimore and London: Johns Hopkins University Press, 2001.

Wulf, Meike. 'The Struggle for Official Recognition of "Displaced" Group Memories in Post-Soviet Estonia.' In Michal Kopeček, ed. *Past in the Making: Historical Revisionism in Central Europe after 1989*. Budapest: CEU Press, 2008.

Wydra, Harald. 'Introduction.' In Alexander Wöll and Harald Wydra, eds. *Democracy and Myth in Russia and Eastern Europe*. London: Routledge, 2008.

Yoder, Jennifer A. 'Truth without Reconciliation: An Appraisal of the Enquete Commission on the SED Dictatorship in Germany.' *German Politics*. 8/3 (1999): 59–80.

Young, James E. 'The Art of Memory: Holocaust Memorials in History.' In James E. Young, ed. *The Art of Memory: Holocaust Memorials in History*. Munich: Prestel, 1994.

Young, James E., ed. *The Art of Memory: Holocaust Memorials in History*. Munich: Prestel, 1994.

Young, Marilyn. 'An Incident at No Gun Ri.' In Omer Bartov, Atina Grossmann and Mary Nolan, eds. *Crimes of War: Guilt and Denial in the Twentieth Century*. New York: New Press, 2002.

Yurchak, Alexei. 'Soviet Hegemony of Form: Everything Was Forever, Until It Was No More.' *Comparative Studies in Society and History*. 45/3 (2003): 480–510.

Yurchak, Alexei. *Everything Was Forever, Until It Was No More: The Last Soviet Generation*. Princeton, NJ: Princeton University Press, 2006.

Zaremba, Marcin. *Komunizm, legitymizacja, nacjonalizm: nacjonalistyczna legitymizacja władzy komunistycznej w Polsce*. Warsaw: Trio: Instytut Studiów Politycznych Polskicj Akademii Nauk, 2005.

Zhurzhenko, Tatiana. 'The Geopolitics of Memory.' *Eurozine*. 5 October 2007. Available from http://www.eurozine.com/articles/2007-05-10-zhurzhenko-en.html. Accessed 27 July 2009.

Zisere, Bella. 'The Memory of the Shoah in Post-Soviet Latvia.' *East European Jewish Affairs*. 35/2 (2005): 155–65.

Zolkos, Magdalena. 'The Conceptual Nexus of Human Rights and Democracy in the Polish Lustration Debates 1989–97.' *Journal of Communist Studies and Transition Politics*. 22/2 (2006): 228–48.

INDEX